Formations of Violence

FORMATIONS

The Narrative of the

The University of Chicago Press / *Chicago and London*

of VIOLENCE

Body and Political Terror in Northern Ireland

ALLEN FELDMAN

The University of Chicago Press, Chicago 60637
The University of Chicago Press, Ltd., London
© 1991 by The University of Chicago
All rights reserved. Published 1991
Printed in the United States of America

09 08 07 06 05 04 03 02 01 00   4 5 6 7 8

Library of Congress Cataloging-in-Publication Data

Feldman, Allen.
    Formations of violence : the narrative of the body and political
terror in Northern Ireland / Allen Feldman.
        p.   cm.
    Includes bibliographical references and index.
        ISBN 0-226-24070-3 (alk. paper).—ISBN 0-226-24071-1 (pbk. :
alk. paper)
        1. Violence—Northern Ireland.   2. Political prisoners—
Northern
    Ireland—Case studies.   I. Title.
    HN400.V5F45   1991
    303.6´09416—dc20   90-47977
                                                                  CIP

Contents

Acknowledgments

Fieldwork in Belfast was made possible by the generosity and hospitality of members of the following organizations: the Whiterock Leisure Center; Dismus House; the Falls Road Felon's Club; the Divis Residents Association; the Andersontown Social Club; the St. James Day Care Centre; the joyriders of the "OK Corral"; Connolly House; the Ainsworth Community Center; the Ardoyne Social Club; Rathcoole Social Club; Taughmonagh Social Club; Woodvale Workingman's Club; the Welder's Club; the Prison Fellowship; Falls Road black taxi service; Shankill Bulletin; Farset Youth Project; Extern Auto Project; the INLA; the PIRA; the UDA.

Fieldwork in Belfast between 1985 and 1986 was supported in part by a Social Science Research Council Western European Fellowship.

Figure 3 is reprinted from *Social Problems and the City*, edited by D. Herbert and D. M. Smith. Published by Oxford University Press in 1979.

. . . imagining those under the hill

disposed like Gunnar
who lay beautiful
inside his burial mound,
though dead by violence

and unavenged.
Men said that he was chanting
verses about honour
and that four lights burned

in corners of the chamber:
which opened then, as he turned
with a joyful face
to look at the moon.

Seamus Heaney, *North*

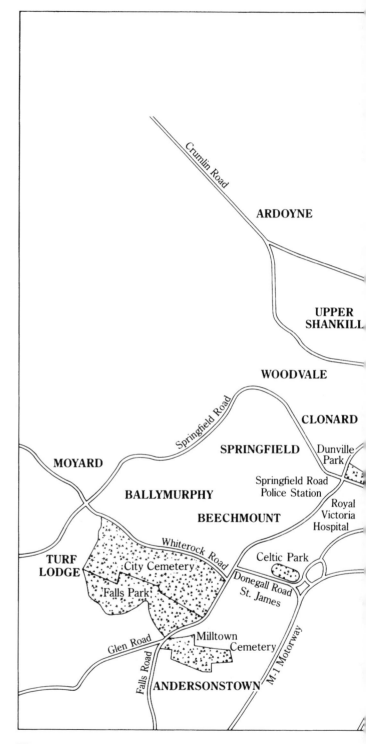

Figure 1.

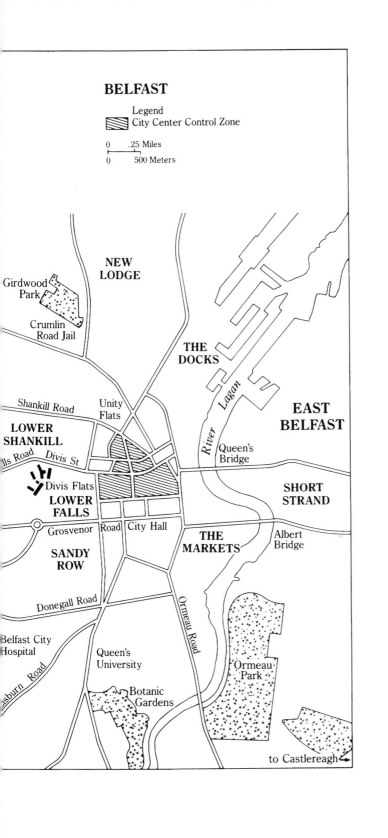

1 Artifacts and Instruments of Agency

This book traces the cultural construction of violence, body, and history in urban Northern Ireland between 1969 and 1986. The oral histories and my commentary encompass events beginning with the intercommunal rioting of 1969 and terminating with the 1981 Hunger Strike in the Maze prison. These events are described in the oral histories from the perspective of the twenty-five narrators during 1984 and 1986. But this book is not an event history; nor is it a social history of ethnic groups, political conflict and organizations. Rather it is a genetic history, a genealogical analysis of the symbolic forms, material practices, and narrative strategies through which certain types of political agency are constructed in Northern Ireland.

My approach to political violence is in keeping with the general thrust of Northern Irish ethnography, which has attempted to identify the underlying structural continuities and cultural reciprocities that mediate the ideological schisms between the Nationalist ("Catholic") and Loyalist ("Protestant") communities (McFarlane 1986). I treat the political culture of these communities and of the state as a material culture and as an ensemble of performed practices. My analysis identifies material reciprocity within ideological exclusion. I look to bodily, spatial, and violent practices as forming a unified language of material signification, circulating between and formative of antagonistic blocs.

The Northern Ireland situation has much to teach us about the problematic of political agency in late modernity. It has compelled me to treat the political subject, particularly the body, as the locus of manifold material practices. The subject is not read here as the unified and underlying originator of actions and values. Political agency is not given but achieved on the basis of practices that alter the subject. Political agency is relational—it has no fixed ground—it is the effect of situated practices. Agency is predicated on self-reflexive, interpretive framings of power which are embedded not only in language but in relational sequences of action (see Warren 1988). Since it is only through practice that subjects and objects become articulated, this book looks at practices of the body and violence to see how the political subject in Northern Ireland is wed to that cultural object known as history. The cultural construction of the political subject is tied to the cultural construction of history. This intersection results in political agency as an embodied force.

The rest of this chapter establishes the theoretical preliminaries that enable the exploration of the material contexts within which the politicized body, violence, and oral history emerge as artifacts and instruments of agency.

Surfaces and Centers

This book is an ethnography of surfaces—those sites, stages, and templates upon which history is constructed as a cultural object. The historiographic surface is a place for reenactment, for the simulation of power and for making power tangible as a material force. These surfaces are frequently located at the edge of social order. Yet they fabricate an edifice of centralized and authorized domination. This erection of authorizing centers—from out of dispersed, regional, and enclosed spaces of violent exchange—is the animating tension in this study. Through this tension between action and legitimation I seek to excavate the different and discontinuous strata of historical time that structure political antagonism in Northern Ireland. Sites of legitimation and authorization suppress historicity through linear, teleological, eschatological, or progressive temporalities. Action, however, unfolds time as difference and as radical heterogeneity. Temporal and semantic tensions can be located between the ongoing deformation and re-formation of material and experiential spheres by violence and the authorizing narrative and/or institution that legitimizes this violence, be it the state, various imagined communities of nationalist and ethnic identification, territorial referents, civil laws, or origin myths. These constructs appear to inhabit a less ephemeral temporal plane than the violent acts of instantiation that supposedly represent, advance, mediate, and materialize these metahistorical sites of legitimacy.

Legitimation can be understood as constructed and mediated by two poles: the site of instantiation and the Archimedean point of the authorizing center. This study seeks to fracture the appearance of lawful continuity between centers of legitimation and local acts of domination. This rupture can be demonstrated in bodily practice and oral history. To simply study power at the "center," that is, from the perspective of formal political rationalities, is to collaborate in the essential myth of formal rationalization: that power distributes itself from some place external to its effects, external to its violence, which is reduced to a transparent instrument. I have turned to the sociohistorical site occupied by the body in Northern Ireland in order to approach power from its point of effect and generation—agency. This is to look at power where it takes a place, in a zone of particularity from which all generalities and universal claims of domination flow.

Thus there is a need to interrogate the mythicizing reception of violence in order to trace the path by which ideological readings of violence engender the subject of the act and the extrinsic site of legitimation in a single movement. Nietzsche's analysis of this fusion was direct and radical: a reversal of the authorial position between act and agent generates a mythic and dramaturgical structure within which actions in time are endowed with a singular, atemporal origin. For Nietzsche, agency was not the author but the product of doing. Yet ideological reasoning imparts to action a doubled structure which resolves into extrinsic phantasmagoria— a counter world of imaginary doubles, agents, and metaphors of moral legitimation—which function as the originary sites of power, of which the act is but a derivative symptom. In his exposé, Nietzsche analyzed the rhetorical construction of force as a passageway to the cultural construction of history. In doing so he presented a performance theory of power in the parable of the lightning flash:

> For, just as popular superstition divorces lightning from its brilliance, viewing the latter as an activity whose subject is the lightning, so does popular morality divorce strength from its manifestations, as though there were behind the strong a neutral agent, free to manifest its strength or to contain it. But no such agent exists; there is no "being" behind the doing, acting, becoming; the "doer" has simply been added to the deed by the imagination—the doing is everything. The common man actually doubles the doing by making the lightning flash; he states the same event once as cause and then again as effect. (1956:178–79)

For Nietzsche, power is not "distributed" from an archic center or a reserved site; rather it is fictionalized as a metonym of doing, the simultaneous site of origin and effect. A mythic refiguration of action generates a perspectivist illusion. Legitimation resides in the construction of a fictive depth, a dimensionality of force which draws consciousness away from the concrete material investment in acts and effects that reproduce domination in time and space. The Nietzschean exposé of cause and effect within an apparatus of domination disrupts neat, unmediated relations of linearity between institution and agent, and does so to arrive at a theory of political subjects. It grants action a semantic and material autonomy that is usually inhibited and denied by legitimation rationality.

Nietzsche counters this denial with a subjectivation of power. Power is embedded in the situated practices of agents. He rejects any site of authorization eccentric to situated practice. Privileged sites, nomothetic domains, or suprahistorical agents are to be interrogated for their fictive construction and not accepted as originary and therefore immune to contestation. The whole semiotic relation of legitimation to the concept of origination falls into crisis. Legitimation becomes performative and therefore contingent.

This framework also calls into question relations of uninterrupted linearity between the *conditions of political antagonism and the relational practices of antagonism.* The moral continuity from given social contexts to practices that intervene to reproduce or transform these contexts becomes suspect when origination metaphors are deconstructed. The conditions and relations of antagonism generate different ideological and practical settings and are subject to diachronic frictions.

Relations of antagonism are mechanisms of ideological reproduction, but they also carve out autonomous material spheres of effect and affect that diverge from formal political rationalities. In Northern Ireland this sphere of material counterrationality is engendered in violence and the body. Republican, Loyalist, and state violence have fused into an enclosed sphere of cognition, exchange, and symbiotic representation. Political violence is no longer fully anchored in ideological codes and conditions external to the situation of enactment and transaction. Political enactment becomes sedimented with its own local histories that are mapped out on the template of the body. Formal political rationalities no longer sustain a singular or determining relation to performance dynamics. Rather instrumental rationality has been increasingly redirected to perpetuating the efficacy of symbolic action. Political action and institutionalized ideology form two discontinuous, significative systems. It is within the interstices that oral history emerges as a representational artifact of violence and the body. This process has important ramifications for the analysis of the political subject, class, and ethnicity in the current political culture:

1. Distinguishing between conditions and relations of antagonism ramifies on the comprehension of political agency. Political agency becomes the factored product of multiple subject positions. There can be no guarantee of a unified subject, as actors shift from one transactional space to another and from discourse to somatic practice. If social space and body space continually predicate each other and if both are subjected to an ongoing reconstruction by violence, the notion of a stable relationship of agency to nomothetic social frames, such as class, ethnicity, or political ideology, becomes problematic. Political agency is manifold and

formed by a mosaic of subject positions that can be both discontinuous and contradictory.

2. Political warfare in the urban sectors of Northern Ireland can be depicted as a Gramscian war of position between fractions of the "Catholic" and "Protestant" working class and between these fractions and the state. Yet though the conditions of this conflict can be traced in part to the relations of production, the *reproduction of antagonism* takes place in other spaces and materialities. In turn, as much as ethnicity symbolizes in part an inequitable cultural division of labor that has precipitated communal violence (Hechter 1975), I have found that violence can effect autonomous and retroactive interventions in the construction of ethnicity (see chaps. 2, 5, and 6). The above dynamics attest to the modernist character of political violence in Northern Ireland, despite all popular and easy characterizations of this situation as an archaicized religious or tribal conflict (see, for instance, O'Malley 1990).

3. The growing autonomy of violence as a self-legitimating sphere of social discourse and transaction points to the inability of any sphere of social practice to totalize society. Violence itself both reflects and accelerates the experience of society as an incomplete project, as something to be made. These processes of autonomization and fragmentation emerged from the ideological, cultural, and material collapse of industrial capitalism in post–World War II Northern Ireland. The development of a sophisticated urban guerrilla apparatus, particularly in "Catholic" working-class communities, can be seen as a political reclamation of the wasteland of industrial culture. The organizational and technical logistics of urban capitalist mass production are now applied to clandestine war. This recolonization of the political sphere by fractions of the Catholic working class is staged with the industrial ordinance, rationalities, and technical proficiencies denied to this social sector throughout the era of industrial expansion by sectarian ideologies. To the extent that the Protestant working class has lost a secure economic base in industrial production, the involvement of fractions of this group in paramilitary violence can also be understood as a staged reentry into the public arenas of social production. Industrial logistics and managerial rationalities can be indexed in the complexities of weapons importation, bomb-making factories and other military-industrial improvisations, the intricate systems of arms "dumping" (storage) which function as both logistical and symbolic capital, and the division of labor known as the cell system where each military operation is divided into specialized segments. These refigured artifacts of industrial culture attest to working-class colonization of entrepreneurial and industrial expertise within a clandestine military context. The instrumental rationality of mass production returns to the

public sphere in the form of working-class violence, where it functions as an emblem of political and not economic mastery. In doing so the transformation of the public sphere of urban social life into a postindustrial wasteland is accelerated. (See chapters 2 and 6 for discussions of the cultural symbolization of these dynamics.) It is no coincidence that counterinsurgency programs of the state introduce advanced electronic surveillance and data-processing technology into the political culture.

Other theorists have located facets of autonomization in the Northern Ireland state's creative hegemonization of Protestant class fractions (Bew, Gibbon, and Patterson 1979), in the long-term effects of spatial order and symbolism (Murray and Boal 1979), and in the role of the counterinsurgency apparatus in the formation of community ideology and identity (Sluka 1989).

4. Touraine (1988) has identified subjectivation as the primary characteristic of political struggle in late modernity. Through the enabling optic of oral history, the body in Northern Ireland emerges as a novel political subject. The historical dynamic of subjectivation speaks to the expansion of the categories of who or what can be a political subject. In turn, the emergence of new political subjects attests to the multiplication and decentralization of the sites of antagonism in civil society. Social antagonism can no longer be solely identified with practices and agents basic to the economic infrastructure. Social antagonisms (including class conflicts) presuppose and construct discursive and transactional settings of wider scope and gauge than relations of production. This would imply that the Marxist dichotomy between productive and unproductive social practices and spheres and between "primary" and "secondary" antagonisms (respectively located in the base and superstructure) cannot hold. The organizational site of social fracture becomes a floating center. Sites of political mobilization and the general possibility-spectacle of historical alterity appear in unexpected places.

If universalized administrative rationalities, and the expansion of socially extractive technologies once segregated man and nature in separate objectified domains, late modernity witnesses the shift of both man and nature from object to subject positions. In this process the anthropological and organic spheres acquire a new self-reflexive relationship. Integral to the historical construction of matter, the body emerges as a political subject. It comes into view as a mise-en-scène with its own genealogy of domination and resistance. The subjectivation of "nature" and the body spins a political and epistemological web that runs through a variety of social struggles including feminism, prisoners' rights, ecological movements, and animal rights.

At first glance the investment in bodily violence, body-as-object, seems at odds with the thesis of subjectivation. Yet new modes of subjectivation engender new object formations. The reverse can also occur. The politicized body traverses both subject and object poles. The body made into a political artifact by an embodied act of violence is no less a political agent than the author(s) of violence. The very act of violence invests the body with agency. The body, altered by violence, reenacts other altered bodies dispersed in time and space; it also reenacts political discourse and even the movement of history itself. Political violence is a mode of transcription; it circulates codes from one prescribed historiographic surface or agent to another. Transcription requires agency, both the communicative activity of the transcriber and the transcribed "object." Struggles will occur over competing transcriptions of the same body and of different bodies. This contest over adversarial transcripts fractures the body as an "organic," "natural" object and thus accelerates the body's subjectivation.

Embodied Transcripts

In his explorations of the nineteenth-century Parisian arcades, Walter Benjamin gravitated to a singular figure who seemed to encapsulate the spectacle of commodification: the sandwichman. The sandwich (board) man stood for the animation of the inanimate; this figure roamed the streets of Paris bearing advertisements of commodity exchange values mounted on the front and back of his body. As an animated text, the sandwichman was an allegory of the body reified by the logic of capitalism.

The Parisian sandwichmen observed by Benjamin were traditionally recruited from the *clochards,* the homeless proletariat, an ejected strata that had been pushed to the margins of society by economic violence. That the most excluded element of society circulated the central social texts of value exchange was an irony crucial to the aura of the sandwichman as a commodity made animate and as a body made into a text.

Susan Buck-Morss's (1989) discussion of Benjamin's sandwichman is literally framed between two period photographs. Through the immediacy of the particular, these images harbor historical shifts of great magnitude. The first photo shows a Parisian sandwichman of the 1930s wearing signs front and back and scaffolding over his head with more ads (p. 306). The second photo shows a German Jew from the same period, marching down a boulevard between two policemen. His shoes and trousers have been taken. This divestiture is compensated for with a new piece of apparel. On his chest he wears a placard that advertises his relationship to the state: "I am a Jew but I have no complaints about the Nazis" (p. 312). In the Nazi procession, the body of the Jew is circulated as a political text. It becomes a point of intersection and ideological instantiation that permits the state and the crowd to exchange messages on the reciprocal constitution of otherness and community. The body as a social type and not an individual is being walked through these streets, and this typification is staged and sealed by the placard.

Commodification imparts its "afterimage" (Buck-Morss 1989:312), its symbolic efficacy to the political form, even as the latter supplants the primacy of economic determination. The political form and the commodity form fuse because, in modernity, political power increasingly becomes a matter of regimenting the circulation of bodies in time and space in a manner analogous to the circulation of things. Power, as Foucault has amply documented, becomes spatialized. It is contingent on the command of space and the command of those entities that move within politically marked spaces. The body becomes a spatial unit of power, and the distribution of these units in space constructs sites of domination.

The juxtaposition of the two bodies in the photographs compels the viewer to consider the political consequences of economic fetishism on the one hand and the economic logic of political fetishism on the other. Both pictures silently address the mobilization of values through the spectacle of the body. In either case the individual body is constructed as a mass article and as a social hieroglyph that opens the possibility of mythical communication with the masses.[1]

For Benjamin the commodity artifact was not phantasmagoric in itself, but rather it was the staging of commodities that generated the imaginary dimension of capitalist experience. The sandwichman and the placard-bearing Jew are staged bodies, surfaces for axial representations. Reserved spaces of political representation and the political formation of the body are coextensive historical developments. Domination's reality is organized through the logic of mythic instantiation, and the body is a central medium of the political instant.

This book is about the instrumental staging and commodification of the body by political violence. It is thus more concerned with the historical implications of the second photo than the first. Yet the linkage between the two images should be maintained historically and analytically. The sandwichman, the placard-bearing Jew, and those bodies violently staged as political texts in Northern Ireland share a uniform genesis: the process by which an entity violently expelled from the social order is transformed into an emissary, a cultural donor and bearer of seminal political messages.

The expansion of the spheres of domination in Northern Ireland in the last two decades can best be analyzed from the perspective of the body as a political institution. This optic discloses the formation of the political subject, the discontinuities between formal ideological discourse and political practice, the performance codes shared between adversaries, and the material conditions within which ideological reproduction takes place. In Northern Ireland the body is not only the primary political instrument through which social transformation is effected but is also the primary site for visualizing the collective passage into historical alterity. The body's material deformation has become commensurate with the deformation, instrumentation, and "acceleration" of historical time (see Koselleck 1985).

In Northern Ireland the practice of political violence entails the production, exchange, and ideological consumption of bodies. Thus I follow Appadurai's (1986) recommendation to trace the life history or social biography of an artifact as it moves in and out of "commodity phases" and passes between divergent "regimes of value." The body accumulates political biographies, a multiplicity of subject positions, as it passes in and out of various political technologies of commensuration (see Foucault 1979; Nietzsche 1956; Deleuze 1977).[2] To analyze this ensemble of practices is to restage, outside of market contexts, the "Marxist" separation of value as an invariant structure (the body as political institution) from the thing-in-itself (the heterogeneity of particular bodies).

From Hegel, through Nietzsche, to Lukács and Foucault, the formation of the body has been treated as the formation of the political subject. For all these theorists this formation has been linked to specific spaces and spatial relations.[3] In Northern Ireland the formation of the political subject takes place within a continuum of spaces consisting of the body, the confessional community, the state, and the imagined community of utopian completion: United Ireland or a British Ulster. The command of these spaces is practically achieved and sustained through ideology and violence. In each of these spaces, claims of power are made and practices of power are inscribed. The spatial inscription of practices and power involves physical flows, metabolic transactions and transfers—exchanges which connect, separate, distance, and hierarchize one space in relation to another. The command of space involves the setting up of novel codifying apparatuses such as the reorganization of the senses, mental maps, topographic origin myths, norms of spatial competance, and rules of spatial performance. The command of space further entails the setting aside of places of imaginary representation: eulogized, purifying, or defiling spaces that mobilize spectacles of historical transformation. A profound discontinuity marks the relations between the conventional social coding of spatial transaction, imagined space, and experiential space.[4] No one space or dimension of spatial practice or representation is determining. With the aggravations of violence, ideological codes in each of these spaces seek continuity and legitimation in the other.

Map of the Book

As asserted earlier, this book is an ethnography of surfaces and spaces. The analyses, descriptions, and oral history trace the genesis of political space in decreasing dimensions. Thus chapter 2 begins with the refiguration of the political space of the confessional community in Belfast during the late 1960s, at the onset of communal conflict. Chapter 3 looks to singular figures, such as the hardmen, the Shankill Butchers, and the Black Man, to chart this process of spatial-political formation in terms of both the historical shifts and transactions between and within adversarial communities. Chapter 4 finds the confessional community shrunk to the space of search and seizure, the enclosure of arrest as developed by the state counterinsurgency apparatus. From there I move to the interrogation center and to the ritual of torture as it traces myths on the surface of the captive body and the ways these myths are rewritten. Chapter 5 enters the prison cell and follows the reconstruction of this instrument by Republican prisoners into an embryo of redemptive contact with Irish historicity. Chapter 6 halts at the body of the hunger striker, where political space attains extreme concentration and its highest level of semantic expansion. Wherever encountered in the book, the shrinkage of the space of political enactment corresponds to the expansion of the acting subject—the increasing correlation of personhood to historical transformation. This transformative application of the person to the fabric of history through the texture of the body is witnessed unobtrusively in oral history. There the body fragmented is reassembled, and this act, the weaving of a new body through language, as much as any act of violence, testifies to the emergence of political agency.

The Politics of Narration

The analyses in this book are primarily based on oral history texts, on the experience of shared talk and shared revisions and expansions of narratives once they were transcribed. I conducted interviews with one hundred people in the Protestant and Catholic working-class districts of Belfast—the experiential, tactical, and ideological center of political violence. Fieldwork in the urban areas was grounded in my prior ethnographic research in rural Ireland. In moving from country to city I remained within an oral culture that exhibited strong continuities as well as discontinuities between the rural and the urban. Fieldwork in Belfast objectively started in the spring of 1984, though I had been exploring the issues of an oral culture of warfare in Northern Ireland for some time before. Before 1984 it was an open question whether there was an oral culture of political violence, whether it would be communicated to an outsider, and whether I would be allowed to document any aspect of it. A second period of directed and specialized field inquiry took place between the fall of 1985 and the fall of 1986. Over a hundred hours of recordings were generated by both periods of interviewing. Obtained in a tense and difficult environment, each interview recorded entailed many more background discussions that never reached the microphone. Though many people consented to be recorded, many more who were willing to talk did not wish to leave any permanent record. Tapes were not allowed to accumulate at the field site and were frequently taken out of Northern Ireland for fear of confiscation. This practice, among other precautions, minimally reassured contributors. All informants were guaranteed personal anonymity. They are identified in this book by their gender, sometimes their age, and by their paramilitary affiliation or the local ethnic classification of their districts. The ethnic designations "Catholic" and "Protestant" are not indicators of religiosity or regular church attendance. The terms "Loyalist" or "Republican" do indicate in a general way the political disposition of persons and places. (All paramilitary informants are male and indicated by organizational affiliation.)

Only when interviews were broken apart and distributed nonsequentially throughout the text, between sections of analysis, did their authors feel that the anonymity had been reasonably assured. The concern with anonymity reflects the intense levels of surveillance in Northern Ireland and the fact that many of the people I talked with had been or were currently engaged in some form of clandestine political practice.

My "access" to certain restricted circuits of paramilitary discourse and culture depended on my recognition of the thresholds of secrecy. This recognition had to be visibly displayed by me in dialogue and in everyday interactions. I had been prepared for a culture of secrecy by my previous encounters with Ulster fiddlers, particularly the virtuoso performers of Donegal. The cultivation of secrecy around performance practices in Ireland is a traditional strategy practiced by musicians, storytellers, "tinkers" and more overt political organizations. In a colonized culture, secrecy is an assertion of identity and of symbolic capital. Pushed to the margins, subaltern groups construct their own margins as fragile insulations from the "center." Secrecy is the creation of centers in peripheries deprived of stable anchorages. Cultural resistance inspires the production of fragments as a counterpractice to imperial agendas.

I met with informants on the border of a political, cultural, and historical situation, and our conversations were transactions of the border— restricted exchanges. The line between *informants* and *informers* was clearly drawn; it marked a division of life and death.

In a culture of political surveillance, participant observation is at best an absurdity and at the least a form of complicity with those outsiders who surveil. I avoided residing in the communities of my informants for these reasons. Neutral spaces were best for talking about the items we agreed to deal with. Long-term visual appropriation of any social milieu was not welcomed. Too much mobility between adversarial spaces, which my nationality facilitated, also proved to be subjectively disturbing. As I became familiar with the topography of confessional communities, I realized that the only other people who were publically moving back and forth in such a manner were the police and the army. I had to constrain the body as well as the voice. Finally, in order to know I had to become expert in demonstrating that there were things, places, and people I did not want to know.[5]

The domain of secret knowledge interposed a certain "spacing" between discourse, between words and acts, between informants. To conduct a dialogue meant apprehending the political necessity of "spacing" and the political impossibility of interpersonal parity. This dialogue with silence generated a contingent epistemology in the "field." I found that the cultural dynamics of secrecy, of editing, became the precondition for the interpersonal construction of meaning. Editing, in the field, is the co-construction of silence and speech. It generates cultural depth through absence. It is a productive and not an inhibiting process. There is an indirect voice of silence that inflects and intensifies the reception of form and content. The editing of transcribed voices in the field and afterward cannot be reduced to a technical, objectifying operation. To do so is to render writing extrinsic to the fieldwork process and thus to exile it from cultural and historical contingencies. Editing can be part of the construction, reconstruction, and simulation of context. Yet editing is often portrayed in recent theoretical discussions as the betrayal of the "dialogical" ethic. In this approach the dialogical is reduced to the positivist model of face-to-face encounter with the other, which is deformed by writing and editing as practices that subtract from the originary mise-en-scène.[6] In Bakhtin, however, the dialogical situation is one in which two or more conflictual, discontinuous, heterogeneous, or polarized social codes are present in the same set of signifiers. These composite signs trace a history of desemanticization: their incomplete detachment from prior references and their realignment with new meanings and inferences. This transposition is in itself a register of historical experience and an editing of that experience by informants and ethnographers. The dialogical relation does not require the physical presence of the other; rather it is all the more powerful in the literal absence of the other, who is present as a violent material and historical effect on language, meaning, and theory (see Seremetakis 1991).[7]

These issues bear on the treatment of oral history and life histories. Watson and Watson-Franke (1985) assert that the text (as editing of the voice) is alienated from the originary subjective intentionality of the informant. Interpretation must trace a regressive path back to original presence, past the interference of the transcription, in order to recuperate the situation where intention and discourse "are practically the same thing" at the scene of dialogue. Subjective intent is considered to be the archic site of truth and occupies a polar position to the transcribed text. This originary intentionality is reachable because life-history texts are primarily self-referential (Watson and Watson-Franke 1985). Yet if the self is the referential object of the life-history recitation, then it is interpellated by that discourse and cannot be prior to it. No discursive object exists outside of, or prior to, a discursive formation. The self is always the artifact of prior received and newly constructed narratives. It is engendered through narration and fulfills a syntactical function in the life history. The rules of narration may perform a stabilizing role in the cultural construction of truth, but then both self and truth are subordinate to the transindividual closures of narrative (spoken or written).

Crapanzano (1984) has made this point by polarizing narrative and social practice. Oral histories and life histories provide an access to narrative dynamics and not to social dynamics that are beyond the text. Yet narrative dynamics cannot be divorced from societal dynamics as easily as Crapanzano claims. The polarization of narrative and "referential event" or "observed sequences of behavior" (p. 957) cannot be sustained if the latter are themselves narrative formations, if the entire concept of the event, like the concept of the self, cannot be detached from the effects of narration with its assumption of causality and agency.

The polarity between text and self and narrative and event cannot hold. In a political culture the self that narrates speaks from a position of having been narrated and edited by others—by political institutions, by concepts of historical causality, and possibly by violence. The narrator speaks because this agent is already the recipient of narratives in which he or she has been inserted as a political subject. The narrator writes himself into an oral history because the narrator has already been written and subjected to powerful inscriptions.

The polarity of self or event and a temporally removed narrative presumes the model of linear time where self or event chronologically precedes the process of narration and is thus considered the site of truth. Lyotard (1973), however, proposes that the relations between event, agency, and narrative are fundamentally *achronic* and not linear (see also Derrida 1976).[8] Narrativity is the condition for the identification of events, agents, and mediating sequence. Event, agency, and narration form a "narrative bioc" (Lyotard 1973: 268) defined as the achronic engenderment of narrative, agency (narration), and event. Narrative blocs are plastic organizations involving language, material artifacts and relations. The narrative bloc of violence puts into play a constellation of events, and discourses about events, as an Event. In turn, any oral history of political violence privileges the event as a narrative symbol or function. The oral history of political violence and the enactment of political violence are differentially positioned and symbiotic narrative blocs. Oral history is a narration of other narratives performed in similar or different media. Thus the oral history of interrogation recounted by paramilitaries is a cultural tool kit, an empowering apparatus that paramilitaries take into the theater of interrogation in order to mediate, and possibly to invert, the interrogator's scenario of violence (see chapter 4). Many of the texts transcribed in this book can be understood as a cultural-political project on the part of their authors and myself, to locate narrative in violence by locating violence through narration.

Narrative blocs may be internally achronic, but they fabricate temporalities and causalities such as linear time, which carry subtle valuations of agents, events, and effects. Sequence and causality are both moral and metaphorical constructs. In turn the temporal relations that exist between narrative blocs can be treated in terms of their synchronicity and dissynchronicity. Social-historical lines of force and fissure become visible in the differential relations and slippage between narrative blocs.

Political violence is a genre of "emplotted" action. Ricoeur (1984), White (1973), and Veyne (1984) view narrativity and emplotment as the organization of events into a configurational system, a mode of historical explanation, and a normative intervention. *The event is not what happens. The event is that which can be narrated.* The event is action organized by culturally situated meanings. Narratives are enacted as well as written. The concept of narrative does not imply the model of the book or of alphabetic signs (see Derrida 1986). Narrativity can be invested in material artifacts and relations that have a storytelling capacity of their own.

If narrativity can be embedded in iconic arrangements of material artifacts and/or actions, one can speak of the making and narrating of history as two sides of the same process. This implies an imaginary dimension to the production of specific performances as historicized and historicizing practices—a process that theorists concerned with symbolic efficacy and oral performance have begun to address:

> These stories Ilongot men tell themselves reflect what actually happened and define the kinds of experiences they seek out in future hunts . . . in this respect the story informs the experience of hunting at least as much as the reverse. . . . Ilongot huntsmen experience themselves as the main characters of their own stories

when responding [in a hunt] to a challenge with speed and imagination. (Rosaldo 1986: 134)

For Ricoeur (1984), emplotment transfigures a practical field through mimesis, conceived of not as imitation, but as a configuring mediation of experience. Through narration Rosaldo's Ilongot hunters perform a mimesis of hunting as they hunt. Social actors inhabit their performances as narrative continua and as units within overarching stories of historical magnitude. This is not a passive process, but the active injection of cultural form that situates agency at the moment of enactment. Enactment can become a medium for locating one's position or nonposition in a narrative configuration.

Ricoeur (1973) sees not only the text but also action as deviating from the intentionality of the actor.[9] In contrast to Watson and Watson-Franke (1985), he proposes that the collective gauge and social truth of an action are dependent on the generation of semantic excess beyond explicit intent. A performance is both the fixation of meaning and the disclosure of nonostensive reference (Ricoeur 1973). The semantic gauge of a performance can open references not built into the intended plotting of action. A performance can exceed the social conditions of its production and thus exceed any particular ideological closure associated with its site of emergence. Multiple and antagonistic counterdiscourses and acts can be attached to the same performance, thereby transforming its semantic efficacy.

In Northern Ireland the relation between performance and narrative has to be understood against a background of profound displacement that engendered both violence and narration. Local oral history emerges in tandem with more formal political discourses, as a narrative genre directly concerned with recording the expanding spheres of domination rather than explicitly advancing domination. The symbolization of domination effects in oral history can be contrasted to the utopian rationalization of domination in formal organizational ideologies. This difference separated oral history, for the main part, from a utopian vocation. The oral history of domination and violence is an atopic narrative. As a discourse without place, it emerged in symbiosis with the primordial scene of displacement—the body. The inability of formal political rationalities to codify their fetishization of the body by violence meant that embodiment became the site for surrogate codes, for censored and excess experience. The overburdening of experience with surplus meaning, the limits of restricted political codes, the routinization of clandestine experience not only generated narratives to be deposited in oral performance, but necessitated oral history in the first place, since no other ideological form could accommodate these experiences without falling into incoherence.

The oral histories may have fulfilled a dual function. These narratives mediated the dissonance between the instrumental imaginary of political rationality and the semantic excess of material violence. But to mediate, the oral histories were committed to recording the presence and the effects of the disjunctive, to registering the limits of official political codes through an imagery of alterity.

2 *Spatial Formations of Violence*

I remember standing in my burnt house, the smell of burnt wood and the smell that covered the city like burnt bodies, but I don't remember the bomb.

—Housewife, St. James District, Belfast

Origin Space

In the political-education classes conducted by imprisoned Republican paramilitaries in the late 1970s, the current political schisms of Northern Ireland were traced to the prehistoric geological division of the island of Ireland from the European continental land mass. The course of instruction treated subsequent historical conflict as the rift between a geographically inspired cultural-economic separatism and outside forces such as Christianity, British colonialism, and capitalism. These interlopers were depicted as undoing what geography had created. This ongoing confrontation was traced in sophisticated political concepts, but its polarized patterning repeated in other forms the geographic splintering of the Ice Age event.

Of the many origin tales of the Northern Ireland conflict that I heard during my fieldwork, this one reduced to elegant simplicity the motifs of all others. In this tale the origin is a separation event, a partition. This sundering of two parts demarcates a historical continuum, expressed as a land mass, within which subsequent events marked by the origin will unfold. Though the origin engenders history, it is located in the prehistoric. The origin is placed outside of time and yet it gives birth to a particular temporality. This temporality repeats the initial act of division in the linear unfolding of subsequent events. The origin, beyond the time it has engendered, is immutable and not open to discussion. In its permanence and remoteness, the origin guarantees all subsequent bifurcations, all repetitions of itself.

There is a Loyalist origin myth that complements this Republic cosmology. Inspired by the biblical allegories of the Orange Order (a Protestant secret society), this story traces the origins and ethnicity of Ulster Protestants back to the ten lost tribes of Israel. Here too the motifs of separation and demarcated territory predominate. In this narrative, the origin is similarly located in a dimension anterior and opposed to secular time.

The two narratives fulfill identical purposes: the origin guarantees the recursive character of history through spatial metaphor. The mimesis of the origin in present events endows the latter with coherence. Linearity and repetition, metaphorized as history, are deployed in these tales to repress historicity—the anthropological capacity to generate dispersal, difference, and alterity in time and space. The use of history to repress historicity is a central ideological mechanism in the political culture of Northern Ireland. And where this occurs, the recursive character of the historical is often expressed and always legitimated by geographical metaphor.

The model of recursive history, of the similitude between causes and consequences, can be found not only in local popular depictions of political conflict in Northern Ireland but in social science analyses as well. Between 1981 and 1987, a debate took place in a British journal concerning the causation of political violence in Northern Ireland from 1969 to 1971. This seminal period experienced civil rights marches by the Catholic community, the violent repression of these demonstrations by the state and the Protestant populace, intercommunal crowd violence, and the emergence of paramilitary violence. The aforementioned debate on these events replicates in a broad fashion the convergence of social science thinking and local popular opinion on the origins of violence in Northern Ireland.

The protagonists of the debate, two sociologists Hewitt (1981, 1983, 1985, 1987) and O'Hearn (1983, 1985, 1987), present contrasting origin theories of political violence that respectively correspond to antagonistic Republican and Loyalist explanations. Hewitt (1981) seeks to challenge the accepted social science explanation of Northern Irish violence (which he equates with journalistic and Republican accounts). This school of thought, according to Hewitt, attributes the "Troubles" to high levels of Catholic unemployment, housing and job discrimination, and electoral gerrymandering. For Hewitt these factors have been exaggerated and are in effect symbolic issues deployed by the true cause of antagonism, inculcated Catholic Nationalism. Ideological tradition is the prime mover of violence. O'Hearn (1983) reasserts the deprivation model. Violence had its roots in socioeconomic inequities perpetuated by sectarian institutions. Despite their disagreement as to cause, both theorists advance identical processual models of collective violence. This is a psychogenetic schema that begins in grievance (material or ideational), moves to expression, and culminates in violence in the absence of redress. In turn their common approach advances a given diagnostic agenda: aberrant cause, pathological symptom (violence), potential cure (elimination of cause). These theorists share in common with the popular ideologies they analyze the narrative model of linear history.

Hewitt (1981) identifies a 5.6 percent discrepancy between Catholic representation on local councils and the actual Catholic population in these districts prior to 1969. He concludes that gerrymandering by Protestants was negligible. O'Hearn (1983) counters that gerrymandering by Protestants was concentrated in larger districts where political control was more crucial; there the discrepancy between Catholic demographics and representation was 12.5 percent. Hewitt (1981) dismisses the charge of widespread public-housing discrimination by Protestants and even identifies Catholic discrimination against Protestants in this area. O'Hearn (1983) points out that though more Catholics than Protestants used public-housing schemes, the Catholic population was more dependent on public housing, and in this area a greater percentage of the needy Protestant population gained access to public housing in comparison to needy Catholics.

Hewitt acknowledges high levels of Catholic unemployment and differential income levels between Catholics and Protestants, but, by using analogous U.S. and Australian statistics, he insists that such variables do not automatically connote discrimination. According to Hewitt the average male Catholic and Protestant wage earner can be identified as a skilled manual worker. O'Hearn presents numbers that demonstrate underemployment for Catholic skilled manual workers and charges that many such workers are employed at jobs below their training levels. He insists that the average Catholic worker be identified as a semiskilled manual laborer.

Hewitt identifies a high statistical correlation between areas that practiced political violence between 1969 and 1971 and high Catholic unemployment. But he also finds a strong correlation between nationalist voting preferences and the occurrence of violence in these districts. He assigns residual nationalist ideology greater causal priority, citing the increase in nationalist electoral support in Catholic districts prior to the outbreak of communal violence.

Hewitt and O'Hearn, like numerous commentators on Northern Ireland, locate political violence as a surface expression of "deeper" socioeconomic and/or ideological contexts. In this perspective the issue of descriptive adequacy is rarely brought to bear on the acts of violence themselves, but only on the putative origin of the irruption. Violence is denuded of any intrinsic semantic or causal character. The sociohistorical depth of the violent event is locatable in zones exterior to that occurrence. Violence is treated as a psychological artifact and surface effect of the origin. The value-imbued character of the origin legitimates or delegitimates violence by endowing social actors with a predetermined normative character that is absorbed, like osmosis, from the origin.

This mechanical causality brought to bear on the act of political violence attempts to sketch a definable historical agent. But here historical agency functions like a hollow space, contoured from without by ideological and environmental circumscriptions. Historical agency eludes diagnostic and symptom-centered theories of violence precisely because these approaches do not locate historical force and trajectory in the act of violence that discloses agency in the first place. Origin and diagnostic theories of violence presume an unexamined theory of praxis as starting point rather than positing praxis as the analytical object to be attained. In the diagnostic approach the conditions of antagonism are conflated with antagonism as a relational practice. The latter lacks any historical status and any autonomy as a determining force.

Conditions and relations of antagonism are not identical and are often discontinuous. Distinguishing between the two levels implies sorting out how contexts for the inception of violence are frequently transformed by their ideological representation and the material reproduction of violence. Recognizing this mutation entails treating violence as a semantically modal and transformative practice that constructs novel poles of enactment and reception. Modal violence detaches itself from initial contexts and becomes the condition of its own reproduction. When this shift occurs, it is because chronic violence transforms material and experiential contexts and renders the relations between structure and event, text and context, consciousness and practice labile and unfixed. Within the ecology of violent practice one cannot, unlike Hewitt and O'Hearn, assume that subject positions are fixed in advance. Novel subject positions are constructed and construed by violent performances, and this mutation of agency renders formal ideological rationale and prior contextual motivation unstable and even secondary.

Both Hewitt and O'Hearn assume that there are domains of experience not organized by ideological representation. Deprivation experiences are thematized as political programs and daily mental maps of the social order only through their mediation by in-place cultural codes, be these nationalist ideologies or some other discourse. The norm of deprivation itself can change from culture to culture and historical period to historical period. At the same time we cannot essentialize the relation between discursive code and experience. The wedding of a nationalist discourse to deprivation experiences can cause the former to mutate just as much as it can alter the conceptualization of the experience.

By treating violence as a derivative symptom, both writers foreclose the mutation of both ideology and experience. By subordinating violence to prior ideological formations and not treating violent practice as a developing ideological formation in itself, Hewitt (1981) omits important factors in the escalation of intercommunal violence between 1969 and 1971. By reducing violence to an idiosyncratic expression of deprivation experiences, O'Hearn denies the status of violence as a residual cultural and political institution in Northern Ireland—an institution possessing its own symbolic and performative autonomy.

The two origin myths recounted earlier contain insights into the genesis of violence that are omitted in Hewitt's and O'Hearn's accounts: the factor of space and the efficacy of spatial symbolism. The Republican and Loyalist origin myths both point to a cultural relation between demarcated spatial continua and indigenous mental maps of historical causation which speak to in-place notions of action and agency. Bew, Gibbon, and Patterson (1979) in their analysis of the gestation period of political violence in Northern Ireland (1966–71) are forced to confront space as a force that can substantially transform the political intentions of social actors, whether they are motivated by economic, electoral, or nationalist concerns. In reference to the civil rights demonstrations of this period they state:

> While these forms of protest—the street march, the sitdown, etc.—had their immediate pedigree in the moderate American civil rights movement and were intended to evoke its image, in practice their impact in Northern Ireland was at varience with this secular inspiration.
>
> In Ulster demonstrations had a distinctly non-secular implication. Marches in particular meant, and still mean, the assertion of territorial sectarian claims. To march in or through an area is to lay claim to it. When so many districts are invested with confessional significance by one bloc or another, undertaking a secular march creates the conditions for territorial transgressions. . . . Quite apart from any independent sectarian attraction such demonstrations may have had for portions of the population, they inevitably had a further tendency to involve involuntarily the unskilled working class, possibly in submission to arbitrary violence. This tendency gave rise to feelings of local solidarity . . . and to the creation of 'militant areas' on the behalf of civil rights. (Bew, Gibbon, and Patterson 1979: 171)[1]

Here ideologies of space disconnect political intent from political consequence; the performative connotations of marching were disjunctive with the ideology of civil space advanced by the organizers of civil rights marches. Marching is an indigenous cultural practice of sectarian space with its own residual political meanings. The conjuncture formed by body and sectarian space in the act of marching triggered non-ostensive references contradictory to the overt ideological ethic of civil rights demonstrations. Protests meant to agitate for civil rights, civil space, and an ethnically neutral jural subject were received as assertions of ethnicity by both their supporters and opponents. The politicized occupation of space possesses a symbolic efficacy that crosscuts other divisions between the Protestant and Catholic working class. Bifurcated space among these groups is a component of a shared material culture that reproduces ideological and ethnic polarities. Bew, Gibbon, and Patterson use the factor of normative space both to account for specific types of political agency and to call into question any theoretical presupposition of free-floating voluntarism unmediated by cultural systems.

In Northern Ireland the adoption of American civil rights tactics collided with the dubious historical status of civil space in that province. Unlike the United States with its constitutional enshrinement of civil space, there were no significant juridical or experiential counterpoints to sectarian space that could relativize this construct and offer alternative cultural models. The rationalized geometry of civil space also ran counter to the hegemonic practices of the Northern Ireland state:

> This was most sharply illustrated in the question of the civil rights movement's 'freedom to march' . . . the right to hold marches was not recognized by a substantial number of Unionists [Loyalists-Protestants], for whom it connoted a decisive modification in the nature of the state. The feeling was shared by at least a segment of the repressive apparatuses, whose reluctance to grant it coincided with popular Protestant opinion. (Bew, Gibbon, and Patterson 1979:194)

The hostility of the Northern Ireland state to the formal equivalence of civil space (subversive of state-supported sectarian institutions from housing to employment), the claiming of an emergent and idealized civil space by the largely Catholic middle-class leadership of the civil rights demonstrations,[2] and residual cultural valuations of space in Protestant and Catholic working-class communities formed a syncretistic cauldron of available and contradictory political frames. Within this admixture, crowd violence and its repression emerged as "articulatory practices" (Laclau and Mouffe 1985) between and within adversarial blocs: "articulation is a practice and not the name of a given relational complex, it must imply some sort of separate presence of the elements which that practice articulates and recomposes" (p. 93).

Partitions

From the middle of August 1969, and in the wake of severe rioting against civil rights marches, a rapid escalation of sectarian violence occurred in Belfast. This resulted in massive relocations of Catholic and Protestant working-class populations. The ethnically mixed working-class sectors of the city and those small ethnically homogeneous districts that bordered on the larger sectarian enclaves of the opposing ethnic group were the main sites of emigration, forced dislocation, and intimidation.[3] Residents left in anticipation of impending violence or were directly forced out after threats or actual violence. Overcrowding and housing shortages in one area due to incoming populations also precipitated the reactive expulsion of ethnic others. Lasting for more than a year, these relocations have been evaluated as one of the largest movements of civilian populations in postwar Europe (Burton 1978:69).[4]

An elderly woman who had been active as a message and weapons carrier for the IRA in Belfast during the postpartition violence of the 1920s compared the two periods of intercommunal violence:

2.1   After the "Troubles" in the twenties, you put those things [the violence] out of your mind. You started to work in the same places with the Protestants and you started going to the mixed dances and you fell in with people who were Protestant. All the Protestants and all the Catholics went to the dances together. Well it gradually came that they all got into each other's districts again. The Catholics went into Protestant districts and the Protestants went into Catholic districts. And everything was forgot about then.

Did I have any bitterness? Oh, indeed I had. A life was a life, nobody should have been killed, but you can't avoid that. But in the twenties, funny enough, that bitterness all left which it won't do now. Both sides wanted to mix together then.[5] In my opinion there's too much hatred now. There hasn't been a family that hasn't suffered on both sides of the fence. It gets into your blood. Too many terrible murders have happened.

In the twenties, the ordinary working-class people did mix and that continued to 1969. Then when the Troubles started again, me and two women next to me were the only Catholics in this estate. It was all Protestant neighbors all around you. I came here in 1952 and it was all good and well. The people you had next door [were] all Protestants, and you couldn't have gotten any better. We were all great friends. Now it is all

different; families come and go all the time in these estates
now. But it wasn't like that in the fifties. The woman next
door to me was a Protestant in the twenties, and I was a
Catholic in the twenties.[6] We got together up here, and it was
great.

In 1969, a wee boy was shot in Divis by the B Specials.[7]
All the Protestants [of her housing estate] moved out. Now,
not one of them was put out. They couldn't say that. They all
left here of their own free will. The woman next door left,
and I couldn't get over that. The man next door stayed on till
Internment [1972]. There was a few strangers [Catholics from
another community] who came into the estate and wanted to
burn him out. They were coming in, just taking houses over,
these people. One woman said, "It's not fair that 'Orangies'
[Protestants] should be living in there and Catholics being
burnt out!" And I said: "There's not a one putting a hand on
that house. He's a decent old man and so is his family. If he's
going, he'll get out in peace." And that's how my daughter got
that house. She was living in Tyndale and the Protestants
were putting her out of her house.

But when they moved that old man, both of us cried; after
all those years and we had to be separated. They were afraid.
I could understand that. If I had been on the Shankill [Protes-
tant area] I would have been frightened. It was the people
who were leaving one house, shifted and moved from the
Troubles, and they were going to new houses where Protestants had been put out by Catholics. These were strangers
[Catholics not from her area] putting Protestants out here.
(Ex-Republican activist in 1920–22, Short Strand; currently
old-age pensioner, Ballymurphy, Belfast)

If populations could not be prevented from entering community
spaces, these spaces in turn were denied to them:

2.2   Every night they were coming up the street further and further burning people out. We went around to the empty
houses[8] with kerosene, poured it on all the rafters, hooked
the light switches to the water tanks or into the toilets. We
cut right through the floor boards and poured kerosene over
that. When they turned on the lights the houses would blow
and catch. That's the sort of thing we done because we were
being taken over. (Protestant male community activist,
Woodvale)

2.3   A crowd on the Falls Road stopped me in '69: "We want your
lorry to move furniture." I went with them; I had no choice;
all I could do was to try to save the lorry. I sat in the lorry,
and they moved all the furniture. All their homes were burnt.
They were Catholics, and they captured me on the Falls
Road, and they burnt out by the Protestants of the Shankill. It
was really pitiful. I had seen the crowds. "This is it, I'm going
to get done [killed] here." There were too many of them,
they surrounded me.
    I done about twelve loads for them. When I got it all fin-
ished they clapped me on the back. They had guns and sub-
machine guns and everything. When I got back to my district
I had four pints and the whole thing went right up on me. My
legs were shaking.
    It was all just heartbreaking and scared the way people
were burnt out, old people and young people. Ruffians were
coming out and ordering them out of their homes. One day I
was moving Catholics out of a district. The next day I was
moving Protestants in. That's the way it went. I was the first
to move the Protestants out of the Ardoyne. The police had
phoned up to move somebody with the police out there. As
soon as he was moved out the whole place went berserk; everybody wanted to move out.
    There was one old lady living at the bottom of the Ar-
doyne. The bullets were flying up and down the streets. We
were lifting furniture in the flames behind the smoke. The old
lady comes up to me, "Mister will you move my furniture?"
"I'll come down in a half hour's time." When I got back she
was dead; a stray bullet hit her. I can still picture that woman's face begging me.
    I was moving people for a year, with twenty lorries work-
ing for nothing on the first week. I moved furniture that
was still smoldering from the fires and the bombs. I reckoned
ten thousand people moved that year; it seemed like that.
I got letters from people months later with five pound notes
in them thanking me. (Protestant male lorry driver,
Shankill)

2.4   When you lived in a Protestant area after '69 and you went
into a shop, all the people would be having their heads together and whispering, and when you entered they stopped
and there was dead silence. And nobody spoke a word till you
went out. (Catholic housewife, St. James)

2.5   I remember standing in my burnt house, the smell of burnt
       wood and the smell that covered the city like burnt bodies,
       but I don't remember the bomb. You didn't want to believe it
       was happening that you no longer had a home. (Catholic
       woman and community activist, St. James)

In reconstructing the historical geography of political violence in Belfast, the social geographers Murray and Boal (1979:151–55; Murray 1982; Boal and Douglas 1982) view spatial constructs as mediating economic structures, class formations, and nationalist and sectarian ideologies. Following the Ecole Annales, they identify politicized space in Northern Ireland as a long-term historical structure with a determining impact comparable to economic or ideological structures. Therefore they reject origin theories of violence for reducing violence to "a dependent variable, the consequences of other processes. Within an urban system, however, violence can be seen as an important factor in shaping spatial structure. The periodic outbreaks of sectarian violence in the city and the enduring memory of them have been a powerful force maintaining high levels of ethnic segregation and territoriality" (Murray and Boal 1979:153).

The geographers identify in Belfast, from the middle of the nineteenth century to the present, a repetitive pattern of territorial extension and residential mixing of Catholics and Protestants. Elements of both groups move outward from segregated ethnic enclaves, mix, and subsequently reaggregate along more rigidified sectarian divisions in periods of social crisis and overt conflict (Boal and Murray 1977:364–71).[9] Permeating surface events and class formations, this spatial cycle constitutes a structural mechanism for the reproduction of ethnicity.

> During years of peace, the relaxation of tensions results in hundreds
> of families venturing out of segregated districts and thus increasing
> the degree of residential mixing. When strife occurs, however,
> these households are among the first victims; direct attacks or
> intimidation forces the local minority group to flee to the security of
> their co-religionists. In this context when the control of space is of
> crucial importance for the securities it offers and opportunities it
> provides, violence becomes a deliberate tool of social engineering.
> It is used as in the case of North Belfast both to define space against
> invasion and to gain new territory. . . . it is a means of ensuring
> social homogeneity. There have been examples in Belfast of orchestrated cycles of territorial violence which begins with group A forcing members of group B into another area. . . . These in turn are
> made room for by their co-religionists forcing members of group A
> out of another area. (Murray and Boal 1979:154)

In this framework, violence is equivalent to the other objectifying instruments by which Protestant and Catholic communities map themselves into specific historical and spatial arrangements, such as kinship, endogamy, and ethnically defined ethics of residence (Harris 1972; Leyton 1974:189–98; Easthope 1976:429–36).[10] Kinship and residence, augmented by a calendrical cycle of ceremonial parades, myth, and historical observances, have been the standard mechanisms, in periods of relative stability, for the demarcation of social space. The intercommunal riots of August 1969 and the accompanying residential retrenchment attempted to reassert a threatened spatial order no longer secured by other residual cultural institutions. (For Protestant communities, transformations in their ideological relation to the state during this period furthered the ambiance of stasis; see below.)

The ideological impetus of sectarian violence in this period cannot be divorced from spatial media. The qualifying character of local sectarian space and ritual calendars endowed the performance of crowd violence with the sanctified aura of historical reenactment. Space itself functioned as a mnemonic artifact that stored repertoires of historical narrative and collective action. The often-mentioned emotional intimacy of the Northern Irish with distant historical events can be accounted for by spatial symbolics in which the past takes objectified form in the immediacy of spatial cognition. The centrality of macroterritorial concepts such as a "United Ireland" or a "British Ulster" and their complex interplay with microterritorial constructs such as the community, the neighborhood, the street, and the parade route reinforces the manner in which geography serves to posit history as a cultural object. Ideological perception obtains a material charge from the force fields of politically codified space that directly mobilizes and channels action. The destabilization of topos instigates the concentration of its value form in symbolic performances directed at the reordering of persons and place.

The investment of topographic detail with precise historical meanings and narrative sediment is prevalent in rural Ireland as attested to by the oral history and etymologies that are linked to Gaelic and English rural place-names (Glassie 1982). In urban Belfast, alongside local oral history, violence emerges as a mnenomic for historicizing space and spatializing history. Historical imperatives are transferred from space to performance genres and the social actor as mobile parts of the spatial whole. There is a convergence in the materialization of historical identity in spatial constructs and the resort to material transformations of the social order through topographic violence.

The anticipated, threatened, and actual violence that precipitated sectarian retrenchment in Belfast during the summer of 1969 aimed at the restoration of symmetry between the current organization of residential space and residual sectarian ideologies, ideologies that had their authoritative spatial referent in the large stable ethnic enclaves to which the residents of the mixed communities fled. Crowd violence colonized and inscribed anomalous social space with sectarian codes. In this dynamic, topography ceased to function as a thing. It was much more than a passive template for the inscription of violence or an object to be manipulated in order to create political representations. Space became a power and an animated entity.

The Interface

Boal and Murray (1977:364–71) term the "interface" the topographic-ideological boundary sector that physically and symbolically demarcates ethnic communities in Belfast from each other. The "interface" is a spatial construct preeminently linked to the performance of violence.

> Because of the physical segregation of the two groups [Protestant and Catholic], most of the inter-group clashes have taken place along the boundaries between Protestant and Catholic areas. The inner parts of these areas have remained relatively free, a haven for the victim of a second type of conflict manifestation, intimidation. (P. 370)

The recodification of mixed areas into confrontational zones transformed them into interfaces writ large.[11] In Belfast the urban interface zone is in symbiosis with the pattern of sectarian residential extension, mixing, and contraction. During periods of residential retrenchment along sectarian lines, the proliferation of interfaces, the dissemination of margins, the formalization of boundaries can be expected.

> The Springfield [road] interface was also prominent in the disturbed period of the early 1920's, and became a major flashpoint once again in 1969. The lack of a change in the pattern is notable and recently has been given an almost total rigidity by the construction of the so-called Peaceline along the interface. This peaceline built in 1969 has been placed at precisely the same location as the site of the 1896 riots and subsequent outbursts. (P. 370)

A report on the 1896 riots that occurred on the Springfield Road interface states: "The great points of danger to the peace of the town [Belfast] are open spaces in the border land between the two quarters of two of these spaces—the Brickfields and the Springfield will be found to have been the theaters of some of the worst scenes of the riots" (p. 370).

Rioting at the interface appears to function as a traditional mechanism for setting and even extending territorial boundaries between Catholic and Protestant communities. As such, it is a variant of the often violence-provoking commemorative parades and the ceremonial marching seasons that characterize the political culture of Loyalism and Republicanism (Easthope 1976:440; Burton 1979:75–76); Buckley 1985–86). Bell (1987:166) views Loyalist ideology among working-class Protestant youths as residing in parades which are a "set of practices . . . a symbolic habitus" where they "explore and repair fractured ethnic identity."

The typical spatial pattern of these parades is the movement from the center of the community (physical and/or symbolic), where the parade audience is ethnically homogeneous, to a march along the boundaries demarcating an adjacent community composed of the opposed ethnic grouping. Marching along the boundaries transforms the adjacent community into an involuntary audience and an object of defilement through the aggressive display of political symbols and music. In periods of peaceful coexistence the Orange Order (Protestant) parades were occasions of great entertainment for Catholics, who often tactfully attended these events from the sidelines. But during periods of ethnic tension, marching at the interface was a predictable and intentional trigger of violence based on the formation of a schismed audience. Ceremonial marches are important in the Catholic communities, but in the Loyalist (Protestant) community they are an axial rite. Among Loyalist marchers there is a tradition of "taking" a new street and incorporating it into the parade route. These new routes are either on the boundary or actually within the recognized territory of adjacent Catholic communities. In the next year's marches, these new routes are vehemently defended from Loyalist incursions by outraged Catholics or the police. In the Loyalist community these parades synthesize historical symbolism, the command of space, and boundary transgression. This synthesis raises the conjuncture of commemorative history and sectarianized space to the heights of ritual resolution. Republican commemorations and, more recently, the public funerals of paramilitaries serve a similar function in Catholic working-class communities. (Though not all working class Catholics identify themselves as Republicans.)

The violence that can result from these space-claiming marches is precipitated by the concentration of antagonistic political signs in a reserved space that had previously been insulated from the accumulation of visible political codes because of its status as a tension-provoking interface. The calendrical organization of these parades is significant, for, given the political climate of the period, it can *channel ethnic violence into specific formats, times, and spaces.* Interfaces function as more or less tacit boundaries and are only formalized at crucial moments (determined by the calendar or the general political climate) and left undersignified at others.

The general intensity of the parade, particularly if it instigates violence, temporarily shifts the symbolic center(s) of the demonstrating community from residential clusters, commercial districts, or church sites to the margins of the community, to the interface. This transference of political centers, temporary as it is, relocates the cathexes of ethnicity from kinship and residence to the parade and to its symbolic and real violence. In turn, the interface–flash point is thereby transformed, as the 1898 report put it, into a political "theater" (Boal and Murray 1977:370). Violence, symbolized or practiced, in this performative context is identified as the appropriate medium for colonizing the outer margins of community space, while kinship and residential structures are reserved as the central ordering apparatuses of the internal community proper.

What occurred in August 1969 was a rigidification of interfaces beyond any calendrical timing, though calendrical observance was one of the initial precipitating factors in this process. The rigidification of space indicated a temporal delimitation of violence.

On August 14, 1968, during the traditional marching season, the following sequence of events took place on the boundary line between the Falls Road section (Catholic) and the Shankill (Protestant) in Belfast:

> From early in the evening on the 14th, the tension was evident in the mixed streets running between the Falls Road and the Shankill Road—particularly on the two, Dover Street and Percy Street. . . . In this atmosphere of tension a large crowd [Catholic] assembled in Divis Street end of the Falls Road hard by Hastings Street police station. Predictably, a few teenagers attacked the place with stones and petrol bombs. . . . the armored cars—this time armed—were ordered on the streets. They drove up and down Divis Street . . . scattering the Catholic crowd up into the "mixed" streets running north. Two of those streets were, of course, Percy Street and Dover Street—down which a muttering Protestant crowd, among them B Specials [police reserve], was gathering. . . . [Later that night] a crowd of Catholic youths . . . marched north from Divis Street up the "mixed" Dover Street carrying the tricolor and singing the Irish Republic's national anthem, "A Soldier's Song." They then cut through into the next "mixed" street. . . . They emerged in full view of the Protestant crowd milling around the Shankill Road. . . . the Protestants were electrified. (Sunday Times Insight Team 1972:133–35)

The next day all the Catholic houses that had not been destroyed by the rioting were evacuated, and Dover and Percy streets ceased to be a mixed area. Many Catholic homes were burnt by their emigrating owners. This tactic, also practiced by vacating Protestants (see narrative 2.2), installs the area as a desolate interface zone.

After 1969 the ritual political calendar could intensify violent interactions, but it no longer wholly determined them. Boundary rigidification and delimited sectarian violence were accompanied by the erection of barricades, some of which were turned into permanent "peace walls" and "environmental barriers" by the government after the British army tore down the first barricades in 1972. The erection of barricades coincided with the formation of "vigilante" groups (community patrols) and the simultaneous or subsequent emergence of paramilitary organizations. The vigilantes were set up as security patrols, and the initial function of the paramilitaries was defensive military intervention.

The barricade/interface, divorced from calendrical associations, was a prescribed place for chronic violence. The subsequent erection of "environmental barriers" by the British government did little in the way of reducing the attraction of violence to this type of space. The politically charged interface ceased to be an expression of community identity and began to regulate community experience. Communities became hostages to their barricades and their ossified boundaries, if not actively violated by their spaces of exclusion:

2.6 The corrugated iron barriers are awful. There are other ways to create distance between communities, but once the corrugated iron wall is there it's a point for people to get at. "There's Taigs [Catholics] on the other side of that!" or "There's Prods [Protestants] on the other side of that!" So they get within a few yards of it and throw bricks over it thinking there's one there they might hit. The next thing you get is fucking petrol bombs and everything coming over. Then some jolly lad decides to come out, stands about twenty yards away from the wall and shouts, "Drop!" Everybody by the wall drops, and he puts two hundred machine gun rounds through it. And it doesn't hit anybody that's been throwing the bricks but hits some old woman up the street that's completely innocent. (Protestant male community worker, Woodvale)

2.7 They put a barrier up, and there's a door [household] on this side of it and there's a door [household] on the other side of it. God help the people that live there because they don't live there long. They live there for a few weeks and can't stick it any longer what with the bricks, the sniping, and the petrol bombs. You'd get twenty houses deserted just because a barrier was put up. (Protestant housewife, Woodvale)

An Ulster Defense Association (UDA) commander who owed his position to these events ironically reflected on their consequences:

2.8   There was just this mass hysteria; there was no political ideology behind it. Being a Shankill man, never being out of the Shankill in my life, we used expressions, "The Taigs are going to kill us! They're going to do us in!" And at the end, looking back now, they [the Catholics] were thinking the same, that we were going to "do" them. Fucking everybody put the barricades up, and if you looked back on it what actually happened was that both sides began to do people in. All because of the barricades. Everybody was sort of intransient in their own districts waiting for the odd "slap" and nothing happened. So out of frustration people said, "All right, there's nothing happening at the minute but they're going to do it. Won't we be better going out to do it first." Then the bombing started and the shooting started and the vigilantes came up and then the regulating organizations [the paramilitaries] all started to evolve.[12] Candlestick makers and bakers were made generals and toilet attendants were made colonels. People who never had any military experience or anything else just came out may it be through some form of aggression, because they could dig [hit] somebody a wee bit harder.

    What you are talking about in terms of the separation of the communities is barbed wire, hurdles, and peace walls at that time. It was like going into a room that has six doors in it, but all those doors are locked up and there's only one door to go in or out, and on the other side of that door you have the fear of a possible hostile environment. You have half a dozen doors and somebody blocks off five of them. People get frightened. There's only one way into a Catholic or Protestant area and there's only one way out. "I'm not going in there." (Protestant member, Shankill)

2.9   In '69 I was working in a factory on the Dublin Road. The barricades were up in Ballymurphy and everywhere else. And this "yop" who came from the Shankill, a real out-and-out Protestant, was waffling on about how terrible it all was. There was this girl from Ballymurphy [Catholic], she was standing on the other side of my pressing machine. She had married a Protestant, and she didn't want to know anything about what was going on in the Troubles. She was telling this

Protestant what it was like living in Ballymurphy and how the barricades were desperate, how bad it was having to give passwords and the rest in order to get through in order to go to work and to come back. Nobody believed it was going to last long at that time. The Protestant woman was asking her, "How the hell do you get to work in the morning?" Your one from Ballymurphy started telling her how she got out of the barricades, what the passwords were and all that.

I kicked her around the other side of the pressing machine. And she let that out of the bag too. I says to her in front of all the Protestants, "You've no bloody business talking about the people of Ballymurphy and their barricades. And better still I'm going to tell the people of Ballymurphy what you're saying!"

A right row brewed over the whole matter. The next thing I hear my husband's voice [he was working in another section of the factory], "Come on, get out of it! If you don't get out of it you'll not only lose your job but your life!"

I grabbed my bag and he had the bus waiting outside.
(Catholic community activist, housewife, St. James)

2.10   I remember the barricades. One of my mates was shot; he was on a barricade at the time to keep the Loyalists from getting into the area. To go from one Catholic area to another there was a password. It was all "bread" or "butter" or "milk." We must have had food on our minds then. It was really exciting as a kid watching those barricades built and actually having somewhere to play. We had trees we climbed not up them, but over them. We'd play hide and seek and "You're the Brits and we're the RA." It was all brilliant. They had pulled the trees down on August 15, 1969. They had put spikes in the middle of the road to prevent cars from driving in. They had dug up all the roads. The barricades got turned into a playground by the children. We had been kept in the house through all the violence and now we were allowed to move. We all got together and went down to the barricades.
(Catholic housewife, St. James)

An elderly woman pondered with amusement on the ease with which the smallest details of daily life were politicized and immersed in fear:

2.11   There were bins across the street for the barricade; then they got concrete over the bins. When they first got the bins out, I said to Dolly [a neighbor] "You for it now! [You're in trouble now.] Because your door number is on that bin, and they [the Catholics] are looking over from the other side to see who got the bins up for the barricades!" She was down at the barricades trying to steal her bin back again! [Laughter] (Protestant old-age pensioner, Woodvale)

2.12 Every street was barricaded all the way down the Grosvenor Road. The McDonald Street barricade was the one that was opened and closed. They would swing it behind you so fast as you were going through that they nearly had half of you in the bloody door. I had to go around to find out who was on the barricades when I was going and coming back from work, so they could open the door for me. When you walked up to it, it was corrugated iron and you had to rattle it and say who you were and where you were from, your name, and on what street you lived. It was rough. After a while you said to yourself: "They have to be there." Inside we had our own shops, even chemist shops and a first aid station. Each street had been given its evacuation plans in case we were overtaken. (Housewife, St. James)

2.13 I was shot on the 15th of August 1969, at a quarter to five. I was shot in the face with bird shot, got peppered in the face and chest. I was standing at the corner of Disraeli Street [near an interface]. A bus was stopped by a crowd from the Ardoyne. They beat the people off with pickax handles. They charged up the street and over our barricade and chased the bus up the Crumlin Road. Three guys walked out of the bus as calmly as you like with twelve-bore shotguns, and they started.[13] I was shot that day for the second time. I had been walking by Ardoyne Chapel; I had decided to walk down the Crumlin Road: "No Taig is going to put me off the Crumlin Road [interface]!" type of attitude, swaggering the shoulder, and this guy stepped out of the chapel and shot me in the ball of the leg with an air pistol. . . . Well the second time by the barricades that finished me. I was taken to the hospital; I got shot because Crumlin Road was a barrier, sort of a dividing line. I knew when I was shot that I had gone blind, everything went black. . . . People will tell you I am a UVF (Ulster Volunteer Force] man. Even my girlfriend doesn't believe that I am not. The UVF claimed me in '69 when I was shot. If I had survived another hour on the 15th of August, I'd have been in Crumlin Road jail for murder. An hour after I was shot about

eleven 303 Enfield rifles arrive here, and that is the one
weapon I love to use. . . . I could be hitting people at about a
thousand yards with that weapon and knock everybody off.
. . . A couple of days later when I was in the hospital a Republican radio station said my name, said they knew which
hospital I was in and [that] when I got out they would do [kill]
me. Then they played that song, "Beautiful, beautiful brown
eyes." (Protestant male, Woodvale)

Not all the violence of this period was limited to the mixed communities and other interface zones, but the spatial retrenchment reorganized
the political-sectarian topography of Belfast—a process that generated
certain preconditions for the autonomous reproduction of violent reciprocity. The cumulative result was the formalization of what had been
heretofore tacit and residual cognitive mappings of the urban topography.
Significant areas of Belfast were organized by an interlocking binary
spatial grid and inside/outside polarities. The proliferation of interfaces,
the barricading, and the influx of refugee populations organized the ethnically homogeneous areas into sanctuary spaces, or at least generated
idealized sanctuary constructs that functioned as mental maps for local
people. The ideological and physical plotting of urban space took the
following form: sanctuary/barricades—interface/adversary community.
This structure was rapidly translated by the paramilitaries into a militarized configuration that could be depicted in the following manner:

Performative Structure

targeted-targeting community	defensive-offensive violence	targeting-targeted community
SANCTUARY	**INTERFACE**	**SANCTUARY**

Spatial Structure

The conversion of communities into "no-go" areas automatically codified the other side of the barricade as an immanent source of transgression. The entire symbology of purity and impurity which impregnated the
polarities of ethnicity received a reifying substantiation in the inside/out-
side division of social space. This division was particularly cogent when
the other side of one community's barricade or wall was a doubled antagonistic community with its own set of barricades and vigilante patrols.
Spatial formation was reorganized into a mirror relation that had a profound ideological impact (Lacan 1977).

In this process, the topographic, the tactical, and the ideological were fused into a mobilizing spectacle which channeled the perception and performance of violent exchanges. Political representation and spatial order constituted a single interactive and mutually sustaining social structure for the reproduction of violence. The fusion of the historical and the spatial by new levels of symbolic investment generated the political autonomy of space. It was upon this autonomization of spatial order that the performative autonomy of paramilitary violence was largely predicated.[14] In contrast to the spatial order that prevailed prior to the summer of 1969, the mechanics of dissected space divided the social order not only into ethnic categories, but also into categories of life and death.

Within this spatial metaphysic, political interest, utilitarian ideologies, and strategies of political manipulation could not be artificially separated from their symbolization in topographic coordinates. Urban space was reinscribed as a radicalized historiographic surface, a terrain of representation that determined the conceptualization of political interest. In this context it cannot be assumed that the formation of political interest precedes the modes of available representation. A political culture, by definition, is organized by prescribed modes of objectification. Political programs are mediated by and conceived within available and recombinant grids of depiction, which means that all instrumental rationality is engendered within a symbolic and artifactual apparatus of representation.

The Sanctuary

The sanctuary/interface/adversary community structure should be understood as both an on-the-ground organization of community space and a system of classification. The creation of the sanctuary cannot simply be viewed as a withdrawal from an anomalous outside, from a violence-prone public domain, in order to create a relatively violence-free haven for confessional communities—a haven that could be contrasted to the bitterness and tragedies of the now-destroyed mixed areas. The sanctuary attempted to mediate violence into certain prescribed channels and not to abolish it. The sanctuary/interface/sanctuary system managed violence in and through spatial devices.

The sanctuary/interface complex was an ideological organization of the spatial dimension of human association and the spaces of violence. It attempted to preserve the subordination of violent enactment to the prerequisites of residence and kinship through the spatial confinement of violence. The sanctum was constituted by a space that was reserved for residence and kinship and by a complementary space, the barricades-interface continuum, reserved for the ideological and material reproduction of community through violence. The cancellation of the calendrical control of violence was counterbalanced by this partition that promoted temporally open but topographically fixed domains of transgression. This arrangement was a very traditional attempt to subordinate disordering historical time (in the form of violence) to spatial enclosure. It also instituted a new tradition: every subsequent intensification and proliferation of violence in Belfast can be interpreted, from the vantage point of the sanctuary/interface ensemble, as an effort to *concentrate violence in manageable but exchangeable forms. Both the rationality and seeming irrationality of chronic violence in Belfast can be traced to the sequential exhaustion of forms that both contained and permitted violence.*

The sanctuary construct, despite its overt defensive rationale, was an explicit attempt to territorialize violence, to maintain the institution of the interface as the prescribed place of violence. Thus, the sanctuary-/interface complex could never be a purely defensive mechanism to the extent that the interface itself was an anomalous zone of reversible violence, a space for defensive and offensive action. The sanctuary demanded the militarization of the barricaded communities which limited the cultural authority of kinship and residential structures, though the latter did much to legitimate this process.

The creation of one community as a sanctuary automatically designated an ethnically opposed adjacent community as a targeting-targeted formation. This relation was passed back and forth between all the barricaded communities, transforming them into instrumental units of a violent system of exchange. This targeting was initially enacted by crowd violence and sporadic individual violence across the interface zone or against individuals of the other ethnic group caught in the interface zone, or found on streets and roads that were technically claimed as part of community territory. Ultimately, violence across the interface was to take on more specialized and covert forms as the paramilitary groups geared into action.

The extent to which the interface partitions the domains of violence from the domains of kinship and residence is currently evident in the abandoned houses immediately adjacent to the corrugated iron peace walls that have replaced the barricades. This sterile zone of boarded-up and sometimes burnt-out shells indicates the withdrawal of the community's settlement line to sectors distanced from the interface. The spaces by the corrugated iron walls are dead zones. Their debris offers the raw material for stone throwing; their abandoned buildings function as natural observation posts for petrol bombings and "snipes"; and the wall itself becomes the malevolent face of the people who live on the other side of it.

Jean Franco (1985) has eloquently discussed the semantics of the sanctuary and its relation to political violence in the context of Latin

America. Her analysis of the sanctuary touches on several important issues that bear directly on the cultural and political dynamics of the types of violence that emerged from this social space in Northern Ireland. Franco, citing Bachelard, defines the sanctuary construct as an immune space, as an expression of "topophilia," a space that is defended against "adverse forces," and as "eulogized" space. In Latin America the sanctuary space is rooted in sharp inside/outside, private/public, family/state, sacred/secular vectorings of social life. As such, typical Latin American sanctuary spaces and spatial personifications are the home (reinforced by the enclosing architecture of Latin culture), the church, the monastery, women, priests, nuns, and children. The sanctuary space in Latin America is an eminently feminized domain associated with the temporal continuities of kinship and other symbolic forms. It articulates, represents, and reproduces territorial ethics, the local command of space, and redemptive forms of sociation (Franco 1985:414–20).

> In Latin America, this sense of refuge and the sacredness that attaches to certain figures like the mother, the virgin, the nun and the priest acquire even greater significance, both because the Church and the home retained a traditional topography and traditional practices over a very long period, and also because during periods when the state was relatively weak these institutions were the only functioning social organizations. They were states within states, or even counter-states, since there are certain parishes and certain families which have nourished traditions of resistance to the state and hold on to concepts of "moral right." (P. 416)

Certain basic continuities between the Latin American sanctuary and the Northern Ireland "no-go" areas are established here despite numerous cultural and historical differences. The emergence of the sanctuary in response to the absence of a strong centralized state was certainly a condition that prevailed in the summer of 1969, a condition that the erection of barricades and the emergence of paramilitary organizations managed to exploit until the development of more effective counterinsurgency tactics by the British army. The close linkage of the sanctuary to the cultural authority of kinship and residential systems based on symbolic kinship can also be found in Belfast. Related to this is the tradition of specific politicized communities, neighborhoods, and families. This was a predominant pattern in Belfast, where many working-class communities were defined by their "hardness"—their collective toughness, predilection for violence, and/or strong political convictions. In Catholic communities a crucial role was played by traditional Republican families who had furnished one generation after another to the IRA in its various incarnations and campaigns.[15] It can also be argued that during the initial offensive incursions made by the army and police, local traditions of "moral right," community, and familial and domestic integrity (rather than fully worked out Nationalist and Republican ideologies) were the ideological bases of resistance to the state by Catholic communities.

For Franco, the cultural hegemony of the counterinsurgency state is advanced by its violent decimation of sanctuary spaces and the colonization of their ethical landscape. This model can provide the basis for understanding the development of paramilitary hegemonization and paramilitary forms of violence within the barricaded "no-go" areas of Belfast in the early 1970s.

In Latin America, the sanctuary as a topophilic space is informed with transcendent, idealized, and utopian resonances that contribute to its ideologies of resistance. Yet these same utopian values such as family, church, and moral community are appropriated by the state *in coordination* with its violent penetration of the sanctuary and the death, torture, and imprisonment of its inhabitants. The signifiers of the mother, the family, feminine purity, domestic purity, and religious solidarity are expropriated and universalized into abstract and, according to Franco, "deterritorialized" sign systems (1985:415). Abstract ideologies of eulogized space are fabricated by the state, in tandem with the erasure of the sanctuary as a quotidian experience.

> This assault is not as incompatible as it might at first seem with the military government's organization of its discourse around the sanctity of Church and family. Indeed these convenient abstractions which once referred to well-defined physical spaces have subtly shifted their range of meaning. . . . This process can be called deterritorialization. (P. 415)

The role of Belfast women in defending community space against the incursions of the state is described in chapter 4. Though the counterinsurgency state in Northern Ireland has functioned as a repeated violator of domestic and community space, local paramilitary groups within these same communities, in pursuit of local hegemony through violence, have also functioned as a deterritorializing force. Ideologies of local territoriality and not only nationalism were the semantic medium by which paramilitary organizations legitimized their specialized operations. Yet paramilitary practice created cycles of violence that exceeded the spaces and performative prescriptions that had been predicated by the sanctuary/interface construct. This space was rapidly instrumentalized by paramilitary organizations as they converted the sanctuary into a base of operations. Chronic paramilitary violence eventually played a pivotal role in the disintegration of the community space as a sanctuary to the extent that it attracted retroactive violence aimed at the confessional space.

Paramilitaries, Populist Violence, and State Formation

State hegemony in Northern Ireland was in part contingent on repressive apparatuses that did not relegate the monopoly of violence to discrete organs of the state. Militarism had a popular sectarian and anti-Catholic dimension promoted by the state. The state did not rarify the command of violence. The repressive apparatuses consisted of the Royal Ulster Constabulary (RUC) and citizens' militia known as the B Specials.[16] These organizations, which were overwhelmingly Protestant in their makeup, were in turn supported by public safety legislation that severely short-circuited civil liberties for Catholics. The sectarian character of the RUC and the state-sponsored paramilitary groups was central to the symbolic management of the class bloc upon which the Unionist state based its legitimacy among Protestants: "populist responsiveness . . . had always characterized the relationship of the Unionist State apparatuses to the Protestant masses" (Bew 1985:17).

Since its inception in 1921, the Northern Ireland state never functioned as a passive instrument of class or sectarian interest. Rather it engaged in autonomous programs of internal hegemonization that generated a receptive configuration of Protestant class fractions. The state sought legitimation in the democratization of violence, which strengthened its affective association with populist anti-Catholic actions and postures. The democratized command of violence was instituted through the Specials, a paramilitary unit with strong regionalist ties to Protestant communities. The state used the paramilitary organization and the RUC to rationalize populist sentiment. This regimented and regimental populism enabled the state to actively collaborate in the formation of Protestant ethnicity. Paramilitary organizations as sites of power constituted by the state mediated the latter's relation to the Loyalist political vernacular (ideology and ritual) as a site of power "included in the strategic field of the State" (Poulantzas 1980:37).

The state's militarist articulation with local Loyalist culture blurred any distinction between repressive and ideological apparatuses. This conflation rendered the social rhetoric of violence and the paramilitary regimentation of the masses internal mechanisms for aligning Protestant class fractions. This situation dramatically changed after the state's repression of the civil rights movement between 1968 and 1971. The partisan role played by the RUC and B Specials resulted in damaging worldwide media attention and became an embarrassment to the British. The Westminster government was forced to push for the disbandment of the Specials and reorganization of the RUC. These reforms, which attempted to rationalize and desectarianize the repressive apparatus of the Northern Ireland state, divorced this organ from Protestant populist identification: "by forcing through the reforms of the police and Specials they [the British state] had severely weakened the Unionist regime, for they had destroyed the crucial relation between it and the Protestant masses (Bew 1985:23).

Voiding the relation of the state's repressive apparatuses to populist sentiment did not eradicate populist paramilitary violence as an enabling ideological form and practical force. That formation has been rapidly shifting instrumental sites since the early 1970s and the barricading in Belfast and Derry. This shift in operational sites occurred in tandem with the incremental collapse of the state's ability to mobilize its populist credibility with Protestants (a process aggravated by the entry of the British army as a nominal guardian of Catholic communities in the early stages of conflict). The collapse of the state's hegemony over populist violence was reflected and accelerated by the spontaneous appropriation of paramilitary practices by antagonistic Protestant and Catholic working-class communities. The fragmentation of a dominant state-sponsored paramilitary apparatus was expressed by the fact that Loyalist paramilitary groups lacked a centralized command and solely identified with their local community base. (This was true in many instances for Republican forces, due to the anomaly that IRA military command during this period was located in the Republic of Ireland and not in the North). The development of paramilitary groups in these districts certainly drew on long standing independent local traditions, but we cannot underestimate the residual effect of the Northern Ireland state in legitimating the paramilitary formation as a populist political instrument.[17]

The emergence of local paramilitary forces presupposed the fragmentation, inversion, and internalization of the social rhetoric of populist aggression historically promoted and centralized by the state. These groups emulated the state's fusion of repressive and ideological apparatuses and implemented programs of somatic regimentation and aggression anticipated by state militarism. Today the mimesis between paramilitary groups and the state is still evident, though it has shifted to the paramilitary emulation of the manner in which violence is bureaucratized and rationalized by the state's counterinsurgency apparatus.

The Runback

The sanctuary space ceased to fully protect or insulate the community as both sectarian killings and state incursions increased in scope, gauge, and number.[18] A profound retrograde dialectic emerged with the proliferation of chronic violence. The territorial violation of the sanctuary became a given condition of daily life, as redemptive ideologies of national territoriality promoted by the paramilitaries assumed greater and greater value.

Deterritorialization of the sanctuary entailed its ideological alienation-abstraction as a nationalist entity in tandem with its material effacement.

Paramilitary organizations exploited the inherited mythic link between microterritorial iconography (the confessional community) and the macroterritorial icons of a "United Ireland" or a "British Ulster" to secure their legitimacy in base communities. This dynamic relegated the reality of territorial purity and completion to the realm of retrospective (Loyalist) or prospective (Republican) utopian projection.

The relative stability of territorial integrity and the ravaging of such constructs during the intense periods of violence differentiated the pre-Troubles confessional community from the barricaded "no-go" areas. This shift was expressed in the ideological transfer of social reproduction from kinship and residence to violence by the paramilitaries. Within the ideological and topographic form of the sanctuary, *experiential deterritorialization emerged as the dominant condition of social reality, as utopian territorial icons emerged as ideological projections of national redemption and ethnic integrity.* The performance of paramilitary violence and its reception by support communities constituted a ritualized reenactment of a social imaginary, an attempt to insert the ideal order of territorial enclosure back into social experience in surrogate forms. The contradiction between the experience of spatial defilement and utopian territorial completion created the *structural* prerequisite for ongoing symbolic violence.

The surrogation of the sanctuary space can be plotted through the emergence of novel topographic constructs. Sectarian murder committed in the space of the other repositioned the interface into the heart of the confessional community and even within the domestic space itself. (The performative dynamics of this practice is discussed in chap. 3.) The patchwork layout of Belfast's confessional enclaves (then and now) encouraged hit-and-run tactics against antagonistic communities. In planning such operations paramilitaries carefully plot escape routes known as "runbacks."

The runback consists of the network of alleyways, double-entry buildings, street systems, and highways that permit the evasion of police/army patrols, checkpoints, and antagonistic paramilitary units. The terminus of the runback is the "safe house," a miniature sanctuary which, in the early and mid-1970s, more often than not was located within the confessional community. Paramilitary units pick up weapons, disguises, and vehicles at safe houses prior to the operation and deposit this gear at safe houses after the operation. Runbacks are usually no longer than five minutes' travel by car from target site to safe house. The timing is essential because at this stage of the "op" (military operation) the paramilitary unit will be in possession of incriminating weapons and a stolen vehicle.

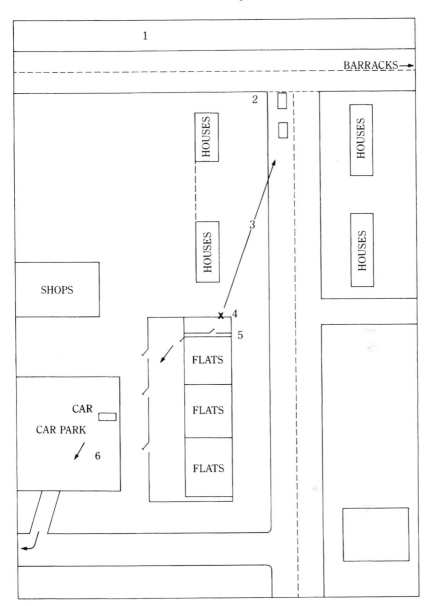

Figure 2. Runback map (based on a drawing by an Intelligence Officer of the Irish National Liberation Army). *Key:* (1) wasteground limiting the possibility for accidental civilian casualties; (2) British Army troop carriers waiting to make a right turn onto main road leading to barracks; (3) line of rifle fire from behind garbage disposal area of the flats; (4) position of attacking paramilitary unit; (5) beginning of runback to location of escape vehicle; (6) vehicle runback to "wash house."

Runbacks display both a technical and a symbolic profile. In an "op" the escape vehicle and the threshold of the runback are positioned at a distance from the actual site of violence. In well-planned operations there will be a series of "cutouts" or blinds that at each stage of the operation visually and physically insulate the paramilitaries from the target, the place where violence is performed, the weapons, the vehicles, and the clothing used by the unit. Visual discontinuity is a tactic essential to an urban guerrilla struggle up against closed communities and advanced surveillance technologies. This insulation of violence through spatial segmentation is analogous to the setting up of a demarcated interface zone—the space that distinguishes where violence can take place and where it cannot.

The safe houses where paramilitaries pick up weapons, receive stolen vehicles, and don disguises, are gradations that detach the agent of violence from "public" identities. The spatial and performative polarity between community space and violent interface inflects the transformation of agency and identity as the paramilitary enters the terrain of political action. This spatial qualification is informed by the stigma of contamination in which violence, as the production of matter out of place, must be confined to a specific space. In performing violence one moves from the terrain of the pure to the impure.

The spatial gradation between the pure (the confessional sanctuary, kinship, and residence) and the impure (the arena of violence) is reversed when exiting the space of death. The safe house that paramilitaries return to after the "op" is called a "wash house." There the unit rids itself of weapons, clothing, and vehicles. It is in this space that the paramilitary is debriefed and the clothing worn on the operation is either burnt or laundered to get rid of incriminating forensic evidence. The wash house is a place for literal and symbolic decontamination. It is the site for the temporary divestiture of transgressive agency. The removal of weapons which are now considered "dirty," having generated forensic traces (particularly if this is not their first use), is the premier event of the wash-house decontamination. The wash house is also a place where jokes are told against the object(s) of violence. These tales are considered by paramilitaries to be psychologically cathartic and are an integral part of the debriefing process. (I was unable to document wash-house stories because informants considered them to contain too much incriminating detail essential to their telling.)

Today safe houses and wash houses are not located solely within confessional communities (no longer barricaded) but are clandestine zones in ethnically mixed and politically neutral areas such as middle class residential areas. Their proliferation as miniature sanctuaries and their association with the logistics of the paramilitary on the run are indicative of the destabilization of the larger, community-based sanctuary by chronic violence, violence that is implemented by the safe house and wash house. The miniaturization and mobilization of the sanctuary construct in safe houses refract the "deterritorialization" of the confessional community. Interiors like the runback, safe house, and wash house first instrumentalized the sanctuary as a military base and then were pivotal in marking the sanctuary as a target for adversary paramilitary groups and the state. Here the miniature sanctum, initially expressive of a larger associative interior (the confessional community), effectively violated the latter. For security reasons, the safe house and wash house were gradually detached from any exclusive topographic contiguity with the confessional community. This physical alienation of part from whole and the eventual dissolution of the whole precipitated intensified symbolic linkages between the two sites that were expressed through nationalist imagery.

The emergence of sanctuary concentrates—safe house, wash house, runback—signaled the emerging sacrificial patterning of violence. Hubert and Mauss (1964) analyzed the sacrificial act in terms of the spatial poles of entry and exit. Entry into the space of sacrifice and exit from it are qualified by contact with impurity and by decontamination rites. The sacrificial destruction of matter and contact with matter-out-of-place calls for strategies of containment. The spatial instruments deployed by paramilitaries in the performance of violence show an analogous techno-symbolic concern for locating the pure and the impure in polarized material and spatial artifacts. Like the arena of sacrifice, the spaces of paramilitary performance also stand in a symbolic relation to a larger, distanced community. But in the instance of Northern Ireland, the part/whole relation that ideally subordinates sacrificial space to communal space could not be sustained in the face of chronic retroactive violence. The runback, safe house, and wash house both aggravated and compensated for the divestiture of the confessional community. Further, the displacement and fragmentation of communal space by the practices of the militarized space engendered a renewed and urgent ideological investment in metaphors of spatial integrity, purity, and completion—a United Ireland, a British Ulster. The local confessional community—caught between the part spaces of the interface, runback, safe house, and wash house and the totalized utopia of nationalist unification—functioned as a mediating, expendable, and sacrificed term.

3   *Hardmen, Gunmen, Butchers, Doctors, Stiffs, Ghosts, and Black Men*

From Hardmen to Gunmen

> It doesn't take a hardman to terrorize people. Anybody can do that.
> You can go in and terrorize your next-door neighbor if you have a
> hammer in your hand.
>
> —UDA gunman

In Belfast, oral narratives express the tensions between residual spatial
systems and deterritorialization by contrasting past and present forms of
violence. Comparisons of violence are encoded in the oppositional figures
of the "hardman" and the "gunman." "Gunman" refers to the paramilitaries, irrespective of political affiliations. The "hardman" was the local
bare-fisted street fighter intimately associated with specific neighborhoods though often enjoying a citywide reputation. The hardman could
have been a semiprofessional trained pugilist (Belfast has a rich tradition
of boxing families) or simply a street tough.

The hardman and the gunman are elements of a folk narrative that
encodes the historical transition from territorialized to deterritorializing
violence. They personify the historical experience of communities that
once laid claim to rule-bound performances of violence, and subsequently
experienced the development of violence beyond traditional social institutions and ethics. The narratives that contrast the hardman to the
gunman are a veiled political discourse on the ethics of violence. In
certain narratives, the contrast between the two figures is used to question the legitimacy of paramilitary violence. Others formalize the historical shift to paramilitary violence in order to specify the explicit political
character of paramilitary practice. In all narratives, the figures of the
hardman and the gunman embody a historical succession in which the
latter displaces the former. Yet the narratives synchronize the two figures in order to classify types of violence.

The hardman stories, in the current political context, measure local
social transformation in the changing ethics and performance styles of

violence. They constitute an oral history of transition between two moral orders. Not surprisingly, it is often the paramilitaries who readily discourse on the hardman as part of a process of performative and political self-definition. For this reason, the figures of the hardman and the gunman, despite their polarity, demonstrate a cultural tendency to personify collective identity and even historical periods through the icon of the exemplary specialist in the use of force.

The British media in reporting on Northern Ireland often refer to the hardmen of particular paramilitary groups. "Hardmen" here refers to fanatic advocates of radicalized violence. Paramilitaries reject this designation not only because they do not want to be characterized as fanatics, but because the term "hardman" explicitly depoliticizes their violence. Keepers of community traditions look upon the application of the term "hardman" to paramilitaries as symptomatic of the desiccation of local ethical systems. The conflation of hardmen with gunmen in media representation and public opinion encodes another level of cultural deterritorialization. By appropriating a traditional term and institutionalizing the conflation, the media reifies unrelenting violence as a "fixed" cultural characteristic of certain Belfast communities. This conflation effaces cultural values in which the imagery of the hardman actually expressed community-based ethics that restricted the performative gauge and objects of violence.

For the keepers of local tradition, old-timers, and paramilitaries, the violence of the hardman and the violence of the gunman summarize different periods, forms, techniques, and intensities of violent practice:

3.1   There is no such thing as a hardman now in Northern Ireland. There used to be before the Troubles. They fought with fists on the street, you see, but when the guns came out the hardmen disappeared. "I don't mind fighting you bare-skin in the middle of the road, but when you bring the fucking guns out, I'm not a hardman now, I'm standing down." That's the way it went. You had the Baggots, the Graves, the McKees and "Stormy" Weather[all]; they're away now. The hardman as such fuckin' evaporated or even emigrated. There are no fuckin' hardmen about now. "I'll punch you but I'll not punch a gun," and they forgot about it. . . . I used to love chasing all the hardmen.

But an era went with them. Because they would have fought stripped to the waist on waste ground and punched each other fuckin' stupid. It had nothing to do with Taig [Catholic] and Prod [Protestant]. Punchy Miller was a wee hardman in his day. He's an assemblyman now and carries a fuckin' gun. They all carry fuckin' guns now. Of course you get older and you get wiser. It's better shooting him than getting punched and having a fair dig at him. The Troubles changed the whole lot. (Officer Commanding in the Ulster Defense Association, UDA)

3.2   It doesn't take a hardman to terrorize people. Anybody can do that. You can go in and terrorize your next-door neighbor if you have a hammer in your hand. It's easy enough to go up to people and knock their doors carrying a shooter and say, "Right this is it!" Scare the shit out of them. Soon as they see the gun they say, "O fuck it's the Boys [paramilitaries]." It's psychological. Say the right words with the right mannerisms and they'll fucking get down on their knees. Maybe I'm going beyond the normal awareness of a lot of people in this situation, but these are the things I picked up over the years. We didn't know what psychological warfare was, we just did it. Couldn't even spell our own names at the time. Didn't know what the word meant. (UDA)

3.3   Each area of the city had its hardman. They were famous, like Buck Alec on York Street who used to keep two lions and was deported from America. He worked with Al Capone, boxed the Yanks and all when they were over [during World War II]. There was all these stories about different men on the Shankill Road. There was this one Shankill man who was well known for being a real good street fighter, and this guy comes up to him and tapped him on the arm and says, "I'm the All-Ireland lightweight champion," and the hardman just turned and hit him once, banged him like that; he never got off his stool. He says, "Well you just lost your title."

The paramilitaries put an end to that because once somebody lifted a hand to punch you, you just stuck a .45 up their nostril and they didn't want to fight then. Them days were long gone. My father he would have said, "If you can't use your fists don't fight." But I remember when he got into a fight with a young fellow who hit him with a chair when he was sitting down. My father says after that he knew that it had come to an end. There was no more of this waiting for your opponent to get up again after you had knocked him down. The hardman fight was more for the excitement than the actual fight, but with the paramilitaries it turned violent here and it was all for to inflict bodily harm.

Pulling out a weapon, that was a whole new ball game, and the hardmen stayed out of it. I've seen it with my own father. He never got involved with the paramilitaries but he would be recognized by many as a hardman because of his fighting ability. He would go to the greyhounds [races] and mix with the dogmen and that both Protestant and Catholic.

There's that generation gap. It's mostly younger men joined the paramilitaries.[1] Today if there's the odd fight in the pub it wouldn't attract the crowds it did years ago. Years ago, "Come on, so-and-so is going to fight so-and-so down at the pub." Women and children would gather to watch it. (Ex–Ulster Volunteer Force, UVF)

3.4 We keep coming back to the definition of the hardman, the difference between a hardman and a thug. Silver McKee and Buck Alec who were the two big names among the hardmen. These men were unafraid; they would have fought anybody. They had a reputation and were willing to stand and fight to maintain it. They were like the shooting men of the old American West.

You had these others who came along like the Caulderwoods, a lower Shankill Family; these were hoods, street fighters. They would have been foot soldiers in the early days of the Protestant paramilitaries. In the early days, the Provos and the Loyalists took on anybody. The Caulderwoods were rated by some as hardmen, but they were just thugs. Today people confuse them with the hardmen.

I see a clear distinction here. You couldn't be a hardman if you were willing to terrorize women or young people or engage in petty thieving. There is a terrible difference between that and the man who stands on his own two feet and says, "Okay I'll take your best man and fight him." Buck Alec was not afraid of anybody, shape or size. Apparently he was prepared to stand toe to toe and fight it out with an equal, irrespective of the gun.

But the gun was used, particularly for sectarian killings which apparently he wasn't adverse to doing. There were sectarian killings in the 1920s at the shipyards, 1920–21–22. The years of continuous sectarian outbreaks. Buck Alec was heavily involved in that. He had such a reputation that people might have been afraid he would use the gun on his own, so he was recruited. The police on York Street were so annoyed with him that they disarmed him because he had such a reputation for sectarian killing at that time. He would walk around with his gun strapped to his waist.

He had a lot of power in this city. He was allowed to keep his two lions at home during World War II. One of the laws was that because of the bombings all dangerous animals had to be kept in the local zoo. He was allowed to keep his lions. That showed you the power he had.

The police wouldn't interfere in a hardman fight. The police here were all very involved in boxing. As long as the fight wasn't out on the road they would have turned a blind eye. . . .

The hardmen generally had a tradition—you didn't use guns. They were the fellows who were willing to fight at the drop of the hat. There was one character, Stonewall Jackson, he'd pick a fight for no reason. Ye had eejits [idiots] like him. Ructious Toal [Tone?] he was beat between drink and getting beat about his head. He used to say the prayers between the beatings Friday and Saturday night, and he started fighting. The police would come and he refused to budge and then fight the police. He would ask for a particular police surgeon and would only give himself up to that doctor.

Stormy Weatherall and Silver McKee were supposed to have tangled at Ormeau Park. They were supposed to have fought for three hours. Weatherall, a big hunk of a lad, boxed at middleweight at 160 pounds. Only had eight to nine fights. As a street brawler he was 170 which was quite big for that period. McKee and Weatherall fought for three hours and decided to call it quits and not to enter into each other's territory. McKee was from the Low Markets (Catholic) and Weatherall was from the Shankill (Protestant).

The average 5/8er doesn't want to fight. The ordinary 5/8 in Belfast is a fellow who works from eight in the morning to five at night. He doesn't want to fight. He's ashamed of it. That's not because he lacks courage. He doesn't want to fight. Now you go into a strange town and you get into a row in some pub or other, apparently not by doing anything specific. It's not the fellow standing there with a collar and tie who's going to come to your rescue. If anybody does come to your rescue, that guy is sure to be the local hardman.

The hardman doesn't get involved in a lot of fights. That type of fellow didn't glory in his reputation. He knew he could take people. There was no fuss about it. Buck Alec and Silver McKee wouldn't have gone looking for trouble. They would be familiar with the people of the area, and they would keep an eye out for people.

They didn't function as policemen; they were just hardmen. There wasn't so much drinking in the twenties, but the hardmen had a rep for being heavy drinkers. That would have set them off from the rest at that time. They would have been a small group within a small group.

This question of the hardman, where does it start and where does it finish? In a pub not far from here, a well-known Republican on the Provisional side, he was very highly wanted by the police. Apparently he had a brawl on this one particular day. Disappeared and came back five minutes later with a .45. He wasn't the brightest individual at the best of times. This individual was a foot soldier, not a general, a man who would commit a sectarian or political killing and would be caught. But the men behind him wouldn't be caught, the generals. They would stay clear. These are the differences. When the gun came in there was no longer any hardmen.

The hardmen would fight just to see who was the hardest. They fought for themselves and nobody else. On the docks, if a fight was on it was just you and him. His mates would stop it if he didn't follow the rules. The question would be, "Is it going to be 'all in' or 'clean'?" It was always a 'clean' fight. 'All-in' was boots, and the head, no weapons. If you decided it was going to be a clean fight and somebody used his head or boots, his own mates would stop it.

Up Sandy Row [Protestant area] or back of the Markets, two hundred to three hundred people around the hardmen, a half dozen fighting each other. Not Catholics against Protestants, but Catholics fighting each other and Protestants fighting each other. Just trying to see who was the toughest.

The Bone was the area for the hardmen, like the Hammer on the Shankill. They were tough guys, working people but they were tough. The yards behind the Markets and the slaughterhouses were the place for hard drinking. One minute they were going to kill you and the next they were going to drink with you. It was the atmosphere of Belfast—a tough town.

The hardmen had this code, "There was no dirt in it." A code of conduct, an unwritten traditional code, and this was accepted. You would have gotten a bloody hiding if you broke that code. You could get yourself in a terrible bloody condition if you broke that code. Your reputation would be destroyed if it was broke. Today I listen to the lads talking, "Five or six of us beat this lad up!" And they laugh and joke about it.

They're not men at all. But a fight between you and me, man to man, personal contact . . . Certainly in the old days you didn't go up six to one. If you had you were destroyed. If this did happen to you, you would've gotten your own mates and gone hunting to solve the problem. If you went up against someone six to one your reputation was mud!

The decision to make it a clean fight or "all-in" was made there and then in front of witnesses. The witnesses were there to ensure that the rules were carried out. They would've also watched for the police. . . . In the dockside there was fields between certain entries and houses, there were railways yards—natural fighting spots. . . . The women would have stopped the fights. They would have clipped you in the ears and dragged you home for your tea!

People of my age [mid-fifties] who were in a good number of fights find it hard to take the brutality of these days. (Catholic male, trade-union activist, ex-resident of the Dockside)

The hardmen's combat revolved around symbolic issues of status and the self-construction of reputation in the willingness to risk the body. In contrast to paramilitary violence, the hardman represented a noninstrumental ethic of violent performance (excepting those particular hardmen who accrued economic rewards for their violence). The hardman/gunman polarity can be read as a techno-ethical opposition—the distinction between violence as a performative component of an individual agent and violence as a mechanized component of the gun, in which the human bodies at both ends of the instrument fulfill purely transitive functions.

In those hardman narratives critical of paramilitary practice, the artifact of the gun evokes the rationalization of violence and the victim. In this perspective, the gun is seen as a diminution of the autonomy of the agent of violence and signifies his self-conversion into a tool. This is based explicitly on the gunman's instrumentation by an organization and implicitly on the gunman's investment in the object relation of the victim. These dynamics are alien to the hardman ethic.

The violence of the hardman is locally perceived as a moral construction of the self through techniques of the body that set the individual hardman apart from others. Between the hardman and the gunman, there is a contrasting construction of the self in reference to both the practice and the object of violence. The hardman's violence represents the extreme individuation of performance. This is based on narratives of the body that construct the hardman's singularity in the community.

Through the self-construction of the self in violence, the hardman came to signify the self-contained and autonomous singularity of his community. The hardmen came from "hard" places like "The Hammer," "The Bone," and "The Nick." As one hardman put it, "I live in the toughest area of Belfast. As you walk down my street, each house is harder than the next. I live in the last house on the street." There was a reversible transfer of moral substance between the hardmen and their communities. The differential relation of the hardman to other men became a metaphor for the relation of the hardman's community to other places.

In certain narratives, the individuation and personal visibility of the hardman are contrasted to the effaced persona of the gunman. The hardmen "fought for themselves," while the paramilitary has "men behind him" for whom he enacts violence on order. The hardman fought to attain a personal visibility. In contrast, the paramilitary is concerned with the anonymous collectivization of violence-the subordination of the self by acts of violence to historical generalities. The iconography of the *masked* paramilitary that dominates the visual propaganda of both clandestine organizations and the state is an expression of this defacement.

Many paramilitaries maintain a personalized and often problematic relation to their acts of violence, yet their propaganda transforms and sublates individual moral commitment through representations of abstract force. In visual propaganda the mask has many more iconic functions than merely protecting individual identity for security reasons. Posters of masked paramilitaries holding weapons are statements about historical transformation and the construction of power. The masking of the agent of force, his depersonalization, identifies this agency with the trajectories of history as generalized forces. The masked paramiliary holding a weapon is a tool holding a tool. This imagery which appears in posters, at press conferences, and at funerals depicts the mechanization of historical intervention.[2]

In the ethic of the hardman, the practice of violence is centered in the self. Hardness is an interiorized quality extracted from risking the body in performance. For the gunman, violence is an eccentric relation, an instrumentality that is detachable from the self, that transcends personal limits and attains magnitude. There is a reversal between the *masking of the face and the display of the gun* in paramilitary visual propaganda. It represents the erasure of the self as agency passes through the gun into the collective magnitudes of historical alterity. The mask is yet another representation of autonomous, collective violence. This recodification of the human face anticipates the construction of transindividual political agency. Through the signification of absence, the mask points to the metonymic circuit formed by paramilitary, gun, and victim. In this circuit, political codes are transferred from one site (agent of violence) to another (the victim) in order to attain collective representation. What the mask hides is that the absent face of the agent of force is worn by the victim marked by violence.

The hardman fought to attain a visibility that was in direct correlation to the diminished visibility (reputation) of the other hardman he defeated. Reputation was founded on scarcity. There was just so much hardness to go around. Hardness was a quality mastered by a few and tied to the immediacy of the hardman's body and fighting techniques. In contrast, the efficacy of the paramilitary's violence is dependent on his remaining covert and his victims attaining visibility. He attains a surrogate visibility through a chain of victims as the mechanized reproduction of the para-military's ideological code. In the cultural shift from hardman to gunman the relations of visibility and invisibility that govern the relation of the agent of force to the object of force are inverted. The hardman attained visibility through the objectification of his own body. The paramilitary achieves political visibility by objectifying the bodies of others.

The ethical shift from hardman to gunman is illustrated in the case of a few hardmen taking up the gun during periods of sectarian violence. When these hardmen practiced sectarian violence, both the performative ethics of the "fair dig" and the dyadic relation to the adversary vanished. The victim of sectarian violence possesses a social-symbolic generality as Catholic or Protestant that is alien to the dyadic confrontation and testing of traditional hardman violence. In the hardman tradition, the opponent is defined performatively. In sectarian murder, the victim is defined taxonomically. The mechanization of violence furthers the loss of the adversary's individuality and completes his subordination to the ab-stractions of ethnicity. (To this phasing of the hardman into the gunman can be added the imagery of both the hardman and paramilitary as social bandits. In Belfast both figures can be associated with protection rackets.)

The cultural construction of the hardmen through oral history ex-presses the collective investment in the topographic segregation of vio-lence that was discussed in the last chapter in reference to calendrical ceremonies and the "interface." The hardman narratives exhibit the tra-ditional tendency to reserve violence for specific spaces and agents de-marcated from other domains of community life. There were "natural fighting spots," back alleys, fields, and railway yards appropriate for the hardman contest: "They would have fought each other . . . on waste ground" (narrative 3.1). The topographic vectoring of hardman violence was extended to the body. The opposition between the "clean fight" or the "fair dig" and the "all-in" limited the techniques of violence to specific capacities and terrains of the body. These rules pointed to the fact that the performance of hardman violence involved a collective moral con-struction of the body for both the agent and object of violence. This moral construction was enforced by the cohort of "mates" and the surveillance of the oral culture of the community. Even the domestic space had a cultural authority over this violence conducted in public space: "The women would have stopped the fights. They would have clipped you in the ears and dragged you home for your tea" (narrative 3.4). This is in sharp contrast to paramilitary violence, which is both directly (in doorstep murders) and indirectly (in the counterinsurgency of the state) linked to the violation of the domestic space (see below).

The displacement of the hardman by the gunman in Belfast in the late 1960s and early 1970s was a minor skirmish in the hegemonization of base communities by paramilitary organizations. But for many paramilitaries and community residents, the imagery of this displacement was culturally central. For the latter the iconography of the hardman encodes certain tensions and ambivalences about paramilitary violence that are not easily expressed in public.

What is significant in these narratives is that the evaluation of paramilitary violence is not based on a negative comparison with nonviolent practice, but in terms of the contrast between two divergent forms and agencies of violence. It was the growing autonomy of paramilitary violence from community contexts, its deepening investment in disrupting the community of the Other, and the increasing separation of paramilitary decision-making from a discursive interface with the community (see Burton 1978) that rendered the hardman significant. The hardman was a singularity, but this quality was jointly constructed by his performances and the oral culture and moral order of the local community. These discourses and ethics could also destroy the reputation of the hardman or place limits on his status and violence. This is a much more problematic situation in reference to the figure of the gunman.

In the present political context, the tales of the hardman have been reorganized around the subtext of territorialized violence—a rule-bound community surveillance of a violence that was reserved for certain spaces and objects and prohibited from others. It was the deterritorialization and mechanical reproduction of both violence and victims in the current situation that foregrounded the gunman's displacement of the hardman. The fact that this awareness of the difference between the two figures is limited to a certain generation of working-class Belfast further intensifies the sense of historical displacement. The shift from hardman to gunman reflected transformations in the cultural construction of violence and the advent of new utilities and styles of violent performance. The paramilitaries narrativize this shift in order to encode a genealogy of their performance styles that is not encompassed in their formal political ideologies. For others the hardman encodes an idealized relation of community to violence that once predicated the community's view of paramilitary practice.

The era of the hardman coincided with the cultural dominance of industrial capitalism in Belfast. The hardman fight and its locales and characters were central to the iconography of industrial working-class culture. The hardman ethic was a revaluation of the body confronted with the power of the machine, not an unusual response considering the relatively recent rural background of the Belfast labor force in the first half of this century. This ethic valorized both physical performance and the moral construction of the body through rules of performance. This was both a counterpoint to the sublation of the worker's body in the mechanization of industrial labor, and a restorative transfer of somatic labor performance to nonmechanized social domains. The hardman's body was removed from commodity circuits through its "singularization" (see Appadurai 1986) as an agency that could not be mechanically reproduced or sold as labor power. The oral culture of the hardman fight was a coded resistance that implicitly opposed the moral construction of the body in the "fair dig" to the pacification of the 5/8er's body in the labor discipline of industrial production. In this context, the displacement of the hardman by the gunman constitutes an inversion. It transformed the moral relation of working-class culture to mechanical reproduction through the imagery of the gun, though in this instance it was not the economic but the political instrumentation of the body that was at issue. The practice of the gunman subverted the somatic singularity and power of the hardman. Political practice subordinated the bodies of the violent agent and the victim to the mechanical reproduction of ideological codes (e.g., Republican and Loyalist). In the critical hardman/ gunman narratives, this inversion appears between the tropes of "pure" violence (the clean fight, the fair dig) and the impurities associated with the automation of violence and victims—the transgression of corporeal integrities linked to the mechanization of aggression.

Sensory Formations

The shift of ideological reproduction from kinship and residence to the mechanical productions of the gun was facilitated by a substrate of corporal symbolism present in both systems and activated by the cultural practice of "telling" (Burton 1979). "Telling" is the sensory identification of the ethnic Other through the reception of the body as an ideological text. "Telling" is a reciprocal ideological formation of the body of the other and of the senses that interpellate that body. Thus in decoding the other it also encodes the self, a symbiosis that renders "telling" a nexus for the construction of political agency. "Telling" constructs a conjuncture of clothing, linguistic dialect, facial appearance, corporal comportment, political religious insignia, generalized spatial movements, and inferred residential linkages. These sign systems cohere into an iconography of the ethnic Other that regulates informal encounters with particular others.

> Telling is a system of signs by which religious ascription is arrived at in practical settings. As a discourse it takes the form of a series of semiological systems whose signs (name, face, demeanor, dress, phonetic and linguistic variations, color, icons, and territory . . .) are connected to confessionally signified groups (Protestant or Catholic). (Burton 1979:62)

Telling is organized around paradigms of ethnic purity and impurity that predicate informal social relations into managed rule-bound situations. This practice provides an analytic access to the everyday construction and reproduction of social dualism. Telling politicizes the senses as historical artifacts. Yet telling is much more than a passive template of overarching sociohistorical codes, for it is precisely a crucial medium that applies ethnic metanarratives as somatic and spatial metaphors. Telling fuels the daily maintenance of a dualistic social order through a system of "common sense" that is in effect an ideological fiction.

As optical and auditory surveillance, telling allows the interpreter not so much to avoid polluting contact with ethnic others as to organize interactions with ethnic others into arrangements of reciprocity and separation that preclude the possibility of transgressive contact. Yet Burton also finds an explicit connection between telling as a residual traditional cultural practice and the emerging patterns of political violence. This implies that telling, in paramilitary practice, is used less as an avoidance mechanism and more as a means for the production of violent encounters through victim specification:

> As a practical discourse the telling signs become inscribed in and influence certain other practices. The discourse helps to order the selective distribution of jobs, houses and more recently assassination victims. . . . Telling becomes a purification filter which orders the potentially polluting contact with a cross religionist. . . . At this level telling is the conceptual ghetto of Northern Irish ideological social relations. (Burton 1979:77)

The ideological construction of the body in the practice of telling is but one component of a historically and spatially informed predilection for the political transcription of the human body. The ethnic texture of the body which is operant in day-to-day informal social interactions attains a particular intensity in traditional political rituals. In this case, it is not the identification of the confessional affiliations of others that is at play but a confessional signification of the self through the text of the body. Buckley's (1985–86) analysis of the insignia worn by members of the Orange Order, a Protestant secret society, reveals complex semiotic cross-references between the political codification of the body (through the wearing of these insignia-badges), sacralized texts, and origin myths. The insignia are worn at Orange Order rituals, the most preeminent being the numerous parades that occur during the marching season of the summertime. Buckley's research reveals a tripartite indexing between the display of insignia on the body during these marches, biblical texts, and the current sociohistorical situation of the Protestant community as perceived by the Orange Order members: "These emblems are not always related to their texts in a manner which outsiders easily recognized. . . . they depict gardeners' tools adorned with olive branch; a seven stepped ladder; a skull and cross bones; a man; a stick with a snake wrapped around it; two crossed trumpets; a square and compasses" (p. 11). The themes encrypted by the insignia, which are worn on collarettes around the neck or on lapels, are the confrontation with alien societies, settlement in promised territory, exile, and faithfulness to religious creed (p. 11).

The major context for public display of these insignia is the parade, a rite that territorializes social space, visibly demarcating inside/outside polarities. The insignia can be seen as territorial codings of the marching body wearing these badges. The marches transfer territorial imagery (note the prevalence of the themes of settlement and exile), from body space to social space (the parade route). The insignia are active components of a total system of historical and spatial inscription that organizes the spectacle of properly coded bodies. The subtext of purity and impurity that informs those insignia concerned with exile, faithfulness, and uneasy coexistence with an alien people can also be found in the boundary-setting intentions of the parade.

The convergence of body space and topographic space is also a crucial component in telling. The proper reading of the various signs of embodiment, including dress, insignia, and speech, creates a circuit that indicates the residential affiliation of the subject and thus his precise relationship or nonrelationship to the social space in which the subject is encountered. Conversely, the placement of the subject in a space with strong sectarian identifications can serve to reinforce and verify the somatic aura of the Other. In this instance meaning and semiosis flow from the coded geography to the body organizing the intrinsic signs of embodiment into a sectarian text.

In the sectarian codes analyzed by Burton and Buckley, categories of purity and impurity and of territorial integrity and transgression figure prominently. In Buckley's analysis, defilement and purity are historicized allegorical motifs, while in Burton's analysis of telling, ethnic contamination and its avoidance are formed by synchronizing body space and social space. This isomorphism uses material artifacts and politicized senses to simulate a historical narrative in the flesh of the Other. Bodies codified in such a manner are no longer biological monads, but emerge from formally constructed social backgrounds encumbered with sedimented semantic weight.

The practice of telling actively constructs sign systems in order to determine of which sociohistorical space the encountered body is a synecdoche. Telling reattaches the spatially mobile body to a homogeneous social field as a mobile part. The purity and impurity which Burton identifies as the moral frame of telling proposes that specific bodies are proper to prescribed social spaces while the presence of others transgresses these spaces. Telling posits an organicist ideology between body and topography, and its daily practice juridically reproduces this organicist ideology through the senses as historical artifacts.

The organic relation between body and topography forms the moral order of the sectarian community. Ideologies of kinship and the practices of endogamous marriage and residence are further applications of this moral order or grid of correspondence between body and space. Transgression of moral order occurs when bodies are out of place, when they occupy territory to which they have no organic contiguity or shared iconic historical or spatial codes. This is particularly cogent when the space being occupied and altered by these out-of-place bodies has a residual link with another collation of "in-place" bodies.

The Butchers

The convergence of telling, space, and violence is self-evident in the atrocity stories about Lenny Murphy and the Shankill Butchers, a Loyalist murder gang that operated in Belfast in the mid–1970s. In these stories, the violent location of political codes in a somatic space specified by telling is in effect a statement about social space.

In the oral culture of Belfast's war zones, symbolic genocide impregnates particular violent incidents and emerges from particular personae that function as condensed symbols of historical possibility. These acts and figures mark an outer limit. This limit was invoked by the Shankill Butchers. For this reason, both Loyalist and Republican paramilitaries are quick to disassociate themselves from this type of violence and do so through stories about the Shankill Butchers. These tales suggest a profound slippage between official political rationality and the performative logic of paramilitary violence.

Shankill Butcher stories push all conventional notions of instrumental violence in Northern Ireland to the background. They privilege the circular relation between the executioner and the body of his victim as a mythic representation. The violence depicted in the Butcher stories records a logic that was bound up with a totalizing investment in the symbolics of sectarian space and the radical reduction of the Other to that space.

3.5   The way the Butchers picked up Catholics was that one of them was in the UDR (Ulster Defense Regiment)[3] and used to walk up to guys in town and say, "You're under arrest," showing him a UDR identification and says, "Right, get into the car!" If your man resisted they just all walked out of the car and hammered him on the street and stuffed him into the car and drove him away. . . . McAllister [one of the Butcher gang] picked up a Catholic and hit him on the head with an ice pick and killed him. Dumped him in a black taxi and drove off to this local pub and had this stiff in the boot of the car while they were drinking inside. They got drunk and one of them says to McAllister, "You fuckin' wanker, you yellow bastard!" Here's McAllister, "Fuck it, I'm a hardman!" He says, "Right, we'll go off and cut this fuckin' guy's head off here." The boy they got was from the bottom of New Lodge [Catholic district]. McAllister says, "I'll cut his head off and you put it up on the fences there in New Lodge." They cut him right to the back to the spine. The people who found the stiff couldn't figure why he was both shot and his throat cut.
    They [the Butchers] done [killed] more Protestants than they done Catholics. *They picked guys off certain streets figuring them for Catholics but they were Protestants* [emphasis mine]. They were doing robberies on the Shankill Road [Protestant area] and the UDA had to disarm them. The UDA went to the UVF and said, "These fuckers are robbing everybody. Disarm them." They disarmed them, and all they had was some old guns that didn't work. After that Murphy said they'd be better off cutting people up. (Catholic male, North Belfast)

3.6   The time the Butchers got caught they done this boy so they did and he didn't die. Cops picked him up, patched him up, and he pointed the Butchers out. I knew Murphy in jail and I says to Murphy, "But what about McClafferty? How did youse make a mistake with McClafferty?" Here's the Butcher, "I don't know why that cunt didn't die," he says really amazed like. "We really did a first-class job on the boy. We slit his wrists up the ways." They defleshed his arms so they did;

"we cut his throat and reversed the car over him a couple of times." McAllister was wearing Doctor Martens [ankle-length work boots, stereotypic footwear of Loyalist paramilitaries according to Catholic paramilitaries]. McAllister took his shoe laces off, tied them together around your man's throat, and used a stick as a tourniquet to tighten the laces around the neck. They had a big stick with a six-inch nail on it, they were whacking it on his head. McAllister had him tied to a chair while "Butcher" Bates was cutting the flesh off his arms, trying to get the vein with a butcher's knife.

And while they were doing this Artie McKay made them all a nice cup of tea. They stopped the torture and gave your man a cut of tea and then started up again! That's true enough. (Member of Irish National Liberation Army or INLA)

3.7   There was a doctors' surgery on Downing Street, and everybody on the Shankill Road knew that in the doctors' surgery on Downing Street the UVF killed Taigs every Friday and every Saturday night. And every cop knew it too—that the Butchers killed Taigs there on Friday and Saturday nights and then dumped the stiffs in the Forth River. And every Saturday and Sunday morning the peelers [police] would send a patrol out to pick them up. But they never sent a patrol around on the Friday or Saturday nights! That's why the Taigs of North Belfast are freaked out of their fuckin' heads. The cops eventually issued a statement that Catholics shouldn't walk certain streets after dark.

There were places in Belfast you never walked! No way on God's earth did you walk them, unless you were completely out of your brains. Milford Street! Union Street! Clifton Street! Up the Antrim Road and the Oldpark! Just forget about the Oldpark Road. If ET had landed on the Oldpark Road someone would have fuckin' stiffed him! It was a fierce place. They would have fuckin' cut ET's head off or at least gone after that wee glowing finger of his!"

ET was definitely a Taig!

Aye, wasn't he Green!

They [the Butchers] were fierce for fighting among each other. One of them got into a fight with another member of the gang and smashed his head with a beer barrel and killed him. His mate [not a member of the gang] shot your man with the beer barrel. The mate who did the shooting was arrested by the UVF and brought up to one of their social clubs and was sat on the stage facing the entire Belfast UVF command. All the rest of the Butcher gang was brought in and sat down in front of your man who did the shooting in the first row. Suddenly Murphy jumped on the stage with a short [pistol] in his hand, saying, "This guy here is a fuckin' eegit." The UVF thought he was going to kneecap your man as a bit of discipline. But Murphy put the gun to his head and blew your man's brains out all over the UVF command. People were freaking out; they were splattered with brain. Murphy was a very heavy guy. The UVF was so angry about it they made Murphy clean the whole mess up. (Catholic male residents of North Belfast)

Loyalist paramilitaries' attitudes toward Murphy and the Butchers are marked by the absence of the black humor Catholics and Republican paramilitaries take out of these events. In response to an "ethnological" question, I was informed by a UDA member:

3.8   They're not "folklore" to our part; they're scum. . . . The Catholic press says they murdered thirteen Catholics, which is a lot of balls. They murdered four Protestants. . . . You had Nookie Shaw. Murphy went up to a club and sat him up in a chair and put a bullet through the front of his head in full view of the whole club, just so nobody would ever testify against them; psychological it was. They were frightening them; they all saw who done it. It was worse than that. He used to ring the *Sunday Press* and say, "I'm Lenny Murphy and I shot so-and-so. It's your job to prove it." He built up such a notoriety somebody had to do him in. But the only thing I had against Lenny Murphy was that I knew Nookie Shaw and there was no reason to do wee Nookie Shaw. And they put him in a laundry basket and left him in a black taxi on the Shankill. (UDA)

3.9   I was talking to one of the Shankill Butchers in prison, and I asked what would you have done if it was me or someone you knew. And he said, "I would have had to kill you." Right up to that point I was ready to go out and start killing again, to go back into it. Then I honestly thought would I want to go out and just kill innocent people. To me it was nothing to kill someone who was IRA, that was good enough reason. But to simply kill people because they got on a road you claimed as yours or walked into your area, or in an area that was Catholic, to kill for the joy of it, I thought I'd never want to be like that. . . . It was a fearful thing for Protestants and Catholics. I remember making sure I was out of Belfast by six o'clock at night. Going down the Shankill Road, making sure I was out of that area before dark. Because everybody knew it was coming from the Shankill Road. It put people indoors; no one was out at night. That was the effect it had. (Ex-UVF)

3.10 I had to go up to the graveyard where Lenny Murphy was buried to see if a headstone had been delivered to the grave of my father-in-law. I took my son with me. We contented ourselves that the headstone was perfectly placed and I says to the son, "By the way, the Shankill Butcher is buried up here in this cemetery." He wanted to see the grave, so we danders up about four hundred yards through the tombstones and we find his headstone. "Aye that's the old Butcher dead and buried." No sooner than had I said it that I felt a tap on my shoulder. An RUC [Royal Ulster Constabulary] policeman in uniform says, "Have you any identification?" I says, "What for?" He says, "I'm asking the questions here." He asked my name and address and where I worked. Two uniform policemen in the middle of a lot of tombstones. I didn't want them to see what I was driving so we walked the other way past my car. We turned around and there they were, two peelers both stood at Lenny Murphy's grave looking at it and looking at it. That's the last thing we seen; we disappeared. (UDA)

The Shankill Butcher stories are organized around the polarity of free-floating, invisible random violence and the gravity of mutilated corpses and defiled space: "everybody knew *it* was coming from the Shankill Road" (3.8). The magnification of the violated body as a spatial unit and the transgressive aura of certain branded spaces are complementary signs of social deformation. Through their violent cathexis, body and topos communicate fearful alterity. The silent horror that grows around deformed spaces subtracts these sites from assumed contexts and anchorages. The disappearance of bodies from specific spaces becomes the sympathetic expulsion of those spaces from their social surround:

> "There were places in Belfast you never walked! No way on God's earth did you walk them, unless you were completely out of your brains" (3.6).

The extraction of part from whole rehearses social transformation of the whole. The Butchers' violence appears to indulge in static binary

messages. But these polarities, as spectacle, plot the passage into genocide. Political violence constructs historical alterity by specifying certain
sites and surfaces as the space where passage is to be simulated. Historical time is encysted in material artifacts to better effect its manipulation, acceleration, and mutation.

In the Butcher's case the tortured and disfigured body encapsulated
the spectacle of collective Catholic holocaust. The encoded body and
killing zone became sites of a transaction where residual historical and
political codes and terror and alterity were fused, thus transforming
these sites into repositories of a social imaginary. These invested surfaces have the semic and sensory potential to trigger the sickening slide
of reality into historical otherness.

The practice of torture in this instance was a *production* that detached
the body from the self in order to transform the body into a sectarian
artifact, an abstraction of ethnicity. Mutilation here is the physical erasure
of individuality as a deviation from an ethnic construct. The ethnicity of
the body is built in its dismemberment and disfigurement. Violence constructs the ethnic body as the metonym of sectarian social space. The
abstraction of ethnic bodies was the decapitation of the confessional zone:
a removal of part from whole. Yet the Butchers' killing of Protestants who
were found in what they classified as "Catholic" space was a disturbing
exposure of imaginary ethnicity rooted in the "telling" discourse.

> In the concentration camps it was no longer an individual who died,
> but a specimen. . . . Genocide is the absolute integration. It is on its
> way wherever men are leveled off . . . until one exterminates them
> literally as deviations from the concept of their total nullity.
> Auschwitz confirmed the philosopheme of pure identity as death.
> (Adorno 1973:362)

For Adorno the post-Holocaust period is characterized by the absolute
impossibility of individualized death. In the violence of the Butchers,
Adorno's theory is paradoxically realized in the detachment of the body
from the self. This detachment is a prerequisite for abstracting the body
through torture and mutilation into a political token. The body is transcribed into imaginary space through the magic of torture which defaces
the body as a singularity and constructs it as an abstract value form of a
spatial referent. In this process, the body emerges as a political construct and the self as apolitical residue, an excess left over from the
process that transforms the body into a political form. The cup-of-tea
episode in the torture of McClafferty (3.5) is indicative of the dissociation
that registers the formation of the ethnicized body as a political commodity, as an abstract invariant that is detachable from the self as an
apolitical unincorporated excess:

And while they were doing this [torturing McClafferty], Artie McKay made them all a nice cup of tea. They stopped the torture and gave your man [the victim] a cup of tea and then started up again! That's true enough!

The story of the visit to Murphy's grave (3.9) gathers together the many strands of corporal and spatial symbolism in the political culture. The site of the grave, the conjuncture of demarcated space, and the corpse refract the historical goal of sectarian symbolization, that is, the moral unification of body and territory—Adorno's "absolute integration." This conjuncture represents the ritual effectivity of the Butchers' violence, the mythic goal that underscored their minute labors on the body of the Other. Yet since it is ultimately a utopian construct, "absolute integration" is concentrated in a singular surrogate. In this story, Murphy's grave is a spatial and political autonomy that radiates power. It has the aura Benjamin associated with the commodity as a spectacle of desire. The uneasy surveillance of the grave by the police confirms this. The polarity of the grave (body and topos) in opposition to the police (the state) functions as a formulaic expression of paramilitary power.

Genealogies of the Dead

In the war-zone communities of Belfast, death has its oral history that is organized around the allegory of symbolic genocide. The genocidal allegory is constituted by part objects and part narratives that refer back to the absent whole, the completed erasure of ethnicity and ethnic spaces. The metaphor is built death by death, and each death expands the negation of ethnicity from the household, to the street, to the neighborhood, until the outer limits of ethnic identity are made to coincide with the outer limits of ethnic erasure.

Any stranger who enters into these communities in search of dialogue is initiated through the recitation of the dead. These genealogies organize the historical experience of political violence into a localized narrative that underscores the overarching codes of Loyalism and Republicanism. Biography, oral familial ledgers, and neighborhood solidarity are organized around the shared genealogical substance of the dead. The dead died in certain places and at certain times that form conjunctures with institutions and events external and internal to the community. The genealogies are calendrical markers that anchor overarching events of historical magnitude in local temporalities and representations. The community marks itself with the cartography of death events—the spaces of the dead. Local history, biography, and topography intertwine through the network of genealogy. In the recitation of the dead, the sense of collective defilement is deposited into historical narrative. The dead are placed at the origin of collective defilement and local history and in their narration continue to bear the burden of this qualification for the entire community.

The genealogy of the dead is a direct inversion of the positivities of kinship and residence, once the central units of the moral order of the inner city neighborhood. The production of ethnicity is partially grounded in the mnemonic recitation. Social reproduction becomes organized around an absence: one's own dead and the dead of the other side. This doubled chain of corpses forms temporal and spatial magnets that sublate and redirect the social relations of the living. The lineage of the dead and the sociation of the living—exist side by side as mirror images of each other. The synchrony of the two social orders is a tensioned trope of the immanent inversion of the living by violence, past and present.

Two components of the genealogical narrative are the banshee or death-warning tale and the ghost story. These narratives are salient because as local iconographies of "bad" death and collective defilement they are directly tied to the imaginary of social space.

3.11　　There have been so many horrendous deaths in this district over the years that there has to be ghosts! (Catholic housewife, St. James district)

3.12　　The night before Francie Legget got dead, a girl from this area was coming from her friend's house. She was passing this wall, a long wall, and there was no houses on that part of the street. She seen a banshee sitting on the wall, and she screeched. John McGorn heard her screeching, and he came down and took her to the house. She said it was a wee small withered woman crying with tears and mourning. He was asking her and asking her about the woman. She said to John, "What are you staring at?" He was as white as a ghost. He said he saw the very same thing when he went to fetch her away from the wall. That was a Thursday night, and on the following Friday morning Francie Legget was shot dead on the spot. (Housewife, St. James district)

Another member of the community continues:

3.13　　Another night a few months before that there was an awful gun battle in our area, and it lasted all over the weekend. They blew Kelley's bar up, and there was a lot of people dead. The Brits changed the regiments three times in our

district, that's how fierce it was. They announced in the
paper the next day that there was sixteen men shot dead. So
we had gone down to get the reporters to go around all the
houses where all the dead were. Time was irrelevant then
to you during those situations. Ye never looked at a watch.
It must have been three in the morning, when the dark is
fading a bit but the dawn hasn't quite come up yet. The next
thing we were covered with mist from the body up. "Suffering
Jesus! Where did that come from?" We were terrified; there
was all this mist out of nowhere in the middle of a summer
dry spell. Some said they could hear something coming from
where the mist seemed thickest. I think it was the 28th, but
I'm not sure because by then time just got wiped out. Daniel
O'Rooney was shot dead at that corner where we were standing that night. (Catholic woman, community activist, St. James
district)

In the community where these stories were collected, the intensified
presence of ghosts since the advent of the Troubles is attributed to the
sheer frequency and randomness of violent death within a limited space
and time. In folk explanation, ghosts are the inevitable excess of the
defilement which emerges from the flooding of social space with death.
This local theory assumes that there is a "natural" balance between the
quantity of death and spatial and temporal dimensions. The intensification
of death within discrete units of space and time beyond the natural
balance transgresses the classificatory order. Transgression is evidenced
by the leaking of the future in the present in the warnings of the banshee
and the return of the past in the present in the reappearance of the dead
as ghosts. In these tales the disordering of space is registered in its
divorce from linear time. The banshee that appears at a certain spot at
which someone subsequently dies or the ghost that reappears at the
place he/she died establishes a synchronized continuity of defiled space
that collapses diachronic difference.

The disordering of time is also transcribed in the nonintegration of
death within the life cycle. The number of youthful dead and the absence
of ritual preparation (particularly for Catholics) that accompanies sudden
death are central to a notion of "bad death."

The transgressive admixture of temporal dimensions in the ghost and
banshee stories is dependent on the atemporal repetitive character of
defiled space. Defiled space never goes away. Its reoccurrence negates
time as distance. It is not only a matter of ghosts reappearing at certain
specified sites, such as the Crying Stairs of Divis Flats, a run-down
housing estate where the ghosts of British Soldiers blown up by the IRA

appear.[4] Killing grounds like the Crying Stairs can easily be recycled in subsequent paramilitary and counterinsurgency operations. They are natural-enough ambush sites. This recurrent possibility is reflected in the British army's sign-posting of sniper holes, alleyways, corners, and hidden entries that have been used in paramilitary actions in the past. They mark these spots with white stenciled signs that say, "Look Here" or "Look Up." The space of death forms a permanent cartography for the local community. Ghost tales also map the history of death in local space.

The appearance of banshees and ghosts at specified locales effects a magnification of place that is tantamount to its deterritorialization. These specified sites are detached from sociological structures of constraint and appear out of place and out of time. The stigmatizing of locale by the initial act of violence and subsequent otherworldly phenomena precipitates spatial autonomization. Through the iconography of the return of the dead, the residual relations of space, time, and body are splintered. If space, time, and the specular body as corpse and ghost appear as detached from customary constraints, it is not an exaggeration to assert that they have been converted into free-floating signifiers. What the ghost, the banshee, and the recursive death site signify is the liminal experience of historical passage. The appearance of confused space and time implies that a residual order that held space and time, life and death, in a differential relation no longer governs, that these constituent dimensions are now in a new uncodifiable arrangement.

Stiffing

There are two entryways into the semantics of political violence in the oral history I collected in Belfast: categories of performance and categories of embodiment. In relation to the latter, the noun "stiff" and the verb "to stiff" are pivotal metaphors for the body encoded by political violence. Prior to the start of the Troubles in 1969, the term "stiff" was a working-class term for a corpse and "stiffing" (murder) would have had purely criminal connotations. Since the onset of civil violence, "stiff" refers almost exclusively to the politically objectified corpse, and thus the term has taken on ideological connotations. "To stiff" and "stiffing" or "stiffed" are all synonymous with political assassination. As a performative idiom, "stiffing" has lost any exclusive criminal connotation in many militant communities where it has been fused with political action.

Dating back to nineteenth century British Isles working-class slang, the term "stiff" is etymologically linked to violence, social hierarchy, and clandestine or duplicit activity. Circa 1823, "a stiff one" meant a corpse, "to stiffen" meant to kill. "Stiff" was also a derogatory term used by the criminal subculture in reference to the working class. "Stiffs" were also promisory notes and forged bills of exchange. Clandestine letters smuggled back and forth by prisoners were known as "stiffs" (Partridge 1961:831–32). Today "the stiff" and its cognates retain some of these residual nuances. Stiffs are subordinate objects; the stiff is a value form that is subjected to clandestine exchanges with other stiffs and the production of stiffs can be looked upon as a simulation of political codes in their transposition from the agent of violence to the object of violence. In both its residual and current usages, the stiff and the act of stiffing engage the issues of value equivalence, mimesis, hierarchy, communication, and clandestine exchange.

In contemporary Belfast the stiff and the act of stiffing are related to a set of indexical terms that infer states of destroyed or altered embodiment. In paramilitary vernacular the targeted male victim prior to being stiffed is "a cunt." To "knock his cunt in" is a targeting phrase that refers to the infliction of fatal violence or a beating. To stiff someone is also to "give him the message." In the working-class vernacular, "giving the message" is a term that predates the civil violence and characterized the male role in heterosexual intercourse. Bearing in mind its prepolitical nuances, "giving the message" now infers the feminization of the object of violence as a "cunt." In turn the "cunt" is understood as a passive recipient prior and during the application of violence to the body. The stiff is an orifice, a uterine space where political codes are gestated. As an orifice the stiff is not only "given the message" but also delivers these "messages" to prescribed audiences.[5]

Other phrases shift the transformations of violence from states or aspects of the body whole to body parts. To "scone" a target is to shoot the victim in the head; this is also known as "the coup" from coup de grace. This practice is associated with face-to-face assassination of political adversaries and with the "punishment" execution of informers and other internal offenders of the political organization or base community. The scone is literally a bread roll and thus a metaphor for the head. A related reference to decapitation is "to top him off," another term for assassination. During their series of prison protests (1976–81), Republican prisoners smuggled out lists of "toppings" which contained the names and addresses of abusive prison staff (see chap. 5).

These phrases correlate to categories of action and consequent transformations of the body. The act of violence transposes the body whole into codified fragments: body parts or aspects which function as metonyms of the effaced body and of other larger totalities. The violent reduction of the body to its parts or disassociated aspects is a crucial moment in the political metaphorization of the body, which in Belfast is a material practice as much as it is a linguistic practice: (1) Metonymic displacement and substitution (parts replacing the whole) express the political instrumentation of the body and thus mark a shift from prior usages of the body, from its prepolitical semantic status. (2) The distillation of the body into parts is the miniaturization of the body. This miniaturization is a mimesis of the concentration of politico-historical codes in the body altered by violence. The body marked by violence encapsulates certain political purposes, mediations, and transformations. The linguistic shift from body whole to body part replicates the performed transposition of political values from social totalities to the singularity of the stiff. Subsequent to this transcription the stiff circulates as a political sign. This effective relation of whole to part is reversible. The encoded body or stiff not only represents external social institutions and ideologies, but its formation as a political artifact permits it to function as a sympathetic (as in magic) manipulator of those overarching structures.

The transitive and value-producing moment of this process occurs when cunts are made into stiffs. This is a shift from the feminized and passive recipient of political codes to the phallic stiff, artifact of power and disseminator of political codes. Due to its local etymology, "giving the message" signifies political mastery through a residual reference to sexual dominance.

The processual dynamics of stiffing can be elaborated from the elemental body imagery described above and recast in overt metaphors of bio-power (Foucault 1980) that equate violent political intervention with curative and medical rationalities:

3.14   There was one particular guy who was very well known about the town for his antic like, and they used to call him "the Doctor," or Doctor Death. He used to have all kinds of fucking names. He was a real header [nut]. When he wanted to stiff a cunt he would say, "I have the medicine here for people. . . . Three pills [bullets] out of this here [the gun] will sort any cunt out" ["to sort out" means to order, to organize]. . . . He really carried the doctor image to the thing, "I'll put the sickness out of the cunt's head." That meant he was going to stiff your man. He used to ring us from up-country: "Hello, have you any cases up there? I'm looking for a bit of work. This is 'the Doctor' on the phone. Is anybody sick up there?" UDR [Ulster Defense Regiment] men, the Brits, the Orangies, they all had "the sickness" as far as he was concerned. (INLA)

Masking the discourse on death with the imagery of medical rectification has numerous analogues in the current conflict. The location of sectarian torture in a doctor's surgery in narrative 3.7 is but one example of medical rationality that permeates the oral histories. Medical iconographies, techniques, and instruments—real or sham—are commonplace in interrogation sessions run by the state and were routinely used against resisting Republican inmates in the Maze prison (see chap. 5). In Doctor Death's repertoire of political metaphor, as in the Butcher's tales, both ethnicity and ideology are literally sunk into the material density of the body, which then provides an instrumental locus for rectification—the elimination and purification of political substance. The essentialization of ideolological codes in the body prepares for the violent dematerialization of the body as the prescribed site for the lodgement and dislodgement of such codes.

Rectification can shift from medical to mechanical metaphors. In the Doctor's vocabulary, violence repairs as much as it cures. To "sort out" a political target is to demarcate, reorganize or to reorder the target. A favored instrument for such repair was the M-1 automatic rifle known as "the fixer."

Doorsteps

Stiffing generates incremental deterritorialization in reciprocating communities. The doorstep murder, for example, transgressed both the domestic and the community space as sanctuary constructs. Because of a now rigidified sectarian residential segregation, it was possible for paramilitary units to mount rapid incursions into ethnically opposed communities, picking off residents with the assumption that the victims' presence in that space was a definitive sign of ethnic/religious and political affiliation. Doorstep murders brought this logic to new stages of refinement and terror. Paramilitaries could drive up to a household and ask for the resident male (whose identity they may have previously researched through surveillance or obtained through prior knowledge of the community). As the victim came to open the door, he was assassinated. A cruder variation was to kill the first adult to answer the door no matter what the person's identity, age, or gender. Most paramilitaries conducting this sort of operation had a distaste for actually crossing the threshhold in search of their intended victim.

Statistics collated by Murray and Boal (1979:152) demonstrate that over half the doorstep murders that took place in Belfast in 1969–77 occurred in North Belfast. The ratio of victims in this area was three to one Catholic to Protestant. This can be contrasted to a citywide ratio of two to one Catholic to Protestant.[6] In 1975–76, this ratio was altered on a citywide basis as the PIRA (Provisional Irish Republican Army) engaged in a systematic campaign of overt sectarian murder (Holland 1981). Murray and Boal provide the following explanation for these statistics:

> This high incidence and ratio are due in part to the religious geography of the area. The map shows one feature that distinguishes

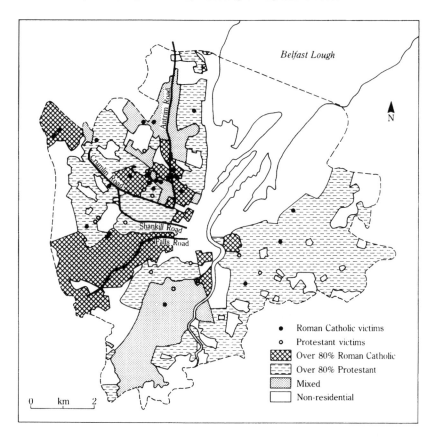

Figure 3. Doorstep murders in Belfast, 1969–77 (After Murray and Boal 1979, p. 152).

North Belfast. Unlike the rest of the city where there is a fairly tidy pattern of segregated and mixed areas the north presents much more of a patchwork pattern. This facilitates sectarian murders in two ways. Firstly the areas are relatively easy to penetrate. Their smallness means that they are quickly traversed while unlike the large ghettos to the south there are few men to provide local defense. (One response of residents in these areas has been the construction of barricades.) Secondly all possible target areas are near to secure areas such as the Shankill and Ardoyne. Murderers can be very soon back in the safety of their own territory. (1979:152)

In Boal and Murray's doorstep murder map, the unstable residential mosaic of ethnically opposed groups constitutes a proliferation of real and potential interfaces between communities and thus a proliferation of the spatial conditions for violent reciprocity. Each district in this territorial mosaic constitutes a defiling presence for an ethnically other district adjacent to it. For the larger enclaves of the Shankill and the Ardoyne, these areas of North Belfast represented an expanded interface for the performance of corrective violence (see chap. 2).

If the moral order of the sectarian space is contingent on the semantic fit or symmetry between bodies and topos, the sectarian killing within the space inhabited by ethnic others can be seen as an attempt to fracture that moral order by rupturing the symmetry between body and place. Sectarian assassinations like doorstep murders deploy "telling" to initially identify eligible victims by their schematic isomorphism with specific topographies.[7] But the resultant corpse, the stiff, inverts that symmetry and hence the moral order of what in the early to mid–1970s was idealized as a sanctuary space. Doorstep murders deploy the stiff as a differentiating and defiling sign, as an interruption code within the moral order of the sanctuary that is built upon encoded bodies. Embodiment as a metaphor of homogeneous ethnic space can be transcoded by violence. The body that was emblematic of territoriality and ethnicity through "telling" is inverted by violence into a sign of deterritorialization. The organic relation between body and topos can be severed, and violence can impart to the body the stigmata of an *adversary* social space. The surrogate victim becomes a detached part of the aggressors' agency inserted into a space in order to introduce polarity within a uniform interiority.

The map displays a multiplicity of binary political codes in each murder location. These locales are signs of both reciprocity and polarity. Each cartographic stigma or "corpse found" bears witness to spatial and material exchanges. Each victim is both a defilement of one community and a purifying intervention for another. Each corpse or stiff is a sign of sacrificial extraction that rehearses the eventual subtraction of the community in which the stiffing took place.

The production of stiffs transfers territorial paradigms from topographic registers to the surface of the human body. A topographic imaginary that cannot be sustained in everyday experience is reenacted on encysted spaces that become surrogates for the display of political claims. For the killers the stiff becomes the emblem of the territorial command that was once invested in a now increasingly anomalous and unstable sanctuary space. On the other hand, the stiff transgresses the territorial integrity of the victim's community. This model implies that sectarian murder was not so much an expression of community consensus as it was a rhetoric of restoration by which social solidarity was formed by focusing social consciousness on politically charged objects, miniaturized referents of more expansive yet unrealizable geographies.

The map plots the structure of sectarian social space and the dynamics of its diachronic transformation. The network of boundary lines charts a symbolic spatial order. In turn, the corpses document the emergence of a political imaginary of space. The symbolic order is fragmented by violence into part objects and surrogates—places to store totality while fabricating its return in a new purified form. The map freezes totality and its fragmentation into a tableau, and in this form it is a fairly accurate transcription of the mental maps of the communities shown. The stiff displaces unstable boundaries and functions for the assassins as a rigid concentrate of the communities located within these shifting borders. The corpse and the border are both points of separation and contact between opposing spaces. These thresholds define the space of political exchange. The corpse and the border form a metonymy that permits political codes and values to circulate. Corpses or stiffs become mobile surrogate borders or interfaces and thus bearers of political spectacle. The stiff is a commodity form of a political exchange. Violence injects spatial and temporal value into the stiff. It activates metaphorical transactions between borders and corpses, exchanges which externalize the internal time of political violence as a history effect.

Political codes are transposed from agent to object. Alterity is simulated in the object through its formation by the detached codes of the Other. This process can be located in paramilitary versions of the telling discourse. In narrative 3.15 the planning of a doorstep murder is discussed. The set of strategies surrounding the "doorstep" is predicated by having to enter alien territory and avoid being "telled" as someone who does not belong. Political identity is only unmasked in the making of the stiff. The narrator begins by discussing the training and military experiences he sees as prerequisites to the successful performance of a "doorstep." He contrasts the doorstep to the guerrilla ambush. The latter implies operating in one's own area or in a sector of one's ethnic group at a distance from the target. The doorstep involves the unsettling prospect of operating within alien territory in proximity to the victim.

3.15   To me you would start off doing snipes, to get you prepared for stiffing people. It's a different thing shooting people at a distance of a couple of hundred yards than walking into his house and stiffing him. There was no deliberate training policy, but to me that's the way it should be. You start off as lookouts, then planting bombs and snipes, and then doorsteps would be the final act of execution. The "coup," it's a different kind of job. You're going to have to enter into a specific area looking for a cop or a Brit, and you're going to have to travel some time for your runback. It's a whole other level of planning. You're going to have to travel into Orangies' [Protestants'] areas, because that's where most of the cops or screws [prison guards] or UDR [Ulster Defense Regiment, local army reserve—mainly Protestant] live. Certain amount of planning involved in the runback, changing cars for example.

If I was going into an Orangies' area I would wear wee Rangers' badges [a reference to the Scottish Rangers, a Glasgow football team that excludes Catholic players]. If necessary I would put a few tattoos on the arm and wear the beatle boots. Orangies always wear beatle boots. You go into the Shankill and Orangies are always big for wearing bits and pieces of military gear, dark glasses, and all the rest, which I'd never do. They're really keyed up. Combat jackets and the lot. Republicans aren't all that into that kind of gear. Republicans bring out that gear for an "op" [military operation] or a parade or a funeral, but not in your day-to-day life. (INLA)

In terms of its target this operation is ideally much more selective than the sectarian doorstep because its objective is a "political" target. This type of thinking reflects the current distancing of Republicans from the negative imagery of sectarian violence. But in the end, the operation, whether structured by "political" or sectarian objectives, reveals the extent to which the paramilitary seeks to violate the spatial constructs that function as armatures of the victim's social order. The narrator continues:

3.16   Doorsteps at the start, particularly the ones done by Orangies, they used to open up the door and whoever came to answer was stiffed. That's opposed to "knock the door, push your way in, and shoot them." The Orangies are very good at doorsteps. The Provies nine times out of ten will bang him as he's getting out of his car and bang him when he's getting into his car or put a bomb into it. But then you have to watch and see does he drive the kids to school and allow for that. That would scrub a car bomb right there and then. If that doesn't work, you're going to knock the door which is harder to do. Because if you knock the door and he doesn't answer, you're going to have to go into his house looking for him with his family all mixed in. If you hurt any of them you count the operation a loss. The political impact is just wiped out because now it's just "criminals terrorizing families," never mind what or who your man is. . . .

. . . It demoralizes the police stiffing them at home. Everybody and particularly a cop wants to come home off the job
and relax, and the doorstep murder fucks up every cop that's
looking for that relaxation. Not only the cop, you take the
wife; the wife is going to demand that he gets out when one
of his mates gets whacked. That's the whole purpose of that
type of operation. You see, they can cope with the violence on
the street in the Republican areas. They expect it there, it's
part of the job, but when you hit the house or the car as he's
coming home from work they hate that. They can't cope with
it in the home. (INLA)

Even at this advanced tactical stage and despite the fact that the
narrator takes great pains to distance himself from any sectarian violence
(as would be implied in the killing of family members of a military target),
the basic spatial components of the sectarian doorstep murder are still
present. The narrator notes the police attitude that violence is permis-
sible solely in Catholic ghettos. He thus identifies the interior of these
areas as functional interfaces for violent confrontation between civilian
Catholics or Republican paramilitaries and the state. The doorstep action
shifts the interface into the policeman's community and ultimately his
home. The community and particularly the home (even in this postbar-
ricade period) function as imputed sanctuary constructs and thus as natural targets of violation. Again, the killing of a surrogate victim is seen as
capable of being elaborated into collective defilement for entire communities of policemen. (Due to the war situation it is not unusual for RUC
members to live in residential enclaves that are also largely Protestant in
makeup.)

Narrative 3.17 concerns the mysterious circumstances of the death
of Lenny Murphy, leader of the notorious Shankill Butchers, whose
violence has already been discussed. Murphy proved such an embarrassment to the UVF that it was believed he was set up by his own
organization for assassination. Yet his death is also attributed to the
PIRA. Some Loyalists feel the PIRA was given the necessary information
and clearance by the UVF or the UDA for this operation.[8] The narrator
deploys the paradigm of "telling" to dispute this. In the following account, the ethnic dissymmetry of Republican paramilitaries operating in
a Protestant neighborhood becomes the basis for the claim that Murphy's
killing did not bear the signature of the Other.

3.17   It was his own done it, not the Provies (PIRA). It was his
own shot him. Provies wouldn't have gone up into Glencairn in
the heart of a Loyalist area and sit there for six hours waiting

for him. No way they were sitting for six hours in a van waiting on him coming. Ambushed him in a 100 percent Loyalist
area! They haven't got the guts to do that. No way. *You smell
them! It's knowing and smelling and instinct.* [Emphasis
mine.] Even a child of three years old would know that there
was a stranger in the area. It's a tribal sort of instinct. They
would know right away there was a stranger in their midst. A
stranger couldn't have sat there in a car for so long. I've
known some brave men, and I can tell you nobody would sit
for six hours in the other community. I've done some fucking
wee tricks in my time, but I never fuckin' sat for six hours.
I'd sit for six minutes and stiff him, but that was my lot.
(UDA)

In these narratives, the dissonance of the agent with the topography
he penetrates and transgresses is but a *preliminary stage in the eventual
transference of this dissonance from transgressor to victim.* Death is the
sign of the transgressor's spatial relation to the victim. *The victim
functions as the surrogate—the inverted and polluting double of the
transgressor.*[9]

Sacrificial Transfers

R. D. Sack (1980:148–49) asserts that mythicized space functions as
both object and force. Following Mauss, Sack identifies three foundational principles of mythicized space: contiguity, mimetic sympathy, and
antipathy. Sack summarizes the logic of contiguity:

> Objects in contact or even in close proximity will share a sympathy
> which continues when the two have separated or that the object
> effects the other at a distance. The two factors to bear in mind are
> these: that things in contact share the potential for cause and effect
> (that spatial contact or near contact is sufficient criteria for cause
> and effect). . . .Original proximity or contact can be thought as
> forming a whole. One part of the whole, the part which is removed,
> becomes a symbol of the whole and because of the confusion of the
> symbol with the referent, it becomes the whole (totem ex parti).
> (1980:150)

Mimetic sympathy also expresses a causal relation between detachable parts and encompassing wholes, though in this case it does not
require original contact but direct iconic similarity and/or schematic reference: "In this case the similitude is based on the sharing of shapes of
spatial configurations, though such likeness need not be precise. There

need only be schematic presentation to produce physiognomic similarity" (Sacks 1980:150).

Spatial antipathy, in turn, involves the repulsion of constituent elements of a spatial configuration and can be seen as resulting from a violation or inversion of spatial contiguity and mimetic sympathy.

Both mimetic sympathy and a metaphysics of contiguity inform "telling" and the performative dynamics of sectarian murder. The sectarian murder victim was either a Catholic or Protestant territorial *artifact* forced into Protestant or Catholic space as an antipathic political symbol. When discussing the sacrificial process, Girard (1977) centers on the victim as a surrogate, an emissary who facilitates the transfer of pollution out of an afflicted community. Sacrifice is a commensuration of the many to the one; it shifts collective disorder to a personified transgressor. The body of the sacrificial victim is the detached part that encapsulates a disordered or disordering whole, and its deformation expresses the passage out of disorder. *The substitution of the whole by the detached part is the basic principle of sacrificial process.* Violent surrogation as the separation of parts from whole is a medium for transforming the whole.

The imaginary of spatial contiguity, mimetic sympathy, and spatial antipathy organizes the ideological construction and reception of the sectarian murder victim. Sectarian murder is a form of code switching which inverts corporal-spatial symbolism and its referential social frames. The victim is targeted by the killers through the spatial and sensory codes of "telling." Telling constructs the victim's mimesis with an assumed space. The sectarian killing fractures this particular mimesis. Within the victim's community, the stiff is marked by violence as an artifact and effect of an alien space. The stiff is both the personalized victim with all the residual associations, linkages, and affectivity of kinship and residence and the simulacrum of the Other who has committed the violence. Stiffing is a graphic act, and the stiff is a political text whose original script of ethnic-spatial symmetry has been effaced by wounding and death. The corpse, its blood, its wounds are quasi-organic signs of a tactile and political contiguity with the Other.

The stiff, as a composite figure of moral inversion, reproduces within the heart of the sanctuary space the territorial signs of an opposed ethnicity. It was upon this antipathy and artifactual status that its function as the bearer of political-territorial hegemony rested.

The transfer of political performance from the level of entire communities and residential systems to the individual body in the sectarian murder is both a ritualistic transfer from whole to part and a rationalization of political violence—an attempt to constrain it within manipulatable mimetic forms. But in this context rationality was grounded on a mythic logic of spatial-somatic causality. The discovery that the brutal killing of a single individual is commensurate in its political and polluting impact to the forced movements of entire communities, that terror has its own circuits of amplification that do not require material destruction on a large scale, is an essential discovery of paramilitary practice.

The Symbolic, the Imaginary, and the Real

A spatial and somatic ideology congealed into a social structure displaces the immediacy of lived experience through symbolic mediation; it channels the experiential through grids of patterned and exclusive representation. This symbolic order is discontinuous with the diachrony of experience.[10] It substitutes formalized signs for experiential flows, rendering the latter into a logical, narrative, and historical order.

The convergence of social structure and symbolic order means that this system of closed reference is bound to have a disjunctive relation to the life-world from which it extracts signifiers of its own intrinsic coherence. The symbolic order is constituted by discrete ensembles of discursive and material practice, each centered on a constructed domain of material reference. The models of sectarian space and the body presented here are characteristic units of material reference by which a symbolic order recuperates its own necessity. Transformation of the symbolic order has been depicted in the last two chapters as slippage and disarticulation between systems of representation and anchoring domains of material reference. How has this slippage been effected?

Violence of a certain magnitude and directed at specific sites of symbolic anchorage is a privileged vehicle for opening a symbolic order to the exigencies of decentering diachronic process. These exigencies are not external to the symbolic order but inhabit this order in the form of its own effects. The symbolic order is condemned to produce an excess of uncoded and uncodifiable experience that cannot be internalized, that resists the conventional categories and practices of representational incorporation. This domain of resistance is "real," yet it exceeds any residual notion of conventional reality and practices of conventionalization.

The symbolic order is never commensurate with the effects of its own violence. In its ideological intentionality and technical practice, social violence functions as a component of the symbolic order, but in its material consequences violence is of the "Real" (Lacan 1977), that outside which exceeds representation. Violence can transgress systems of classification and produce discontinuity within a symbolic order by effecting a slippage between systems of restricted designation and the "opened" domains of material reference. Violence alters the residual character of the system of material reference and detaches this domain from the domestications, the conventions of the symbolic order.

With the advent of chronic violence, terrains of material reference begin to exceed the classificatory systems that formed these domains.

The sphere of material reference leaks out of institutional closures into uncharted semantic terrains. A social imaginary appears in discourse and act that tries to mediate the slippage between social order and internal violence. The social imaginary draws on the revenants of residual significative systems and recombines these into new semantic configurations in an attempt to reconcile the symbolic and the Real.

The uncoded excess of the desymbolized material domain solicits the resymbolizing entries of violence. In the scripture of violence, a system of designation obtains an immediate fixation, a validating duplication in matter. This process of simulation constructs a mirror relation between ideology and the material world. Through violence, matter is semioticized in order for it to feed back narratives of historical transformation and political dominance that duplicate ideological discourse. Violence enables and enacts a one-to-one correspondence or isomorphism between discourse and the material world. Yet this dissimulation or denial of difference is constantly threatened and rendered contingent by the excess effects of the very violence that institutes the mirror relation between ideology and matter. I term this particular mirror relation, the instrumental imaginary. The instrumental imaginary uses violence as discourse to affect the political rationalization of the material world. Political violence reorganizes the material world into a phantasm, into a spectacle of historical transformation.[11]

The attempt through violence to inscribe symbolic time and space (ethnohistory and ethnic space) onto the register of the body is a fundamental suppression of historicity. History is not lodged in the body but in the act that constructs the body and locates it in a metonymy. That act has a genealogy. But this is effaced by the metaphorical displacement of the transcribed body in official nationalist rationalities. The transformation of somatic and other material domains into symbolic time and space by violence and ideology forms a closure that represses historicity in favor of the mimetic and the recursive. Yet in this process by which ideological time and imagined space are duplicated in matter, the body acquires its own clandestine history of alterity.

The tearing down of the "no-go" barricades and the occupation of these zones by the British army in 1972 were events of both practical and symbolic centrality. The subsequent escalation of doorstep murder and other sectarian violence was much more than an opportunistic response to the removal of physical impediments. The barricades were removed but the symbolic space and its damaged cognitive-political margins remained. The removal of the barricades and occupation by the British army were events that confirmed the instability of all local territorial designations. Paramilitary violence had to reinscribe the imaginary of social space in surrogates. The "stiff" was thus caught up in a progression that was intricately bound to the deformation of social space.

The absence of a stable sectarian spatial order and the dispersal of symbolic totality furthered the investment in part objects as substitutes and supplements of the absent whole. These part objects, "stiffs" and "cunts," were detached signifiers of a desired command of space. The absent spatial order magnitized the value relations between the micrometaphor of the corpse and the macrometaphors of nationalist imagery—the utopian fetishes of ideal spatial totality. The loss of residual symbolic infrastructure and the advent of profound experiential discontinuity resolved into a polar conjuncture: *the derealization of space and the hypostasis of the body.* The reappearance of the dead and their stigmatization of certain locales were mirror effects of this conjuncture.

The Black Man

The incursions of transgressive others, the crystallization of a tangible terror around arbitrary victims, reversible violence and defiled space were personified in the "Black Man". Burton (1978:25–29) collected Black Man stories in the early 1970s, and I was able to recover similar tales about this figure and associated events more than a decade later. The Black Man was a rumor, a cultural elaboration of terror. He appeared wearing a black cloak or hood and an upside-down cross, and he "sacrificed" dogs in arcane rites of black magic. He was simultaneously "Man," "Devil," and "Prod," and was associated with the entry of the First Paratroop Regiment into the Ardoyne, a Catholic area of Belfast known for its militant Republicanism. He visited the houses of recently killed IRA men, leaving black candles. He was both elusive and indestructible. He is depicted as a figure of aggression, butchering dogs and frightening people, and then in other narratives he is the object of collective violence, chased by the IRA and shot at by the British paratroopers. He is subjected to beatings but never killed; bullets pass through him, and though he is chased away he always returns. Sometimes there is only one of him; other testimony asserts there were two Black Men. It was conjectured that since his appearance coincided with the arrival of the paratroopers, he would leave the community when this regiment departed.

Burton dismissed these tales as essentially an adolescent prank, since it was among the young that these stories circulated when he collected them. Yet the Black Man tales are a reworking of violent agencies and their cultural effects. More than a form of gossip or a technique for keeping young children home at night (as Burton suggests), the Black Man stories harbor a dense web of political polysemy.

The paratroop regiment locally known as the "First Paras" has a notorious reputation in both Republican and Loyalist communities. They were known for casual, indiscriminate brutality, covert assassination, and the killing of neighborhood dogs and cats.

3.18   We trained our dogs to bark when the paras were coming. So they used to kill our dogs. (St. James district)

3.19   They tried to get me for shooting a para. . . . They brought me to a street where there was a Saracen stationed, and all the paras were there waiting on me, queing up on me. They gave me a desperate beating with rifles. Later they came and told me they knew I didn't do [kill] the para, but they wanted me anyhow. Three weeks later they came and said they had orders to shoot me on sight. The next day they kicked an old dog to death and threw him on my front step. It was their way of saying I was next. (PIRA, Ballymurphy)

3.20   In the early 1970s there was a period when there was dead dogs everywhere. There was dogs found everywhere with cut throats. They were cutting dogs in Dunville Park. They even crucified some dogs and cats. The paras were digging stiffs out of the cemetery and throwing the bodies around. At the same time the dogs and cats were getting done, they found a wee fellow sliced up on the Ormeau Road. At first they thought it was a sectarian murder. But there were goats that looked ritually slaughtered by the body. They brought in an expert on witchcraft who said the only time he seen markings like that was at black magic ceremonies. They did find on your man's body signs of ritual slaughter. Some dogs were burnt on crosses. It was all black magic. There was a lot of black magic stories going around the early seventies. We all thought the Brits were playing on superstitions. When the First Para came in, any dogs that were giving them hassle, the first thing they would do would be to shoot them or cut their throats. People automatically connected that with the black magic. (PIRA)

Senseless arcane atrocities committed against animals are powerful depictions of both surrogate victimage and boundary transgression. For the surrogation of animals in place of human victims, or in anticipation of a human victim, incorporates the explicitly apolitical domain of nature into the political (see 3.19). It is the extreme disengagement of animals and nature from the political domain of men that renders these figures evocative allegories of arbitrary victimage. The entanglement of nature with the violent political life of men is a profound confirmation of boundary collapse and deterritorialization. In turn, domination of the animal body is a metonym for the politicization of the human body and its unfixing from all customary social references by political violence.

In narrative 3.21 the transgression of nature functions as a metaphor for the disruption of kinship and residence in the imagery of the disturbed birds' nests.

3.21   There was a shooting one night, and we were out giving the soldiers tea. And this nest fell at our feet. Dolly looked at it. It was wee broken birds' eggs, and there were wee birds in them. And Dolly said, "It's that bad here, the wee birds are having miscarriages!" (Protestant female old-age pensioner, Woodvale)[12]

The Black Man had a factual basis in the counterinsurgency practice of the First Paras. Central to the Black Man stories was how this modicum of fact was rearranged in combination with other signs to codify most of the symbolic dynamics that have been discussed in this and the previous chapter. The Black Man as a figure of inversion, polysemy, and indeterminacy can be considered as a central condensing myth of the experience of reversible violence and violated space. He was a signifier of random violence that gravitated to emblematic victims and locales, raising these units of transcription and surrogation to phantasmic intensities.

His mimicry of Catholic religious iconography establishes him as a figure of inversion (i.e., the upside-down cross). The characterizing "blackness" associates this figure with the grease-blackened faces of the paratroopers on infiltrating night operations. His dark hood evokes the dark woolen ski masks worn by the IRA (and other paramilitary groups) during operations, military funerals, and parades and the hoods worn by sectarian murder victims. His invulnerability to British bullets links him to the imagery of guerrilla evasion. And his designation as the devil echoes the stereotypic Church condemnation of the IRA.

The Black Man occupies alleys and other obscure, darkened passages that are the typical locales for acts of clandestine violence. He evokes the shimmering negativity of specified killing sites that has already been encountered in the Butchers', banshee, and ghost tales. He visits the house of recently killed IRA men and is thus linked to "bad death." But foremost he is explicitly associated with the sacrificial dynamics of arbitrary victimage in his killing of animals, entities without any political status. At times the Black Man is a figure of transgression, sacrificing the innocent (animals). At other times he is the object of scapegoating violence. Feared yet hunted, he is subjected to attacks by both the IRA and the British. He is pursued by crowds of young men armed with hurley sticks. He is linked to the paratroops, and his expulsion is a symbolic rehearsal, a substitute for the more problematic departure of the British army.

The Black Man is a divided figure, linked to the sacrifice of surrogate victims, but also an object of violence himself. The fact that he is beaten but not killed indicates that he performs a ritual function. As an operator of sacrifical signifiers he is a necessary presence. He participates equally in the imagery of paramilitary violence and state counterinsurgency. He is victimizer and victim. That is why he is both singular and dual. He is essentially a trickster-scapegoat who in his own multiple relations to violence codifies a collective insight into the reversible and mimetic character of local violence. His chronological position coincides with the early periods of intense warfare and establishes the Black Man as a figure of entry, a limen, a threshold. His equivocal relation to the IRA and the British paratroopers and his unstable shifts back and forth from agent of violence to object of violence indicate that he mediates adversaries and polarised subject positions. In his codification of mimesis and reversible sacrifice, the Black Man is a theater of mirror effects that reduces all the forms, agencies, and objects of violence to relations of sameness and value equivalence. In this manner he personifies the infrastructure of violence as exchange.

4 *Being Done: Rites of Political Passage*

On the street you know you can go to prison or you can die. . . .
You can't dwell on it when you go into the street with a weapon in
your hand.

—PIRA gunman

When they come to lift anybody they do a profile on them. Where is
he at this moment? What's happening with him? What way is he
performing?

—UDA gunman

Endocolonization

The experience of arrest and interrogation is central to the political
culture of violence in Northern Ireland and has a vital narrative presence
in the oral culture of paramilitaries and their support communities. The
violence experienced in arrest and interrogation is as socially determining and biographically significant as the experience of paramilitary violence. Life-history accounts of paramilitary careers reveal an obvious
symbiosis between the two domains of practice. Paramilitary practice and
the state's machinery of search and seizure form interdependent structures that determine the autonomization of violence in Northern Ireland.
These practices increasingly take each other as their ideological reference point and develop performance repertoires that permit the exchange of ideological codes within a closed circuit.[1]

To understand the relation of arrest and interrogation to the enculturation of violence in Northern Ireland, it is necessary to abandon the
accustomed concept of arrest and interrogation as procedures in the
disclosure and rehabilitative punishment of the individual offender. In
Northern Ireland, arrest and interrogation are integral components of an
overarching counterinsurgency strategy. These mechanisms facilitate
the endocolonization of society by the state, that is, the occupation and

infestation of insurgent and delinquent communities by systems of surveillance, spatial immobilization, and periodic subtraction of subjects from homes and communities. Through arrest and interrogation the state imposes a kind of information taxation on society.

Arrest and interrogation validate the sociological assumptions that animate terrorist ideologies and practice. Like paramilitary violence, arrest and interrogation contribute to the coercive collectivization of social life—a process that prepares the sociological and cognitive foundations for the collective ritualization of violence and the elevation of terror to the dominant symbolic logic of social life. Arrest and interrogation, like other forms of terror, transform social life and historical experience into encysted ritualized enclosures.

In Northern Ireland the state apparatus, from policing, incarceration, social welfare, and urban planning to public housing, conceives of governance in terms of counterinsurgency. This is not only a required bureaucratic response to violence but a symbolic posture that supposedly differentiates the violence of the state from all other forms of violence it seeks to eradicate.[2] Arrest and interrogation are both symbolic and instrumental modes of hierarchization. The analysis of arrest and interrogation forces one to read the state not only as an instrumental and rationalized edifice but as a *ritual* form for the constitution of power; in turn, one is led to the central role arrest and interrogation play in the performative construction of state power in Northern Ireland.

The Collectivization of Arrest

On August 9, 1971, the Northern Ireland government introduced internment. In a series of predawn house raids the British army and the Royal Ulster Constabulary (RUC) arrested 342 Catholics who were supposedly active Republicans and/or secret members of the IRA. In fact IRA leaders and membership, having been forewarned about the internment order, largely evaded arrest. Because the selection of internees was based on out-of-date or inaccurate Special Branch files, numerous men, uninvolved in paramilitary activity and in numerous cases politics of any kind, were arrested and in instances subjected to violent interrogations. Within six months of the initial internment order a total of 2,357 people, mainly Catholics, had been interned.[3] Internment rapidly became a technique for confining "suspected terrorists" against whom court convictions could not be obtained (Hillyard 1983:37; McGuffin 1973:86–87).

In 1972, attempts were made to depoliticize internment by shifting the authorization of internment orders from the executive government to the courts. This transfer signaled the gradual reorganization of the judicial system into a counterinsurgency apparatus. Subsequently, this transformation was formalized by a series of legislative acts that, on the advice of several government commissions, redefined common rules of law and civil rights guarantees as technical rules subject to suspension in emergency conditions. Common law had been identified by government investigative commissions as the primary cause for the inability of the policing and judicial systems to obtain convictions against "terrorists." Two complementary results stemmed from this reduction of common rules of law to technical procedures: (1) political violence was redefined as a jural problem; (2) paramilitary activity was criminalized and depoliticized. Reorganized around legislation that permitted three to seven days of preventive detention without formal evidence, the state's police and jural and penal apparatuses were rapidly integrated into an overarching counterinsurgency apparatus (Hillyard 1983:48–53).

These strategies can be traced in part to the proposals of British army general Frank Kitson, who, although not the only source of this policy, certainly gave it its most eloquent and public expression (Kitson 1971:10). Kitson stressed the role of intelligence as the key to the successful attrition of guerrilla and terrorist forces. The culling of accurate intelligence was essential to both the military defeat of covert guerrilla organizations and the demoralization of terrorist-support communities. Intelligence constituted the primary medium for the restoration of state hegemony via the informational and technological colonization of insurgent communities. Kitson conceived of military/policing procedures as "low-intensity operations." The primary function of these operations was the cultivation of an ongoing flow of "contact information" through the surveillance of individuals, families, and communities by electronic monitoring, field observation, sociological surveys, computerized data collation and cross-referencing, and preventive detention and interrogation.

In Northern Ireland, the implementation of this approach meant that there was no one-to-one correlation between arrest/interrogation/ongoing criminal investigations and actual criminal prosecutions. Although arrest and interrogation did lead to prosecutions, by and large they functioned as components of the information economy of the counterinsurgency forces. Community-centered surveillance involved foot patrols, helicopter overflights, video scanners mounted on traffic lights, taps on private and public phones, long-range sound monitoring and computerized data banks that collated the private life of entire populations.

Massive importation of advanced surveillance technologies, the routinization of house raids, and the frequent arrest of males of military age and members of their families were as much displays of techno-political power as they were functional methods for securing a data base. In this context, search-and-seizure practices mobilized the state as spectacle. As such, arrest not only constituted an expansion of the spheres of domination but functioned as a self-recuperating exercise by which the state apparatus effected its reproduction through performance. This ritualized aspect assumed greater centrality when outright military defeat of paramilitary organizations proved unattainable.

According to Hillyard (1983:41), at a peak level in 1973, 74,556 houses, one-fifth of all houses in Northern Ireland, were subjected to police and army raids. Hillyard's 1979 survey of court defendants revealed that two-thirds of Republican prisoners and two-fifths of Loyalist prisoners were apprehended in predawn house raids (Boyle, Hadden, and Hillyard 1980:29). The Bennett Commission revealed that between September 1977 and August 1978, 2,970 people had been arrested and detained for more than four hours under the Emergency Provisions and Prevention of Terrorism Acts. Between January and October 1980, 3,868 people were detained. In the detainee group surveyed by Hillyard in 1979, 35 percent were charged by the authorities; in the 1980 group, only 11 percent were indicted for specific offenses. With no more than a 35 percent indictment rate from detainees subject to prolonged interrogation, and with as little as an 11 percent indictment rate, it is obvious that interrogation served more as a screening and data collection technique than as a means for direct criminal prosecution. The prolongation of interrogation after confession (Boyle, Hadden, and Hillyard 1980:45) also reinforced the intent of arrest and interrogation as intelligence-gathering operations. These factors would have influenced the lack of selectivity and discrimination in reference to who was and was not arrested.

The collectivization of arrest by the state proved to be a problematic mode of hegemonization. There was an inbuilt contradiction between the information-gathering needs of the counterinsurgency forces and the camouflage of these practices behind juridical facades. In ostensibly liberal democracies such as Great Britain, juridical intervention and correction, from arrest to trial to prison, is predicated on individualization— the creation of a juridical subject through documentation and examination systems, and spatial confinement. The collectivization of arrest and interrogation, and their dissemination as routinized features of day-to-day life violated the jural principle of individualized accountability for criminal acts. Arrestees were extracted as insignias of dangerous and conspiratorial collectivities that extended from the paramilitary organization to the entire ethnic community. The functional redefinition of criminal agency had a decisive politicizing impact on specific communities. In these zones, arrest was dialogically restructured. The imputation of collective criminal agency was inverted into collective action directed against the legalities and technical rationalities that sought to isolate and segregate the political subject from his or her community base.

Resisting Arrest

In Belfast, the characteristic sound of police and army Landrovers echoing through the deserted night streets is infamous. The whine of Landrover gears at that time of night is automatically read as the signal of a house raid. These predawn arrests are spectacles that elicit subject positions by commanding complicitous silence and passivity. The predawn house raid by the counterinsurgency forces is a display of colonizing power and the command of territory; it reclaims a temporality and geography of subversion. This claiming of territory and time moves to the command of domestic spaces and bodies. Each appropriative stage, from its timing to its culmination in the subtraction of the suspect from his home and community, functions as a disciplinary incision onto populations and topographies.

Arrest in Northern Ireland is thus analogous to Foucault's description of public execution: "a policy of terror to make everyone aware through the body of the criminal, of the unrestrained presence of the sovereign. The public execution did not reestablish justice; it reactivated power" (1979:49).

Arrest as a performative display reactivates the political potency of the state which has been suspended by the "terrorist" act. Because the restoration of state hegemony must proceed via the commission of violent and violating acts, the essential issue that confronts the implementation of arrest is differentiating state violence from antistate violence. The legitimacy of the arrest event depends on this capacity to hierarchize state violence. It has proven to be a fragile hierarchy. If the essential logic of terrorist violence is arbitrary victimage, the legitimizing rationales of arrest events were subverted by activating the same logic. Through arrest the state reduced itself to another "paramilitary" presence on the streets of the community. In their performative logic, which is independent from their divergent ideological rationales, the terrorist act and the state's arrest presuppose collective objective guilt.

4.1   There was this massive shooting going on in the Shankill. Jesus Christ it was wild! There was this pub called the Bricklayer's Arms, it was brilliant, real old fashioned from the year dot. We were sitting there and the fucking shooting starts. Of course I wasn't involved in it! [Laughter.] The bar manager decided to blow and give me the keys [more laughter]. The First Para shot two people dead that night. They were getting hit back though. We were sitting in the bar—do you know the whine of the Saracens when they put them into low gear, they have twenty gears in them—we heard the whine, "Weeeee!" Then, boom! The whole building started shaking. Those wee stupid Englishmen had backed the Saracen through the door of the pub. "Let's get out! Let's get out!" We ran out the back door and realized the whole fuckin' place, because it was the Shankill Road, was wired off so we couldn't get out. We couldn't get over to the place next door, because if we went over the wall the alarms would have gone off and we would have been shot. We were done for. So all nine of us backed into the wee toilet. Here's me, "I'll go in first." [Laughter.] So, I goes in first and everybody goes in behind me. So we're all piled into this loo and I'm way in the back.

The First Paras meanwhile had reversed the Saracen through the stone wall and came right into the bar. They opened up the Saracen's door from the back, piled out and kicked the loo door open. Now, one of the things about Paras is their flak jackets. The Paras keep them underneath their tunics which make them look like American football players. "Fucking look at that boy there, the size of that wee fellow there, he must be doing some weight lifting!" It's all psychological. Now there was this guy, one of my men in charge of my teams, and we were very like each other, only that he was older. So they gets this fellow who is about third from the door [in the toilet] and who looks like me, line him up against the latrine and say [imitating a Cockney accent], "Ollo Mr. _____." Whack! "Nice night Mr. _____." Then another one hits him. Whack! He says, "I'm not _____." But even though he was under pressure he wouldn't say where I was. They touched no one else, only him. He denied knowing me! I had not come out of the toilet then; they were still taking us out one by one. (Later, what they tried to suggest was that the pub was the base of operations for the shooting. Of course, the brewery that owned the pub said I was one of their part-time employees and I was only there for the beer.) They brought us all into the bar, "Stretch out spread eagle!" The intelligence officer came over to me, pointing, "This is Mr. Fucking _____here!" The Paras all went sick. They were so frustrated beating the shit out of the wrong guy that when they came to me they didn't touch me.

While all this was going on the phone rang. The Intelligence Officer picks it up. He comes over to the colonel. "Somebody wants Mr. _____here." So I goes up to the bar to the phone. The I.O. puts a fucking gun to my head and says, "Will you answer the phone right?" So it happened to be the late Tommy Herron [commander of the U.D.A.] calling. Now what had happened as that this fucking stupid English soldier answered the phone first. He was so excited he lifts the phone and says, "Hello what do you want?" Herron heard the fuckin' English accent. "Hello is _____there?" The Brits expected to hear him ask, "How many Paras have you shot?" But they didn't. Herrons heard the accent and became the stupid Irishman: "Is that you _____?"

"Aye."

"I heard there's a lot of trouble on the Shankill Road. Could you not try and stop it?" [Laughter.] "Because for the good and welfare of the country it's important that we stop this trouble. Could you not get them fucking UVF men to do that?" [Laughter.] [The caller and narrator are UDA.]

The Brits get everybody to line around the bar. There was a couple of dipsos and winos and everything in the bar. This was all part of my thing; I sort of looked after them. They were no use to anything that was a security risk. They all lined up. I wouldn't spread eagle, "Fuck off!" The Brits bring everybody around to a table and they get their names and addresses.

I says, "What about me?"

"We fuckin' got enough on you; we don't need fuck."

So the next thing it is, all the Paras go into the counter behind the bar. I says, "What the fuck do youse think you're doing?"

"Searching."

Cartons of cigarettes and bottles of drink into the flak jackets. The Bricklayer's Arms was a very long bar, about thirty-five feet, and all the Brits were sitting one up against the other on the bar, dangling their wee legs. You couldn't have put your hands between two Brits.

They told all the lads but me to sit down. I'm standing alone, thinking, "What the fuck's going on." I wouldn't do nothing for them, you see.

"Dance Mr. _____ . Do an Irish jig."

"What!"

"Can you do an Irish jig?"

"Fuck off."

They turn the radio on and get an Irish tune, "da, di, di, da. . . ."

"Can you do an Irish jig?"

"I'll do no fucking Irish jig."

One Para pulls the bolt of his Sterling down: "Ye either get it that way or get it this way."

What am I going to say? "I don't even know one."

"Make an attempt at it."

I get into the middle of the floor and all these Paras shouting and clapping their hands. It was fucking sick, and that the first and only time the fucking Paras ever got me and they were loving it. (UDA)

4.2 Even before I joined I can remember getting picked up by the Brits and getting fucking hammered like. They really created this situation you know. At that time they could fucking stop you in the street, put you up against the wall, frisk you, search you. You might have got that any time of day. It was a real military situation, no question about that. Complete street raids, blocking the street off, and searching every house from top to bottom. Mass liftings, fucking major gun battles, thousands of rounds being fired. We were throwing nail bombs as if they were stones. You started off throwing stones, progressed to petrol bombs, to nail bombs, and then so on and so forth. You were getting done by the Brits and peelers [police] all the time. There was no pussyfooting. They were knocking the stones out of you—fucking bad diggings. So it was a natural thing to do, the violence. I remember going down lodging complaints dead official and all. Police making you fill in these forms, "When did you get lifted and what happened." Really thinking you would see a bit of justice and all. Four weeks later a cop comes around and says, "Sorry, there's no grounds for complaint." So, if you couldn't get anything one way, you went the other way. There was no way at that time that you could get a fair crack of the whip. (INLA)

4.3 If there were shootings on the Falls Road, the Brits would just lift the whole fucking area, three hundred to four hundred people in a night. They used to bring four-ton trucks in to fill them up and bring them down to Grosvenor Road barracks for interrogation. They'd take whole streets. You'd see thirty guys from one street being marched from the Falls Road to Springfield barracks. They tied cunts [male prisoners] to the

Saracens to prevent them [the soldiers] from getting bricked
by the kids. (INLA)

Arrest on this scale and intensity severely disrupted the social structure of the targeted community. New forms of collective identification
appeared: the reincorporation of the arrested suspect into the community and the reappropriation of judicial assessment by the populace. The
subtraction of one body from the community mobilized the corporate
body.

The repeated violation of the domestic space by the house raid was a
major precipitant for the countercollectivization of arrest by targeted
communities. With the juridical erasure of the domestic space, the affective linkages and sociative potentials of the latter were remapped into
the street which became increasingly inflected by ethics of privacy, personal territory, and closed interiority (see chap. 2 and 3).

The following narrator addresses the continuing violation of domestic
spaces and boundaries. The walls of her home function here as a defiled
border, a register of the crumbling boundary between the inside and the
outside, the private and the public. The wall, rendered a political artifact,
silently stores a history of violence and is a physical connection between
the witness and the victims of violence:

4.4   You see the nature of these troubles was that no matter what
        hour of the night, I would have fellows getting spread-eagled
        against the walls of this house. They were getting knocked
        about on my walls! One night going out there I heard a com-
        motion. The taxi was sitting at the end of the road, and four
        fellows were getting done by the Brits. It started at my door,
        and they were getting hammered. I went out to let the Brits
        know I wasn't frightened of them. I went out to the lads
        spread-eagled and gave them a cigarette. And this big Brit
        comes flying down, "Who gave you permission?" "Son," I
        says, "We're not in Russia. I can talk to these lads and I can
        give them a cigarette." I knew most of the lads. He says,
        "Get in and turn your lights out." If anything ever happened
        around here I would put my light on front, rear, top, and bot-
        tom floors. The Brit comes down to me, "I'm having a look at
        you," he says, "and I'll remember you and I'll be back." And
        all their dirty talk, the worst dirty talk you ever heard in your
        life. (Female pensioner, Short Strand)

Arrest establishes a *cordon sanitaire* around the suspect, his house,
and around entire communities in which the arrest occurs. This partition
is the essential mechanism for hierarchizing the violence of the arrest

event in relation to other forms of violence experienced and practiced by the community. This cordon sanitaire is the state in miniature. At the same time that it disrupts public/private allocations of personal and social space, this zone presupposes the juridical division between civil society and the state. During arrest, the counterinsurgency forces expect the community to avoid the event, to stay off the streets, to close the lights and curtains and withdraw into privacy.

The narrator intentionally violates the cordon sanitaire that maintains the arrest as a politically neutral and technical procedure. Her very movement across these boundaries transforms the arrest into communal space. She becomes the out-of-place entity in a tableau in which all participants are supposed to occupy fixed positions. The automatic response of the commanding soldier is to incorporate her into the juridical space through a threat that renders her as visible as the men laying spread-eagled on the sidewalk. Arrest divides the populace into the visible and the invisible, a division that objectifies and produces the jural subject. But violence as well as panopticism is crucial to this production. The soldier draws the narrator into the space of arrest as a continuum of immanent violence. In turn, she registers violence and defilement in her remarks concerning the abusive language of the soldiers.

Events like that described above were repeated innumerable times in the Catholic ghettos of Belfast during the first ten years of the Troubles. Anonymous in themselves, their repetition and commonplace enactment contributed to the architecture of collective resistance.

The countercollectivization of arrest by targeted communities exploited the performative contingency of this part-space of the state. The arrest spectacle attempted to create a periphery of the state in the domestic space and the community. The command of local space, always an overdetermined concern in Northern Ireland, inspired mass mobilization as it had in other instances of visible territorial violation. This process constituted an ideology of collective experience that contributed— more than the formalized ideologies of nationalism—to politicization:

4.5   When the Brits moved into these districts to lift people, the first thing they done was to smash all the street lighting. Our ones [the IRA] were breaking the lighting as well. At night most of the districts were pitch black. The Brits had what we called "duck patrols." They were moving into the areas in black-painted Saracens [armored cars]. The soldiers' faces were blackened, and there was no street lighting. The Brits were coming in, and nobody knew where they were.

It started first on the Falls [Catholic district]; the local women in each district operated "hen patrols" as a response to the Brits' "duck patrols." The women would come out with pots, spoons, and bin lids, banging them and following behind the Brits. The noise was everywhere. You always knew when the Brits were raiding through the districts. That's also when the paint bombs started.

The black Saracens were coming in so we were throwing white paint bombs so they would show up the black jeeps. The Brits started painting all the walls in the Falls black up to a certain height. So when the foot patrols were moving along the streets they were blacked out. There was no profile coming in. You couldn't snipe them; you couldn't see them.

Our crowd started going out and painted all the black walls white. The Brits would repaint them black. This was going on for weeks, black/white black/white, back and forth.

The Brits got fed up and got their water cannons; they smashed people's windows all along the Falls with high pressured water. Then they shot black paint through the people's houses all around the kitchen walls. It was fuckin' murder that night with rioting: "You can do anything but don't you touch the inside of my house!" (Falls Road male resident)

4.6   When the troubles started around here, the women were immaculate. They were great. When people heard the doors getting kicked in they rattled the bins in their yards. If anybody was getting arrested in this street, into the yard I was, banging pans. On every anniversary of internment—the bins. That will never die out. There were too many people killed here.

When the women all gathered and all got together they played a great part. One Sunday the Brits came in and lifted a brother and sister and her infant. The pots were banging and the women rushed out into the street which was lined with Saracens. The Brits had backed a Saracen right up to the front door of the house that was getting done. So you couldn't get into the house to see what was being done to these people. You wouldn't have seen this street or known it for the armored cars and water cannons. The Brits said if we didn't get off the street they would turn the water cannons on us. We told the Brits to turn it on. What's a taste of water? The people all rushed—all women. If any wee lad or boy was there they would have been lifted. It had to be the women. When they started they got more than they bargained for. There was no shooting, but with bottles and stones against their rubber bullets.[4] We had a big black dog on this street. He would have went up the street where the soldiers were and brought back every bottle that hadn't broken and would pick them up and carry them back to us. No one knew what happened to that dog. He disappeared. Some say the Brits did him in. (Housewife, Short Strand)

Narrative 4.5 is organized around a series of spatial, chromatic, gender, and sensory oppositions that encode the political polarities of the arrest process. The destruction of the street lighting by both the PIRA and the British army shifts public space at night into a liminal condition. On this dimmed stage, a series of alternations between qualities of light and dark codifies the exchange of transgression and countertransgression. The black vehicles, faces, and walls of the army are countered by the white paint bombs of the community. The narrative is organized around visibility and invisibility, light and dark, white paint and black, silence and sound, knowledge and secrecy, inside and outside, men and women. It is focused on the maintenance of exchange in a state of balanced equivalence. The transgressive force is persistently neutralized by the defensive strategies that counter the defiling effects of invisibility, darkness, secrecy, the outside, and invasive men. This emphasis on balanced tension and reciprocal inversion suggests that the narrative codifies a cultural construction of warfare that is prerevolutionary—a holding action by both the community and the state attempting to test and to maintain specific topographic claims. Ritualized exchange is overturned by the spraying of the domestic space with black paint by the British soldiers, that is to say, by the excessive entrance of the defiling male outside into an interior that is associated with women. The structured tension of gendered oppositions collapses, and in place of dyadic exchange an unrestrained and indiscriminate rioting breaks out.

This depiction of nonmilitary, community-based resistance is centered on women as defenders of the neighborhood, an expansion of their role as the defenders of the domestic space. Transgression and resistance are thus marked out with visible and invisible gender presences: the maleness of the invading British army—the duck patrols; the women defenders—the hen patrols; and the absent men of the community who remained marginal figures in the narrative. They are in effect the absent cause of the gendering of public/popular resistance. Local men are missing for two fundamental reasons. They are the natural targets for arrest, and many of them are active members of the PIRA.

The story thus documents the complex dynamics that organize the relations of a specialized and clandestine military organization with its community base. It maps out a gender division of political labor in which the feminine metaphor totalizes the community against the state. The collectivization of resistance by women is the transformation of the local and national community into an associative topos analogous to the idealized domestic space. "Communitas" now becomes the feminized inside in relation to the externality of the colonial state.

Bin-lid banging (4.6) in the working-class communities of Belfast is a modern-day variation of "rough-music" or "charivari" by which many British Isles communities once registered protests against the state and expelled polluting presences. Rough music has an explicit historical association with protest against jural institutions and with gender inversion.[5] In many cultures, ritualized collective noise-making signifies defiling temporal shifts and death (Seremetakis 1991). Bin-lid banging in urban Northern Ireland is a resistance technique almost exclusively associated with women and children. Beside banging lids in the confrontational space of the street, the other spaces for this performance are the backyards and interconnecting alleyways behind the brick houses, which are also the customary spaces for women's networks and for gossip. Bin-lid banging communicates not only a warning, but also signals that the community has been moved into a liminal and defiled state due to the presence of the Other. The linkage between pollution, death, and lid banging is particularly strong. Bin lids are banged to mark the anniversary of internment and the deaths of the ten 1981 hunger strikers.

Capture

Resisting arrest was enacted against a sense of isolation: the isolation of the arrested individual, his family, and community, which became ghettoized through the process of repeated and routinized raids. The individual arrest functioned as a structural model of political process in Northern Ireland that was easily extended to the political/juridical situation of the entire paramilitary support community. Thus it is crucial to understand the function of arrest as a biographical experience capable of generating collective political meanings.

In Belfast and Derry since 1969, crowd violence and territorial mobilization have been a given experience and model of agency for many since childhood, via constant exposure to street riots and military training by various youth organizations, such as the Republican Fianna and the Loyalist Boys Brigades. Arrest and interrogation, and not violence, therefore, serve as the seminal experiences that demarcate political maturity. Male children under a certain age are seen as eligible to take visible part in street actions because they are not liable for arrest. Arrest and interrogation tend to function for paramilitaries as biographical markers that precede the intensified involvement with organized paramilitary violence.

Bazin (1984) identifies the fusion of both ritualized and instrumental procedures in the process of capture. Capture is analyzed as a mode of production, as a form of social death, and as a rite of initiation, all of which originate in an "initial act of violence" (pp. 111–12). Bazin reconstructs capture as a limen. In the same moment that it signifies constraint and immobility, capture can also mark the production of new legal personalities and mediating subject positions.[6] The Northern Ireland situation extends Bazin's theorization of capture by illustrating how the coerced movement of the captured from defined to undefined identities affects the reproduction of collective violence and political subjects. Subject formation, a pivotal mechanism for the production of political ideology, can be located within the biographical conjuncture formed by arrest/interrogation experiences and the construction of the body. This intersection is a crucial point of inception from which the performative autonomy of violence in Northern Ireland derives much of its symbolic logic, codes of exchange, ideological content, and personal agency.

4.7   When they came for me . . . I was up at half five in the morning. I had been up the same time the Monday and Tuesday before. Though I hadn't been involved for some time I knew they were coming for me. I'm thinking, "Will I keep the door open?" Here's me, "Sure, when they come I'll rap the window for to let them know I'm expecting them." I went back to sleep for an hour, woke up and told the wife to get up because the house is getting done today. At a quarter past six I hear the Landrover coming up the street. Before the peelers could get to the door I jump up and rap the window.

     The peeler says to me, "How did you know that we were coming?" Here's me: "I'm psycho." He says, "If you're psycho, you could have saved me from getting out of my bed and coming down to lift you. You could have come down to Castlereagh [interrogation center] yourself." He got me on that one. I says, "You think I'm going to fucking do your job for you?" I was asked again and again in the interrogation, "How did you know we were coming for ye?"

     So they came through the door. "Are you ____? What color are your eyes? Date of birth?" I says, "You're overexceeding your powers under the Emergency Provisions Act." That stops them. They're now thinking, "This guy knows his stuff!" As soon as they come through the door the first thing I have in my hand is a card for writing notes. And if they come over to look, I say, "Fuck off mind your own business."

     They come through the door and the first thing I'm at them

right away. I don't threaten them. I just abuse them. Once you're arrested that's all they looking at. The manner in which you're getting done. If they thought I was sitting down here crying with nerves and shouting, "No don't take me!" They'd say, "He's cracked, hit him with a slopper in the ear." But I say, "Fuck off you bastards."

I says to the wife: "Give me the breakfast." Because I'm one up on them now. I try not to show off to the wife. It's very easy to shout, "Get me my fuckin' breakfast!" That would show them I'm getting at her because they've annoyed me. So I ask for the breakfast quietly. There is this detective woman sergeant. The first time they brought a woman. I was insulted. She came to arrest me and here's me in a robe. The next thing this bird asks me, "Do you normally have your breakfast this time in the morning?" I'm thinking, "Only normally when bastards like you come and get me out of my bed." But here's me: "Why? Are you refusing to let me have my breakfast?" She says, "Oh no, no." She now has doubts; she's saying to herself, "Is he allowed to have his breakfast?"

I'm eating the breakfast and meanwhile the guy across the street is getting done the same time as me and on the same charge. What are they doing to him? They're fucking pulling him out of bed, putting handcuffs on him and dragging him in the street without his clothes on. It's a profile they have. When they come to lift anybody they do a profile on them. Where is he at this moment? What's happening with him? What way is he performing? (UDA)

"Getting Done"

In both Republican and Loyalist paramilitary support communities, being arrested is known as getting "lifted," "scooped," and "getting done." Getting "lifted" and "scooped" refer to the physical act of the arrest event. The metaphor of physical removal that these phrases evoke encapsulates the subjective experience of forced extraction from one's residential and community contexts. Being "done" has more complex semantic associations. To be "done" in Northern Ireland refers to the qualitative impact of arrest on both the subject's cognitive and physical states of being.

In chapter 3, I asserted that there were two passageways into the political culture of violence in Northern Ireland: categories of the body and categories of performance. Paramilitaries, of course, see these domains as continuous. "Stiffing" (see chapter 3) is a sphere of action that primarily encodes violence from the perspective of transformed embodiment. Stiffing infers unambiguous domination of a political agent over a made object: the stiff or "cunt" (male target). To stiff someone is to "do" the victim, and to be stiffed is to be done. To do and to be done are pivotal categories of performance in paramilitary culture and extend beyond the absolute dichotomies and terminal states of stiffing.

Other forms of the verb "to do" such as "doing" and "the doings," also refer explicitly to the enactment and media of violence. In the decades preceding the current civil violence in Belfast, to "do" someone meant to inflict a beating on him. To "do him up" or to "touch him up" are variants of this phrase. During the same period, to do a house or commercial premises meant to commit a robbery. From the late 1960s, the verb "to do" has undergone a politicization that reflects the expanding spheres of domination in Northern Ireland. Currently, "to do" someone can range from inflicting a beating to arrest, guerrilla ambush, and political assassination. Reciprocally, "to do a house" means not only to rob but also to raid a house for inflicting violence on its members or for their arrest by the counterinsurgency forces. Both paramilitaries and the counterinsurgency forces regularly "do" houses for their respective purposes. "The doings" can refer to acts of violence and to weapons and their associated technology. (Weapons are also known as "gear.") The current usage of "doing" or "getting done" still retains the sense of direct face-to-face interpersonal violent interactions that the original meaning of inflicting or taking a beating possessed. Thus, "doing"/"getting done" does not usually apply to the enactment or receipt of collective violence in such situations as riots where one-to-one and face-to-face interactions are at a minimum.

"Doing" and "getting done" are highly charged phrases that in their didactic brevity refer to complex semantics of personalized interaction. To "do" violence is a tautology in the local idiom. The absorption of the grammar of enactment by the inflections of violence implies (1) that the general gauge of salient social agency has been conflated with the enactment of violence and (2) that norms of performance inform the commonsensical reception of violence. The verb "to do" seals the instrumental, reductive, and pragmatic construction of violence—a construct that is ideological. A distinction between ideology and experience can be posed here because the performative symbiosis of doing and being done subverts any pragmatic and utilitarian depiction of political violence. Thus at the same time that ideology attempts to integrate violence into the quotidian through terms like doing/getting done, the effects of violence increasingly contradict utilitarian and pragmatic accomplishment. Because of the insistent ironic subtext of performance experience, the unmediated instrumental construction of everyday reality becomes problematic.

The contemporary paramilitary usage of "doing"/"getting done" activates sedimented meanings that connect the performative and the violent to certain pertinent cultural institutions and practices. These semantic strata document the extent to which the current structure of violence is grasped through residual cultural categories, which in turn become decentered and altered in their application to novel historical experience. In the Lowland Scots dialect (which predominates in Belfast), the phrase "to do" refers to several action domains: to cause, to give, to perform, to administer law or justice, to exert power, to put in place, to put away, to put out (Craigie 1937:175–78). In the nineteenth-century underworld slang of the British Isles, "to do" someone was to cheat, to swindle, to attack, and to punish (the last two terms are also found in boxing circles). To "be done" was both to be cheated by a confidence man and to be hanged by the state. In military parlance, "a do" was an attack and "the doings" referred to the material of warfare (Partridge 1961:226–27, 233).

To do and to be done are rural and working-class terms that commensurate the performative dimension of several social spheres: the criminal, the juridical, the military and contest. These verbs effect certain exchanges between these domains. To claim that someone is *done* by a criminal and by the state is to infer certain equivalences between "illegitimate" and "legitimate" violence. The verb "to do" applied to the exertion of force detaches the performative dimension of power from formal legitimations and institutional facades. In contemporary Northern Ireland, paramilitary violence and state violence are rendered commensurate through the axis doing/being done.

Doing and being done refer to types and domains of violent action and also characterize typified social relations between adversaries. Paramilitary experience is frequently characterized as an alternation between doing others and being done yourself. It is a continual exchange between active and passive, domination and subordination. Anomalies and ambiguities abound in this relation because political identity autonomously circulates between these two poles and is never fully containable within one phase or the other. One's position on the scale of doing/being done is never fully controlled. To do others is to enter into an anomalous continuum dominated by reversible violence that can culminate in "being done." These positions are also intersecting trajectories that form the metaphorical body of the paramilitary as a constellation of subjectivities, insofar as they are concerned with polarized dispositions of the same politicized body, be that the body of the victim of violence, the agent of violence, or the instrument of violence.

This manifold formation of the body as a political agency and political object is at its most visible in the paramilitary discourse on contact with weapons. Doing as a type of action is inseparable from weapon use and is linked to the "doings" or the "gear" (weapons). As paramilitaries put it:

4.8   Whenever you're fucking with the doings, you're taking your life in your hands. (INLA)

4.9   On the street you know you can go to prison or you can die; its not something you dwell on in your own thought. . . . I knew that from experience, having been interned in 1972 and having been shot at by an SAS assassination squad in 1975.[7] You can't dwell on it when you go into the street with a weapon in your hand. (PIRA)

The body and the weapon occupy interchangeable and isomorphic positions in the conversion of doing into being done. The handling of, and contiguity with, weapons is riven with life/death, domination/subordination polarities. Defiling contact and personal history with weapons are the biographical metaphors for ironic, fatal reversal. To be caught with weapons by the counterinsurgency forces is considered by paramilitaries an automatic death sentence in the field. To possess a weapon establishes the paramilitary as a legitimate target for a "shoot-to-kill," whether he is offering resistance to the arresting authorities or not.[8]

The weapon as a signifier of political mastery and resistance is also the conduit into the position of the victim, the subaltern, the "cunt," and "the stiff." While conducting operations, paramilitaries deliberately minimize the duration and space of physical contact or contiguity with weapons. Under the cell system[9] used by the PIRA and INLA, each stage of the "op" is divided into sanitizing "cutouts": weapon delivery, arming and weapons use, and disposal after the completion of the assignment. The "safe house" where arms are divested is known as a "wash house" (see chapter 2). Guns that have been used are considered "dirty," that is they accumulated a forensic history with the police and are doubly incriminating due to their past and present usages. Such weapons are used with trepidation and distaste by the paramilitary.

To wield a weapon is literally *to take one's life in one's hand.* In violent praxis the fate of embodiment ("life") is detached from the self and transferred to the instrument of violence. In turn the weapon as a political and forensic artifact of both the self and the Other is encoded with the reversibility of doing/being done. To pose the weapon as an artifact of the body and as the conduit of reversible violence is to conceptualize both the body and the weapon as heterogeneous sites of mediation and exchange. The weapon artifact is associated with the interpenetration of active and passive, being and nonbeing. The weapon incarnates the body's political alterity and endows violence with a cognitive structure, with a biography. If somatic positions are deposited and exchanged in the weapon, it is because the individual body is effaceable and the collectivized weapon endures; it is a hardening (reification) of the body. Thus if embodiment is sublated by the weapon, if weapons become bodies, then bodies can be reciprocally metaphorized as weapons. Both "hardmen" and "stiffs" are bodies transformed into weapons (see chapter 3). The weapon, with all of its multivalence, is a cognitive map of material exchange and violent action. In doing/getting done the exchanges between the body and the weapon are historicizing devices and a means for conceiving political alterity.

The semantic circuit of doing/getting done is encountered in both weapon use and in the arrest event. The identification of the verb "do" with violence, weapons, and death reinforces the qualification of arrest/interrogation (getting done) as a form of social death. Arrest is a portal for the cultural construction of violence in Northern Ireland. For the paramilitaries, arrest is a transaction where doing is inverted to being done. The formation of arrest as a limen is the result of this reversal.

4.10   If you are caught in a house, the normal procedure [for the police] is to come up in a disguised van or furniture lorry. Without warning the front door is broken down with a sledge hammer. They just fly into the house, and the first person up gets hit with the sledge hammer. It's all just quick impact to make sure the people in the house don't get a chance to "open up" [fire their weapons]. Last week the peelers hammered down a flat but they didn't move in quick enough.[10] They just got unlucky, and they got shot dead.

In a car transporting weapons, or coming to and from an operation, the car is rammed or stopped at a roadblock. In a built-up area like this you're dragged out of the car with the arm up the back and searched, then kicked about, and then thrown into jeeps where you would be beat about with batons by both the army and the police.

If you're caught in isolated circumstances like Sean Quinn or Eugene Tolman last year [1982],[11] then it's a shoot-to-kill policy whether you're armed or not. Three hundred shots fired into Tolman's car, and he was hit with a hundred rounds. Most times you'd be lucky to get caught where there would be seventy or eighty witnesses on the road, where it's unacceptable and they can't gun somebody down. Though they have executed people in Belfast while lifting people in operations, numerous people. (PIRA)

The entire sequence leading up to arrest and its aftermath is experienced by paramilitaries as a process of incremental enclosure that can culminate in the ultimate isolation of violent death. The relative levels and intensities of isolation move the arrest event toward the paramilitary's death. For the paramilitary the public/isolated, visible/invisible dichotomization of arrest stands for life/death alternatives predicated by the presence or absence of the community of witness.

This division of arrest into public/isolated, visible/invisible, life/death oppositions reveals the extent to which violent practice, depending on its performative settings, is perceived to be governed by informal rules. In the instance of arrest, the rule-bound practices of violence by which the paramilitaries gauge their proximity to death are usually expressed by such phrases as "acceptable" or "unacceptable" levels of violence. (These terms originated with the counterinsurgency apparatus but predictably have been taken over by paramilitaries in a deflating mimesis of state rationality.) Another variation is "excusable" and "inexcusable" violence. These classifications demonstrate the extent to which the enactment and experience of violence are based on shrewd assessments that elicit a formal structure beneath the rapidity and disorder. These rules emerge with the accumulation of personal experiences of arrest as rough guidelines by those who have survived repeated arrest and who are aware of how their colleagues have died from the same procedures. To the extent that these oppositions reflect the need to inject order and limits into violent interactions, they also express the awareness that the paramilitary operates, lives, and dies in demarcated zones.

The heightened awareness of operating in a separate continuum of discourse and action is evident in the differentiation of settings of violence and the levels of violence these locales authorize. The fear of the isolated arrest, bereft of collective witness, projects an image of the state as an underground apparatus by virtue of its capacity to exploit or to create enclosed situations of invisible punishment. This enclosure of state violence is aggravated by systems of secret knowledge. Both the army and the police forces deny an unofficial shoot-to-kill policy, despite the number of deaths that have occurred in highly ambiguous circumstances. The practice of shoot-to-kill procedures in isolated arrest events is the ultimate cordon sanitaire and is the standard by which the paramilitaries and their support communities evaluate the more public and possibly less fatal cordons that cloister state practices.

Shoot-to-kill stories are also disgruntled recognitions of the formation of a shared material language and political culture between state and paramilitary. The autonomous reproduction of reciprocal violence in Northern Ireland is informed by a mimetic identification which endows all clandestine violence with a tacit jural status—a unifying valuation for all antagonists despite ideological borders.

The bifurcation of arrest into life/death polarities is part of the generalized division of the paramilitary career cycle into doing/being done. The paramilitary career is experientially and cognitively structured around two polarities: imprisonment or violent death leading to political martyrdom. Ideological and eventually existential acceptance of these two options are an essential component of the formal initiation into the paramilitary organization and of the eventual professionalization of the paramilitary.

4.11   I was told, "Join the movement and you have two options. One of them is death and the other, if you're lucky, is jail. You can be sure of one of these two things. Now, if you don't like jail, go out the door." I was lucky. I went to jail; other guys died. If you are totally committed as many claim to be, jail won't annoy you. There have been guys inside, out, and back in again as many as five times, all the way through the Troubles. It says in my deposition that I was an "active member, a *very* active member." I didn't get killed but that was because I was careful. That isn't to say I didn't come close to it, looking through the back window of a car and seeing the fucking cops closing in and they starting to open up with their gear. (INLA)

The life/death polarities that govern both the cognitive mapping of the arrest process and the overarching paramilitary career cycle also polarize symbolic and instrumental forms of political action in Republican ideology. Military death in combat is considered by the PIRA and INLA as a pragmatic inevitability whose efficacy is easy to identify in its contributions to the Republican struggle. In contrast, the processes of arrest, interrogation, and imprisonment are seen as frameworks for types of resistance that can be identified as symbolic and expressive, though Republicans do not use these categories. Rather, they codify this polarity as the opposition between the "physical force" strategy and the "political strategy."[12] The political strategy is all resistance and insurrectionary activity that does not involve the use of weapons and military violence. This opposition between the instrumental (military) and the symbolic (political) is a longstanding one in the Republican movement. Republican history, and the ideological development of the IRA in particular, has been bitterly divided between a physical force policy and a "political" policy. Within the Official IRA, the Provisional IRA, and the INLA there have been repeated conflicts over whether the military council or the political wing of the organization should define and direct the overall revolutionary strategy of the organization (Coogan 1980:14–15).

The liminality of the arrest event refracts its dual position in both instrumental and symbolic activity. Arrest stands at the juncture of the life/death military/political, instrumental/symbolic polarities that inform the direction of the paramilitary career. Arrest functions as a passageway to violent death or as the corridor that opens up paramilitary praxis to a self-reflexive framing of power, agency, and the body.

Arrest and Death

The routinization of imminent violent death is a determining condition of paramilitary life. In turn, the support community during the course of the war has been socialized to the repeated occurrence of abrupt violent death. The paramilitary organization partially secures its legitimation within base communities by disseminating an ideology of "acceptable levels" of violence. The paradox is that this ideology, once internalized, also causes the deaths of individual paramilitaries and their more visible supporters to be received with decreasing levels of collective disturbance. The paramilitary funeral has gradually become an extremely rationalized ceremonial response to violent death. The gradual shift of emphasis in popular street action from the collectivization of arrest to the collectivization of death in the funeral is a shift from an interventionist to a commemorative mode of political symbolization, even if both can touch off riots. For the living paramilitary, the politicization of his death in the funeral is tempered by the fact that the same ceremony ritualizes the inevitability of that death. Advanced thinking in the PIRA sees the general acceptance of inevitable Republican deaths being exploited as a depoliticizing tool by the counterinsurgency forces. (This is particularly cogent in the wake of the ten hunger-strike deaths in 1981, where the imagery of fatalistic death was deliberately cultivated by the PIRA.) As in the double-edged and reversible defilements of weapon handling, the ideology of "acceptable levels" of violence can turn against the paramilitary and capture him in its miasmic logic. The dialectic of doing/being done, as a dominant symbolic logic of the culture of war, operates within its own self-directed circuits and economies. The closed circuit of violent reciprocity facilitates an acceptable level of distancing by communities in which the paramilitary lives and for whom he claims to die. This dissociation from violence and death through the ethic of the "acceptable" territorializes violence in the body of the imputed paramilitary. This confinement of violence suits state practice insofar as it transforms the latter into spectacle and the paramilitary's community into passive spectators. The political code of "acceptable levels of violence" indicates that both the state and the paramilitaries share a sacrificial logic of political hegemony based on the subtraction of parts from the whole. Social-political formation is predicated on the creation of visible zones of somatic disappearance and violent exchange. Political formation is grounded on excluded negativity, on the expulsion of experiences and persons.

4.12 If a house is getting raided three times a week and some guy is constantly being taken down to the Reagh for interrogation and the next thing that happens is that this guy in the house gets banged [shot] by the Brits or the Orangies, people think nothing of it. The Brits set people up all the time that way. If an RA [IRA] man, or someone people think is an RA man, is stiffed, people will say, "It's bad but you take your chances." The Brits know this is the thinking in the area, and they'll create that situation when it's necessary for them.

   If I got shot dead tomorrow by the Brits, I might not have been doing anything at all. But I have enough background so that the Brits can justify it. The fact that I can drive through a red light and they can shoot me, the fact that I drive through that red light doesn't matter. The fact that I have been shot dead is justified by whatever files they have on me. (INLA)

4.13 There's a process of installing in people's minds that the IRA are terrorists, which ultimately makes us fair game for shoot-to-kill operations. It has been totally acceptable for people who come out and condemn IRA attacks to find it acceptable for IRA volunteers to be assassinated in situations where they are not offering armed violence. On a day-to-day level, through a long period, the Brits have built up their intelligence. They know to a fair degree who are and who are not Republicans. They know who are and who are not threats to them. They build up the media image that Sinn Fein activists defend the violence of the IRA so it's excusable when they're assassinated by Loyalists, so that's setting them up for Loyalist assassination. But there is a more sinister approach, used by the RUC in particular—the Divisional Mobile Support Units. They're supposedly crack antiterrorist RUC men who trained with the CIA in Central America. Their approach is not simply technical but political. It's a political decision taken by political and military strategists.[13]

   Take Sean Quinn who lives in Ballymurphy. Let's say he was interned in the 1970s. You have a fair idea that he has Republican sympathies. He goes to marches; he buys the *Republican News*. Then his house starts getting raided all the time, and he's lifted. People think to themselves, "He must be up to something." It's the first reaction. He becomes stigmatized. The stigmatization is further enhanced by the regular stopping of him on the street in front of people without asking his name. Now people say, "They know him well." It isn't vocalized; it's thought. People's perception of him becomes that he is one who is actively involved. He is an open target for harassment. People who associate with him get harassed; people he drinks with get harassed. So people begin to move away from him, begin to get careful in his company, and he becomes isolated. The only company he can keep are people of a similar background. But if they're really active they'll stay away from him too; he's a red light. No one's hostile to him but they're wary. What the Brits do bring about in people's minds is that he's someone to be avoided because they've created the atmosphere that he's a likely or prospective military target either for Loyalists or the shoot-to-kill squads. People's perspectives are there—that this guy is likely to get shot— and he ultimately is shot. It won't cause a ripple.

Now the IRA has always claimed its volunteers, no matter what circumstances they're shot in, even if they're shot unarmed, even if they're shot in their beds. The number of people who have been shot in the shoot-to-kills been roughly fifty-fifty active service volunteers and noncombatants. There has been as many political activists as military activists shot. It's been targeted for case-hardened volunteers but also for political activists. (PIRA)

4.14   I suppose I was classed as the most wanted Protestant terrorist in Northern Ireland. It is very easy for people to put a label on you and to justify it within their own organization. Then you look back and say to yourself, what I have been doing is in no way by any means as extreme as much as they are trying to suggest I am. So you look back and say at the end of the day, these bastards are trying to set you up and to get you bumped off. Here I am years after I've retired and they're still doing the house, and I'm still being taken down for [police] interviews. It doesn't matter what you do or try to achieve or strive for. You will never be forgiven, and there is no way on this matter that you will ever create a balance.

I'm not talking about the other side [IRA]; the other side doesn't worry me, just the security forces and the government. Regardless of what you do or tried to achieve they'll always come after you. (UDA)

4.15   When they lift you, they stop you and put you through a "P" check.[14] If your color comes up red you're lifted for no reason. Just because your color is red, and that means "Suspected Terrorist," they take you in a jeep right through the town. Everybody is staring at you. Shouting at you, "They're terrorists!" I'd say, "Well fuck you I'm no terrorist!" (Teenage girl, Catholic, Short Strand)

In Northern Ireland violence is covertly performed by clandestine organizations and thus characterized by invisible webs of causation. The public construction of a suspected terrorist by the state, through the performance of arrest and subsequent political assassination, creates a personifying imagery of the origins of violence and disorder. Arrest envisions the "terrorist" in order to process this juridical object through various systems of expulsion and erasure that include breaking the suspect under interrogation, imprisonment, and covert assassination. This rhetoricized construction of the stigmatized (the terrorist) and the creation of an aura of immanent doom around this object function as an imagery of contamination through which the counterinsurgency forces predetermine the legitimacy of their operations. Being repeatedly questioned and stopped on the street, having one's house subjected repeatedly to raids by the security forces, supplants the necessity of courts, testimony, and evidence. The techniques and rhetorics for specifying, "redlighting," and neutralizing a suspected terrorist can thus be applied equally to practicing paramilitaries and to arbitrary victims chosen by the state for political theater and the periodic advancement of hegemony. Arrest no longer requires an overarching juridical edifice or legal code by which to secure its claim to truth.

Arrest is the political art of individualizing disorder. The surveilled and harassed suspect is termed a "redlight." The continued harassment of the redlight is called "being tortured," a characterization that documents the colonization of social life and private space by the logic of the interrogation cell. In the former space the redlight's social life is turned inside out; in the latter space the redlight's body is unfolded and exposed. This "tortured" subject is the walking panoptic presence of the state in a community that wishes to evade full panopticism. The redlight is a body suborned into a mobile instrument of state surveillance. Through the redlight, diverse people become caught up in a net of objective guilt. Made visible as a source of pollution, a danger to himself and to those who are linked to him, the targeted subject is isolated from his community and from other associations. He is incorporated by repeated arrest, into the "acceptable levels" of attrition and fear.

Jacobo Timerman (1982:52) has referred to the collective "silence" that hovered over the "disappearances" caused by the Argentine death squads, the reorganization of social and political life around the doubled negativity of the political victim and contamination avoidance. As in Argentina, this silence in Northern Ireland expressed the need to avoid polluting contact with the economy of violence, with the exchange systems of death. This silence troubles the paramilitaries because they have played a central role in routinizing it as a socializing force within their own communities. This is the backgrounding of violence, that is, the emergence of violence as the assumed basis of entire domains of social interaction and of the informal ideologies of everyday life. In Northern Ireland, the distancing that is associated with the execution of suspected or known paramilitaries and their active political supporters is a part of routine prophylactic rules—regulations of the commonplace that cause people to avoid certain streets at night, abandoned cars, and unclaimed parcels—those customary and, by now, banal signs of prospective death in Northern Ireland into which the targeted paramilitary is assimilated.

4.16   What's it like to be on the run? [Pause] Nobody wants to know you. Because if you get caught in their house and get turned over, nobody wants to speak to you. They've got the psychological thing that you might shoot them eventually because you think they're an informer. And you don't trust anybody. You are always saying things to yourself: Are you looked for? What can they prove on me? Who spotted me doing what, when, and where? Who's telling yarns on me? (Ex-UDA)

Interrogation: Ceremony of Verification

The politicizing of judicial procedure in Northern Ireland transformed the temporal relations between the law, criminal activity, and societal order:

> The evidence is therefore unequivocal. The powers of arrest and interrogation in Northern Ireland are being primarily used by the police to collect information on individuals and communities rather than to charge and prosecute. Policing in Northern Ireland has therefore moved from a retroactive form where those suspected of illegal activities are arrested and processed through the courts of evidence obtained after the event, to a pre-emptive form where large sections of those communities which are perceived as being a distinct threat to the existing status quo are regularly and systematically monitored and surveilled. (Hillyard 1983:46)

Boyle, Hadden, and Hillyard (1980) link the institutionalization of interrogation-torture procedures with the reduction of common rules of law to technical practices. They are particularly concerned with common law that dealt with the defendant's right to silence, the admissibility of confessions in courts of evidence, and the limits of legitimate judicial questioning. Common law contravenes "many of the techniques of interrogation in Northern Ireland and elsewhere. Interrogation in this sense is perhaps best defined as prolonged and persistent questioning in which the suspect's right to silence is implicitly if not formally denied" (1980:36).

It has been ascertained that in the early and middle 1970s, officers of the Special Branch in Northern Ireland received special training in interrogation techniques from British army personnel of the English Intelligence Center. This training disseminated techniques that had been deployed in Kenya, Aden, Cyprus, and Malaya during periods of guerrilla and terrorist warfare. The central objective of these techniques, as described by psychologists, is the personality breakdown of the suspect, what army experts described as "softening" the subject for interrogation. The techniques used in Northern Ireland are modeled on established and well-known KGB methods (Shallice 1973:386–87), but in contrast to the Soviet procedures, "Ulster methods are more severe versions of the isolation technique. . . . the components of the process are therefore: isolation, sleep deprivation, non-specific threat, depersonalization, inadequate diet and in many occasions physical brutality" (p. 390).

These procedures were combined as the "Five Techniques," which were supposed to have been formally abandoned in 1972, after the publication of the Parker Report which described their use during internment. This report concluded that the Five Techniques were justified given the special circumstances in Northern Ireland, but that they should be officially reintroduced and regulated by formal legislation. The Diplock Commission of 1972 advocated the suspension of common rules of law concerning the right to silence and the admissibility of evidence. For the Diplock Commission, these rules were "hampering the course of justice in the case of terrorist crimes" (Boyle, Hadden, and Hillyard 1980:37–38). The Diplock Report recommended the admission of statements by the accused obtained in violation of common rules of law, provided that these statements had not been secured by "degrading, torturing or inflicting forms of inhuman treatment on the subject." The classic maxim advanced by this commission, which the RUC has rhetorically adopted, is that interrogation should "build up an atmosphere in which the initial desire to remain silent is replaced by an urge to confide in the questioner" (p. 38).

Hillyard (1983:49) identifies the institutionalization of coercive interrogation procedures in Northern Ireland with the opening of Castlereagh and Gough Army Barracks as specialized interrogation centers in the mid-1970s. Their establishment also coincided with the ending of internment and the phasing out of mass population screenings. With the opening of the two interrogation centers, complaints of police brutality increased dramatically. The Bennett Committee report of 1979 recommended the installation of video cameras in the interrogation cells which would be monitored by Special Branch personnel in order to curtail what the committee had identified as individual abuses of interrogation procedures. The committee also recommended time schedules for interrogation sessions and a code of conduct for the interrogators (Boyle, Hadden, and Hillyard 1980:39).

Taylor, in his interrogation study *Beating the Terrorists,* provides us with this account of Castlereagh interrogation center, which emphasizes its formal functions as a data collection center:

> Castlereagh has thirty-eight cells and twenty-one interview rooms—some of them the old rooms with the pegboard walls that survived the Provisionals' bomb attack. On any day, suspects, connected with three separate investigations can be interrogated under the same roof. Each group is questioned by a team of detectives, usually from HG Crime Squad, Belfast Regional Crime Squad and Belfast Divisional CID. . . .
>
> An intelligence collator, often a Woman Police Constable, monitors the progress of the interviews. On the wall of each collator's office is a huge chart. Down the left-hand side are written the names of the detectives who work on the team and against them the code numbers they are given to ease collation. There were twenty-seven detectives involved in investigations on the INLA sweep. Alongside the detectives' names are listed the names of the suspects. The times and duration of each interview are then entered in a square. On the basis of information received from each interview, further permutations of detectives and suspects are worked out, which are likely to yield the best results from the next session. (Taylor 1980:154–55)

In this description, the image of the interrogation center as an efficient enterprise in rationalized administration is exactly the model of technically neutral juridical processing that the security forces use to legitimize counterinsurgency practice. There is no hint of anything political or coercive about the work being done at Castlereagh. It is simply a data collection center dependent on human subjects, a combination of technical administration and crisis management.

From beneath this facade, another tale emerges. Taylor was covertly informed by Castlereagh personnel that it was accepted almost every where in the world that the beating of a suspect was often a quick way of getting him to talk . . . that the atmosphere in the interview rooms was "indescribable" and only the Provos (PIRA) knew what it was like. They admitted that the allegations they [the Provos] made were sometimes based on first hand experience and agreed that many of them were true. . . . They said they were getting results and that was the standard by which their work was judged. (1980:156)

From Boyle, Hadden, and Hillyard's survey of confession statistics in 1979, we are given the following description of the interrogation process:

The first interrogation session would be unlikely to take place much before noon. But from then until late that night the suspect would be interrogated by two or three teams of detectives in continuous sessions of up to two hours. In some cases a new team of detectives would take over without any effective break in the interrogation, so that from the suspect's point of view the session might last for three or four hours. A similar pattern of interviews would be held the following day, starting about 10 A.M. and continuing again until 10 or 11 P.M. In the case of those arrested under the three-day power the series of interviews would be likely to come to an end in the later morning or early afternoon of the third day, when the suspect would be taken to an appropriate police station for formal charging. In the case of those arrested and held under the Prevention of Terrorism Act the series of interrogations might continue for five or six days. (1980:41)

Boyle, Hadden, and Hillyard go on to note that a statistical survey of defendants from January to April 1979 reveals that 43 percent of Loyalist defendants and 59 percent of Republican defendants underwent from four to nine hours of interrogation, and roughly 10 percent from both groups underwent ten hours or more. In the same period, more than half of both Republican and Loyalist defendants were charged on the basis of statements made in interrogation sessions, as opposed to indictments based on forensic evidence or the testimony of a witness (1980:42–45). A more recent study by Walsh documents that 90 percent of suspects taken in for interrogation were released without charge, while for 75 percent of those who were charged, indictment was based mainly on confession (O'Malley 1983:213n).

Boyle, Hadden, and Hillyard's survey (1980:41–45) establishes that half of the indicted suspects made their confessions within three hours of interrogation and a further one-fourth within six hours of interrogation.

Despite the fact that these figures indicate the decreasing productivity of prolonged interrogation, the authors note that the vast majority of suspects (charged or not) underwent interrogations that exceeded three hours. The RUC preference for techniques that induce rapid confession becomes clear. We need only correlate the declining productivity of prolonged interrogation with the police's certitude that violence generates quick confessions in order to confirm that violence must be an accepted and regular practice at the interrogation centers. It is also evident that the general physical and psychological ordeals of interrogation are designed to have lasting effects on suspects, independent of any criminal prosecution. Crucial to data collection and rapid confession, the factor of violence must be included in the interrogation process, not only as a technique, tool, or symptom but as a determinant of the social space and symbolic relations engendered by the interrogation.

Interrogation is crucial to what Taussig (1984:469) has termed the cultural elaboration of fear and terror. In interviews with the RUC, Taylor (1980:158) was informed that, though rumors about violence in the interrogation cells were false, the dissemination of these rumors in the community were instrumental in softening individual suspects for interrogation. To this we might add that such "myths" of violence function to "soften" entire communities (see 4.19).

Scarry (1985), in her literary study of the political construction of pain under torture, identifies the myth of instrumental rationality that legitimizes the interrogation/torture procedure as an extension of the fictionalization of the body by torture. For Scarry, the process of torture converts body pain into imaginary "insignia" of political power. A crucial component in the fictionalization of power is the falsification of motive, a dissimulation of the physical, symbolic, and ritual components of the torture/interrogation process:

> The display of the fiction of power, the final product and outcome of torture should in the end be seen in relation to its origin, the motive that is claimed to be its starting point, the need for information. . . . This false motive syndrome is not adequately explained by the vocabulary of "excuse" and "rationalization," and its continual reoccurrence suggests it has a fixed place in the formal logic of brutality. The motive of torture is to a large extent the equivalent . . . of the fictionalized power. (Scarry 1985:56–59)

The central ethnological issue confronting the analysis of interrogation and torture is not how a ritualized symbolic process leaks into the rationalized objectives of the political institution, nor how instrumental rationality, through its rigidification and reification devolves into a ritualized form in which the ends are absorbed by the means, but rather how the ritualized and the symbolic provide the foundations for the rationalization of power and thus the fictionalization of its violence. This entails not only the fetishistic interna!ization of instrumental rationality, but also the rationalization of the fetish. The central fetishes fabricated in the interrogation room are the state and the body as the authorizing sources of interrogation violence and political truth. In this context, interrogation and torture are practices for the self-mimesis of power by the state and the respective interiorization of power by those who act for the state and those who are compelled to function as "material" witnesses to this reenactment. Interrogation is a ceremony of verification, not only of crime but of agency. It revolves around techniques of encapsulation and transubstantiation that render power tangible, immediate, and circumscribed. The performance with its ceremonies and regalia is committed to the simulation of a center. The state is politically recharged by local apparatuses that specialize in the construction of center-effects. The force of the center is forged at its extremities, validating peripheries, like the interrogation room, where power is spatialized and the referentiality and externality of the governing origin are manufactured in performance.

The performance of torture does not apply power; rather it manufactures it from the "raw" ingredient of the captive's body. The surface of the body is the stage where the state is made to appear as an effective material force. Two metaphysical intangibles collide, intersect, and synthesize in the body of the captive—the force of disorder and the force of the state. The captive's body encapsulates both. It becomes a political orifice, a dual passageway into the state and its Other(s). For Foucault (1979) and Poulantzas (1980), the primary productive enterprise of the state is the body as political institution. The production of bodies is the mechanism by which the state apparatus detaches ideological parts of itself, reassembles itself in alterity, and then recuperates itself in this alterity through the extraction of narratives and artifacts of power. *The state (m)others bodies in order to engender itself. The production of bodies— political subjects—is the self-production of the state.* The rooms of torture are like Ceausescu's endless maze of underground tunnels, a uterine space where the state considers and ensures its reproduction.

The Name and the Eye

The rationalization of interrogation procedures in Northern Ireland coincided with the inception of the "Criminalization, Ulsterization, and Normalization" policy that sought to depoliticize paramilitary activity and to foreground the police and the judiciary as the central intervention forces against paramilitary violence (see chapter 5). This process was initiated in the mid-1970s. Thus, in the following narrative concerning events that took place in 1972, the interrogation practices deployed do not display the levels of refinement and psychological insight that came to be associated with Castlereagh from the mid-1970s onward. Yet even at this early stage, techniques that were to be refined and extensively employed later in Castlereagh were operative. What is perhaps more important is the fact that in this particular account some of these techniques occur not as substantive practices but as rhetorical symbols of domination and coercion. Thus, the procedures recounted in this text disclose the historical priority of ritualized form over rationalized objective in the interrogation process:

4.17   In 1972 I was captured with an M-1 carbine. I was only seventeen at the time. The interrogation started on the spot on the street. We were spread-eagled on the pavement—three of us. The lance corporal in charge of the patrol came down across the street, and he grabbed me by the back of the hair and stuck a "sub" up the back of my neck. There had been a guy with us who had escaped, and the Brit wanted his name: "Right, who do you call the bastard?" "I don't know; I only had a lift in that car." He laughed. "Cunt, you only have three seconds to tell me the name of the bastard and then I'm shooting you." The first thing that entered my mind was that no way he was going to shoot me. The possibility of death to me then didn't enter into it, with the bullets all missing me like the way they always do in the movies. The first thing that came into my head was, "Dead on mate," though I didn't say it.

The next thing he let a scream out of him, and he opened fire. Right up across the top of my head with a sub, right up alongside me and into the grass we were lying near. All I could see were the muzzle flashes and this fucker screaming. What was banged into my head right away was that I was hit. I'm shot, and the common thing you hear about getting shot is that you don't feel it.

I was looking for holes when he grabbed me by the ankle and flipped me over. "Start talking!" I just lay looking at him. But he walked up to my mate, and he was carrying a high-powered Browning pistol and stuck that in the back of my mate's head. He cocked the pistol and pulled the head back by the hair and says: "Talk or he's dead." I hadn't made a sound; I was still trying to figure out whether I was alive or dead. I didn't know where I was. He just raised the pistol up over the mate's hairline and fired. He was getting pretty frustrated by then.

He sicced the whole patrol on us, who then proceeded to boot us to fuck. We went from there to being spread-eagled against the Saracen jeeps. Now, I had forty .45 rounds in my pocket. I don't know how they hadn't found them. They searched me but they never touched my coat, and it was lying on the ground with this bag of rounds. It was flying through my head to get fuckin' rid of them. I was saying to myself, "If they find these rounds, no sweat about it, I'm getting five in the chest." But I was the last one fucked into the Saracen, and I was thrown on top of the pile. The Brits were sitting with their rifles jammed against my hands. They were standing battering the fuck out of me because I was the top of the pile. I couldn't get my hand in my jacket.

They put us into the army barracks and said to all the Brits there: "Here's three fuckin' scumbags caught with an M-1!" And the whole regiment was there at the bar drinking and at the snooker. The only thing that saved us was the fact that there was too many of them. They were really trying to get at us. They dragged me by the ankles through the barracks, and others were running after me booting the back of the fuckin' head out of me. There was one with a big needle and he was trying to stick it in. One of them shouted, "Bring the bastards somewhere we can wash the blood away!" Here's me, "Of fuck!" a rake of things flying through your head, "These fuckers are going to tear me into bits." To make the situation worse, that night one of their mates had the eye shot out of him by an IRA man with an M-1 rifle. It hadn't been us but that didn't matter a fuck. They were going fuckin' nuts. "We've got these fuckers!" They were screaming about their mate. They were crying their eyes out trying to describe to us their mate's eye which was lying in the middle of the street. I was in the middle of hysteria. I was standing there terrified at what these ones were going to do.

They brought us to the showers, and they held me outside the shower stall and put my mate in, banging the fuck out of him, trying to get the name and banging his head off the wall. And I'm still standing there with this bag of ammunition in my pocket. This went on for about a half hour when the mate suddenly gets dragged out with his trousers and his trunks down about the ankles. They just lifted me and fucked me in. They had these wooden boards in the shower, and they had fucked this red stuff all around the floors and the walls. The first thing they produced on me was two big knives. One Scotch fucker say, "Right laddie, you're getting your balls cut off." I had long hair at the time, and he grabbed the front of my hair and just sawed it off. They got my coat, and the cunt felt the weight of my coat: "What's this laddies?" They got the bag of rounds. He just exploded, and my trousers went down and the trunks went down and the knife went up under my "bobby." "Right laddies, a fuckin' name quick." I was petrified and that's what kept me from saying anything. He took the knife around my back and he pricked me with it, and I near went through the ceiling. They said to me, "That's your mate's blood." The knife disappeared, and they put me down on the boards and battered the fuck clean out of me. They got cheesed off after awhile, and they fucked me out into the corridor. I was lying in the corridor, and I couldn't get up. By that stage I was booted senseless.

They brought us down to Springfield barracks, and the peelers started battering the fuck out of us, but I didn't feel nothing. I was numb. By that time I didn't give a fuck; they'd wallop me and I couldn't feel it. My mate's ribs had been busted, and when we got into the barracks a peeler comes in, "Do any of ye want a doctor?" My mate turned around and said, "Ye fucking black bastard, you can stuff the doctor up into your hole."[15] Here was me: "Jesus, what are you saying!"

Two Branch men came and caught me by the ankles and pulled me straight out into the doctor's surgery. There was nobody in the surgery bar these fuckers that brought me in. They stuck me down in the chair, and I had bare feet. The fucking ankles and feet were cut to ribbons. The biggest of them stood on my feet and just went up and down on them. And I couldn't feel nothing. "Right, a name." At this stage all I could do was stare at what he was doing. I couldn't say anything. He was down looking at my eyes and he says, "This bastard's full of dope." And he grabbed me by the throat and he was shaking my head, "Are you on dope you bastard? I'll give ye some dope now."

This was the time of the early seventies, and they were using truth serum in the interrogations: "You have a choice, you're going to give me a fuckin' name or I'm going to give you dope and have everything in that fuckin' head of yours out." I didn't believe for a minute that he was going to inject me with anything. But the bastard came over with the syringe, "Roll your sleeve up." I put my hand out to him. He looked at me and run over to the fuckin' jar of alcohol that you rub on the arm before they would inject you. He just

dipped the fucker into it. "You're in for it now you bastard!"
As he came toward me I smashed the syringe up the wall with
my hand that I was holding out for the needle.

So they held me up against the radiator and were cooking
me and punched the ribs out of me. I just dropped down to
the floor. That all happened between 8:30 at night to 5:30 in
the morning. There was no subtlety to that interrogation; it
was slap, bang, and wallop. Which was the sort of method
they were using around '71 to '72. They hadn't got the psychology of interrogation yet. They let their own frustrations
get the better of them. (PIRA)

This account of an interrogation offers what appears to be an interminable series of irrational and brutal episodes wholly unproductive in
terms of the ideal goals of interrogation—information retrieval. As the
beatings overlap, the capacity of the narrator to deliver information de-
creases radically; the beatings literally reduce him to silence, pound him
into inert flesh beyond language. For the narrator, the cumulative sequence of beatings and attempted mutilations becomes a narrative of
survival—a journey past language and the body and a return to language
and the body that coincides with the recitation of the oral history. The
recovery of the violated body as a political artifact takes place through
the storage of the body in a surrogate medium: language and memory
double the effaced flesh. The body subtracted by violence is reconsti-
tuted and replotted through oral history.

These incoherent episodes of mob violence contain a formal structure that reveals the lines of development of what was to become
several years later an ostensibly more manipulative and medicalized
approach to interrogation. This narrative describes a protostructure of
cathartic violence that is never wholly abandoned by subsequent rationalization.

The interrogation begins with a reference point that the narrator can
comprehend—the "name," to be confessed; but as events proceed, his
increasing dissociation from the violence enacted upon him, his sense of
being given over to arcane interventions and transformations in which he
plays no active part, is readily apparent.

The narrator's capacity to survive is dependent on surrendering his
body to the objectifying violence that is inflicted upon it. The body,
appropriated as an object of ritual, is divested of any sense of self and
invested with the collective meanings it encapsulates for his interrogators. This elementary divestiture of the body, as much as it presages
death, also becomes the condition of resistance. The visible target of
inquisition and the potential volitional agency of confession become bi-

furcated. The self remains at the margins of the body and the interrogation process, both of which are increasingly experienced as spectacle.

The captive's point of entry into the void of interrogation is opened by the lance corporal as he screams and fires an automatic rifle off the side of the captive's head. The corporal organizes the interrogation scenario as a life/death, speech/death opposition, and then in a gesture that marks entry, simulates death through disordering acoustic and visual effects. Here the gun, insignia of the state, suborns and absorbs the captive's body. The visual and acoustic effects of artificial death flood the captive as he lays immobile.

The reaction of the PIRA captive to this performance attests to both his dislocation and the effects of simulation: "I hadn't made a sound. I was still trying to figure out whether I was alive or dead. I didn't know where I was." At this juncture, the dialogical splintering of the interrogation process begins. The captive maintains his silence, and he is also stunned into silence. He mimes the condition of the corpse, of the disembodiment that had been deployed as threat against him: a detachment of self from the body, and a separation of the body from language that is both voluntary and involuntary and that exploits the very violence which overwhelms it with prospective death. From this point on, the captive's silence is equated with a series of secondary deaths that he will undergo. This silence, this involuntary mimesis of death from without into a death from within, begins the prisoner's transformation into a cipher to be broken. The violence of the soldiers is complicit in this cryptology. The interrogation requires this alterity as the legitimizing pole of its violence. Silencing the captive inversely elevates state violence to discourse, and this empowers the body of the captor.

Language, death, and silence are the three points of the interrogation triangle that governs the relations between the interrogator and his prisoner. Each figure will move to and occupy one of the three positions in this configuration as the interrogation proceeds. Each will use language, death, and silence to counter the position of the other and to decipher the other's strategy. Each will view the other as a code to be broken.

For the captive, his silence is his initial step toward self-objectification, his exchange of his body for the absence of language. This evokes Adorno's theory that the human acquiesence to thinghood originates in the miming of death as a camouflage strategy or as an identification with the aggressor. For Adorno, the identification with thinghood and/or with the force of domination is an elementary stage in the process of reification (Cahn 1984:32–33). The interrogatee offers up his body as a mirror-thing to the interrogator. This self-objectification of the resisting captive has to be analytically differentiated from the objectifying violence that is inflicted upon him, although he in fact exploits this violence to further his body-objectification.

The greatest fear of the experienced interrogatee is the acceptance of the central illusion promoted by the interrogation space that it is absolute reality, that it is the interior structure of his being, his origin and terminus, his body. The arena in which the interrogation is played is abandoned by the captive to the interrogator. His body becomes the origin and the terminus of the state and, therefore, other.

The PIRA captive is removed to a British army barracks after his initiation. At the barracks he is presented with the central motivating myth/history of his interrogation. One of the soldiers, resident in these barracks, was blinded just that night by an M-1 rifle wielded by an IRA sniper—the same weapon that the narrator has been caught with. In this story, true or false, he is presented with the history, with the immediate origins of his interrogation for which "the name," his confession, will be the resolution. Thus, the secondary closure of the interrogation space— after the initiation by violence—is set. The theater of interrogation is organized by its own internal histories that endow all subsequent actions, discourses, and violence with a syllogistic order.

The type of surprise attack that has blinded the soldier is known to paramilitaries as a "one-shot wonder." The rapidity of the single-shot snipe leaves the victim(s) wondering where it came from and thus amplifies the invisibility and potency of the attackers. In addition, a sniping attack that mutilates rather than kills is considered by paramilitaries as the most demoralizing form of attack because it reveals a capacity for precise isolation of targets. The remote-control bomb experts of the IRA pride themselves particularly in being able to pick off an individual target with a bomb. This demoralizing effect of the combined one-shot wonder and mutilating snipe is confirmed in the behavior of the soldiers at the barracks. They respond to the IRA man as a traumatized community, as an undifferentiated mob without military order or hierarchy, that has suddenly discovered the singular source of its contamination.

The narrative depicts a scene of violence in which the soldiers exchange the mutilation of their comrade for the attempted mutilation of the PIRA captives. The exchange may be predicated on their probable knowledge that the IRA men are not directly responsible for the mutilation. Because of the presence of surrogate victims, violence is channeled into symbolic forms. The entire action oscillates at the boundaries of spontaneous violence and fabricated performance. This differentiation remains blurred throughout the entire interrogation procedure.

As surrogate victim, the captive is subjected to an explosive procession through the barracks. The structure of this performance/nonperformance, the dynamics real or pantomimed, transform the British army into a mob. All this coincides to a remarkable degree with the violent unanimity described by Girard (1977) that occurs when a community becomes divorced from its traditional hierarchies and social order through the experience of defilement and turns on a victim-substitute in a rite of purification. The signs of physical and medical purification proliferate throughout the remainder of the narrative, from the location of subsequent violence in the showers to the location of the doctor's surgery in the final episode of violence, and from the alternation between blood and water to the threat of a cathartic psychoactive drug and the display of medical technology.

The PIRA captives move from the parade of mutilation and mob violence with its attendant scenes of weeping and anger to the showers, where supposedly any violence enacted against them can be masked by the washing away of blood with water. At this juncture, the supposedly spontaneous violence of the barracks procession is transformed into the overtly theatrical beatings of the shower stall, where the signs of surrogation dominate the logic of the interrogator's actions. Red paint masquerading as blood is thrown around the shower stall before the arrival of the prisoners. Again, the theme of mutilation appears, initially in the threat of castration and subsequently in the surrogate action of shearing off of the prisoner's hair. Interspersed with mimetic violence are beatings that serve to diffuse the boundaries between the real and the imaginary.[16]

Throughout the interrogation, the prisoner's physical removal from and insertion into different spaces is coordinated with different treatments of the body: the mimicked execution on the street, the mob violence of the open space of the barracks, the threats of castration and the scalping in the showers, and finally the pretended administration of a mind-altering drug in the police barracks. Different forms and intensities of violence are associated with different spaces. Space and violence are synthesized into a single interrogatory structure of continuous dislocation.

The final episode occurs in a doctor's surgery, in the police barracks. The prisoner has moved from the military to law to medicine; his interrogation transforms him into a tourist of state rationalities—an itinerary of all the different and specialized things the repressive apparatus does to bodies. Doctors' surgeries have a particularly ominous association with violence in Belfast where this narrative takes place. As discussed in chapter 3, a Loyalist murder gang devoted to sectarian torture and killing conducted their torture sessions in a doctor's surgery, and the notorious INLA operative, known as "the Doctor" or "Doctor Death," used medical terminology in discussing weapons, covert operations, and his victims.[17] In the present narrative under discussion, when it becomes obvious that simple brutality has not produced a confession, but rather immunized the captive to further physical coercion, the police turn to a symbol of the next technical interrogation stage—the psychological assault on the captive's mind. Despite the selective use of psychoactive drugs, interrogation as a form of clinical and psychological intervention has not been institutionalized at this particular time, but medicalization as a rhetoric of intimidation have already been interiorized by the interrogators. This scene captures the transfer of the prisoner's selfhood to the instrument of violence and via this instrument to the state. The needle, a medical symbol of the state's capacity to intervene in the structures of the self, not only injects a coercive substance into the body but extracts interior substances from the body and renders these substances accessible to diagnostic scrutiny. This is explicit in the policemen's threat to "have everything in that . . . head of yours out."

White Spaces

For Foucault, it is the architecture of discipline that rationalizes the offender, that embarks offenders on their rehabilitative passage (1979:200–204).

> The Panopticon is a privileged place for experiments on men, and for analyzing with complete certainty the transformations that may be obtained from them. (p. 204)

> The structures of compulsory visibility and architectural coercion in the Panopticon are designed to force the body to carry out tasks, to perform ceremonies, to emit signs. (p. 25)

The panopticon is an automaton for the production of automatons if we retain the original meaning of the term—self-acting instrument. For Foucault (pp. 202–3) power is an action upon the action of another. From its point of origin to its terminus, power presupposes and requires agency. The architecture of the panopticon is thus an action upon the active body of the inmate which constructs complicity and elicits agency. Thus power is invested in the intersection of space (architectural and corporeal), perception, and action. The panopticon as architectural technology is a sensorium of the body; power is formed spatially through the formation of the senses, which are vectored and specialized by the edifice.

The oral histories of interrogation return again and again to the spatial order and human ecology of Castlereagh, which are remembered with compulsive and microscopic detail:

4.18   The vehicles bring you inside the gates. Where you get out of the vehicle it's like a courtyard, an enclosed courtyard with one door up on the extreme left hand, and you're brought in through and brought immediately to your left to the commital desk. At the commital desk your name and address are taken, and then you move up to the corridor to another desk where they take your property. Off this corridor, again to the left, there's a number of rooms used for fingerprinting. Afterward you're taken to holding centers. They're laid out in a series. There's one inside the main block of the building. If they're into disorienting you heavily, you're held in there, because you have no access to daylight or electric light so you can't see.

The interrogation cells are on down to the left of that. There's also a separated holding center outside. You walk though an enclosed walkway where you come to a series of holding cells. There is a grilled enclosure where there is an airlock gate. Beyond that there is a desk. As you look down the corridor your immediate impression is that all the doors are flush; there's no breaks along the doors. It's like two sealed parallel walls running down forever with no end to them. Each door has nothing on it but one minute spy hole, a centimeter in diameter. On each door there is a recessed lock in the middle of the door. The doors are painted light gray. Once you walk into the cell the dimensions are square, about ten feet by ten feet. You pace it. Along the back of the cell itself there are two parallel heating pipes about five inches in diameter running from the next cell. These run right along each side of the cell block through all the cells. Through the heating pipes there is a chain, and the chain is connected to a leg iron on the bed. As you come through the door into the cell, the bed is in the extreme left-hand corner. Some cells have a chair; some don't. In the corridor itself the lighting is kept gloomy, and there's no natural light anywhere. The lights are all centrally controlled by the cops. They control your perception of night and day. It's fairly important, and it's a thing they extended into the organization of the H-Blocks.[18] Control of light is in the hands of the screws with their over-riding switches. During the winter when it's dark at 3:00 P.M. you would most times eat your evening meal in the dark.

As you go into the holding cell itself, if you look at the wall, the opposite walls are blank, no fixtures, with light gray moldings that are only a shade darker than the white walls. The mattress of the bed is an imitation leather, and that's white. The sheets are white and the blanket is white wool. There's no other break in colors save white and light gray.

The floor tiles are off-white as well. The heating pipes are painted white.

Normally there's dead silence in the cell block. When they leave you in your holding cell you'd go up to the door and shout, "Is there anybody here?" It's a very strong moral support when you hear an answering voice. If they're too afraid to answer at the door you'd start tapping on the pipes.

In the cell itself, you have the impression of completely blank walls with no dimensions on it, completely flat, except for the heating pipes running parallel behind the bed. It's down under here you always find the names. Sometimes it's the names of people you know who died in Castlereagh or people you know who have been tortured in Castlereagh. It has a very strong effect on you when you see those names scraped on the wall under the bed.

The ceiling itself is pure white. The paneling around the door is light gray and the door is white. High in the top corner of the wall there's a circular light. It sits out there about three inches from the wall. The light has a circular red plastic rim around it. It is controlled from outside the cell. It can be dimmed or brightened at their will; invariably when you are showing signs of activity they'll dim it. When you're beginning to relax or to sleep the light is brightened.

As you look at the door there's a wee spy hole in the middle that you can't look out of. The only thing that you can do with it is that there is a metal cover on the outside of it, out on the other side of the door. You can hear that being slipped aside, and you get the impression of an eye watching you. The only other thing you can hear is the squeaks of their rubber-sole shoes and the keys. The keys are attached to the screw's chain by the belt, and the keys fit into their trouser pockets. The clink of keys and the clink of the metal spy hole is the trigger for fear. When you hear the clink of metal and the movements outside of the door, that means that they're coming for somebody. . . . You wait and wait and the sound passes your door, and you hear it stop and you hear the word "Interrogation." And you know that some poor bastard's away for it. It's always that clink of metal.

The interrogation room is roughly the same dimensions as your cell. There's no protuberances or breaks in the interrogation room, except that there's a desk. Like your cell, everything is painted white. There's a desk or a rectangular table attached to the wall. It always reminded me of a school

desk. There are several chairs against the wall. High up on
the wall on a bracket is a movable camera, and it's meant to
scan the interrogation. The Branch men just hang their coats
over the camera lens and tell you, "You know who mans these
cameras? It's us, so don't be worrying about the camera."
(PIRA)

Beneath the lack of architectural relief, a political organization of human space can be located. The preliminary process of interrogation, "the
softening up," is actualized in this architecture of coercion. The isolation
and the silence, the airlock gates, the surface topography that resists any
imprint of human use and sanitizes the fear and violence that inhabits its
cells and corridors, are juridical codes. There is a relation built into the
edifice between the architecture of coercion and the dynamic of confession.

The text of the edifice and the idealized text of the confessed self are
intertwined here. The light that prevents sleep and dreaming as sheltering recesses of the self—as counterpositions to the interrogation
world—and the voiding of time reinforce the sense that there is no
outside and no exits. The interrogation space is a plane of total integration with no difference, variation, or gaps. All passageways lead back to
the same room. There is no possibility of changing roles and identities by
changing locale or dispositions of the body. From the cell, where one is
interrogated, to the cell in which one attempts to rest and escape interrogation, there is no real alteration of architectural intensities, only the
unceasing process of being led to confession. The removal of time and
sleep is the effacement of any possibility of transition or distancing from
the absolute spatial power of interrogation.

The circularity of the interrogation space, an expanse without any
variation, reaches its highest expression in the subverted function of the
video cameras. The interrogator's remark that the cameras are in fact
blind and do not limit the violence of the interrogation because they are
manned by other interrogators points to another fiction of power. The
fabrication of an "outside" with the use of cameras is in actuality the
fabricated interior space of interrogation redoubled and mirroring itself in
an endless refraction. The blinded cameras are a symbol of total enclosure. The cameras are mere effigies and a patently redundant technology
because the entire edifice of the interrogation center is itself a massive
lens, an infinite optic of power reproducing itself in a series of recursive
magnifications that feed off the visibility of the body.

The absolute whiteness of the interrogation space exemplifies this
topos of the same and the undifferentiated. White is the color of total and
exhaustive exposure in which nothing can be hidden or disguised, in

which there are no recesses or depths, only the self reduced to a figure against a ground—a diagram. Absolute whiteness is the visual metaphor of the confessed self.

The chromatics, architecture, topography, and optics carry an explicit political message: the entry of physical violence into the body of the prisoner is prefigured in the transformation of the spaces and colors of confinement into instruments of encompassment and penetration. The edifice itself is a massive and clumsy indication of the state's desire to incorporate itself into the sensory ecology of the captive body. The architectural machinery of interrogation is nothing less than a mechanized adjunct of the human body infested and inhabited by the state.

The tendency of interrogation veterans to refer to their sojourns in Castlereagh with precise topographic details signifies much more than the boredom and fear experienced there. These descriptions convey the reduction of the detainee's perception to architectural effect and the formation of the senses by alien enclosure. The intimacy of environmental detail in the oral histories is an intimacy expressive of an internalized relation to the spaces of coercion, of an other self who is the unavoidable construct of this space. In describing the architecture, spaces, and colors of coercion, the paramilitary inventories the insignia of the state; he is describing an iconography of the state as it appears from within its machinery of affect.

The centrality of compulsory visibility, the hypostasis of the "eye," disembodies the agents of discipline and tends to preclude blatant forms of physical intervention. Of course, inasmuch as the optical paradigm of power reveals certain dynamics of penal regimes, we must also consider this "eye," like the Castlereagh video cameras, as a myth. Within a system that is dependent on the alternations between embodiment and disembodiment, visibility and invisibility, power is defined in terms of increasing distance and disengagement from the body. Optical forms of surveillance, the intervention of the corrective "eye," constitute the narcissism of power and its central fiction. Occular power conforms to the sanitizing and purifying mythology of the program of compliance. The mythology of optical power "purifies" the coercive structures of the closed institution and mystifies the "dirty" manual violence of enforcement. The imagery of pure structural force within the state is a myth of technological determinism, an ultimate reification that removes both the state and the human practitioners of coercion from any form of responsible agency.

In the history of technology, the myth, rhetoric, and falsification of the automaton (to which the panopticon belongs) always prefigured the actual technical capacity to make functioning automatons, precisely because the future promise of the automaton is always a politically masked statement about desired social transformations of the subject and the body in the present. Anthropomorphic technology is always prefigured by the socio-technical instrumentation of man. Institutions concerned with the production of automatons (as political subjects) are in effect speaking to their own automatic reproduction as self-directed instruments. The automaton is driven by the logic of mimesis and self-reproduction. These categories—the self-acting instrument, mimesis, and reproduction—are political values and the axes of coercive practice and ideological discourse.

The Sensorium of Death

The state occupies the site of power, in a single self-constituting rush of violence, seeming to emerge from the very architecture of coercion itself and establishing its dominance in a total immediacy that distributes all the participants of the interrogation into their appropriate spatial, political, and historical positions:

4.19   As soon as you come straight into the interrogation room, the door flies open like a whirlwind and in come these two Branch men, and they beat you around the room. They don't say a word, they just beat you rabbit punches, squeezing the testicles, anything at all. Just general brutality. Their favorite was standing people against the wall for long periods, resting the entire body on the weight of the fingers. Your fingers would become numb, and every time you fell they are all battering you and making you stand up again.

They made people squat on their haunches, made them do press-ups until they're tired out, physically exhausted. Then they would put them through a two-hour stretch of intensive questioning. They'd go through your family history, throwing up all sorts of filthy stuff, discrediting your family, blackmailing, and the rest.[19]

They showed me explicit photographs of friends that had been killed, closeups of photographs of them blown up or shot, photographs of peelers shot in the head. They just try to break you down. They take you out of the interrogation room and then brought back in by these other two Branch men who say, "Look, we're only doing our job. We don't agree with this brutality. Why don't you talk to us." The soft attitude. The battering police build up hostility so you're not going to talk to them ones, but they go out and in come the two soft guys. And they're going to ask if you want a cup of tea, do you want a cigarette—all this type of stuff to make you feel at ease and break down your resistance. They say, "Look, if you're not going to talk to us we can't do nothing. We're going to have to send these other two guys back in." It's a continuous process between the heavies and the softies.

The first time I went in, the beatings were bad; the second time if you already have been in and out of Castlereagh and they know you won't talk they call you case-hardened. They let you sit and try to wear you down with constant questioning. They take away your sleep and your relaxation. I was brought into an all white cell, no windows, and the light on all the time. You haven't a watch and no idea of how long you've been in there. They take you to an interview room with a clock that says four o'clock, or they let you see their watches. You're held there to six o'clock and then thrown back into the cell. You're lying there in the cell and you imagine that you've been there for a couple of hours. They take you out again and let you see a watch or a clock and it says 6:15. Though you were sure hours have gone by. It's a disorientation process.

After awhile when they get you, they realize there's no way you're going to talk and they'll let you sit. You sit like that [hunched up]—pick a spot and watch it and you don't talk. You just give your name and address and sit and think on a book you read, a holiday you took, or something you went through. You blank your mind to what's being done to you and you try to remember. To remember anything. You can sit it out, and they get frustrated. The only reason you get beat then is the Branch man sitting continuously questioning and questioning and you're not looking at them and they come over and grab your face, saying: "I think he's stupid," or "I think he's ashamed. He can't talk of what he done. How are these men patriots that don't admit their deed? They're not proud of their deed. I'm proud of what I've done. Are you not proud of what you done?" You just sit and ignore all that. The frustration gets to them, and they pull you out of the seat and start beating you with a baton.

The joke about Castlereagh is that after Brian Maguire was killed there—he was hung in his cell—according to the police he hung himself: he had to climb a twelve-foot ventilator to hang himself. After that they installed cameras in Castlereagh. But the cameras are manned by Special Branch men, and there are Special Branch men interrogating you. So it's a joke.

When they come into the interrogation room and just lift their coats off and hang them over the lens of the camera, that's the sign of the beating session.

In the Diplock courts the police will say, "These terrorists are so ruthless that they will go into Castlereagh and kick themselves unconscious before they could talk." You have a judge sitting there saying: "This shows how ruthless and dedicated these terrorists are, that they would come in here and inflict all sorts of injuries on themselves to discredit the police." He believed the police joke.

People on the outside hearing all that and seeing fellows come out where the bruising and swelling was unbelievable, were really getting terrified of what would happen in Castlereagh. When they got into Castlereagh the first day and got beaten around, they were saying, "My God! I've seven days to stick all this. How am I going to stick it?" The whole thing broke people down. Everybody has to accept it that the Brits are fighting a guerrilla war here and they have to use every method they can. (PIRA)

4.20 The routine doesn't change when they lift you. They bring you to Castlereagh. You see a doctor. They fingerprint you and they photograph you. They put you up in a cell. It's four walls painted white, a floor, a ceiling, a light on all the time, a rubber mattress, a rubber pillow, two paper sheets, and if you're lucky a rubber blanket.

You're usually lifted at half six in the morning; you're photographed, fingerprinted, examined by the doctor, and in your cell by nine o'clock. They come in at ten o'clock, and they take you down to the interview room, which is the exact same room as your cell, white, only there's a table and two chairs and a radiator. Ten [o'clock] to twelve [o'clock] they start constant interrogation. At twelve they usually let you go back and eat. You're back again from one to six—constant interrogation. They change Special Branch men on you all the time. Two Branch men every two hours. Then you get the night shift. They finish you between 10:00 P.M. and 2:00 A.M. It was heavy going.

There was some very witty Special Branch men. Two come bounding into the interview room and your man says to me: "I'm Starsky, he's Hutch."

"Hello Starsky," I says, "what about you."

"No, we're really not Starsky and Hutch; call me Newell.

And he's French, Durex French." [Durex is a brand of condom and French letter is vernacular for condom.] All this old carry-on—you should've heard them. One of them walks around behind me. The next thing I feel is a Browning 9mm in the back of the head: "Going to blow the fucking scone off you, you cunt."

I laugh, "Dead on."

"I'm going to scone you, you fuck."

And I'm saying to myself, "They're not allowed to have guns during interrogation." Some of them were very witty like.

They were interviewing me and they were saying: "Do you go out?"

"No I don't go out."

"Do you go with girls? What's wrong are you a homosexual?"

"No, I'm not a homosexual either."

"Suppose you don't curse?"

"No I don't curse either."

They're looking at my name, Michael Stephan, looking at the date of birth. "December 27, St. Stephan's Day! A fucking saint we have here! Doesn't drink, doesn't smoke, doesn't curse. A fucking walking saint! What are you in here for son?"

"I don't know. Somebody's accusing me of shooting a policeman."

"Who the fuck is accusing you of shooting a policeman? Tell us where he is. Get that man around here who's accusing this boy!"

Really fucking good they were. You're sitting there the whole time waiting on the big fucking digging [beating] in the side of the ear. Their favorite was busting the eardrums you know.

Interrogators basically boil down to three types: the ones who are nice to you, the ones who scream at you, and the ones who come in silently and knock your cunt in. Those three. Anything else doesn't really matter. The last time I was in for an interrogation I never got a finger laid on me. I tried to provoke them into fucking digging me so I could get the hatred up. "Ah fuck, they're not going to beat me into giving them something." But the ones who are being nice lower your defenses: "Do you want a cigarette? A coke? For fuck's sake, wise up, this old violence is no good." Probably speaking the truth from their point of view.

I was a great Gaelic man when I went into Castlereagh for interrogation. I went in very proud of my national identity and culture. A lot go into Castlereagh, and the police have things in common with them. That used to break down their defenses. You see guys come in for interrogation and they're as English as the English, except they claim to be Irish. They have a lot in common with the police; they break down and become informers. If they had the culture and the Gaelic stronger, they could hold out. If you don't have any culture, how are you different from the Brits? You're fucking just the same. I went into Castlereagh; I hadn't that much in common with the Brits. In the Reagh a Branch man would sit down and talk to you about football. I'd have no interest in soccer, only hurly. They would talk about discos; I wasn't interested in it. I only listened to Irish folk and traditional music. It was as if you were two completely different people and lived in completely different worlds. The Brits haven't got it so they can't understand it. (INLA)

4.21   When they take you in for interrogation you're supposed to be allowed to call for your own personal doctor for an examination within two hours after being arrested, to check you in case of having prior bruises. So your doctor can say whether or not you get any [bruises] later during interrogation. But they won't let the doctor in. They won't let your solicitor in. They won't let anybody in to see you. They won't even tell anybody where you're being held. So even if your people could send a doctor or a solicitor, they wouldn't know where. They have military doctors to examine you. But I've only seen them after two days of being inside. They will ask you where you got a bruise or injury. You might be bruised on the ribs, but the Branchmen interrogating you will say, "If you tell them it was me done that, you'll end up worse." So what can you do? Do you take the chance and say they done it, in case the doctor can do something about it, or say they didn't and avoid another beating? It's a catch-22 situation.

In interrogation they'll keep you blindfolded and in total silence for hours, and your mind does honestly start to wander. You don't know who's there or if anybody's there, or after awhile whether you're really there. You might be sitting trying to resign yourself to the fact of your situation. I personally start reciting the alphabet backward to try to keep the mind ticking. You'd be there thinking to yourself for hours in silence, the next thing, a big whack on the back of the head.

They do simple things to you where they're not trying to mark you. But mentally it does affect you. Mentally you don't know where you are. You're in a cell with the light on all the time, painted white ceiling to floor. You're naked, and you think hours have passed and it's only an hour. They strip you of everything. These bastards are walking in the cell never saying anything. You get the head down, "Right, I'll have nap." As soon as the head is down they're in right away and start interrogating you again. As soon as the head's down they're on you and you're lost. They'll interrogate you for a couple of hours, bring you back into the cell; you get the head down again and they're in questioning you.

A few of us have different tricks for surviving it. I was in one cell that had tiles. So I started counting the tiles, doing them backward, diagonally, row by row. Pick a point and stick to it. Try to remember all your family's birthdays, when did someone die, anything at all to keep the mind functioning.

Their temper eventually frayed after a period of time. They say: "This bastard is not going to fucking tell us anything." So that's when you usually get the diggings. They get more frustrated than what you do; that's the way to beat them. Frustrate them before you get frustrated. It's difficult, don't get me wrong. You see anybody that's cracked under interrogation, I would never run them down.

When they lift me they try to break the wife. They say to her: "We're putting him away for fifteen years for the shooting of Gerry Adams."[20] So she doesn't know what sort of statement I might have made. Then they're coming to me: "The boys are down at your place screwing your wife." And: "We've taken the kids in custody for the welfare officer." Trying to make me say, "Look, I'll tell you anything you want, just as long as you make sure the kids and the wife are all right." They're trying to break up the family; they're trying to fight terrorism with terrorism. Many times I've come back after seven days of detention and interrogation and the wife's nerves are shattered.

I remember one story where a guy suspected of IRA terrorism jumped out of a window and killed himself. Now I hate the IRA. Some of the Republican politicians said the soldiers done it. I said, "A lot of piss, he was trying to escape, didn't know he was so high up and killed himself." After I had been taken in for interrogation a couple of times I said to myself maybe he did get thrown out the fucking window. If a Catholic said to me such and such had happened to him while being

interrogated I would honestly believe it. I would believe him
before I'd believe the security forces if they were denying it.
It's as bad as that. (UDA)

4.22   You know before they arrest you that they've sat up for a
week with your file. They know who I am. They know what
they want to do to me. They know what responses they're
going to get. So you know that everything they're doing follows a pattern. When they come in you can say this is the
nice guy, this is the bastard, this is the drunk, this is the rabid Free Presbyterian foaming at the mouth to get at Catholics, this is the total anti-Communist. You can pick out all the
different roles.

   The drunk is the one who comes staggering into the room
wanting to knock your cunt in, wanting to get at you. They'll
throw him out of the room. One of them goes out and you're
given the impression he's trying to calm the drunk down. The
nice guy says, "Fuckin' nasty man out there, if he gets at you
you're done, you'd better talk to me." The Free Presbyterian
is the rabid anti-Catholic. He'll come in foaming at the mouth
telling you, as he beats you, that this is a chastisement from
God. It's retribution for your evil activities. What he's doing,
he says that even in the short term, though it seems like he
hates you, it's not his hate showing but his love. "You're on
the road to destruction." He's trying to convert you using religion. Living in this society you understand that the extreme
bigots don't give a damn—it's making the psychological link to
the Shankill Butchers, the whole genocide thing. You're supposed to thing, "Oh fuck, this guy is prepared to do anything." The variation on that is the born-again Christian. He'll
give you paternal shit and hold out his arm, "Grab that there.
That's a rock for you to hold on to! You're a drowning man;
you need the rock of faith!" Everybody is there—the whole
of Northern Ireland Prod society. The thing that puts you in
control is that the guy who's acting the drunk for you is the
nice guy across the corridor three minutes later, and on
down the corridor he's the sectarian bigot. He's acting out a
role, and that role is there to instill a specific response, and if
they get those specific responses they step up to the next
phase.

   About one out of every three interrogations you'll have the
weapon pulled out. Once I was arrested with another guy; we
were both eighteen. We were being interrogated by the same

Branch men, but it was his first arrest and I was "case-
hardened." Their approach to me was that I got very few
beatings. In his interrogation they were pulling guns out.
They build a heightened sense of some big impending calam-
ity, some big disaster about to befall you. Your whole mental
reserves are fighting against it. And at that point they say,
"There's a way out; sign this statement." My mate signed his
statement, but as soon as he signed the statement the pressure increased: "Who gave you the gun? What type of gun?" The
peeler pulls out a Walther, and sticks it up against my mate's nose:
"Was it this type of gun?" And they got the automatic reaction,
"No!" Here's the peeler, "So it wasn't a Walther; what type of gun
was it? Was it a semiautomatic. How was it loaded?" If my mate
describes these things to them, obviously he knows something
about guns, so he knows more than he's telling, and they start
building up from there. (PIRA)

4.23   Lately, when they arrest you they don't arrest you alone, but
along with a member of your family. The interrogations have
taken a slight shift. If they're dealing with someone who'll not
break, the interrogation techniques are not centered on him,
but on his family or a specific member of his family. The peelers are always exonerating themselves from blame; the onus
is always put on you. "Do you know what you're putting your
family through?" It's a necessary duty for them to be interrogating your family. It's that shift of blame installing in you
that you have the ultimate control of the treatment of those
members of your family that are in along with you. They
took ——'s girlfriend, dragged her into Castlereagh while he
was under interrogation. Stormed into his cell with a soiled
sanitary towel that they took off of her and said, "Do you
know what you're putting this woman through here?" It was
to degrade her and to degrade him. She broke and she made
statements. (PIRA)

4.24   They're trying to make you feel that people outside don't
want you—that you are not a member of an organization, that
you are a basic criminal, that you're only out to do this for
yourself. In interrogation they would tell you the people of
Turf Lodge don't want you. What they'll try to do is that they
pick up on punishment shootings and tell you that people of
such and such an area don't like it. They would present it to
you as if you were maiming your own people. Hijacking cars

and stuff you're taking your own people's cars. Which to a
certain extent is true. It would be much better if we could go
up the Malone Road [Protestant and Catholic middle- to
upper-class area.] and hijack cars, but the Brits stop that from
happening. (INLA)

4.25 It's fairly impossible to fit all the interrogation techniques in a
seven-day period, but anybody going in has had the fear built
up to such a level that they think all the interrogation techniques are going to be used against them. Their fear is automatically played upon by the cops. "You know where you are?
This is Castlereagh! You've heard the stories about here. We
can tell you that they're all true. . . ." Your vulnerability rests
on their capacity to confront you all the time with your immediate circumstances and to make you feel that you're isolated
from everything. You see, if your mind is not in Castlereagh,
you're not in Castlereagh and you can overcome them, no
problem. (PIRA)

Interrogation synchronizes techniques of transgression in order to
generate truth. The interrogators construct a coincidence between pain
and memory in order to make transgressive action and knowledge visible
through language. Instrumental torture is a method for mimetically reproducing the imputed past in the present of the body. The violence of
the interrogators constitutes their encoded discourse that enters into the
body in order to emerge at the far end of interrogation as the discour-
se/confession of the prisoner. The prisoner's confession is the interrogator's violence reaudited and redoubled as truth.

The past act of transgression and knowledge of the past are defined by
the interrogators as an absence hidden by the presence of the body
within its own depths and recesses. Confession is the inversion of this
relation between the absent past and the body's present. The body is
unfolded in order to expose the past in discourse. Violence encodes the
body into a textual apparatus for the production of texts. Power is based
on this proliferation of texts, textual doubles, textual substitutes, and
transcriptions. There is no opposition between violence and discourse,
language and silence. The silence of the prisoner, like his body, is a
discourse, a code that overlays and stores the discourse of the confession. More than anything else, the confession text signifies the erasure
of the body; it is the substituted presence of the prisoner in a domesti-
cated and sanitized medium.

The fundamental processual dynamic of interrogation is the disordering of time. This begins in the holding cells with the manipulation of the
electric light and the erasure of any access to normal temporal passage.

Time is also removed as a foundational cognitive referent through the trickery that distends or shrinks the "real" time of the prisoner through the manipulation of the wall clock and other distortions.

This disordering of time is crucial for the Castlereagh interrogators. One of the central anchorages that the prisoner possesses is his certitude that he has (depending under what law he is detained) two to seven days of interrogation to endure. This legal time limit provides him with an ostensible resolution of the various negating experiences he is in the process of undergoing. It relativizes the permanence of the interrogation space and indicates its margins. This is countered by the manipulation of time by the interrogators. In a self-enclosed ecozone exiled from time, in which no day or night exists, where six hours can be made to appear as one hour and one hour as six, the legal limits placed on the time one can be held for interrogation are meaningless. The time of two days or of seven days belongs to a lost order of temporal measurement, a delusional reality. The disordering of customary time is also a prerequisite for the mythic histories of the confessional.

The removal of time is the simulation of death. Supplementing this are techniques of petrifaction such as sustained silence, darkness, hooding of the head, and holding the body in rigid postures of immobility. The state's fabrication of the body begins with this sensorium of death—the provision of sensory reality to a condition devoid of sensation. The sensorium of death is then given its specialized history—a genealogy of death—in the form of the photographs of mutilated corpses, murdered policemen, and dead comrades which are displayed to the prisoner in the intervals between episodes of physical violence.

There is an explicit relation between this visual record and the erasure of time; it inserts a novel and qualified thanatological temporality into the interrogation session. The interrogators display a historiography of violence in Northern Ireland plotted out in various exhumations of deformed embodiment. The captive is made to know that his body can easily be inserted as the next photograph in the chain. The pictorial series of wounded bodies is meant to be read as a domination text transposable to the viewer's own body. The body as political commodity easily circulates between flesh and icon and icon and flesh. It possesses an infinite transposability. The stiff, which is the subject of the photographs, functions as the abstract invariant that is superimposed on all bodies, living, tortured, or dead, as their past or future. Whether violence occurs outside the interrogation space or within it, the stiff is a political form that facilitates the circulation and exchange of bodies: an action that permits certain claims of power to be made.

If the history that is insinuated in the photographs uses the stiff as an agent of commensuration, it is then also a record of exchange. Two organizational genealogies are laid out here along with the effects of their intersection: the stiffs of the state and the stiffs of the paramilitaries. Each set of stiffs is in a reciprocal relation to the other; each set has been "given the message," and the convergence of the two series bears witness to the formalized history of the exchange of "messages" given.

The joking categories of interrogation set the poles of discourse and death. Confession and death are codified in the rapid alternations between questioning and violence, between wordplay, psychological sparring, and the sudden gun to the back of the head. These alternations move the interrogation in a circular fashion from one phase to the next. The division of juridical labor between the "soft" and the "hard" interrogator reflects the dichotomization of interrogation between confession and death, language and violence. Within this opposition gradations are introduced: the anti-Catholic bigot, the anti-Communist, and the demoralized vengeful drunkard are culture-bound figures that seem prone to irrational violence. They confirm the disengagement of the interrogation process from any rationalized procedures and objectives. These characters are played to indicate the interrogator's immersion in cathartic and arbitrary violence. They also inadvertently disclose how much of ethnicity is constructed around stereotypic repertoires of violent gesture and inference.

Breaking the Interrogation

Within the triangle of interrogation in which the interrogators and their prisoner move together and alternatively from silence and death to language, each of these vectors is structured dialogically. I have attempted to reconstruct one pole of this intersection—the techniques of domination. But there is another pole to the interrogation process which is constructed by the experienced prisoner's counterinstrumentation of his body, in which, to invert Foucault's formula, the prisoner makes his body the principle of his dissociation from the rituals of domination. The experienced interrogatee learns to manage the interrogation through his management of his body and other techniques that subvert domination effects.

I have asserted that the experienced captive exchanges his body for silence. He mimics his death and transforms himself into a cipher. This exchange between body and silence, the prisoner's own investment in the appropriation of his body by the interrogators, is the initial counterinstrumentation of his body. In this process, the prisoner literally autonomizes the body and sends it out into the space of interrogation as a detachable part of his political agency.

Experienced, "case-hardened" paramilitaries have devised techniques and postures for turning the interrogator's violence against their ostensible objectives. A common lexicon of violence, a doubled political technology of the body, is formed out of the interrogation process, which turns interrogation into a shared political arena. The experienced paramilitary extracts a sacrificial strategy of the body that bifurcates the violence.

4.26   To a certain extent they [the interrogators] have this thing that everybody coming into Castlereagh was worried about getting beatings. This is their ace card: "We can slaughter you; we can beat you." Whereas if you provoke them into beating you, they're playing their ace card right away. They've blown it. Sometimes you don't have to provoke them into it; they'll beat you anyway. But how is that going to work the next six days when the beating hasn't worked on the first day? When you provoke them you're making them declare their big card right away. They have nowhere to go from there.

I was a contrary cunt. I would've come in and they would say sit down in that chair, and I would say, "No, I prefer to stand," and stood for a while. They says: "You're not going anywhere right away so take your shoes off." "I'm not taking my shoes off; if you want my shoes off you take them off." When the cop bent down to take them off, I says: "Can you not shine them while you're down there?" Really aggravating the situation. You found whenever you were getting fuckin' dug [beaten] you didn't want to talk, whereas when they were being nice to you it broke down the resistance. The thing about not taking your shoes off was to make your stand as you go into interrogation. Because that's the first thing they ask you to do is to take off your shoes. Not only to say, "fuck you," like but to rub it in. I was lowering them before they could lower me. It's the same as whenever you go to jail. You dig [beat] a screw even though it might mean a beating and you having to go down to the boards [solitary confinement]. If you do it two or three times, you'll have an easier time the next few years from the screws. It's the same in interrogation; it makes your time.

The most dangerous interrogator is the friendly one. If somebody was being friendly to you, you will talk. Last time I was in Castlereagh I never got a finger laid on me. They had my file; they knew my profile. I tried to provoke them into fucking digging me so I could get the fucking hatred up. "Ah fuck, they're not going to beat me into giving them something!" Twenty times before I got diggings. I've got the complaint files and medical records to back it up.[21] But they were into being nice; that's in order to lower your defenses.

I was trying to sleep through the interrogation and your man turns to me and says: "Are we boring you?" "To tell you the truth, yes." He says, "What would you like to do?" "To be honest, I think I'll go to sleep here." I went to sleep on the floor. It was hard but I did go to sleep. The cunt woke me up. I was just lying on the floor. Your man starts questioning me again. I says, "There's a better conversation going on in the next cell." I could hear it through the wall as I was lying on the floor. There was some guy from Derry, and he had broke and was fucking telling them a heap. The peelers say to me: "What are you talking about?" And I start telling him. "Do you like that conversation?" Here's me: "Aye, as a matter of fact I just think I'll bring it to an end." The peeler says, "What are you talking about?" Here's me, I start banging on the wall with my fist. Smacked the fucking wall and near enough broke the knuckle, on this interrogation going on next door. I shouted in, "Hey boy! Say fuck all! Say nothing to them!" Here's the peeler: "Fuck up! Fuck up! Stop that banging!" The next thing two Branch men were in from that room next door: "What the fuck's going on? Can you not keep your own eye on your own suspect!" It broke the isolation they had been building, and they were really fucked up about it. (INLA)

4.27   When you walk into the interrogation cells you can attempt to sit down, but at the end of the day they'll put you where they want you. I just usually sit on the floor. If you try to take a seat they'll just pull it away. If they want to hold me against the wall they'll have to do it with their own hands. I know that three of them holding me against the wall are going to get sick and tired as I am standing against it. A lot of people believe compliance to where they tell you to sit or stand will save them from getting beat. But it's not; it's usually the prelude to getting beat. If they say to you, "Stand against that wall," and you stand against it, they say to themselves, "This guy is pliable; we can use him." That's when the beating will start. If you walk in and lie or sit on the floor and your whole attitude is "I know what you're about here and I don't give a fuck," then you'll get the beatings of frustration from them. You can sense their frustration and that makes you feel good.

You know then that you're in control. If you're dictating to them when they beat you and when they don't, you're totally in control. If it's them that's dictating the basis of the interrogation, it's them that dictates where you sit and where you stand and what demeanor you'll have. They're in control of your emotions and can carry out a given procedure and get a given response.

But if you're lying on the ground and you know they're going to crack up and pick you up and throw you against the wall and then hold you against the wall by force and getting very frustrated with it and then they say, "Fuck the bastard, let him lie." You know then you're in control. You're in control of yourself, and in turn you are in control of them through your control of yourself.

The beating is inevitable. You're going to get it one way or the other. All you have left to defeat them is to show them you don't give a fuck and that you've psyched them out even to the extent that you know when and why they're going to beat you. They've lost their tool. When you dictate to them when the physical violence is going to be used against you. Then it isn't coupled in with a big buildup of psychological pressure. The gradual buildup of psychological pressure leads to the point where your mind is preparing itself all the time for this violence. When the violence does come it has a massive psychological effect, which is, "Jesus Christ! I'm going to have to go through this for seven days." (PIRA)

4.28   They try to make you feel as if you were nothing, screaming into your face, "You smell, you stink, you're a criminal." They take all our clothes off. They give you a loose boiler suit which makes you feel not secure. What I learned being in and out of interrogation rooms: you will always have a device or means to break any interrogation; what I had was an old television set sitting in the corner. What I had in mind: "If you go under big pressure here you're putting your head through that TV. All right you might carve your face up, but you'll go to the hospital right then and there." That was my safety device; that was me secure. (PIRA)

4.29   Big Ronnie Bunting was the best I ever heard of in interrogation. He was the son of Major Bunting who led all the campaigns against the civil rights in the sixties, a real staunch

> Loyalist who was responsible for the Buntollet massacre, and his son turned out to be a fucking Republican.[22] Ronnie had done all these psychology courses and all the interrogation courses, so he ended up teaching the anti-interrogation courses for the movement. The Special Branch would be questioning Ronnie and he would have said, "Oh I see, you're trying such and such a method." So they'd try something else, and he'd name that one too. It fucked the Branch up completely because some of them didn't even know the names for what they were doing and he did. The Orangies banged him and his wife, so they did. (INLA)

Although the strategies for breaking the interrogation vary from paramilitary to paramilitary and from interrogation to interrogation, a common pattern emerges in handling the relation between violence and the hidden temporality of the interrogation. By deciphering the temporal patterns of the interrogation that anchor the surface disorder, by skillfully assessing the intensities of the interrogator's violence, the paramilitary begins to restructure the interrogation. Deciphering the order that mediates the apparently random and unpredictable assaults on the self becomes a powerful countertechnique. The simple naming of the interrogation techniques, which is the introduction of visible differentiation, order, and hierarchy into the violence, can derail the process.

While it is possible to describe the formal logic of inversion that animates resistance, it is difficult to project oneself into an experience that offers such few alternatives that security, control, and self-integrity depend on the capacity of the prisoner to time and determine when he will be beaten.

> If you are dictating to them when they beat you and when they don't, you're totally in control. . . . You're in control of yourself, and in turn you are in control of them through your control of yourself. (4.27)

Resistance is predicated on the restoration of time in the sensorium of death, where time has been banished. The return of time brings with it the restoration of agency, now directed to the manipulation of the interrogators' time as presented through their gradation of violence. The restoration of time and agency is registered in the premature violence the interrogators inflict on the body. They beat new modes of agency and embodiment out of the flesh of the captive whose posture has triggered the violence. The restoration of time, and the emergence of a new body forged as an instrument by the captive, signals the transformation of the interrogation experience into a political rite of passage.

If one can direct the interrogators through the direction of the body, it is because the body has become the shared construct of the participants in interrogation. The paramilitary redirects the body-automaton assembled in the sensorium of death by the interrogators. The body is identified as the privileged site of ideological reproduction. Even for the paramilitary the instrumentation of the body is not the direction of an unmediated pristine capacity; rather it is a transfer of political will and agency to a surrogate, alien double. By instigating the interrogator's violence, the captive performs a mimesis of the interrogators' body-object. The interrogators' body-artifact is mimed by the captive in an act of violence that appears as the interrogators' violence. The use of mimesis here implies that resistance is understood by the experienced captive as counterfeiting the state's trajectory of ideological reproduction. Thus the premature escalation of violence in disrupting and forging the timing of interrogation sequences disrupts the time within which ideological replication takes place.

Case-hardened paramilitaries can bifurcate the violence of the interrogation. This indicates that the body that first enters into interrogation is not the same body that emerges as the product of successive interrogation episodes. Interrogation transforms the body into a bivalent instrument codirected by the interrogators and the paramilitary. Reversible instrumentation of the body has been previously encountered in the paramilitary discourse on the weapon. If we consider that interrogation has traditionally been a radicalizing experience for prospective paramilitaries and veteran paramilitaries alike, then we must recognize the link between the reversible objectifications of the body in the violence of the interrogation and the instrumentation of the paramilitary's body as a conduit for military violence.

When questioned about the functions of the body in the military operation, in the breaking of interrogation sessions, and in the Hunger Strike of 1981, when ten Republican prisoners willfully starved to death, Republican paramilitaries made no essential distinctions between these various political usages of their bodies. Either the body was extended by the technology of weaponry in the military operation or it was extended into a weapon in the interrogation center and the prison. At each of these sites of political conflict, the paramilitaries saw their bodies as occupying and exploiting a single political and performative continuum.

Scarry (1985:56–58) identifies the creation of state hegemony in the process of torture as based on the detachment and transfer of political meaning and significative capacities from the body of the tortured to the instruments of torture which become fetishized symbols of the state. The apparatus and instruments of domination form a vector where state and body meet, intermingle, and exchange substance. Like Foucault,

Scarry sees investiture and divestiture of the body as modes of domination when performed by the state. Both Foucault and Scarry abandon the body to the monopoly of the state apparatus. Yet in Northern Ireland, within the performative domains of paramilitary and state transactions, a similar series of semic transfers, displacements, exchanges, and substitutions characterizes the cultural construction of power against the state. The circuit, in the instance of terrorist violence, traces the following route: agent of violence (self) → weapon (instrument) → victim (other) → stiff (the corpse as a political text and defiling double and ideological concentrate of the paramilitary) (see chapter 3). In interrogation, the circuit of semiotic transfer ideally proceeds as follows: interrogators (state) → various instruments and media of violence → the prisoner's body → the confession text (state artifact and purified double of the captive body).

In the terrorist act, the bivalent weapon as the invested object of political agency establishes reversible exchanges between the agent of violence and the condition of the stiff. As the consequence of contact with the weapon, defilement and violence are perceived as traversing manifold directions, encoding the intended victim, the original object of the terrorist act, or decoding the agent of violence, the weapon handler, by transforming this agent into a stiff.

An inverting exchange of violence also takes place in the interrogation in the strategies of resistance deployed by the "case-hardened" paramilitary. Through the self-detachment of his body, the resisting paramilitary moves from being the object of violence to the subject position of the codifying agent. The prisoner exploits the transcription of his body effected by interrogation violence in order to commit a clandestine act of inversion against the interrogation which both simulates state violence and empties it of its ideological content. *Was this exchange what Adorno was searching for in the mimesis of reification—the extraction of a modicum of resistance in the death-like parody of domination?*

The substantiation of power in the inversions of embodiment/disembodiment links the terrorist act and the interrogation. In both domains of political action, the body is invested and autonomized by violence. The body becomes the medium, the origin, and the telos for the graphic of violence. Violence flows out of the body or enters into it in order to create political value. Transactions of the body encode social institutions with signs of power, or social institutions bear down upon the body with violence and invest it with political value. The manifold formation of the body by violence, political technologies, and jural ritual renders it into an inscribed text and an inscribing agent, into a defiling and defiled instrument, a "doing" and a being "done." This bivalent construction of the body and its establishment as a political form are coeval with the institutionalization of violence as a mechanism that perpetuates itself by exchange and mimesis.

Battle-proofing

Paramilitaries' recoding of interrogation as a rite of political and military passage is underscored by the resemblance between their narration of interrogation violence and the rites of "battle-proofing" practiced by warrior sects and military organizations in diverse cultures. Techniques of "battle-proofing" are deployed in military rites of passage that use corporal mortification, divestiture, and pain to test and to harden initiates. Heald (1986), in her analysis of ritual mortification in male circumcision ceremonies among the Gisu of Uganda, identifies battle-proofing as the central objective in subjecting the initiate to violence and other transgressions. Battle-proofing uses somatic defilement to inure the Gisu initiate against pain and fear; it also releases aggressive energies, which sets the initiate apart from everyday social domains.

In Vietnam, novice U.S. soldiers were forced by combat veterans in their units to engage in mutilations and mortifications of Vietnamese corpses. For the new recruit who had to mutilate a single corpse tied to a tree or a pile of dead Vietnamese, the experience was one of overwhelming personal defilement and a reciprocal depersonalization and abstraction of the dead (personal communications). However, combat veterans viewed this practice as acclimating the initiate to combat and violent death. The recruit who had undergone this rite of defilement was seen as beginning the socialization process that would turn him into a reliable partner in war.

These practices are analogous to the "case-hardened" paramilitary's appropriation of the mortifications of interrogation as a form of resistance and as a rite of political agency. Interrogation recodified into a battle-proofing ritual would confirm its structural linkage to the reproduction of political violence outside the interrogation space. If the arrest/interrogation process is seen as culminating in the reordering of political identity through the political reconstruction of the prisoner's body, then a formal processual initiation schema can be discerned in the oral history of arrest and interrogation in Northern Ireland. The ritualized character of paramilitaries' passage through the corridors of arrest and interrogation is particularly evident in the progressive sequence of temporal structures that inform each stage of the arrest/interrogation process. These simulations of death and restoration mark the shift in coercive intensities and the transformative movement of the political actor through the interior of the state.

In his cyclical and repeated movement from the street into the interrogation center, from the interrogation center into the street, from violence inflicted onto his body to violence inflicted by his body on others,
the paramilitary remains locked within a demarcated continuum of corporeal mimesis, a serial circuit of bodies coded and recoded, folded and
unfolded by violence given and violence received. This production and
reproduction, this distribution and circulation of bodies formed and signified by violence and signifying through violence, constitute the vast
economic enterprise and structure of exchange that is warfare in Northern Ireland.

5 *The Breaker's Yard*

But the feces are not the cause . . . feces give rise to a character [*abscheu*] only if the subject lives them in such a way as to find them a dimension of being.

—Maurice Merleau-Ponty

Nothing had its right name in the Blocks.

—PIRA Blanketman

Prison Regime

Since the introduction of mass internment in 1971, the prison system of Northern Ireland has become a domain of action, discourse, and symbolization that has time after time escalated communal violence and precipitated new waves of politicization among the imprisoned and their respective communities. Prison resistance is seen by paramilitaries in Northern Ireland as symbolic or "political" action, and is differentiated from the functional immediacy of military violence. The military struggle on the streets is reflected, for paramilitaries, in the shadow play of discourse and expressive action in the prisons. Yet precisely because political resistance in the prison has worked with different media than those of the military domain, it has defined the ideological content of the war at crucial historical junctures. With the advent of the 1981 Hunger Strike, the Republican prison struggle actually wrested temporary precedence for itself away from the military campaign.

In the first decade of civil strife, the prison became the center of ideological advancement and a subculture of resistance that incessantly produced collective symbols of political incorporation for insurgent communities outside the prison. Between 1976 and 1981, ideological development and refinement of symbolic media in the prison became almost exclusively associated with Republican paramilitaries in their protests against the removal of political status by the British. Loyalist prisoners underwent many of the same experiences as Republican prisoners up to the initiation of the Republican political status protest. However, the major political focus of the Loyalists remained the issue of religious segregation in prison, an issue that corresponded with existing Loyalist ideology on the streets, and which did little to advance Loyalist political thinking in the prison (Tyrie and McMichael 1981:4). Because of this division in the ideological formation of Loyalist and Republican prisoners, an analysis of the Northern Ireland prison system as a domain of symbolic political action and discourse inevitably gravitates to the experiences and concepts of Republican inmates. They surpassed not only their Loyalist coprisoners in the development of novel political ideology and symbolic war, but also their Republican comrades outside the prison. This uneven ideological development within the Republican movement between the prison struggle and the military campaign on the street owed its existence to complex institutional processes. These can be traced to the separation of the prison from the outside world and to internal structures of confinement, both of which facilitated the cultural reconstruction of the prison into a theater of political allegory by Republican prisoners.

The prison system developed in tandem with the intensification of violence on the streets. Its institutional and juridical profile, from 1968 to the present, changed radically, particularly as the Northern Ireland and British governments rationalized the law enforcement complex into an intervention mechanism for combatting terrorist violence. The prison system along with the arrest/interrogation process and the courts became the frontline in a counterinsurgency strategy that increasingly abandoned overt military defeat of paramilitary organizations for their juridical attrition (Hillyard 1983).

By 1976 the prison system attempted to depoliticize paramilitary ideology and practice. The Northern Ireland judicial and penal system positioned itself between the paramilitaries and their existing and potential support communities in order to restructure the latter's perception of paramilitary practice. The government sought to shift the political comprehension of violence to a juridical reading that consigned paramilitary practice to criminal agency. Republican paramilitaries correctly concluded that the procedural criminalization of insurgency implied a corresponding but camouflaged politicization and militarization of the judicial and penal systems. Republican prison resistance strategies were addressed to the total destruction of the juridical/penological facades that masked the actual politicization of the courts and prison.

The transformation of the prison system was initially precipitated by the massive increase of the prison population. In 1968, before the start of the Troubles, the prison population was 727. By 1971 it had increased to 944; in 1974 it reached a high of 2,650; and in 1980 it leveled out to

2,500. There were 1,300 inmates at Long Kesh, the center of prison protest. To accommodate this politically embarrassing increase, new forms of incarceration and judicial processing were devised (Boyle, Hadden, and Hillyard 1980:88).

The development of penal institutions and procedures directly reflected the state's conception and image of the political conflict in Northern Ireland. As these conceptions changed, so did the corresponding penological strategy employed by the state. The government reinterpreted the Northern Ireland conflict from a short-term, resolvable crisis to a long-term social pathology of particular and identifiable segments of the population that had become profoundly ruptured from civil order and the state. From 1972 through 1976, the penal system moved from a policy of recognizing the political and ethnic origins of the prisoners to a criminalization policy that denied all historical contingencies that had led to the formation of what was a totally new prison population (Boyle, Hadden, and Hillyard 1980:43–48; Coogan 1980:51–59; Hamill 1985:217, 222).

Criminalization

In 1972, as a result of protests by Republican prisoners, incarcerated paramilitaries (Loyalist and Republican) were granted Special Category status. Commonly known as "political status," this designation exempted paramilitaries from wearing prison uniforms and engaging in prison labor, while granting the right to free association and political education within penal facilities. The paramilitaries understood "free association" as authorizing residential segregation in prison in terms of ethnic, religious, and political ascription. The ideology and practice of residential segregation, enhanced by the Nissan huts of the compound system at the Long Kesh penal complex, facilitated the development of self-governing paramilitary communities. Political internees and sentenced paramilitary prisoners lived under this segregationist system, as much for protection as for ideological reasons. In "The Cages" as the compounds of Long Kesh came to be known, paramilitary prisoners observed strict residential and communicative segregation from what the penal regime called the Ordinary Decent Criminal (nonpolitical prisoner).[1]

By 1975, due to the numbers of "political" prisoners, the prison system stood on the verge of a large-scale legitimation crisis. The official response to the growing prison crisis coincided with planned policy that required the acceleration of court prosecutions and the development of new penological strategies and architectures. The prison system became irrevocably committed to playing a central role in the counterinsurgency campaign (Coogan 1980:56–59):

5.1   At that time [1975–76] we all thought the war was over because the Brits were pulling out. All the big British companies
were folding. We were putting out the posters, "Victory in
'76." Everything was over. One day we were all up on the
roof of Cage 11. It was a good summer; we were lying on the
roof sunbathing. The cranes below were just munching away
building down at the bottom of the camp. Everybody's wirelessing [gossiping]. Somebody up at the far end said, "Do ye
reckon the Brits are going to declare they're going soon or
what?"

 And Gerry Adams said: "Excuse me, look down there!
What do ye see?"

 "Them workmen."

 "And what do ye think they're doing?"

 "Building something."

 "What do you think they're building?"

 "I don't know."

 "Well try and think. What would they be building there?"

 "Prison cells?"

 Here's Adams, "Aye! And who do ye think they're for?"

 We all started looking at each other. Then we sat, staring
at the skeleton of the H-Blocks. (PIRA)

The period between 1975 and 1976, indeed, appeared to offer a de-
escalation of the conflict, if not its resolution. The IRA had declared a
truce, and the British government had entered into a series of negotiations concerning the status of paramilitary prisoners. Imprisoned paramilitary leaders were brought on inspection tours of the H-Block facility
in the process of being constructed at Long Kesh.[2] A prisoner's welfare
office, in which both the government and the paramilitary organizations
were supposed to participate, was in the process of being set up in
downtown Belfast. The paramilitary organizations had agreed to make
the area in the immediate vicinity of the welfare office a demilitarized
zone. The British government stated it was prepared to invest a hundred
thousand pounds for such prisoner welfare services as transportation for
prisoners' families to Long Kesh. The paramilitary organizations seemed
on the verge of being recognized by the British government as legitimate
political entities. By the end of 1975, the IRA truce had collapsed and a
new policy of police primacy had been implemented. The IRA now un-
derstands the overtures of the British government as a smoke screen
that facilitated a retrenchment of the counterinsurgency campaign. Certainly Gerry Adams, future head of Sinn Fein, held no illusions about the
intensification of war during this period. Prior to this, Adams, Bobby

Sands (leader of the 1981 Hunger Strike), and a number of other prisoners had theorized the advent of a new counterinsurgency policy that came to be known as "Criminalization, Ulsterization, and Normalization" (Coogan 1980:60–64).

The Diplock Report of 1972 had recommended the introduction of "extra-judicial" processes for the bringing of paramilitaries to trial: special courts without juries, enhanced powers of arrest and interrogation, and new rules concerning the admissibility of evidence. The burden of proof was to be switched from the prosecution to the defendants in all cases involving firearms and explosives. The Diplock procedures were implemented as an alternative to internment, which had become a highly politicized issue and had never attained any juridical legitimacy (Hillyard 1983:39–40). (See chapter 4.)

As the Diplock procedures were introduced, the prison population correspondingly increased. With this rapid increase in the prison population, the Special Category status became a political embarrassment, as it officially confirmed that the British government held a large population of political prisoners. The Gardiner Report of 1975 urged the abolishment of Special Category status. At the time of its publication, there were 1,119 prisoners with "political status" incarcerated in Northern Ireland. The report recommending the building of cellular prison accommodation stated that the compound system of incarceration had served only to further radicalize paramilitary prisoners by allowing them political indoctrination and military training. The report correctly identified that the spatial layout of the compound system, known as "The Cages," removed prisoners from strict disciplinary regimes of the prison administration. What this report did not discuss was that the social organization of the compounds must have contributed to the lower recidivism rate there as compared to the recidivism rate of cellular modes of incarceration on the British mainland during the same period (Hillyard 1983:53–59; Coogan 1980:55–59; Boyle, Hadden, and Hillyard 1980:89; Bishop and Mallie 1987:274).[3]

In November 1975, the Secretary of State for Northern Ireland declared that any person found guilty of a scheduled offense after March 1, 1976, would not be granted Special Category status. The removal of political status in this manner meant that there were now two forms of incarceration for paramilitaries in Northern Ireland. There were still paramilitaries scheduled to serve out sentences under the Special Category rule well past the March deadline. These same prisoners, convicted of a past offense after March 1, 1976, would serve their new sentences without political status. Paramilitaries released from the Cages and convicted for new crimes after the deadline would also return to prison without political status.

Aborted Initiations

The PIRA had threatened dire consequences, including the shooting of prison officers, if Special Category status was taken away. Yet while recognizing the surface implications of the removal of political status, the PIRA did not fully appreciate its ramifications combined with the new system of cellular incarceration in the H-Blocks. There was certainly no ideological or tactical preparation of IRA activists who faced the imminent possibility of entering prison without political status. For most paramilitaries, the compounds and the H-Blocks belonged to the same undifferentiated penal system. They were unprepared both as individuals and as an organization for the radical transformations of the prison situation and its new psychological, political impact on inmates.[4]

The paramilitary's prison-based social organization—the brigade command hierarchies and training programs—had been tailored for "The Cages," with their collective living situation and prisoner-of-war psychology. The first IRA men to enter the H-Blocks encountered a regime that refused to recognize any social unit larger than the individual inmate. The depoliticization of the paramilitary's formal penal status conversely meant his extreme individualization and a refusal on the part of the prison administration to recognize his organizational affiliation. The paramilitary's social space was reduced to the prison cell, the prison uniform, the prisoner's identification number, the "black book" (the prisoner's file), and the inmate's interactions with prison staff. Paramilitary organization and ideology had no reserved place in this structure. The cell, the uniform, the number, the file, and deference to prison staff were intended by the prison regime to be the sole registers of the paramilitary prison identity. The paramilitaries' emerging awareness of their changed position in the prison is evidenced by the centrality that formal institutional induction procedures occupy in their recollections of the early days of the H-Block regime. When paramilitaries discuss the Cages, the initiations that figured prominently in their oral histories were their own organizational debriefing and the various practical jokes played upon the new prisoner by their peers. In contrast, their oral histories of the H-Blocks trace the violent encounter with the typical Goffmanesque assaults on personal identity that are associated with the total institution.

5.2   I went on the Blanket in October 1976. The decision to go on the Blanket was taken from us by the Brits when they removed political status. Anybody arrested after March 1, 1976, was going to be treated as what they call an ordinary criminal. I was arrested on April 6, 1976. Even on remand we were in a new system. Prior to that, on remand you had political sta-

tus. You had your own system in the Crum [Crumlin Road
jail], operating under your own command structures. We found
ourselves going into a wing in which there was only twenty-
five other Republicans. While there were two hundred re-
mands with political status being held in A-wing separated
from us, we were all isolated in C-wing.[5]

I met the reality of the loss of political status right away. I
was in prison five minutes and I ended up on the boards [pun-
ishment cells]. The first thing they do is that they put you
through reception, give you a bath, and then march you
straight into the Prison Officer's office. My experience of
Prison Officers was that you didn't take any shit from them:

"Name?"

"Mc ____ ."

"Mc ____ , sir!"

"Why don't you go fuck yourself, sir!"

My feet never touched the ground. I was away straight into
the boards [isolation cell]. The next morning they took me
out. I had been in the Crum in '72. The first thing I realized
when we got to the grills that the whole wing had been
changed, redecorated and repainted and all cleared out. We
were standing between the grills, and there was screws there
who recognized us from our sojourn in '72, when we were
running the jail under our command structures. One screw he
shouted: "Fuck me, it's fucking 'Evil'!" That's what he called
Big Jim McCauley who was in along with us. He ran down the
stairs to the grill and says: "Fuck you yeeze bastards. It's all
changed in here now! You're getting a rough ride."

It was then that it hit us that it wasn't going to be the
same. The first thing they did was to hoist us into a big cell
full of screws. The top screw says, "This is the setup.
There's no IRA in here. There's no organization in here. Each
one of youse is an individual. You'll address me from here on
in as sir." We were all standing looking at each other. They
put us into our cells. It was six hours later till we got out to
go to the canteen where we had our initial discussion. We
knew that we were going to have to take some sort of stand.
It was then that we started discussing seriously the implications of the removal of our status. Right away we knew that
we as political prisoners were not going to wear prison uniforms which were symbolic of a criminal. The suit itself didn't
mean an awful lot. It was just material. The suit of clothes
doesn't make the prisoner, but it was symbolic. We were re-

fusing point-blank then and there to put a uniform on which
would give anybody a visual of us being different whatsoever.

It was an easy guideline: "Don't wear the uniform. We
don't work. Political prisoners don't do menial type of work
they want you to do." We got the boys in a discussion. "Look
whoever's first sentenced here [September was the earliest
anybody was due for sentencing] will refuse to wear the uniform."

On remand we wore our own clothes. In September we
went to court, got up, and refused to recognize the court.
They threw us out and put us back a week. Two weeks later
they banged [convicted] Kieran Nugent. He came out, and he
refused to wear what we call the "monkey suit." He ended up
in a cell down in the H-Blocks. There were four other guys
waiting to be sentenced, and they all followed suit.

The first impression getting down into the H-Blocks at that
time was from the outside it didn't look like a prison. It was
all built on ground level in the form of an H, with big windows
on the cells, concrete pillars, and no iron bars. The pillars
were behind the panes of glass, not on the outside.

We first went into the body of the H, which was called the
circle even though it was a square shape. It was all white;
everything was painted white. The bars were green. The
screws were screaming at us. We had refused point-blank to
even touch the "monkey suit." They asked us all our sizes,
and we refused to give them our sizes. Before they put us
down into the cells they lined us up in the circle. We were
watching all around us because we were expecting a tanking
[beating]. There were six of us, and we says to each other:
"The first time they lift their hands get fucking into them.
You're going to get murdered, but fight or we're going to get
tortured. If they frightened us now they'll be torturing us for
the rest of our wick [time]."

Davey Long, a rotten bastard of a screw who I knew in
'72, came up to me and says, "I don't need to tell you nothing!" That's all he said to me. They took us down to the cells.
When we first hit the wing it was like going underground, an
underground well. There was very little light. Everything
seemed dead squeezed in and compact. Everything was
painted white with green cell doors. I went down into the cell
and the screws came in. "Strip!" We strip. They had their
"monkey suits," and they threw them on the bed. "Put your
suit on."

"I'm not putting it on." I was standing bollock naked.

It was then that Davey Long came into my cell. "This is the crack: you've got your orders and I've got mine. This is the way the situation is. These are my screws and my cells. You'll have no contact whatsoever with them; you don't speak to them. Anything you want you request the Prison Officer." Away he went, and they all trooped off the wing. It was fairly spontaneous. You felt very vulnerable standing in a cell, so I just lifted the blanket off the bed and put it around myself, and that was to be my uniform for the next five years. (PIRA)

In *Asylums*, Goffman advanced the now-classic model that the induction into the closed institution parallels rites of passage. These procedures are intended to be identity-fixing events for both the inmate and his keepers, a performance that establishes the total gauge of discipline in the institution. The induction is an unavoidable rite of defilement for the new inmate, who is stripped of many of the outward components of his preinstitutional identity. In many instances the new inmate, once bereft of these identity components, has very few resources left with which to counter this massive socializing onslaught (Goffman 1961:18–30).

In contrast, the paramilitaries possessed significant barriers to the impact of induction procedures. They imported their political and ethnic solidarity and their military command structures into the prison. Conforming to the prison regime was for them a form of depoliticization, a "breaking" of their political will and identities. The most common expressions associated with this process in the oral histories are "isolation" and "individualization." These terms signified the forced extraction of the paramilitary from his organizational and ideological frameworks.

The paramilitary hierarchy in the Cages was by and large legitimized under political status. These command structures and their attendant ideologies of collectivism were the central targets of the new H-Block regime, where political status had been removed. The induction procedures are portrayed by the paramilitaries as an attempt to destructure paramilitary hierarchy at the point of entry into cellular incarceration. The prison officer who admonishes the narrator to only make requests or to speak solely to him and not to his subordinates is in fact reversing the formal relationships between warders and paramilitaries in the Cages (narrative 5.2).There the guards had to communicate to each inmate through the mediation of the paramilitary OC (Officer Commanding) of each compound.

The central mechanism of hierarchical incorporation by the prison regime was the wearing of the prison uniform. The paramilitaries perceived the uniform as a physical stigma that fixed the paramilitary firmly into the criminal population of the prison and irrevocably subordinated him to prison hierarchies. The wearing of the prison uniform was an erasure of classificatory difference between the paramilitary and the Ordinary Decent Criminal (ODC). The paramilitaries in both the Cages and the H-Blocks observed strict segregation from the ODCs. They came into contact with the ODC only to assert their dominance and higher position in the prison hierarchy. Sex offenders were considered particularly polluted and were a common target for paramilitary violence.

For the paramilitaries, identification and cohabitation with the ODC population were the ultimate forms of defilement, and this judgment was encoded in their reaction to the "monkey suit." So the issue of hierarchy recognition related not only to the legitimation of their brigade structures by the prison regime but also to the position of the paramilitaries as a social grouping in relation to other prisoners. Prison for the paramilitary was thus seen as a mosaic of polluting contacts that had to be mediated by structural distancing. Status segregation from the ODCs and recognition of paramilitary command structures by the guards minimized the individual paramilitary's polluting contact with criminals and the prison administration.

Wearing the "monkey suit" negated these hierarchical concerns and was equivalent to contact with sex offenders in its defiling impact. The incoming Republican prisoners not only refused to wear the prison uniform but refused to touch it or to give their body measurements. In this, they refused to establish any relation between their body and the prison uniform. "We were refusing . . . to put a uniform on which would give anybody a *visual* [emphasis mine] of us being different" (narrative 5.2).

This reference to the negative visual dynamics of the uniform is crucial to understanding the dynamic of resistance. Foucault (1979:195–216) identifies hierarchical observation as the axial practice of somatic domination and transformation in the penal regime. The captive under hierarchical observation is manipulated by his body's visibility; the body is thereby transformed into a text to be read by authoritative observers. Among the optics of domination practiced by the prison regime, which range from the cell cubicle to documentary systems of personality assessment, the prison uniform occupies a pivotal place. The cell functions as a mounting site for the fixed body of the inmate, the documentary systems of behavioral evaluation medicalize the prisoner's psyche, but the uniform is crucial to the visual serialization and training of the prisoner in the disciplinary regime. It has been worn by others before his incarceration and will be worn by others after his release or death. The uniform evokes the clothes of dead men; it is an artifact of used bodies. It belongs to both other bodies and bodies othered, and as such it transforms the body of the self into an alterity. As the apparatus through which the prison regime comes into direct physical contact with the inmate, the uniform is a stigmatic action upon the body, a second confinement of the body. The uniform as lever inserts the prisoner into the machinery of incarceration as an identical and interchangeable component. In reference to stigmatizing serialization, the Republican prisoners identified the refusal to wear the prison uniform with the refusal to answer to the prisoner's designated number.

The Republican paramilitaries described in narrative 5.2 associated the violation of the prison uniform with the violence of the prison guards, who encircle the paramilitaries in a claustrophobic grip. In the prisoner's thought this is analogous to the enclosing defilement of the uniform.[6] Both the uniform and the collective violence of the guards were perceived as initially reducing the prisoners to an undifferentiated mass in order to isolate, individualize, and segment the prisoner as a divisible penal unit.

The refusal by the Republican prisoners to wear the uniform was thus a refusal to enter into "compulsory visibility" (Foucault 1979). Their denial of the elementary modes of penal objectification meant that the prisoners disrupted the penal regime at the margins of its central rite of ideological reproduction—the initiation. The Blanket Protest, as it came to be known, aborted formal entry and passage into the prison. The "Blanketmen" were thus in and out of the penal institution at the same time. They were to remain in this anomalous position for five years before they consented to enter. Both the development of the Blanket Protest and the violent reaction of the prison administration to this protest must be viewed against this aborted initiation and jural incompletion.

The transformation of the rites of induction into a terrain of political warfare and the objectifying effects of hierarchical observation are the dominant themes in the following account of the first days of the H-Block regime. This account foregrounds the prisoner's number, the cell as a theater of observation, and the enforced silence as steps toward the transformation of the prisoner into a disciplinary text.

5.3   I mind on the first day getting to the door to try to shout across the wing, and immediately there was a line of screws in that wing. They were into my door, "All right, fuck up! No talk!" They were trying to enforce a rule of silence. We didn't want to push the issue then. But we were tapping at the pipes and communicating very quietly at the pipes. They were threatening to tear everybody to pieces, so rather than take a stand and get brutalized we decided to bend to the rule of silence. Your bed was taken out every day, and you were constantly observed through the hatches to see if you were staying on your feet or sitting in the chair. You had that sense of real isolation building there and then.

Right from the very beginning searches were very important to them for attacking you, for making you feel vulnerable.
Although they knew you couldn't get anything in when you
were naked, under twenty-four hour lockup and had no visits.
You had no contact with anybody or anything. Still and all they
were coming in strip searching. It was very clear then strip
searching wasn't a method for finding anything; it was an op-
portunity for them to do whatever they were going to do on
you.

How we dealt with the isolation? You walked up and down
the cell constantly thinking, "How do we get our status back?
What are we going to do?" There was no answers coming but
"Resist." The attitude of the screws to me then became a
personal thing. I'm not going to let them bastards see me
walk out of that door with that "monkey suit" on. They were
constantly at it for us to wear it. (PIRA)

The fact that the Republican prisoners in the early months of the
H-Block protest did not realize the extent to which they were dealing
with a restructured and autonomous prison regime markedly different
from the Cages added to the liminal experience of their present incarceration. A significant number of the new H-Block residents had served
time with political status in the Cages, and that experience reinforced the
intentionality of the protest as an attempted return to a prior form of
incarceration. The political development of the protest was inhibited
because the Blanketmen did not acknowledge that two different prison
systems existed at Long Kesh. This was eloquently reflected in the fact
that despite their concern over the formal recognition of their command
structures, the incoming Republicans of the H-Blocks had subordinated
their command structure to the PIRA OC of the Cages:[7]

5.4   In the first year we had subordinated ourselves to the com-
        mand structure that was in the Cages. We had a wing OC and
        a block OC, and the OC of the H-Blocks had subordinated
        himself psychologically in his mind to the Cages staff struc-
        ture. We still looked on it as one prison, and they had a com-
        mand structure going as we came into the prison that we
        would automatically go into. We resolved at the door that it
        wasn't working; we were psychologically subordinating our-
        selves to the Cages. We resolved at the door that it wasn't
        working—that we were in a different situation and that we
        would have to have an independent command structure of our
        own.

We were slowly starting to get more men drifting in, ones and twos, and our numbers expanded. Nobody wanted to put a date on how long we were going to be the way we were. It became a battle of wills. You were getting that much stick [harassment] and hammerings [beatings] from the screws that it was just a blank out there, a wall. "I'm not walking out there with that suit on to let them bastards walk up and down my back." One month went into the next. There were different wee issues coming and going, resolved and unresolved, right the whole way through. There was very few communications with the outside at that time. Very few were taking visits because to take the visit you had to put on the uniform. Yet we believed wrongly that people were aware of what was going on in here. We never even thought for a minute how they were supposed to know. But for some reason or the other we all wanted to believe that there was a whole lot of people getting their act together to get us out of the mess we were in.

What brought it home to us was the Mass. We were under twenty-four hour lockup because of the protest, and we only got out for the Mass. It happened to us at the Mass two weeks in a row. The priest was blathering away. He was saying things like, "When you are mixing with one another, having conversation out in the yard or canteen or over a cup of tea during free association, think about this or think about that moral issue." We were all looking at each other! Sitting like madmen with hair down to here and bruises all over us and he's blathering on about wee cups of tea and all. [Uniforms were worn for Mass.]

Here's us: "Hold on a here, wait a minute. We don't get free association, we're the Blanketmen."

He says, "The what?"

"We're on the Blanket like."

"What do ye mean, what's happening?"

"Did you not hear about us?"

Here's the priest, "Oh aye, I might've heard something." We knew then that he was bluffing. And the exact same thing happened to us a week later with another priest.

We went back to the wing, and everybody that evening was up to the doors shouting: "Nobody knows we're here; nobody knows what's going on. We're not going anywhere. We'll be lying here for the next twenty years and they'll not know even we're here." This was the first sort of serious debate in the wing. The common consensus was that we're going to

have to get into the headlines. We're going to have to make
news. We had reached the stage that in order to get the word
out we had to take visits.[8] But to get out on a visit you had to
put the monkey suit on. That ruled out visits for the first eighteen months. Establishing channels of communication with the
outside world meant once a month putting on that monkey suit.
   We had to do it remembering it wasn't the suit that made
the man. Our whole approach until that moment was because
something in Republicanism, like not wearing the prison uniform, is tradition; you followed tradition, no matter what it
meant in practical terms right back through to all the campaigns. We realized a principle is a principle, but don't let it
blind us to the extent that we were cutting our own
throats. . . . If we could use the uniforms to further the resistance against criminalization, then we should put it on and
take a visit once a month. The blanket was a technique for us
at the very start of the H-Blocks. We had to make an impact;
we had a status symbol. We had the blanket and we were naked. That became our badge, our blanket. We became known
as the Blanketmen. By eighteen months we had already won
that much. The whole system knew that we had taken our
stand. It was then that we could talk among ourselves to
change the tactic to suit ourselves. (PIRA)

These decisions were belated recognitions of the political uniqueness
of the prison situation and reflected a growing sense of separateness
from traditional IRA strategies and hierarchies. These recognitions
marked the acceleration of the prison conflict into a resistance that incessantly churned out unique symbolization. The blanket, their nakedness, and their bruises had been tatooed onto their bodies as a visual
code that successfully repulsed and neutralized the stigmatization of the
uniform and the number: "we had a status symbol. We had the blanket
and we were naked. That became our badge. . . . The whole system
knew that we had taken our stand" (5.4). The Blanketmen had used the
blanket and their nakedness to interrupt the optical circuit of domination.
They had generated a countertextualization of their bodies, a self-
inscription that could not be effaced by defiling contact with the prison
uniform. They could with impunity now put on the uniform to take a visit.
They had placed themselves in the position to use the uniform as a
political tool rather than be used by it. As the culture of resistance
became systematized, the prison as a totality would become subject to
the same reversal as the uniform.

The generation of Republicans which passed through the ordeals of the H-Blocks views the current political/military situation in Northern Ireland as a continuation of an ongoing struggle that goes back to the 1916 rebellion, if not further. These Republicans pride themselves on the development of new strategies, tactics, and ideologies that correspond to what the IRA terms "different phases of the campaign." Their decision to reconstruct the Blanket Protest into a system of political representation directed to an audience outside the prison and to set up a separate H-Block command structure involved the recognition that the H-Block situation had imposed upon them a new campaign phase. This entailed much more than the development of new ideologies and new tactics. The H-Block situation forced a reevaluation of the entire concept of the tactical and the ideological in the Republican movement. The imposed rupture from earlier forms of incarceration instigated a hidden ideological break within the Republican movement, a break that remained tacit solely because its chief ideologues remained incarcerated in prison.

5.5   Bobby Sands made an impassioned sort of effort to make us understand his conception of the "Breaker's Yard." He would say, "No matter what we win and lose in here is not just won or lost for us. It was won and lost for the generations to come because what the Brits are into building here isn't just for breaking us. What's happening here is that the Brits have a closely worked out psychological approach to prison. They're trying to build a 'Breaker's Yard.' " That was the term Bobby Sands used. The idea of the "Breaker's Yard" is that they'll get IRA volunteers into jail. They'll isolate them from the struggle by putting them through the fucking mill. Even if the brutality is not there, they'll get you in and individualize you and isolate you within the prisons. They'll divorce you from your structures and divorce you from your roots. They'll turn out apathetic people who'll be doing nothing but watching the gate for their day of release, and when they do get that day of release all that's going to be in their heads, "I'm not going back in there." No matter what happened on the Blanket or in the aftermath, we had to ensure that even if they break us down to five per wing, that within those five we could ensure our organization. We had even analyzed the number of prisons the Brits had, the number of us, so that we knew that they could never break us down to less than seven per wing. Even if they split us right across all their jails. Even if they mixed us in with the criminals and all the rest. With those seven we were talking about building a cell organization. (PIRA)

Bobby Sands, in his thesis of the Breaker's Yard, not only summarized the rationale of the Blanket Protest, but also shifted the paradigmatic topos of the Republican struggle from violence on the street to resistance in the prisons. He did not challenge the final legitimacy of military violence but exploited the notion of "campaign phases" to relativize its strategic centrality for the moment. Sands simply redirected the stream of Republican tradition into the prison struggle which has its own traditions of martyrdom and sacrifice (see chapter 6). Sands challenged the traditional dogma that the political was subordinate to the military and that full politicization of the Irish masses was predicated on a preliminary military resolution of the conflict. Sands' thesis introduced a new periodization into the current IRA campaign, and this periodization challenged the uncontested primacy of the military campaign. Sands asserted that the very reproduction of the IRA, its ideological survival, and its conservation of an active and experienced membership were anchored in the prison situation.

There is a finessed movement in Sands' thesis. If the prison was to be the topos in which the reproduction of the IRA would be put into crisis, then it was also the topos in which new forms of ideological and organizational development would occur. On one level, there was a self-evident logic to this model. In the view of the IRA activist, the paramilitary career cycle culminated in either death or imprisonment (see chapter 4). Sooner or later, the "active service volunteer," if not killed, would end up in prison. According to Sands' thesis, the prison cadres were as strategically crucial as the active service units committing violence on the street.

The notion that new ideological and tactical perspectives emerge from prison experience is not a novelty in the IRA. Key figures of the present military leadership of the IRA had been heavily influenced by their prison experiences in the late 1950s and early 1960s, that is, when they met with imprisoned Cypriot insurgents and adopted General Grivas's terrorist strategy for defeating Britain in a guerrilla war. It was IRA graduates of the Cages who instigated the replacement of the old brigade system, whose security was easily penetrated, by a cell system in which a rigid division of labor facilitated the maintenance of secrecy (Coogan 1980:39; "Provos Have Second Thoughts" 1982:4–5).

Sands' model, by establishing the tactical equivalence between military action on the street and political action in the prison, inserted the Blanketmen into an emblematic and sacrificial structure of action. If new forms of ideological and organizational reproduction were to appear, they would literally emerge from the incarcerated and brutalized bodies of the Blanketmen. The Blanketmen were to be the hinge upon which the new ideological advancement of the Republican movement turned (Sands 1981:67).

Republican violence, particularly its current forms, legitimizes itself within a conceptual framework of historical reenactment. The IRA guerrilla anchors his violence morally and historically in the traditions of past insurrections. Sands' thesis shifted the historical direction of these traditions of Republican violence to the prison, and thus shifted the topos and genres of historical reenactment.

But there are strong discontinuities between Sands' analysis and the oral history testimony. The sacrificial logic introduced into the prison dynamic by Sands' analysis emphasizes the voluntaristic and rationalized impetus of the prison struggle. The structures of resistance in the prison are presented as acts of pure political will, animated and charged with the weight of Republican tradition and the sacralized historical direction of Irish nationalism. What is excluded from Sands' analysis and what does appear vividly in the oral history accounts are the uncontrollable material elements of the Blanketmen's situation—the coercive violence of prison discipline which imprinted an unalterable cultural logic of the body onto the political consciousness of the Blanketmen. Both the violence endured by the Blanketmen and their strategies of resistance revolved around this developing cultural logic of the body. It is from this political fetishization of the body that Sands' tactical centralization of the prison struggle found its condition of practical possibility.

The genealogy of political action in the H-Blocks returns time after time to the discontinuity between the restricted codings of official Republican discourse and the more elaborated semantic codes present in the forms of everyday life in the prison. This discontinuity was constantly camouflaged by the evolutionary schema that the Blanketmen theorized concerning the relationship of their resistance to the great repository of Republican tradition. This tendency by both the Blanketmen and other Republicans to assimilate the H-Block situation to residual Republican ideology can be seen as an attempt to ground the emergent and highly alien culture of the current prison struggle in the entrenched discourses of the Republican movement. A partial break with the traditional assumptions and strategies of the "physical force" school was first effected when advocates of the H-Block ideology forcibly took over the PIRA Army Council in 1979 ("Provos Have Second Thoughts" 1982:4–5). But the subsequent development of the new "bullets and ballot box" (military and electoral) strategy only furthered the necessity of anchoring novel H-Block ideologies in traditional Republican precedents. Given the isolation of incarceration, this need to integrate emerging prison-based practices that were often alien to, if not discordant with, traditional Republican values and myths was both a political and psychological necessity. Yet the assumption of a seamless evolutionary continuity in the development of Republican ideology and tactics obscures the particular experiential basis of their resistance and its symbolic systems.

The oral history of the H-Block protests reveals that Republican and Gaelic tradition functions less as the ideological precipitants of resistance and more as the idealized and prospective goal of political action in the prison. The Blanket, "Dirty," and Hunger Strike protests were informed by the need to eventually recast a collective situation of loss, separation, and social death into emblematic performances that could forge a utopian cultural sensibility. The overwhelming theme of the prison protests was a *future reunification* with rediscovered submerged Republican traditions, with a precolonial Gaelic cultural order, and with the Irish people as a historical/ethical/linguistic agency to be created. This prospective reunification was tied to the accumulation of paradigmatic acts of resistance that would transform their bodies and thus engender the cultural-historical alterity of the Blanketmen. The ideology of future historical reunification was a significant contribution. Rather than tying the political ideology of the Blanketmen solely to the negative history of cultural loss and political betrayal, the ethic of future reenactment shifted their entire set of actions and discourses into an eschatological framework. Full historical reenactment as a form of political and cultural decolonization had a *prospective* rather than a *retrospective* impetus in the H-Blocks.

Despite the rhetorical incorporation of the prison struggle into established Republican frameworks, the veterans of the H-Blocks confess to an unreconcilable sense of being alien, of inhabiting places and situations that cannot be fully comprehended by the nonprisoner, whatever his political identifications. In the wider Republican community, to this day, an unassimilated aspect to the prison struggle remains; this incomprehension is encountered in the painful silences that surround the events of the Hunger Strike, the silence of unhealed wounds, unresolved hopes, and fragmentary understanding. Between the official discourses of the Republican movement and the oral histories of the H-Blocks, there is a conceptual opposition of *event* and *structure*. The chain of events has been duly historicized by the official ideologies, but the cultural structures from which these events emerged remain Other:

5.6　　This is what's frustrating about the H-Blocks—that people to this day don't understand what was going on in the H-Blocks. They don't even start to understand. We recognize ourselves that nobody who's not actually been there cannot know what it was like. When people ask me, I find myself at a loss for

words, to find words to portray what I really felt. I remember
telling people who were always talking about the "protest" we
were in, "Hold on a minute. This was more than a fuckin'
'protest!' This was a way of life for us! It was no longer a
protest with a visible end to it. That's how we experienced it
at the time. This was our life-style for two, three, four, five
years. It had become an alternative life-style for us and not
one we wanted by choice like. (PIRA)

Scatology

To understand the symbolic systems of the H-Blocks one has to abandon
the notion that political symbolization expresses an objectified reality that
is somehow external to or independent of systems of representation. To
comprehend the political formation of the H-Blocks it is also necessary to
abandon the view of symbolization as a purely expressive activity (the
base/superstructure model of symbolization) and to take up the notion of
symbolization as an affective and determining material performance that
reflexively transforms self and social structure. To refer to symbolic
action in the H-Block protest is redundant. In the H-Blocks, symbol and
action neither were opposed to each other nor complemented each other;
to symbolize in the H-Blocks was to act politically and with finality.

In the H-Blocks, there was no reality outside the various systems and
countersystems of representation and objectification that were violently
hurled back and forth through the recesses of the prison. The capacity to
symbolize and to encode a given reality was the basis of political resistance. Domination, in turn, was predicated on desymbolization. The body
was an essential component of the material conditions of confinement;
any semantic and performative alteration of the body reciprocally altered
the material conditions of incarceration. Resymbolization of the body in
this context can hardly be considered an expressive activity in contrast
to effective practice. The H-Block struggle moved rapidly beyond the
stage of a simple protest and far beyond the point where the media
expressing this protest referred to a stable objective referent. Symbolization of the condition being protested transformed that very condition
and constituted a vortex of active material transformation. As much
violence occurred over the modes and methods of symbolization constructed by the Blanketmen as occurred over the issues being symbolized. Symbolization in the H-Blocks was forged in violence, it was often
violent in itself, and it never failed to engage life-and-death issues.

The H-Blocks became a site of intensive culture-building by the prisoners. Within the enclosure of the prison, further partitions were
mapped out, dialogical domains defined by the antagonistic and intersect-

ing ideological imaginations of the inmates and the prison guards. The prison became a bifurcated space, but this bifurcation did not permit the protagonists of the conflict to remain on either side of a pristine ideological border but rather divided the prisoners and the guards to the very depths of their bodies and being. The H-Blocks became the scene for the development of dramatic biological and semantic reorganizations of the human body, secret languages, ritualized temporalities, surreal ecosystems, and unique technological adaptations. The H-Blocks had their myths, local histories, performance spaces, carnivals of violence, symbolic kinship, death rituals, and animal totems.

As in many other alternate societies studied by anthropologists, the culture of the H-Blocks could trace its origin to the recodification of the organic. The prisoners' bodies were divorced from any known "natural" norm or experience of the body to be found in society outside the prison. The symbiosis between prison discipline and political resistance culminated in a *literal inversion* of the body, in a dissected body turned inside out.

Foucault (1979) asserts that all prison revolts occur on the level of the body. The H-Blocks teach us that within the ecologies of violence, knowledge, representation, and cultural genesis begin and end in the body. The bodies of the imprisoned became the "degree zero" for all cultural constitution and demarcated the outer margins of the inner world of the prison. The margins between prison and body were submerged and erased; the cell became the extended body of the prisoners, and their bodies became their temporary prison:

5.7   At the start when we went on protest, it was strictly no work and no wearing of the prison uniform. We were under twenty-four hour lockup, no free time outside. You were locked up the whole time, because we wouldn't conform, and you had only one visit a month and one letter a month. The screws started messing us about. You had two towels at the start. You used to get washed with one and kept the other one wrapped around you at the showers, so you weren't standing naked in front of the screws. The screws took the one towel off of us, saying use the towel you had wrapped around you to dry yourself off. So in other words you had to stand naked whenever you got washed. So the guys said to the screws: "We're not going to do that. We'll stay in the cells as a protest and get washed in the cells." So we were getting washed in the cells for awhile. Now there were no mirrors in the cells as there were in the showers. So the screw starts throwing you in a razor and says shave. Without a mirror that was impossible to do. So we says all right, no problem, we'll fucking grow beards. It was the same with the hair cutting: fucking let our hair grow, no problem. It was the whole harassment thing building up. The thing with the toilet was that you may be shouting for an hour to go out to the toilet. The screws would be saying: "Ah yes, but you were there yesterday. What do ye want to be going out there today?" When they did let you out to the toilet you had to walk up the wing to get to the toilet, and you were getting strip searched. The screws were giving you a strip search as you were going up to the toilet and as you were coming down, really fucking you about.

In the showers the screw would put a mirror on the floor and tell you to stand over the mirror attached to a sponge, and they said put your hands against the wall. We wouldn't do it. So right then and there you got a fucking digging [beating]. They pushed you against the wall and battered the head off the wall a few times and then said to you, "Squat." We didn't squat; they kicked the back of your legs to make you go down. That meant you were squatting over the mirror. They parted the cheeks of the arse and looked up them and all the rest. You always got the screw who struck his finger up your arse and hooked about, and they said to ye, "Open your mouth," to see if anything was there. And the screw used the same finger into your mouth, this same shitty finger searched your nose, your ears, and searched your beard. All with the same finger. Some of them went to the extreme, and this is true as fuck, to search below the foreskin. They were bastards of the first order. The only place they never searched was your belly button. They were looking for letters. At the time they made the excuse that there were screws' names and addresses going out for assassinations. But it was all going out verbally anyway, because that's not the kind of thing you write down.[9] It was all just to fuck guys about trying to break them.

We says no problem, keep fucking us about and we'll not use the toilets; so we stopped using the toilets, just used a slop bowl in the cell. At that time we were throwing the shit out the window and pouring the urine out under the door. So the screws had to mop it up. The cells were still basically clean. So then the screws blocked off the windows. So you couldn't throw it out the window. They started squeeging the urine back under the door into the cells. So the guys said all right, we'll just put the shit in the corner.

At that time the screws were doing about five cell searches a day. We were getting these cell searches, and all our gear was in the corner. The screws would have come in and all the shit and urine was in the corner. They lifted your blankets and fucked it into that corner and walked the shite all over your blankets or fucked the mattress into a wad of it. So the only effective way of combating that was to spread it on the walls. Get it off the floor and then the screws couldn't put it on your blankets.

I had several birds coming up to visit me, but after awhile on the Blanket you didn't want to go near many women or take visits from your family. You were stinking, and you were conscious of it. Your breath was rotten because you weren't brushing your teeth; your sweat was stinking. We used to smash the cell windows to let the fresh air in. It was great in the summer, but in the fuckin' winter it was cold. You were fuckin' lying, and the snow was literally on your blankets. You had no clothes, only three blankets to keep you warm. (INLA)

5.8   I was on the Blanket for five years. I was arrested in May '77. I had only just been released from political status seven and a half weeks earlier. I was arrested, charged with possession of an Armalite [rifle], and sent through the courts, and in that seven and a half weeks I all of a sudden became a "criminal." In the Blocks you go into reception, and you would say straight away, I'm a political prisoner and I refuse to wear a prison uniform and I refuse to engage in prison work. They'd have all the clothes stripped off of you and that was the last you saw of your clothes. We were brought into the "circle," the middle of administration wing of the Block which has four wings running off it in an H shape. You're brought in there, and then again you had the humiliation process, "You're number 289, you're a criminal, you're not a person, you're in there and we're going to break you and you're going to do prison work." There had been none of that in the Cages. You went in from there into the "circle" and made to run a gauntlet of screws from there to your wing, through batons, punches, and kicks. And when you got into your cells they threw in your prison uniform and slammed the door. The only time after that that your door got opened was to allow you to go on a monthly visit of a half hour[10] and once a week for an hour on Sunday for Mass.

They were treating us like a special category right from the start, and they refused to acknowledge it, that they couldn't

deal with Republican prisoners the way they could deal with
other prisoners. With the ODCs it was a one-to-one relationship, but when they came to talk to us, if a screw had to
come to me to say something about visits I'd have told him to
see the OC. They just couldn't break that down. To communicate with us they had to recognize our staff structures. . . .

You were thrown into your cell, the door was locked, and
you paced an eight-foot cell, and that was your world for the
next five years. You never got out, no books, no radio, no
TV. All you had in the cell was three blankets, a pillow, a mattress, a chamber pot, a container for water, and a Bible, nothing else. They had to give you the Bible. It's part of the
Geneva convention; you're not allowed to deny a prisoner
freedom of religious practice. Outside of that, there you had a
Perspex up the window so you couldn't see out and just a
small strip of clear glass again at the top of the Perspex, again
because the Geneva convention states that they are not allowed to refuse you so much directional light into the cell.
They just left the bare minimum. Right down to the basic
whatever they could do. They fed you by opening your cell
and putting your plate of food on the floor; you had to eat on
the floor. Everytime you left the cell you were stripped naked; if you were going to Mass or on a visit or if it was a
wing or cell shift, there was a mirror set on a sponge and you
were spread-eagled over the mirror naked and then kicked
down over the mirror. If they suspected you were carrying
something, they had a sixteen-inch medical forceps and they
would give you an internal examination.

We were getting searched like that every time we went out
of the cell to wash; that forced us to wash in the cells and to
use the chamber pots in the cell. But that began to stink up
the cell. We would push the shit and urine out under the
doors into the aisles, and the screws were throwing the shit
and urine back under the doors. The whole thing escalated
until you had nothing left in your cells that wasn't stinking. We
started emptying the chamber pots out the windows; soon
you could smell the stink coming from the yard. In retaliation
the screws would come down the wing with a big bucket and
collect all the chamber pots and all the contents in a big
bucket and then open somebody's cell and throw it all in.
(PIRA)

5.9   The orderlies were washing down the outside walls of the cell
because we had been putting excrement on them. We just had

the windows smashed out with the cell furniture to get some air in. They were hosing down the walls, and a screw passed by just when I was about to throw the excrement out the window. I got hit on the side of the head with the hose. After that I got a kicking from the warders which I had expected anyway. I was brought to the boards for three days. When I got out, the screws were getting uptight. They started moving us from dirty wings to clean wings. When we were shifted from one wing to the next we heard that the beatings were going on all over the wings. We were told to squat down over the mirrors which we refused to do. They used to beat us down over the mirrors—sometimes they would have kicked you down behind the legs; other times they would just beat you till you went down. We were told not to offer any overt physical resistance but also not to comply. The cells by that time were in a bad way. We were lying on urine-soaked mattresses on the floor next to the excrement and the urine because during cell searches the screws would kick over the chamber pots. The food was very bad, and some of that was going on the wall to dry with the excrement because it was inedible. Guys would be making designs on the wall with the porridge and the excrement. Each morning we would lift the mattresses and chase the maggots out from under them. The food had been cut down to small punishment proportions. It angered us that we were getting starved as well as beaten. The screws said it was because we had thrown the food all over the walls and into the corners. In our cell we didn't throw that much away, just the crusts of stale bread and the porridge, but in other cells they were throwing everything away. The prison authorities cut the portions to stop that. There was one wing on our block H3, and at that time they were down about to their skin and bones for not eating. They were getting very thin. Eventually the prison doctor had to order for them to get more food. (INLA)

5.10   We had decided that we would refuse to cooperate in any way with the screws. We sent a message up to H5 about what they thought about noncooperation. They talked it over. "Dead on we'll go ahead." So what the two blocks done that Monday morning was when the screws came around, "Clean out your cell."

"No, I'm not brushing it out. This is a protest against the conditions we've had to endure up to now. We're getting hassled going up and down the corridors. There's guys getting beat up and having urine thrown around the cells." They would stop guys and they would knock the pot out of his hands, and if the pot didn't go all over him it would go all over the corridor and into each cell under the door. Every time you left the cells it was a flashpoint. You hated leaving the cell. Because you had a sense of security in the cell and once you got out past that threshold you were in enemy territory. Anything could happen. Sometimes you got back without nothing happening but verbal abuse; other times they would have kicked your balls in. This sort of thing was building. So we said, "Right, we're not going over the door. We're not emptying those buckets so you could throw it around us and kick our balls. We're not going to those sinks because every time we go up there somebody's beat up. It was March 17, St. Patrick's Day 1978. We refused to wash and to slop out. The escalation was very slow. Everything we did was all defensive mechanisms.

The screws were giving us these basins to wash in, and the first thing they done was take nails and knock holes into them. Water was leaking and the screws were laughing. So we would break them. They kept replacing these basins till they sussed [figured out] that we were breaking them. (PIRA)

5.11 We smashed the windows the winter of '78. You'd wake up in the morning and you would have wrapped the blanket around the back of the heating pipes to keep the heat in and you woke up many a morning buried under snow on top of the blanket. It was wild cold. At that time there was a bit of fencing around over the protest.[11] The screws were saying if you do this we'll do that. We could get washed for a visit, and our people could come up with our clothes so that we could wear our own clothes for the visits. So we nominated two wings to go through this procedure to see how far it would work, to test the screws. We knew if we called the whole protest off and everybody went into clean cells, it would make it that much more difficult to revert back to the Blanket Protest, if the screws went back on their word. So we left everybody else on the protest and took two wings off as a trial. There was a wing in H5 and our wing in H3 that decided to go ahead and test the situation.

We went through the procedure and got cleaned up for the visits, got the cells cleaned up as well. At the end of the day

they did the dirt on us and refused point-blank to take the
clothes into the jail that our people had brought. There was
TV cameras watching the whole thing, and it was a point
scored for us. We had been accommodating and had gone as
far as we could. That night we reverted back to the same
level of protest as everybody else. As part of the experiment
we had been given new furniture in our cells. That night we
smashed a heap of it up and banged it out the windows.[12] So
around came the heavies. Dragged us straight out of our cells
and had our booters kicked in. They dragged us straight
across the circle and into a wing on the Dirt Protest that had
been shifted that morning. It meant us being bucked into cells
that other guys had just been moved from. The cells were
stinking. Now it was okay when you were in your own cell
with your own crap on the wall. It was all the worse because
for the experiment we had been washed and felt clean for the
first time in years. We were bucked in at 12:00 at night.
There were no lights on in the wing, and they wouldn't put
the lights on. The cells were flooded with piss, and the walls
were black with shit. They had taken our blankets and there
were none in the cells. The bastards left us bollock naked.
You couldn't sit down because the floor was soaking; all you
could do was stand in the middle of the cell. The windows had
been knocked out and the wind was blowing through.

We were all saying they'll come down soon and give us a
blanket; they can't leave us like this all night. By three o'clock
we sussed out that they weren't coming back. They left us till
about 10:00 A.M. till they threw us in a blanket. They moved
us up into H6 with empty cells again that were freezing. It
was 7:00 P.M. that night before they gave us a meal. We were
going into eighteen hours from when we had been bucked into
those pits. All day long as soon as you heard the keys: "Dinner's coming; they'll throw us some blankets in." No blankets
with the breakfast and no blankets with the dinner, and no
blankets when they came to lift the dishes. Everybody
thought they'd thrown them in with the water buckets:
"They'll have to throw them in at the fuckin' tea time with the
chips." No blanket at the tea, and we were fucking shattered.
And when we finally did get the blankets they were soaking
and we had to dry them out on the heating pipes.

I never felt more reduced as a person than I was then.
With everything else that they have done to you, you could

fuckin' fight them. You could do something. But this was just beyond our control. (PIRA)

5.12 The Blanket was something else. When you went into jail you knew you were going on the Blanket. You knew what you were going to be doing. But see, when you walked into the cell for the first time it was a shock, make no mistake about it. You went into this cell, and there it was covered with shit from top to bottom and I mean everywhere: ceilings, walls, doors. It was fuckin' unbelievable. The first cell mate I had, the first impression was that he was white, totally fuckin' white from head to toe; a drawn face, big beard, hair down to his shoulders, and just a blue towel wrapped around him. (INLA)

The failure of the prison regime to imprint the bodies of the Blanketmen with the disciplines of the prison uniform and the prison number gave way to further penal inscription. The prison regime turned to new arenas of regulation that extended the logic of compulsory visibility from the surface to the interior of the prisoner's body. The interior body of the Blanketman was unfolded and exposed by the colon-ization of body functions—of the digestive and elimination tracts of the imprisoned.

The chronology of this project of colon-ization illustrates the deliberate and systematic manner with which it was implemented. As early as November 1976, the prison administration attempted to enforce a single-towel rule at the showers. The Blanketmen, refusing to wash naked under the eyes of the guards, decided to wash in their cells. The administration relented and restored the second towel for the showers. Then late in 1977, the single-towel rule at the showers was reimposed. At the beginning of 1978, the mirror searches were initiated and the physical harassment that accompanied the Blanketmen's trips to the toilets intensified. During this period, strip searches became routinized both in the cell and in the corridors. On March 17, 1978, the Blanketmen refused to leave their cells, and on March 18, the Dirty Protest began. During this period, the inmates' feces were thrown out the windows and the urine was shifted under the cell door into the corridor.

By April 1978, due to the violence of the guards as they entered the cells, the Blanketmen were spackling the walls and ceilings of their cells with feces. In December 1978, the guards initiated the regime of forced washes. During this period of escalation, the Blanket population fluctuated between 360 and 400 prisoners.[13] The Blanketmen were almost completely segregated from the rest of the prison population. They occupied the blocks known as H3, H4, H5, and later H6. Each block housed a hundred cells, and each wing contained twenty-five cells. (In February 1980 thirty-two IRA women went on dirt protest at Armargh prison.)

The bodily interior of the inmate was detached from his control and transferred to the skeletal machinery of administration. This established a correspondence between institutional performance and biological performance. Two systems of penological training converged—coercive economic exchange and optical exposure of the body. This colon-ization of the prisoner's body was intended to force divestiture, to divorce the prisoner from what little sense of somatic mastery he had managed to retain in prison. The beatings of the prisoner that transformed his use of the toilets and showers into a trial by ordeal as well as the violence that accompanied the delivery and removal of food trays were the mechanisms that propelled him into contradiction. Intimate biological functions over which the Blanketman had little control became zones of betrayal that intensified his exposure to the state. His body was now a periphery, a margin of the state.

The Mirror

In the Blanketmen's own recollections, the beatings were a predictable and routine element of prison life and did not attain the debasing level of the "mirror searches." These searches became a central emblem of the logic of defilement and biological warfare in the H-Block conflict. The mirror searches, more than any other practice of prison discipline, retained a rhetorical appearance of technical rationality, while they activated the most ritualized and metaphysical elements of the disciplinary mind:

> The examination combines the techniques of an observing hierarchy and those of a normalizing judgment. It is a normalizing gaze, a surveillance that makes it possible to qualify, to classify and to punish. It establishes over individuals a visibility through which one differentiates them and judges them. That is why in all the mechanisms of discipline the examination is highly ritualized. In it are combined the ceremony of power and the form of the experiment, the deployment of force and the establishment of truth. (Foucault 1979:184)

The rectal mirror examination was a ceremony of defilement and the highest expression of the prison regime's optical colon-ization of the captive body. Ostensibly the mirror examination was intended to find contraband messages, tobacco, cigarette papers, and writing implements that were being smuggled in and out of the prison, but it was, in effect the reorganizing ritual upon which new strategies of compulsory visibility and hierarchical observation revolved. The rectal mirror search replaced the prison cell as the central theater of observation. The prisoners' refusal to wear the uniform has been the first interruption of optical circuits. The guards responded by transforming nakedness into an obvious surrogate tool of visual degradation in place of institutional clothing. The No Wash Protest by the prisoners reclothed their naked bodies with a new and repellant surface of resistance. The fecal cell, which the guards tended to avoid and mainly entered to inflict quick terror, also interrupted compulsory visibility. In its soiled condition the cell was no longer a unidimensional and totally transparent optical stage. The stained walls and the stench endowed the cells with a sensory opacity, resistant depth, and blackness within which the prisoners could shelter. There was a strong analogue between the hiding of contraband by the prisoners in their rectal cavity and the withdrawal of the Blanketmen into the repelling depths of the scatological cell. Denied the surfaces of the inmate's body and the interior of the inmate's cell by fecal defilement, the prison regime extended its optic to the colon-ization of the physical interior of the prisoner with the rectal mirror search.

The inauguration of the Dirty Protest was the period that witnessed the intensification of mirror searches,[14] and the mirror searches raised the institutional synthesis of interpersonal degradation and administrative violation to new heights. The guards who kicked the No Wash protester over the mirror, who spread the prisoner's buttocks and then gazed intently at the reflection in the glass, examined an imaginary spectacle of penal logic. The mirror's penetration of the prisoner's rectal passage reflected back to the guards a purified specular double of the inmate. The images shown by the mirror were icons of a dominated, sanitized and transparent subject—an idealized and desired effigy of interiority, a physical analogue of subjectivity under the grid of compulsory visibility. This purified double secreted an imagery of control and power.

The paraphernalia that lent this ideological exercise a technical aura—the sponge attached to the mirror, the sixteen-inch forceps, and the plastic gloves—mimicked the medical examination. This pseudomedical imagery identifies the rectal mirror search as a rite of purification/sanitization, a curative intervention and an exercise in the production of desired institutional truth. The functional contribution of the mirror search to the detection of contraband was wholly subordinate to its ideological structure, which arranged guards and inmates on either side of the glass in a performed hierarchy. With the mirror search the relations of domination/subjection shifted from a stable structure within which agents acted to a contingent structure that had to be reenacted.

The mirror belongs to the category of coercive doubles by which the penal regime manipulates, trains, and documents the inmate: the uniform, the number, and the prisoner's records, known in the H-Blocks as the "black book." In the context of the mirror search, the following account furthers the aura of ritualized performance that was associated with the examination in the H-Blocks:

5.13   There was one asshole in particular, McGill. He was a senior prison officer. Whenever they were shifting you between wings he would check your thumbprints against your file in your black book. Everybody was accompanied by their black books, and in the black book there was a breakdown of your charges, your personal profile, your scars and other identifying marks, and your thumbprint. This asshole would stand there and examine your thumb and then give a quick look at your thumbprint in the black book with just his bare eye, and say: "Yeah, that's him." He was making sure that it was you who was really going across.

There was an argument among us about whether he could really tell just from glancing at your thumb. He would look at this and then he would say: "What's your prison number?" Once the issue of the number was raised, that was always the signal for violence. (PIRA)

The Body as Weapon Artifact

Nietzsche analyzed the body as a "political structure" (1968:492) and political structures as bodies. This was not an organicist thesis. The Nietzschean "body" is the factored product of the unequal and differential effects of intersecting antagonistic forces:

> Whether chemical, biological, social or political . . . any two forces being unequal constitute a body as soon as they enter into a relation. (Deleuze 1977:80–81)

Deleuze traces Nietzsche's model of the factored body to Spinoza's theory of affectivity. The extent to which the body forcefully affects self and other is determined by the investments of external forces:

> Spinoza in an extremely profound theory wanted every quantity of force to correspond to a capacity for being affected. A body would have all the more force so far as it could be affected in a greater number of ways. It is this capacity that either measures the force of a body or expresses its power. . . . the capacity for being affected does not necessarily mean passivity but affectivity. (Deleuze 1976:94–95)

Such a cathected body assumes not one form but as many forms as there are powers orienting it. It passes back and forth between subject and object positions, because it has internalized these positions as interlocking poles of the self/other power relation. Power applied to this factored body at the very least empowers the body to simulate this application. Spinoza's model suggests that the mimetic formation of the body by external forces is an open-ended and fecund process that is sustained by subjective practice that acts on and transforms the normative character of the original fixation.

The intersection of forces (political practices) coheres into an economy of the body. The body is a cumulative effect of exchanges between agonistic forces.[15] Economy here speaks to both the production and regulation of subject positions through transformative exchange. Nietzschean economy treats exchange as the recursive passage of the subject into alterity and the mimetic formation of the subject by alterity. Exchange historicizes the subject, fixing it and unfixing it into determinate but manifold forms. The subject as a definable site is the result of the unstable convergence of forces. The subject is the economic effect and self-reflexive framing of accumulated transactions between bodies.

> Economy is a metaphor for energy . . . where two opposed forces playing against each other constitute the so-called identity. . . . Economy is not reconciliation of opposites but rather a maintaining of disjunctions. Identity constituted by difference is economy. (Spivak 1976:xliii)

Foucault's analyses looked to one side of this economic formation—the application of force to the body. But even in this instance, power only attains efficacy by functioning *as an action upon the action of another*. Power is the formation of agency, and in Foucault's thought it was the agency of the body that is both presupposed and formed by power. In the Nietzschean framework, agency is manifold and reversible. Magnified and even fetishized by the investment of forces, the body is never fully determined by a singular static force. This would remove the body from history. The historicized and historicizing body is a pluralized site of torsion and contestation. But it is not a passive site. Exteriority folds the body, but agency, as a self-reflexive framing of force, subjectivates exteriority and refolds the body. It is not only a matter of what history does to the body but what subjects do with what history has done to the body (to paraphrase Sartre).

If the body is an economic grid, a point of transaction, it is because it is fetishized by the exchanges between antagonistic forces that require a fixed body in order to become present to each other through a shared terrain. The body conjeals the respective practices and codes of oppositional forces. In Foucault's model, the inmate is bifurcated through the internalization of alien disciplinary representations of the body and the self. He internalizes the application of alien force onto his body; the action of the Other is metaphorized as his own activity:

> A real subjection is born mechanically from a fictitious relation.
> . . . He who is subjected to a field of visibility and who knows it,
> assumes responsibility for the constraints of power; he makes
> them play spontaneously upon himself; he inscribes in himself the
> power relation in which he simultaneously plays both roles; he be-
> comes the principle of his own subjection. (Foucault 1979:202–3)

The state reproduces itself by transcribing alterity. In this situation the Other (of the state) is always the detached part of the state that has been invested with alterity. The state recuperates itself in the Other by techniques of violent extraction and ideological consumption. But this construction of the Other (by the state) is a transfer of force, an empowering investiture of alterity, that can be played back against the state, so that the "copy" can affect the "model."

Foucault does not acknowledge that it is precisely the *self-bifurcation* of the prisoner, the mimesis of alterity, that is the basis of prison resistance and revolt. The body as the terminal locus of power also defines the place for the redirection and reversal of power. In revolt, the prisoner *also* bifurcates and objectifies the body as an instrument of violence. The prisoner's capacity to resist exploits the principle of auto-domination and auto-punition that Foucault identifies with panoptic penal regimes. In assuming "responsibility for the constraints of power" and "making" them play spontaneously upon himself, *he inscribes himself into a power relation* (Foucault 1979:202–3). This relation both objectifies and subjugates the prisoner but also involves the subjectivation of power as exteriority. The formation of the subject and the somatic manipulation of political technologies become a single process. Foucault identifies the mimesis of empowered otherness as the principle of self-subjugation, but mimesis not only repeats the model but counterfeits it. (There is no power in the panopticon outside of it's [power's] mimesis. There is no originary act of power, only interlocking circuits of mirrored replication.) Subversive mimesis (see Cahn 1984, Taussig 1987, Buck-Morss 1989) subjects the "model" to the detours and diversions of simulation which can detach mimetic practice from any external or originary reference. This detachment, this transformation of power's re-presentation into novel political presentation, becomes a project of self-emancipation.

In the H-Blocks, the body of the resisting inmate became a shared topos that permitted the reception and recirculation of violence through its semic reorganization by both the guards and the prisoners. The actual violence of the prison regime and the redistribution and political inversion of that violence by the prisoners created a composite body whose liminality became the precondition of its symbolic fecundity. The prisoner's body became the mimetic site in which the violence of the guards and the counterdefilements of the prisoners were made commensurate, and this established the body as the invarient for all political valuation and exchange in the prison.

The H-Block narratives contain the prisoners' tacit recognition that what was done to their bodies by the prison and what they did with their bodies to the prison encompass an experience that cannot be incorporated into their traditional political ideology. "We recognize ourselves that nobody who's not actually been there knows what it was like. . . . I remember telling people who were always talking about the 'protests' we were in, 'Hold on a minute! This was more than a fuckin' 'protest,' this was a way of life for us!' " (5.6). And from another Blanketman, "The H-Blocks broke all your inhibitions about your body. It made you more aware of your body" (5.34).

5.14   The H-Blocks changed the whole way you thought about your body. . . . From the moment we hit the H-Block we had used our bodies as a protest weapon. It came from the understanding that the Brits were using our bodies to break us. (PIRA)

The ex-inmates of the H-Blocks as well as veterans of the interrogation centers admit that in negotiating these spaces of domination they deploy their bodies like weapons. This analogy between the political instrumentation of the body and the gun is significant. It establishes the weapon and the body as both central and interchangeable political artifacts of paramilitary culture. The cognitive structure of the weapon as a medium of political exchange and historical intervention informed the paramilitaries' self-codification of their bodies as political instruments. The handling of weapons, "the doings," or "gear" in paramilitary cognition is linked to an anomalous domain of political performance in which empowerment and victimage are intertwined (see chapter 4).

The gun, as the body in the H-Blocks, is associated with an admixture of active and passive states of being and nonbeing. The use of the gun is both the highest expression of the voluntary and the involuntary. The weapon artifact is essentially a limen, a Janus-faced gateway into historical mutation and social alterity.

Isomorphic to the H-Block body as a polluted-polluting political instrument is the recirculated weapon. Paramilitaries store active weapons in arms "dumps" or "camels' humps" as they are known in the local rhyming slang. These weapons are redistributed to active service units as they go on operations. The arms dumps are both functional methods of storing the armament "capital" of the paramilitary unit and expressive of the paramilitary's need to maintain a sanitizing distance between himself and the tools of his practice. The gun that has been used on operations, that has been recirculated back and forth between active service units and their arms dumps, is termed a "dirty" weapon because of its accumulation of violence. Paramilitaries view the use of a "dirty" weapon on an operation with distaste. They like even less being caught in possession of a dirty weapon. Dirty weapons can be weapons used by others within the same organization or used by the same paramilitary on previous operations. The ballistic record of such a weapon is essentially a history that can link the weapon handler with operations distant in time and space. Paramilitaries are very familiar with the histories of their unit's dirty weapons. The incremental "dirtiness" of the recirculated weapon encodes a history of violence that endows the weapon with an artifactual status and a reified autonomy. The weapon carries both empowerment and victimage within its own cognitive structure. The perceived "dirtiness" of the well-used weapon and the anomalous reversible violence that the contact with any weapon is seen to generate involve valuations that informed the manipulation of the body as a weapon in the "Dirty Protest."[16]

The weapon is the composite construct of the interaction of antagonistic forces; its "dirtiness" is a code for its historical relation to such exchanges. It bears the trace of the Other and mediates the political agent and the Other. The body in the H-Blocks is "dirty" to the extent that it also bears the trace of the Other, that it is not purely proper to the self but is the place where self and Other come into contact and exchange affects. If the state practiced a forensics of the weapon, then the Blanketmen engaged in a forensics of the contested body. To the same extent that the penal regime left traces of itself on the outside and inside of the body, the Blanketmen left scatological traces of the body on the prison.

The imprisoned body participated in the multivalence associated with weapon use outside the prison space. In both performative domains a curious reversal occurs. The self is sacrificed, sublated to the political instrument which gains a significative and performative autonomy, yet at the same time the political instrument, the artifact of violence, becomes increasingly fragmented, polysemic, and liminal. Instead of a unidirectional vehicle for goal realization, it becomes a dialogically structured nexus of opposing actions, values, and discourses.

The Blanketmen's subsequent strategies of resistance were predicated upon the anomalous structuration of their bodies in prison. The naked body and its biology, which had suddenly become a passive source of defilement and coercion with the new levels of harassment and violence, had to be reinvented as an actively defiling and therefore power-laden agency, thus restoring the political potency of the prisoners.

The Blanketmen had denied juridical order to the prison, and the guards reciprocated by denying biological order to the Blanketmen. But rather than rejecting this imposition, the Blanketmen turned it against the guards and the prison regime. The somatic defilement that was supposed to signify their vulnerability became the basis for empowerment. The excreta went up on the cell wall as a historical record of the conditions of their imprisonment. Like the shaman or sacred clown who ingests polluting menstrual blood, urine, or feces and transforms these substances into power-laden medicine, the Blanketmen recodified their feces as the basis for an exclusive cultural identity and a renewable cultural power (Makarius 1970:47–50).

Through the mirror searches, the prison regime had turned the prisoners' bodies inside out. So the Blanketmen reciprocated by imprinting this defiled interior of their bodies onto their cell walls. The defiled prison cell became a symbolic appendage of the violated body of the prisoners, a cognitive mapping and a spatial representation of the captive body under the impact of H-Block discipline.

The individual Blanketmen could tolerate his own defiled cell, but when he was moved into the newly vacated cells of other Blanketmen on the Dirty Protest, he found the alien fecal matter in the cell revolting. In a negative fashion, this reaction demonstrated the extent to which the personal defilement of the state's cell rendered the latter an organic extension of the individual prisoner's body.

The Dirty Protest did not constitute a resolution of the Blanketmen's situation. On the contrary, it accentuated the cyclical and cathartic performance of institutional violence and magnified the liminality of the protestors beyond all previous levels. They now lived outside of all "civilizational" standards of biological order. The Blanketmen had propelled themselves into an alien condition, the cognitive and biological implications of which they could not anticipate or control.

The Dirty Protest finalized the transformation of prison resistance from instrumental political action with objective goals toward a systematic cognitive and cultural otherness. No one expected to live in these conditions for five years. There was a tacit expectation among the Blanketmen that the fundamental disordering of their physical environment had set a biological clock ticking. As they realized the full implications of living in a scatological ecology, the prisoners initially experienced the Dirty Protest as a death ritual, a final act that would resolve their predicament in a biological eschatology of disease and possible death. Their condition of fecal disorder was to be an escape from the suspensions of juridical time—a fundamental structure of their oppression—and an entry into the resolving finitude of biological time.

5.15   We had sent out on the visits to get medical opinions and all. We were told we would get scabies, dermatitis, dysentary, scurvy, blood poisoning, and all sorts of infections. We used to picture ourselves being carried out on stretchers and taken to hospital with all sorts of foreign diseases. For the first time it hit us that we might die in prison, that we would never get out. As soon as the No Wash Protest started, the screws isolated a wing to be used as a hospital to fit large numbers. It was never used. They must have been expecting the same thing we were expecting. (PIRA)

5.16   At the time everybody would've thought we'd soon come down with all types of strange diseases, but apparently your sweat washed out your pores. Three things were very common: worms, maggots, and dysentary. You didn't feel like moving no matter what you ate; it would just run through you. The grub was horrible because they used to halve all portions. They really starved you, deliberately trying to break you. Conditions were bad but it made you all the more determined. (INLA)

As they transgressed customary biological boundaries and adapted to the scatological ecology of their cells, the Blanketmen began to extract political lessons from their relative biological immunity and survival. The scatological began to cohere into a system of positive meaning that defined their relationship to the prison and to the outside world. The fecal body and cell began to function as an encoding mechanism from which a variety of political texts could be mined:

5.17   Through all the dirt and shite everywhere, eating food without washing your hands, in general nobody suffered any sort of diseases, body rashes, or lice in the hair. We used to say to ourselves that maybe the screws were lacing the food with antibiotics or chemicals. We had heard about a group of Jews in the concentration camp, they were all psychiatrists. The point was that none of them had washed their teeth for four or five years, yet no one in this particular group ever got a tooth ache, whereas the rest of the camp their teeth were rotting abscesses. It had all been put down to the frame of mind of that particular group. They had the will to resist which kept them in some degree of health. And I always wondered if there was a parallel between us and them Jews. (PIRA)

5.18 One day a TV crew came in, coming up the yard. We had wire grills on the windows, like a box built right around it. There was plenty of activity in the yard. I'm up clinging to the wire trying to screw out through the wire to see out what was coming on. Now when we had gotten people to come up from the media, in case they weren't allowed to speak to us we would've shouted at them from the window whatever we could get across. I started shouting: "We're getting tortured, we're getting brutalized." Your woman directing the TV camera pointed to my window and your man comes over with the camera and a big boom microphone. Now, in those sort of conditions, with the isolation, when someone comes toward you with a TV camera it's frightening. I sort of flipped and as the word went up the whole wing was also flipping. I was standing on a heating pipe and the pipe was roasting and I was dancing up and down. You had that much in your head that you knew you had to get out, and there was that much in your head that you knew the boys wanted you to get out. My mind was flying from one point to the next. At one point I said: "And we're going to beat the bastards back into the sea." Behind me I hear my cell mate going into hysterics [laughter]. I jumped off the pipe like a scalded rat. I was panicking. They moved away from the window and they came into the block then. When my door opened I near dropped dead because they were coming in with these big TV lights into the cell. I felt like a rat in the corner. Thinking: "What is this," running like an animal in the corner when the cage is opened. When they went in, it was just "You're civilization. You're people who are not obviously biased against me. You're not obvious enemies." Living outside civilization, that you weren't functioning in the real world was something you were conscious of the whole time. (PIRA)

5.19 It's amazing how you just got immune to the shit. All these assholes coming in from the Board of Visitors, British M.P.s, all the big wigs, Clement Freud.[17] All these guys on the outside who have such a high idea of themselves. They brought Humphrey Atkin's wife [then secretary of state for Northern Ireland] in to see the cells. They were going around opening cell doors without warning as if we were animals in the zoo. They opened one cell and this guy Leonard Fern was sitting shiting in the corner and the door opened on him. He made no attempt to move, and he just looked up at her: "What about you, Mrs. Atkins?" [informal Ulster greeting]. Her whole fuckin' facade just sort of collapsed. She just shut the cell door and left without a word. (PIRA)

5.20   At one stage they were moving us very quickly from one cell to another so the cells didn't get in too bad a state. I found myself in a cell of my own and I'm saying to myself, "How am I going to get these walls covered. There was only one of me and they would be moving me soon. They would steam clean the walls and spray paint over the wall, with white paint covering the Irish and all the political slogans scratched in. So I shat in the pot and put some water into it diluting it. I started to bang it around the walls, and I was looking up at the ceiling. The shite was all splashing over me from the ceiling. At that moment the door opened and in came a priest, the Prison Officer, and the Governor of the jail. And here I was standing with the pot covered with shit. They stopped dead and just looked at me all frozen like. Finally the priest says to me: "There's a whole lot going off the protest."

"I'm not going off it."

He was looking at the ceiling shaking his head. "I don't know what they're going to do with you."

I looked down at the pot full of watered-down shite and all I said was, "More miles to the gallon!" They had come in to try to wreck me with the story that somebody had left the protest. And here I was standing on one leg with what was left in the pot and the rest of it dripping off the ceiling around me. That was it. They shook their heads and closed the door. (PIRA)

The H-Blocks with their all-white decor and their cellular incarceration were an architectural continuation of the sensory deprivation experiences of the interrogation cells at Castlereagh. For the Blanketmen, this architectural continuity signified a political continuum. The all-white interrogation cells of Castlereagh had been designed for coerced confession, betrayal, and the conversion of the paramilitary into an informer. The monochromatic color scheme signified the interrogation space as a topos of political sterilization. The H-Blocks shared in this architectural semantic, a pattern fully recognized by the Blanketmen.[18] The whitewashed cell, in paramilitary culture, had taken on an overdetermined political significance because of the accumulated experiences of interrogation and the H-Blocks. The Blanketmen were now able to shit on this white history, this blank law.

Mechanical Bears

The material conditions of imprisonment and the human body had been invested with an overpowering symbolic charge that heightened the negativity of matter. Intensification of material debasement in the prison increased the level of symbolic investment and semic transmutation by the Blanketmen. The animation of the material structures of imprisonment and the concentrated flow of symbolic investment to these templates were accentuated by the dead time that accumulated between moments of heightened confrontations—those interstitial periods before and after the enactment of violence when life in the cells settled down to the monotony of tombs.

It was against this background of dead time that the prison as a physical entity seemed suddenly to come alive, to take on a malevolent persona that was unleashed in the particularized violence of the guards. The guards themselves seemed to recognize this incorporation of their individual identities into a personification of the prison. The prisoners' name for the prison guards, besides "screws," was "bears." The most repressive group of guards, who trooped on and off the wings in military formation, *called themselves* the "mechanical bears," as if to signify their incorporation as components in the automaton of violence.

The two groups, the guards and the prisoners, despite their unrelenting antagonism to each other, rapidly learned to speak the same biosymbolic language. This co-acquisition of a biosymbolic idiom of physical/political action facilitated the distribution of violence through commonly constructed yet ideologically bifurcated symbols. The dissemination of a biological idiom by both the guards and the prisoners was the central impetus behind the mimetic reproduction of violence/defilement in the prison. The prison guards' reaction to the Dirty Protest took the form of strategies of literal and symbolic purification—literal because their tactics involved the forced washing of prisoners and the cleaning of cells by high-pressured steam hoses, and symbolic because, as in the mirror searches, these apparently instrumental interventions attempted to simulate and restore penal rationality.

Forced washes and the wing shifts that allowed the prison staff to clean a dirty wing while moving prisoners to a clean wing grew to be the most dreaded experiences in the H-Blocks. The wing shifts combined biological decontamination and the cathartic dynamics of brutal violence with the physical erasure of symbols of resistance. The forced washings and wing shifts were in effect replays of institutional rites of induction. They were failed initiations, endlessly reenacted in a futile attempt to incorporate the prisoners. The penal regime had thus been reduced by the prisoners' resistance to its most elementary administrative procedures. As failed replications of once efficacious bureaucratic norms, the forced washes and the wing shifts signified the demise of any functional form of prison administration in the protesting cell blocks. They were rhetorical performances that reduced prison administration to cyclical violence. These practices re-created, in an almost stereotyped and certainly exaggerated form, an idealized iconography of penal hegemony. They should be appreciated as reenactments, and they belong to the same genre as the mirror searches.

5.21   They always kept three wings full and one wing empty, and when they wanted to clean your wing they shifted you. One of the most violent wing shifts happened the morning that Governor Miles was assassinated by the IRA.[19] We were due for wing shift that morning. That morning at seven o'clock you could hear all the screws of the block filing into the yards and from there into the circle. You could hear the gates being locked. They all gathered in the circle and they began beating the batons against the bars, "CHUK!—CHUK!—CHUK!—CHUK!—CHUK! CHUK!" They started beating the batons slowly against the bars in a steady rhythm, then it gets louder and louder and faster and faster until it builds up to a crescendo. You hear that noise and the psychological buildup begins. It's the trigger for fear. People thinking. "Oh fuck, here they come!" You hear the opening and the closing of the gates, getting closer. You hear the sound of the bolt locks shooting, opening the cell door, getting nearer. On a real bad wing shift you would know what it was going to be like because you could hear beatings of the ones before you. You heard the batons working away at the top of the wing; they would then come down and took each prisoner individually. They'd tell you to collect your "personal belongings," which would be a set of rosary beads, your towel, and your Bible. On this day they set the examination table at the top of the wing in the middle of the landing. You were grabbed by the arms, and the two screws would run you toward it. Your towel is ripped off so you're naked. You're runned until you're slammed by the waist into this rectangular table, which forces you to bend over. There's the table and the sponge with the mirror for the anal search. You're ordered to spread-eagle over the mirror. You refuse to comply so they kick you down over it. Your anus is searched. A torch shined up your anus, your mouth, your nose, and in your ears. When you come out at the top of the wing you turn the corner out of the airlock gate and into the next airlock gate. There would be a bunch of screws waiting for you around that corner. You had to run the gauntlet. From that point on, it's just punches and kicks until you get to your new cell. The morning Governor Miles was shot the screws pulled their batons out, and some of them were carrying mops and broom handles.

One of the worst wing shifts was when Prison Officer Terry was executed by the IRA.[20] He was in charge of our wing. On that shift four men ended up in the hospital. Mc-Cluskey got his nose smashed. They smashed Martin Hurson's leg continuously between the gates and broke his leg. Hector McNee had been shot. He used a walking stick for the shot leg. They took the walking stick off of him and beat him over the head with it. Clinkie Clarke was dragged in between the showers and the sinks and came out with internal bleeding. (PIRA)

5.22   The reason wing shifts were so violent was that the screws in large groups never had access to us to beat us. There was only the few screws on the wing doing their particular duty tour. But for the wing shifts, you had upward of thirty screws from all over the blocks coming in for the wing shifts. This was heavy-pressure time. They all had access to you then. Outside of that we never left the cells except for wing searches. The wing shift was definitely part of the breaking process. You knew ultimately that every three weeks you had to go through this. That this was a constant feature. There was this constant living on the edge of your nerves because of the shifts.

The violence of the wing shifts was specifically linked to incidents of violence on the outside. In the aftermath of Warrenpoint where eighteen British paratroopers died or when Mountbatten was assassinated, the wing shifts on the morning after were particularly violent.[21] They had control over the timing of the wing shifts. After Miles was killed and after Warrenpoint, the wing shifts were brought up in schedule just for that. After Warrenpoint they were beating their batons, shouting and yelling, "Bring on the Provo bastards!" You would hear the table being brought out, and the next thing you would hear was the "Whoop!" of the metal detector running over the body for contraband. What you heard from the first cell was always a big indication of the level of violence that morning. You would hear them come down the corridor. As soon as you got outside of the cell door the first indication would be the door opened out to the right. You might have seen two screws standing in front of you, but over behind the door there could have been four screws. As soon as you stepped out you would have gotten a big "Whack!" in the back of the head. You'd have hit the corridor with the force of it. They would get into you then and there. Right then and there the rest of the wing knew what the shift would be like. As you got up to the end of the corridors there was this wash area and a wall with a blind corner. Now around this blind corner there would be a whole group of screws standing there waiting for you. Their favorite was spread-eagling you against the roasting hot radiator. They would cook you on it.

You could always tell when a wing shift was on from certain signs that was used by the screws as a psychological pressure buildup. They would give you the impression that a wing shift was on the way even if one wasn't, because they knew how it affected people. Your first sign of an impending wing shift was no water. Your water container was taken out of your cell at 7:00 A.M. at the first count. Your first indication of the wing shift was if the water container wasn't filled and brought back to your cell. You'd know then that a wing shift was coming. Though sometimes they would do that and not shift you. (PIRA)

5.23   They had to get a doctor in to lie that we had lice to use it as an excuse to force wash us, which was an excuse to batter us. There was no single piece of the prison that wasn't used to break us. They all colluded. This lice doctor we called "Mengele"; the other doctor they used was the one who examined us after interrogations. The whole approach of that doctor during the forced washes—they would drag the men out like cattle, kicking men up the wing—the doctor would be standing there in a white coat and two jumped-up screws beside him pretending to be medical orderlies. This man is supposed to be a doctor and he's standing there watching us get beat, holding his dispenser stick and having a conversation with the two orderlies as if nothing was happening. There were guys getting dragged, kicked, and batoned up the wing, and he would look at you from a distance of ten feet and just say, "Lice infested, shave him. Lice infested, shave him. Lice infested, shave him," over and over again. That formality had to be filled. (PIRA)

5.24   In the forced washes you were held down and your head was shaved and your body hair was shaved off. You were forced into a bath and scrubbed with stiff brushes. People had the skin lifted off of them. You were dragged out of the bath, and then they held you up naked and painted you with a solution that was meant to stop infections. It all happened with a set pattern. Two screws, Billy Hood and "Vomit Face" (we had names for all the screws), would always soak the beds when they were gathering the piss pots. They came around one morning; I heard the door bolts being shot up the wing and a splash and a scream. I thought they were soaking the beds. Next door the same, and when they got to the third cell I heard someone yelling, "It's roasting!" They were throwing boiling hot water on people in the cells. They worked their way down the wing, and when they got to my cell they yelled out the number of the cell next to me and opened my door. It was to catch you off guard. I was standing with my back to the door and the blanket wrapped around me so the effect would be minimized.

"Vomit Face" tore the blanket from me, and Billy Hood said, "This is just to show you that you can't indulge in these bad habits. This isn't punishment, this is corrective medicine. We're just here to ensure that you tidy up your bad habits."

And he fucked this pail of boiling hot water, and it hit me on the back. I had sworn I wouldn't scream, but it near lifted the skin off me and I screamed, "Jesus!" I could feel the blisters forming on my back. (PIRA)

The medicalization of discipline inverted the form/content relations between the theater of domination and rationalized prison administration. Rationalized administration had from the beginning incarnated itself in the performance of violence and the stylized theatrics of domination. These displays functioned as the effective surface for rationalized administration. The advent of various practices of decontamination accelerated the retrograde transformation of administration into a ceremonial camouflage for cathartic and cyclical violence. The wing shifts and forced washes were manufactured events that reinforced social solidarity and institutional identity among the prison guards. It was their carnival. The guards gathered from all the different prison blocks; they beat out the ceremonial tatoo of the batons and arranged themselves in various covert locations, which transformed the prison corridor into a labyrinth of sudden beatings.

Perhaps the strongest indication of the emptying of rationalized administration into a purely rhetorical procedure was the deployment of medical paradigms in these ritual purifications. The prison doctor who stood beside the examination table verifying imaginary lice infestations in order to sanction violent decontamination was a figurehead, a token holdover from the prescriptive and rehabilitative norms of modern penology. The doctor provided a medical legitimation for collective violence in the wake of the almost total delegitimation and dysfunction of the rehabilitative paradigm in the prison.

The medical caricature of the mirror examination imparted its logic to the wing shifts and forced washes. Like the mirror searches, the wing shifts and forced washes were exercises in the ideological imagination of the prison guards. The new wings to which the Blanketmen were moved soon became dirty. The effects of the washing and the chemical baths were also temporary. In attempting to colonize the biological system of the prisoners, the guards had unleased a flood of defilement, an unstoppable momentum from the very biological processes the guards had sought to limit and manipulate. The prisoners enacted an ecological revenge. There was no way to limit the flow of excreta, urine, or the accompanying stench into the prison short of the death of the prisoner.

At this juncture, the guards knew that the violence of the wing shifts would at most drive a few men off the protest without ending the protest itself. The functional gains of such actions were paltry. The very absence of such gains verifies the extent to which their carnival was a temporary respite from the perceived hardships of guarding the "Blanket Blocks." For a brief period, the prison officers took back their prison in a theatrical exercise by which they gained the temporary confirmation of inserting shaven and decontaminated prisoners into clean cells.

The prison guards were caught up in events and indeed became prisoners of their fabrications. This can be confirmed in the recollections of a prison welfare officer at the H-Blocks who found himself caught between the internal warfare of the Blanketmen and the guards. In the following testimony the clash between rehabilitation and the prison as a site for cathartic violence is readily apparent. This clash should not obscure the interrelationship between rehabilitative norms and institutional violence. I cannot hold with the view that the violence of the H-Blocks was a deviation from penological paradigms of corrective training. The choice of the prison as a strategic topos for counterinsurgency intervention was not an accidental or fortuitous choice.

5.25 Among the staff it was understood that it was government policy to lower the status of political inmates. The status of prison officers in Northern Ireland society outside the prison is very low. They manage their identities by subordinating inmates to them. It was in the interest of the prison officers, in terms of their own status within the prison, to put political prisoners down who showed a much higher level of resistance than ODCs [Ordinary Decent Criminal]. For the prison officer the major difference between the ODCs and the political prisoners dealt with the negotiation of their living conditions in prison. With the ODCs the prison officer had a lot of power because negotiations were covert and were transacted between the officer and the criminal leaders of the ODC population on an almost one-to-one basis. The negotiations between staff and paramilitary leaders were overt. The whole basis of staff/inmate transactions were transformed. A lot of the very distasteful and bizarre negotiations were absent, which meant a loss of individual power for the prison officer. So there was a built-in need to lower the political prisoner. It was fortunate that this conformed with government policy to criminalize political prisoners. There were explicit instructions to this effect, but it met with the disposition of the prison officers.

The instructions to break the prisoners came from the highest levels of government because the policy was criminalization to be implemented by prison staffs. The actual term was "conform," to make them "conforming prisoners." There were in place formalized mechanisms for breaking down the morale. Various blocks had different regimes or systems. A lot depended on the Assistant Governor and the chief prison officers. In comparison to English prison staff, the Northern Ireland staff weren't that professional. English staff would adhere to official rules much more than Northern Ireland staff. The local staff in addition were 95 percent Protestant, and that was a major factor in the handling of Republican prisoners. In turn, there was a covert understanding between Loyalist paramilitaries and prison officers that to the extent that they were Protestant and living in Loyalist communities or coming from communities that Protestant paramilitaries came from, that pressure of a violent kind could be exerted on prison officers.[22] The Republicans obviously did not have this kind of leverage.

When it got to the stage of the Blanket Protest, things like the prisoner's nakedness became a means for discrediting the individual. He would have to ask permission to go to the toilet. Permission may have been refused. He'd have been laughed at, his nakedness forcibly exposed. Then the Blanketmen were taken on stupid trips to see the Governor. A naked man would have to stand outside the Governor's door for an hour with his face to the wall. Humiliation was a big weapon. Prisoners were constantly propelled into an infantile role. You could see the Dirty Protest as virtually resistance to toilet training in a bizarre way. . . .

The harassment was seen by the upper echelons of the administration as a temporary situation. "The quicker we break the men, the quicker we can bring in a humane system." It was seen as a transitory step toward normalization, the acceptance of the prison uniform and of prison rules in their totality. They may have been naïve. I think it depended on the psychologist who was advising them. I've heard that everything that went on in the H-Blocks were reported directly back to London, that Governor Miles was a figurehead, and that there were various key people, government ministers, psychologists, and sociologists who were handling the situation.

Brutality and mistreatment was justified by many prison officers as getting the thing resolved as expeditiously as possible. If we make life totally intolerable for the next week it will be over and we'll go back to normal. As time went by, more and more frustration set in and more and more pressure. The abuses became more excessive. Yet they had to keep the goal in sight. "We'll win next week" was a common thing to hear from the prison officers in the beginning. Obviously morale among the staff eroded as the weeks and months went by and it went into years. The fact that the prisoners were convinced that they were going to win and their convictions in the righteousness of the cause constituted pressure on the way prison officers treated inmates.

Then there was demoralization stemming from the outside. People in the Loyalist community were also protesting prison conditions. The prison officers felt isolated in their own communities. They tended to escape the consequences of their violence mainly through drinking, through cyclical destructive cycles. There was a fairly high dropout rate. One way they had to avoiding it was transferring men to the compounds or to Crumlin Road prison where the H-Block type of situation didn't exist. There was special leave given and financial allowances, but the marital breakdown rate among prison officers was extremely high. Money was the big incentive for staying on. You had prison officers earning the same salaries as a general practitioner. It was an attitude of making hay while the sun shined. There were some officers who, because of community isolation or marital situations, felt more at home inside the prison.

During the Dirty Protest you never really got accustomed to the stench and the atmosphere of the place. For a prison officer who was in for a twelve-hour shift and who then went home, he would usually have to spend about four hours trying to get the smell off of his uniform and his body and then go back into that situation twelve hours later. That became a daily barrier that he had to overcome, both returning home and entering back into the prison. The inmates didn't have that adjustment. You could actually see, as I saw and the inmates must have seen, the revulsion of the prison officers as they were coming onto their shifts. The smell would stick to his uniform and to his body and was hard to get off. Even the disinfectant they used on the wings had a very penetrating smell which made the situation worse. The prison officers did feel defiled because it extended into their private lives, their bodies, their sense of cleanliness, their marital relations, and their relations to their children. It became a personal conflict. Physical contact with the prisoner and the cell was abhorrent. It was bound to be a factor in the violence against the inmates. The prison officers were alienated, but unlike the inmates they had much more limited outlets for venting that alienation.

They could not admit the role of their violence and humiliations in escalating the protest. "Prisoners brought this on themselves." They played no role in the conditions that brought the Blanket or the Dirty Protest. These were seen as self-inflicted conditions. It was the same attributions as government policy.[23]

At the same time the psychology of the Dirty Protest was so alien to them: "Human beings don't do this to themselves." They didn't understand it. They didn't understand the group solidarity; they didn't understand the culture, the Gaelic. They didn't understand how group morale could be kept so high. They couldn't understand the conviction. The worse things became, so the officer felt, the more the inmates liked it. Some of the relationships of the men who shared cells together were closer than what they [the guards] had seen in their own marriages. There was very close bonding through the suffering, and the prison officer didn't understand it. I personally saw the merging of entire personalities based on that sharing.

There was one event that stuck in my mind. I had a very good relationship with one of the Republican OCs who would come into my office for conversations. I would always offer him cigarettes while we were talking. He was on the Blanket. The Prison Officer used to always look in on us. It was always a very mysterious process for them what went on in the Prison Welfare Office. The POs [Prison Officers] would be constantly looking in through the spyhole of my office door and on several occasions would burst into my office on some pretext. Now there was nothing in prison rules that said you couldn't give a cigarette to an inmate. But this prisoner, rather than get me into trouble when the PO intruded, would put the cigarette out with his bare foot! That always stayed in my mind. What sort of bizarre bloody system am I involved in when a man has to do that. To protect you from the system because you gave him a cigarette. From the staff viewpoint that would be seen as clear symbolic collusion with the prisoners.

A colleague of mine went to someone very high up in the prison administration during the Dirty Protest, and he said: "Do you realize that prison staff are going to be killed?"

The reply was: "They're expendable, what are you worrying about?"

After that I got out. "Fuck this game, I'm not in this league." (Ex-Prison Welfare Officer, Cages and the H-Blocks)

The above account describes the devolution from a long-term strategy of rationalized administration to what appeared as the day-to-day spontaneous performance of violence. The prison officers initially rationalized their violence "as a transitory stage toward normalization . . . as getting the thing resolved as expeditiously as possible" (5.25). As this situation moved into a long-term struggle with the Blanketmen, the guards "could not admit the role of their violence and humiliations in escalating the protest. Prisoners brought this on themselves. These were seen as self-inflicted conditions. . . . From the point of view of the prison officers there was no sense of continuity or totality they were working toward on a day-to-day basis" (5.25).

The guards' denial of accountability for their own violence demonstrates the extent to which the polluting aura of the inmates as Catholics, Republicans, terrorists, and No Wash protestors had reached such metaphysical proportions that the guards experienced their own violence as an organic elaboration of the defiling body of the Blanketmen. The guards had not only been reduced to functions of the disciplinary machinery of the prison regime, but they had also become functions of the machinery of pollution that emanated from the body of the prisoner. To describe the prisoners' conditions as totally "self-inflicted," as the guards did, was not only a mystification of the actual dynamics of the prison situation but the guards' inadvertent admission that their own agency had become a function of their ideological construction of the prisoners.

The mystification embodied in the notion of "self-inflicted" violence signaled the elevation of miasma to the reified origin of all action and signification in the prison. The guards, in their violence, saw themselves as passive registers of this autonomous miasma emanating from the prisoners.

The impact of the Dirty Protest came to encompass the total social situation of the prison guards inside out outside the prison:

> For the prison officer who was in for a twelve-hour shift. . . . He would usually have to spend four hours trying to get the smell off of his uniform and his body and then go back into that situation twelve hours later. That became a daily barrier he had to overcome, both returning home and entering back into the prison. . . . The prison officers did feel defiled because it extended into their private lives, their bodies, their sense of cleanliness, their marital relations, and their relations to their children. (5.25)

In this proliferation of pollution, a reversal had occurred. The prison guards had sought to dominate the prisoners through colonization of the prisoners' bodies. The protesting Blanketmen now determined the working conditions and private lives of the prison guards through the contagious emissions of the very bodies that were the object of domination. The guard who spent four hours every working day attempting to rid himself of the stench of the H-Blocks, and who had to bring that stench home to his family, had become an inadvertent emissary of the Blanketmen.

In their attempts to encode the bodies of the inmates, the prison guards had transmuted their own bodies into a text that displayed the signs of unavoidable polluting contact. This process worked its social effects on the prison guards, who were gradually isolated from family and ethnic community. They were inserted deeper into the closed systems of the prison situation, the only social institution in which they participated in an unambiguous, fixed social relation.

The intensified incorporation of the guards into the negative space of the prison mystified the Blanketmen. In the following descriptions the status of the guards as intimates or even doubles of the prisoners is implicit in the prisoners' fascination with the "screws":

5.26   We would wonder about the screws. What sort of people are they. You open that door and there they were in the morning. All your waking hours they were there, and they closed the wing at night. We used to ask ourselves what type of existence to voluntarily imprison yourself. One fuckin' screw, he was there at 7:00 A.M. on the dot. He must have deliberately got up early and rushed into work to get your mattress ten minutes early because he knew it affected you. We knew he lived in Ballyclare. He had to arrive at the front gate at 6:30 to get through their security systems. He must be getting out of bed at least 5:30 A.M. to come in. He stays to seven o'clock that night, goes for his dinner, and is on the wing to nine o'clock that night. He never left our wing till nine o'clock. By the time he gets home it was 10:00 P.M. He is knackered, goes to bed at 11:00 P.M. The next morning he's up at half five again.

We were sitting there constantly plotting what their lives must be like. We realized that the difference between us and them as far as the prison goes was that they go home at night to sleep and we didn't. Some of them couldn't even do that because when the RA was stiffing them they had to move into the camp. Some of them were working double shifts. I used to wonder what do they spend the money on. By the time they get home, there's no pub, no crack, just straight to bed. We were their crack [entertainment]! (PIRA)[24]

Many Blanketmen also recognized the symbiosis they were caught up in. If the prisoner had become the central object of the screw's pleasure, what had the screw become for the prisoner? These prisoners admitted with horror the dependence of their political identities and motivations upon the figure of the screw:

5.27   I hated the screws. I would have sconed them no problem. Used to live for the fuckin' day that I got out. I would have taken three days over a screw before I killed him. I was wrapped up in the hatred thing, and it wasn't political motivation at all. (INLA)

5.28 The hate, I found out what hatred was. I used to talk about hate on the outside, but it was superstitious, it was depersonalized. There were wee people you didn't like. But it was in there that I came face to face with the "black" hatred. It frightened the life out of me when I seen it for what it was. I thought, "Hold on. Don't let that into you mind; don't go in that direction. Because I knew that direction. It was real "black" hate. When you thought of getting your own back on the screw, how much you would enjoy it, it really frightened you. It was bogman talk, bogman thinking. You just blacked those thoughts out your mind. Looking at them ones as parts of a machine, like robots. If we can't overcome that, we're nothing. At the end of the day I knew I was smarter than the screws. But I knew the road of "black" hatred. I just got a glimpse of it. It scared the balls clean out of me. (PIRA)

5.29 You see screws would come in for the first two weeks, and you could see they couldn't understand what was going on. They tried to talk to you, to do this or that favor for you. But after two months they became the worst bastards. Then there was the hard cases. They called themselves the "mechanical bears." They were the ones who force washed ye. They used to march down the wing in military time. The senior officers who wore the white shirts were called the polar bears and the governor of the prison was the "Big Bear." When Governor Miles got whacked by the RA [IRA] we all sang "Big Bear off the air!"[25]

One of the mechanical bears was Skelly from the Shankill; he was a bigoted Orange man [Loyalist]. It was the time the RA had started sending letter bombs to the screws' wives. Now Clinkie Clarke hears Skelly coming down the wing and says, "Hey there, rat face!"

Skelly says to Clinkie: "What do you want scumbag?" because he was as cheeky as Clinkie.

Clarke says: "Hey, got your name down here on the hit list."

"So what? What do you want me to do?" He knew he was getting banged anyway. Clinkie gives Skelly his full name and address. Just letting him know they had sent his name out to the organization. Anybody else wouldn't have said anything about that to a screw because they would slaughter you with beatings.

Skelly says: "I don't give a fuck, send it out!"

Three weeks later Clarke called Skelly over. "Hey rat face, I'm just letting you know that I took your name off the hit list."

"What do you want me to do, fall down on my knees and thank you?"

Clinkie says: "I don't know whether you will or not. I put your wife's name down instead." And he gave him his wife's full name and gave a description of her.

Your man went berserk; he cracked up! "Anything happens to my wife, Clarke, you're getting done!"

And they did send her a nice letter bomb. Clarke didn't give a fuck. He done the same with Governor Miles when Miles accepted full responsibility for the mirror searches. Clarke sent the word out about Miles's admission of responsibility about having full knowledge about the level of violence, and the RA stiffed him.

A lot of the information about screws for the hit list actually came from the Orangies [Loyalist paramilitaries]. They didn't have the balls to do it. The screw to be banged might be living next door to them, and the Orangies passed the info on to the RA where they lived. (INLA)

The assassination of the prison staff by the IRA "outside" also confirmed the pivotal role of the abused bodies of the Blanketmen in a political system of generalized value equivalence and exchange. This retaliatory violence enlarged the symbolic gauge of the defiled body of the prisoner beyond the secluded space of the prison. This process anticipated the logic of the Hunger Strike, where the body of the dying hunger striker exerted a determining political presence that exceeded the structures of confinement. With the screw assassination campaign, the body of the Republican prisoner assumed a status approximating the value of the defiled Republican community in the IRA military campaign.

Techniques and Discourses of the Body

The political capacities of the body were not limited to the fecal. Various other sectors and sensory capacities of the body were reorganized into politicized zones. This vectoring of the body was the dialogical product of disciplinary interventions. The body and the cell had both been subjected to continuous assaults that attempted to reduce these spaces to one-dimensional disciplinary texts. The creation of a scatological ecology of the body and the cell recoded these interconnected appendages; from pure externalities, they became cavities that harbored opaque and resistant depths. The Blanketmen's scatological withdrawal into the cell established that recess as a relatively protective shelter.

The reconstructed body was a mask of abjection that stored a politicized and resistant interior. The prison regime had attempted to colonize the digestive and waste elimination functions of the prisoners' bodies. The Blanketmen converted the interior of the body into a zone of trickery and a medium of communication with the world outside the prison. The rectum, the foreskin, the navel, the mouth, and the nose, like the cell, became protective and sheltering recesses that repulsed the optical penetrations of the prison regime. These cavities were used to smuggle messages and other items in and out of the prison. Typical incoming cargoes were cigarette papers (used for both writing and smoking), tobacco, Parker pen refills, flints, and the occasional quartz crystal radio (especially designed by a Swedish technician for the Blanketmen).[26] IRA communiqués were written on the cigarette papers with the highly valued "Ronnie Barkers" (Parker pen refills). Proficient prisoners could fit up to four thousand words on each cigarette paper. The rolling-tobacco papers were folded as tight as possible, sometimes wrapped in silver foil, and then inserted into one of the body orifices favored by the particular prisoner. Each prisoner had his techniques for smuggling contraband and his preferred cavity. This orificial specialization was reflected in the renaming of these body parts by the prisoners. The penis and its foreskin were renamed the "fagin" after the Charles Dickens character. This was later expanded to the "faginbush" to account for the contributions of pubic hair in the hiding of contraband. The rectum was renamed the "bangle" because of its circular shape, and all smuggling that used the orifices of the body came to be known as "bangling."

5.30   I smuggled Bobby Sands' diary out [see chapter 6]. You had to wrap it in silver paper and stretch and seal it. It was all written in dead minute writing on cigarette paper. You had to bring it out in your anus, or under your lip. It was called bangling, a bangle being a circular ring or hole like your anus. A lot of that language came from the jail into the community. These days, for instance, if you have something that someone wants and you don't give to them, they'll say, "You fuckin' bangle it then!" It means stick it up your ass. (PIRA)

5.31   They never searched your belly button. I had a big belly button when I was arrested, but I can tell you, it's much bigger now! You got a cigarette paper and wrote dead minute writing. People had to use a magnifying glass on them. You'd wrap the paper dead tight and put it in your belly button. Then you would put a bit of fluff from your blanket over that to look like hair. When you went down to the visit you wore your shirt out and you would open the button as you sat talking, took the note out, put in your mouth and pass it on as you gave the "bird" a kiss. No problem, that's how it was done. (INLA)

5.32   When the screws came on the wing you had to bangle all your writing equipment, the tobacco, the striking wheel from a cigarette lighter, and the flints for lighting cigarettes. Everything you had that was of any value you bangled or fagined or foreskinned. I had a comb for my beard which was giving me skin rashes; it was part of my personal equipment, and even that had to be bangled. We called the penis a fagin from a character that was a real droopy looking and sinister fucker. Then it went from there to being called faginbush for the pubic hair. Nothing had its right name in the Blocks. Guys who bangled things under the foreskin were called hammerhead sharks because of the bulging of cigarette papers under the foreskin.

On the bangling, there was a guy who worked as Bobby Sands' aide, Malachi. He was known as "the Suitcase." Bobby Sands would go to Mass. Mass was the big time for "coms" [communiqués] and passing "Ronnie Barkers" [Parker pen refills]. Everywhere Bobby went during the Mass, right beside him was "the Suitcase." People would come up to Bobby and give him a "com." Bobby would say, "Malachi!" Bingo! He had it bangled. (PIRA)

5.33   I had to take out the list of screws for the "toppings" [assassinations]. We had this hit list, and they were giving me all this fuckin' wired-up stuff about it. So the "Dark," who never took a "com" out in his life, says to me, "You better not get caught with that. It's fuckin' *iontach, iontach tabhachtach* [very, very important]." Stick them up your nose—that's the best way. I'd rather take them out in the faginbush. That's the way I always take them out. I felt safe with my routine, and they were breaking it. But they insisted it go up my nose. It was all screws names and addresses, very dangerous thing to be caught with. I was tossing all night about it. If I fagined it and did get caught with it, I'd have the balls chewed out of me for disobeying orders. So I put the "com" up the nose. Coming out the screw says to me, "Alright, search." He shines the torch over the mirror for the anus. He tilts the head back and shines the torch in the nose. "What's that up your nose?"

I shout out in Gaelic, "They've got that fuckin' com!"[27]

He gets a hanky and says, "Blow your nose."

So I held the nostril as I blowed. He tilts the head:"It's still there."

I know the cunt will get the medic, and the medic will take it out with forceps. Banjo! I fuckin' hit him with the flat of my hand on the chest and blew it out to get it and swallow it. It hit my hand and bounced off to land under the table. I'm under the table after it, and there's screws booting me and everything. Got it swallowed and got it fucking down. "What was that you swallowed?"

"I swallowed fuck all!" (PIRA)

5.34   The H-Blocks broke all your inhibitions about your body. It made you more aware of your body. You never thought you had so much fucking space up there. You look at your body and you think it's a solid mass. I never knew anything about my body, but in the Blocks you become dead aware that you had a sphincter, a colon passage, a bowel. You never knew it before. You appreciated there was a hole in it. I've lost all inhibitions about the body. I would frolic in the street naked, no problem, if I could get away with it. (PIRA)

As sectors of the body were politicized and acquired technical characteristics, "personalities," and names, they amplified the symbolic and pragmatic capacities of the body. Within the architectural immobilization of the prison, these specialized techniques of the body were not simply functional acts but avenues of empowerment. The sheer possession of an adaptive technology meant a significant reorganization of the sociopolitical space of the prison. Technological adaptation by the prisoners was not only instrumental but also communicative and expressive; it was a structure upon which crucial moments of social solidarity among the prisoners depended.

5.35   We had heating pipes that ran through the wall and an expansion collar around the pipe. There was a wee bit of space between the pipe and the expansion collar. We would have made a wick out of the strands of the towel or from the blanket. We would unravel it and make what we called the "choochoos" and get it pulled through to the other end in the next cell. When you got the wick lit, with some flint and a lighter wheel that had been bangled in, the guy next door would have pulled it through from his end and get it touched off [lit]. He'd have a wick sitting on the other side of his cell in the pipe and would have touched it, and that would likewise have been pulled through. We called it pulling the choochoos. Then there was shooting the choochoos, which was when you had to shoot [the wick] under the door across the wing corridor to a cell opposite yours. It had meant that we had only one source of fire on the wing and that person was the keeper of the flint and the wheel—the "keeper of the fire." Well, that day the "keeper of the fire" lost his standing, and if it hadn't been for Willy Deke in the cell with me I'd have cried my eyes out.

The screws read a statement in the paper where the IRA said if they didn't lay off of us they would be forced to take action against the screws. We were roused out on that night for a wing shift, with the screws singing a chorus of the "Old Orange Sash." This was their response. They were standing in the "circle" banging their batons. It was just a mob singing and yelling. They had this white surgical tape stuck to the floor right back to the wall. We were ordered to run over it, toes on the line, hands on the wall. There was no way your hands could reach the wall. The next thing you were down on your face and they were booting the spooners clean out of us. It was just a screws' riot.

I was carrying at the time the small wheel out of a cigarette lighter for lighting fags and a piece of flint. We would have struck the flint against a wheel to get a spark. I used to carry the wing's wheel and the flint in the navel. I have a deep navel. There was that much messing about that I was somersaulted down the corridor and I was booted into this cell. Willy "Deke" was in the cell, and Deke was lying in the corner and he was looking at me and he had the big eyes on him. And I was looking at him. He started just chuckling and laughing. And that was it. I started laughing too. I mind Deke's words, "Fuck them! Get that wheel out! We'll see if we can get a smoke."

Here's me, "Willy I've been booted around that fuckin' corridor and it's lost!" We were shattered.

It was then that Clinkie Clarke got the boys up to the doors to sing. He had us all sing "Provo's Marching On."

They had beat us all around the place and the boys were still singing. I had the hands wrapped around the bars at the window and I rested my head, and I never came so close to fuckin' tears in my life. I looked down at the Deke and he was just staring into space and it was dead poignant. But then I see him looking around the floor for the wee stones that would fall off the edges of the window. He gets a wee bit of stone. He says, "Give us the flint." We used to hide them in the pipes or in your mouth. We unraveled a bit of towel to get a wick, spread it out, and we would just keep striking the flint against the stone or the wheel until she lit for ye.

So we got the wick done and were banging away for five minutes, him and me down on our hands and knees with our noses right up to each other. The next thing, "Whoosh! and up it went. And Deke let a yelp out of him. And I let a scream out of me. We were dancing around the cell like two maniacs, yelling and shouting and laughing. We usually had the wick up the line to give everybody a light. The rest of the lads were shouting, "Get the blow, make the fags! Make the fags! We're on the air!" But we hadn't made the choochoo because we didn't think it was going to work with just the stone and no wheel. We made the wick but we couldn't get that choochoo lit again. We lit the short wick at dinnertime; by eight o'clock that night the fingers were wore clean off of us trying to get the blow lit. By then our fingers were bloody.

The Deke said, "Fuck it!" and threw the flint off the wall. Him and me didn't speak another word to each other. Off we went to the mattresses, laying staring at the fuckin' ceiling and the boys all screaming for the blow. It took me two days getting over it. We had completely psyched ourselves out over a fag and the point that we hadn't got a light. We were psyched out up to a million. (PIRA)

There is a strong continuity between the technology of the "choochoos" and the technical adaptation of the body in the various techniques of "bangling" and "fagining." Both these techniques display a built-in ideology of somatic communication and empowerment—obvious reactions to the cellular interruption of social life in prison. The general technical adaptations of the prisoners involved the extension of the body outwardly (the choochoos, the radios, the microscopic writing on cigarette papers) and inwardly (the bangling and fagining). These extensions mediated the immobilization of the body by the cell and the surveillance systems of the prison. This movement of resistance into exterior and interior spaces and the autonomization of various physical and sensory capacities of the body (which are discussed later) were essential building blocks in the cultural reconstruction of the prison by the Blanketmen.

The progressive politicization of the prisoner's body constitutes a moral genealogy not only because it involved serial transformations of the body that were masked by normative constructs of law, violence, and emancipation, but because a new corporeal morality emerged from the interplay of these forces. The most crucial dynamic of this process was the causal relation established between ideological development and new reorganizations of the human body. *Each stage of politicization and ideological attainment corresponded to a radical deconstruction and reassemblage of the body.* Thus, there was the visual opposition between the prison uniform, the number, and the nakedness of the Blanketmen; the attempted colonization of biological functions followed by the Dirty Protest; the intensification of compulsory visibility through the mirror searches, strip searches, cell searches versus the trickery of bangling or fagining. These were breaks with customary conceptions of the body, and through the body with the prison. As each break was effected, the conceptualization and gauge of the political struggle changed: new political representations and insights emerged that could be traced directly to the technical and semic reorganization of the prisoner's body.

In the H-Blocks we only encounter various fragmented projections of the body, each of which had to bear the semantic weight of the absent totality of the human body. If this totality emerged at all, it appeared only at the moment of its total disappearance in the death of the hunger striker. This continuous incompletion of the captive body in the prison, its permanent liminality and fragmentation, was the precondition for cultural constitution and genesis. The body fragment and the absent totality formed a novel dialectic. Fragmentation of the body became a political technique that enabled the signification, the evocation, of absent wholes: the eventual unification of the prisoners with their political organizations and support communities, with a United Ireland and a postcolonial and separatist Gaelic speech community (see below). Hunger striking was posited as the last act because in its consumption of flesh it was the ultimate fragmentation technique that finally invoked the body whole in a shimmering moment of historical clarity. This invocation of the body whole also elicited the presence of other deferred and desired totalities.

Each reconstruction of the body was experienced by the prisoners as a radical break with prior conditions of imprisonment. The preceding structures of resistance and imprisonment functioned as diacritical markers for the present condition. The inmates looked back on these earlier stages of the protest as mirrors of a lost self that had been irrevocably abandoned as new somatic investments and resistance strategies emerged. This consciousness of perpetual rupture and present dislocation was the basis for the historicization of prison experience by the Blanketmen. Despite the evolutionary expectations of the prisoners' political program, the sense of alterity and dislocation broke through the necessities of ideological cohesion.

5.36 At the start of the Blanket Protest you'd think, "My God! How am I going to stick with this! Then you would look at the Blanket Protest from the position of the Dirty Protest. "Well we had our wee bogs [toilets] and showers. Then what were we complaining about?" Then when the Hunger Strike started we were thinking, "For fuck's sake, the Blanket Protest was allright. What were we complaining about?" (PIRA)

Jameson's (1981) formulation of sociocultural transformation under capitalism centers on the economic and sensory reorganization of the body which divorces the body from precapitalist forms. Jameson links the modernist reconstruction of the senses into specialized, autonomous powers to the hypostasis of language as an "autonomous object, power or activity" (p. 63). Cultural genesis in the H-Blocks among the Blanketmen traces a circuit of autonomization that, like Jameson's account, proceeds from the segmentation and specialization of the senses, and other components of the body, to a culmination in empowering linguistic constructions of social reality.

In Foucault's analyses, the emergence of modern rationalization is characterized by the endowment of vision with an autonomous power of transformation and reconstruction; this hypostatic vision can constitute its objects and generate its specialized systems of knowledge and discourse. The optical paradigm of power in prison also proceeds through a stratification of sensory capacities and sensate subjects. The prison regime that relegates to itself the privileges of hierarchical observation, in turn, denies vision to the observed object. The men in the Blanket Blocks were under twenty-four hour lockup, and they had no freedom of direct physical association with each other (with the exception of cell mates and at Mass). The prisoners had a limited view of the prison yard and an even more constrained view of the corridor through the cracks between their cell door and the adjacent wall which they had chiseled out with their bare hands. The prisoners as the specified "observed" were basically denied full vision as a sensory capacity. For the Blanketmen the limitation of optical mobility was experienced as a denial of survival information and as a disruption of sociation. This absence of a crucial sensory capacity heightened their sense of confinement and was a major source of anxiety as it severely limited their capacity to anticipate the movements of the guards, which were frequently preludes to violence.

The denial of vision to the prisoners meant that new forms of sensory mobility, and specialization were developed in order to orient the prisoner to random violence. Thus, the hegemony of the administrative "eye" was countered with the sensory acumen of the "ear." In this process of sensory substitution and reversal, the prison regime and its violence were converted into auditory texts:

5.37   You never saw each other except on Mass on Sunday. I still meet people in the street that I know from the H-Blocks. I know them dead well, their names, their voices. I've talked to them for hours, and yet I don't know them because I never saw them face to face. I'll bump into people and I go, "You're not——?" I'm just starting to know faces of people I had lived with for years. (PIRA)

5.38   The routine of the prison day was based on sounds. And sounds mean either normal routine or a break in the normal routine, which almost always meant a higher level of violence than what you were getting. The first thing when we woke up we would hear the crows. We would say it's the crows with their lunch boxes out to do a day's work. The crows always went across the yard just before the screws came on the wing. You could hear the crows, and you knew that meant the screws coming soon. You could hear the screws coming through the big metal gates out from and into the circle. We would hear the twenty-five perimeter gates right around the blocks getting closed and checked. Then you would hear the screws parade in the circle. Vaguely in the distance you could hear the Prison Officer detail the day's duty. You heard them after the parade was dismissed coming out of the circle and coming down the wing. The first indication that the day wasn't running on a normal routine would have been the head count. They have to see you to count you.

There was roughly a five-second space between each door opening and closing. And you could time the rhythm of the count from that. If it was just a straightforward routine count you could hear the door bolts shooting, "Ssssh!—One!—Bang!—Sssh!—Two!—Bang!" They went right down the wing doing this. If there was an untoward break in the constant flow of that rhythm it meant that they were coming into a cell to kick somebody out from under the blanket. You might be sleeping or just trying to keep warm, but they had to actually see you to count you. They would give you a hefty wallop, and when you moved, "Ah, that bastard's still alive." And on they would go kicking people.

That finished and you would hear the screws, "C wing, numbers fifty-two. They would ask the screw if he got his numbers, and they would all respond. "Right there CD grill, carry on!"

Then the breakfast would be given out. You could hear the wheels of the food van coming down the corridor. Some of us were able to punch holes in the side of the door so we could see the van. Breakfast was either porridge or cornflakes. Porridge was a downer. It was always hard as cement. The first guy who got the breakfast would shout out in Gaelic, "Porridge on the air!"

As people or things came on or off the wing, because everything was done by sound, they were either "on the air" or "off the air." "Bear's on the air" meant screws on the wings. When Miles the Governor was killed they were singing "Big Bear's off the air," which meant that the governor was dead. So the porridge, which everybody hated, was pebble splashed onto the wall with all the shite. If it wasn't good enough for eating, it was good for the wall. As you heard the breakfast dishes being collected you heard the water gallons being filled with your statutory daily three pints. With all those noises you would be tuning in for normal procedure. The bolt shooting on the door, the dishes rattling, set on the trolley with a bump, the plastic containers being set on the ground all in about fifteen seconds. If there was a break in that routine it could mean violence would be happening. Again in Gaelic somebody hearing the break in the timing would shout out, "What's happening?" and the reply in Gaelic would come, "No problem, just checking something." There was a whole regular sound pattern that either meant or did not mean violence.

At half ten the visits would start. You would hear the clink of the cage that was the first indication that they were coming toward us. You could hear the clinks of the keys as the screws were just moving around. But when you heard that different sound of the keys being drawn from the screw's pocket that was an indication that they were coming toward us. Every time you heard that sound the whole wing would go quiet and the tension would build. If nothing happened it was shouted out in Gaelic, "It's okay!" or "They're battering!"

That would set the pace of the visits for that day. Now if someone was getting a heavy beating you could hear it. "Oough! Oough!" It was one of the worst feelings in the H-Block, one of the worst experiences to sit and listen to somebody getting beat. Because you were totally powerless, and you would always get somebody shouting at the door, "You shower of bastards!" It was always a crowd of screws and one or two naked men in a cell. They had total control.

From ten to twelve noon the routine was silence from the screws, interspersed with the sounds of people coming on and off visits. If you had smuggled out letters or bringing something in, everybody on the wing knew that you were carrying stuff. As you came off the visit you walked through the front gate. We would stand on top of the heating pipes looking through the glass into the main yard. People would shout in Gaelic, "There's so and so back again!" As soon as he came back in he would shout, "I got the fags, or the parcel," whatever he smuggled back in that he had gotten through the search. When stuff got out safely or got in safely it was a victory for us.

At half twelve, Henry the VIII, a screw, would come on the air with the Happy Wagon, which was the dinner, the best meal of the day. They fucked about a lot with the food. A screw would say, "Is that the dinner there? Right, how many containers of chips? Five containers? Right, put three away; they'll do my greyhounds. Two's enough for these bastards." They were always fucking you about. Now, you had regular medical requirements. Once a month each prisoner is entitled to one ounce of salt and one ounce of sugar. Normally you would get your ounce of salt fucked over one dinner during the month. They would say, "There's your statutory requirement" and fuck all of it over the same dinner. The dinner was ruined. They made sure you got what you were entitled to, but they made sure you got it the way they wanted you to. Within the three pints of water they were scrupulous not to give you any more. "There's your three pints. We don't want to give you any more because you just piss too much and throw it out in the corridors."

Around half twelve a deep silence would come because the screws had gone off to their dinner. That silence told you that was them away, that it was safe. We could start the Irish classes then. The one screw who was left on the wing wouldn't interfere. If they did it usually meant water or piss being mopped in under the door of the cell. At two o'clock the noise pattern was exactly the same as the early morning. At that point we would slop out and throw the piss out under the doors. There would always be a fuck about then. Trying to push the piss back into the cells or trying to hose the cells down. From half three to four there would be more visits. At four the tea would be brought in with a same routine as the dinner. From five onward you didn't expect any noises. The screws had no call to come onto the wing or near the cell doors. So any noises you heard then signaled violence or a confrontation. People were always tuned for that.

One of the biggest indicators of violence was the sound of the bolt being shot on a door that was leaving the door opened so you couldn't pull it closed. "Sssh! Sssh! Clank!" That would be for them coming into a cell for a beating, a cell search, or a cell shift. If they saw you were getting on too well with your cell mate they would split you up. The last thing at night is the final night count. The first indication that lockup is completely safe is that you could hear the night guard come on and a little alarm ring as he clocked in every hour on the hour for the entire night. If they came in on you at that time it was always to fuck you about. (PIRA)

The prisoner's perception of the prison's topography was mapped into opposing danger and safety zones. The cell and the body's interior were the relatively safe sectors in the prison. The corridor beyond the cell door, however, was experienced as an anxiety-provoking space of violence; so was the "circle," the crossbar of the H, where the prison officers had their administrative and observation area. The aural coding of the prison regime by the inmates was similarly dichotomized into danger sounds and safety sounds. No sound was neutral. Every sound had a diacritical relation to the sounds preceding and following it. The ear of the prisoner converted the prison routine into a schema of relational sounds and corresponding actions. The slightest alteration in the routine patterning of sounds signified acts of violence. The prisoners did distinguish between predictable and random violence. Random violence magnified feelings of uncontrol beyond all proportion and was the most feared form of administrative intervention. The inmates translated the structure of prison hegemony into auditory signs which, in turn, reduced the functions of rationalized administration to the acoustics of violence. These acoustics were simultaneously inscribed onto their bodies and into the atmospherics of the prison. On the other side of the cell door, a malevolent, invisible, and transcendent domain existed that could only be penetrated by the ear, the imagination, and the warning shout.

The prisoners' metaphorization of sound should be seen as a further textualization of the dynamics of imprisonment that originated with the fecal imprinting of the cell. Violence was recorded on multiple levels of the body; this involved the internal body organs and the web of sensory perception and imagination. In this multiple registration the continuum of embodiment became a sensorium of violence in which each particular sense was dialectically formed by its perceptual object.[28]

In face-to-face conversation with ex-inmates of the Blanket Blocks, one often hears the ritualized interjection, "Are you listening?" repeated automatically several times during the course of a conversation. This phrase is a holdover from the time when discourse meant carrying out conversations with disembodied voices and faceless partners. The collective discourse of the prisoners emerged from the dialectic of the immobilized, invisible defiled body and the supplementing intensity of the disembodied voice.

The centrality of the disembodied voice is evident in the prison slang "on the air" and "off the air." To be "on the air" was to be a subject in communication, to break the limitations of cellular isolation. A related, anglified Gaelic term was "scorcher," the inmate who shouted messages between wings at night. To be "off the air," meant much more than to be silent. It was equated with the special silence of the social death of incarceration and with physical death. The presence and absence of vocality and sound signified life/death, active/passive, social/asocial oppositions. The voice and the ear became autonomous organs of political practice. The dematerialization of the prison space into malleable specular representation originated in the torsion between the effaced body, the autonomous ear, and the disembodied voice that was always "on the air," free and transcendent. This collective voice penetrated the recesses of the excreta-stained cells, the walls and locked doors, and it dominated the nights of incarceration. This vocality not only bridged spatial segmentations, but also moved backward and forward in historical time. Under the heavy burden of the symbolization it was forced to carry, this collective voice generated historical myths and identified itself as not only that which represented, but also that which was historically *representative*. It was a vocality that sought to reaudit a lost history and to be the origin of a new history. This collective voice, learned and devised specialized and secret languages, and thus established the utopian foundations of political community in a linguistic community.

In the H-Blocks, the two sides of this dialectic, the effaced body and auditory presence, became the interlocking poles of the prison culture.

Both the linguistic and the biological separatism of the Blanketmen and hunger strikers can be traced to this dynamic polarization:

5.39   The first time I heard Irish spoken in the H-Blocks, it was like magic. It was a Cages man who was shouting over to the other wing. What actually had happened was that somebody shouted over with a message, but it was in Gaelic and nobody in the wing could understand it. Tom Bush said for us to tell him to get up and shout it across. That was done, and he said, "Right got it," and then bent down to the pipes and passed the message up the cells in English.

We were all sort of amazed: "That was good!" It was like a magician's trick to get a message across from one wing to another. We got up and started shouting, "Talk some more!" The more you heard, the more incentive you had to learn it. There was something magic about listening to these guys waffling away with each other in a tongue that was once ours, that identified us as somebody separate. You would think, "I'd love to be able to do it." You were thinking about the effort, that you couldn't learn another language. But then it became something practical. Going on a visit if you couldn't get up close to a guy to whisper a message to him you were beat. Whereas with Gaelic you could shout right across the visiting room and he would have got it! The way it was put out then it was in the interest of everybody. It was a concrete way forward here, if everybody started to take lessons.

It was like a massive jigsaw puzzle. We were getting a piece of the puzzle now and again. You got another verb and the picture was starting to fill in. We were spending hours on it just writing everything on the walls. The men were using nothing but a piece of metal or a piece of lead to scrape on the wall. There were no textbooks; everything was just shouted out of the door. You always left a patch away from the shite on the wall for the Gaelic. If you look at a cell, the pipes run along the back wall and your mattress was on the floor. Up along the walls you had two feet off the ground that was left blank for the writing. Everything else but that was covered with shite.

You would get shifted into a new cell, and there was this massive amount of Gaelic on the wall. You got a whole new vocabulary that you didn't have before. You were expanding your Gaelic every time you were moved. And you would add your Gaelic on the wall for the next guy who was getting all that combined. There was *sceal* [news] and whole stories written on the wall in Gaelic. Some cells were like a big book. You had nothing to read, no books or newspapers, no TV, you had all that time to sit at that wall trying to figure the Gaelic out. You would check with the rest of the wing, does anybody know what the word means.

Before I knew it I was able to communicate, to waffle. You got to the stage when you had half a message in Irish and the other half to bail you out in English. As long as you were able to get the message across without the screws knowing what you were actually saying. Then it got to the stage that you were using half Gaelic and half English up at the door without even thinking about it. Then it came to the stage that the biggest bulk of what was being spoke was in Gaelic. The cell door was no longer a door but a *doiris*. It was no longer a window but was automatically a *fuinneorg*.

There were four guys, Tom Boyd, Sid Walsh, Jackie Mc-Mullen, and Bobby Sands, who were fluent Gaelic speakers in the whole prison at the start. And from those four guys it went out and out. Within two years everything that was said out the door was in Gaelic. There was one guy who was real anti-Gaelic, "There we go again, there goes Paddy Irishman." He had you really believing he despised the language. By the time the protest ended he couldn't speak it and he didn't attempt to learn it, but he could understand it despite himself. There were a whole lot of people like that who picked up just by being in the environment, constantly exposed to the sound and beat of the language. (PIRA)

5.40   In the Blocks the main way you communicated was shouting out the doors. So that was one of the reasons that the Gaelic became so prominent was that you had no way of communicating except by shouting out the door in Gaelic. Gaelic gave us a language of our own. There were screws coming down asking people for the Gaelic word for screw. We gave them the word *faolean*, which meant seagull. And the screws would be running around calling each other seagulls. It was ludicrous; they were very naïve from that respect.

The way we learned it was that a fellow got up and shouted the lesson out the door, the spelling of the words. It was just a methodical thing. You had a set of rosary beads, a screw, or a nail, and you scratched the lesson on the walls which were whitewashed. The beginner's class was Monday, Wednesday,

Friday between 12:00 and 1:00 P.M. Tuesdays and Thursdays
from about three to five you had advanced classes, and on a
Sunday from 12:00 to 2:00 P.M. you had the class for the
teachers, where the teachers all got together and improved
each other's Gaelic. At the end of the week you would set
aside a day of storytelling, and then I done the history, Irish
history all done in Gaelic from the head. The Gaelic was part
of a whole education program that Bobby Sands initiated, and
it was all done from the head and by shouting out the doors.
Some of us had been trained in the Cages for this. Bobby was
the main advocate of cultural separatism. That was the message that came from inside the jails out to the whole community now. Bobby told us that the proof of the pudding was in
the eating. The jails proved that when you become culturally
separate it breaks the enemy, that it builds walls they can't
cross and people within those walls.

It was a long day in jail. You'd wake up at 7:00 A.M. in a
black depression, lying there in your cell, "I can't go on with
this here." But most of the time because of the Gaelic and
other education classes you were that caught up in what you
were doing and you believed what you were doing was so important for the fortunes of the struggle that you refused to be
broken. To maintain the integrity of the Republican movement
by maintaining resistance in the jails. The Gaelic kept the
whole thing together. The education programs traced the history of Ireland right back to the Ice Age. How Ireland as part
of the European continent separated and right the way down
through the history, the Viking invasions, the British invasions
right down to the development of Republican ideology. When
we finished that, we went into all the different political
philosophies—capitalism, Marxism, Leninism, Maoism, Western Socialism, Cuban Socialism, and all that.

When that was finished we'd go back and pick specialized
subjects, for instance, that Christianity right from the start
was associated with British invasions of Ireland. St. Patrick's
position in Ireland had been endorsed by a synod of British
bishops. That Christianity was the first foreign philosophy and
wasn't a religion as such which brought in the whole thing of
breaking down your culture, the breaking of the power of the
Brehons and the bard schools. We would trace that right down
to the coming of the Vikings, when you had the beginnings of
the decline of Irish culture and the old Irish law, right on up
to the Norman Conquest and the imposition of a new eco-

nomic era. How the Vikings and the Normans brought in the money system, played the money trick on the Irish people, and enslaved the Irish people economically. (PIRA)

5.41 The Gaelic we were learning, we spoke with our natural accents, which is rough. This woman after the protest was over came up from the Free State she was the first Gaelic news reader on RTE [state-run television]. She had a terrible elitist attitude toward the language. She once said to me, "When I hear the Gaelic spoken here in the Blocks it makes me shudder."

I said, "When you hear the Gaelic in here you're hearing it as a living language. It's spoken and evolving in a natural environment. Your Gaelic is put in a glass case as a showpiece. We have a living language. Yours is an artificial thing. For you it's an academic achievement, while for us it's something that lives, and that comes from our day-to-day situation. We had no choice but to learn Gaelic; it was a matter of survival."

With the Gaelic you began to get back in touch with political and ideological concepts. For instance *cealachan*, where in the Brehon laws to express a grievance against an injustice a guy sat outside the wrongdoer's house and starved himself to death. Now *cealachan* had a whole moral import to it that it wasn't a hunger strike as a protest weapon; it was a legal assertion of your rights. The hunger strike was a legitimate and moral means for asserting those rights, and it had legal precedents dating back to antiquity. You found that there was literature that was untranslatable from the Gaelic that could never be expressed in the cold English. (PIRA)

5.42 We fucked the screws; we even changed their vocabularies— their talk changed. They all started using our language as much as we did. Some of them even tried to learn the Irish. They called themselves bears and the rest, talked about bangling and "wirelessing." We changed the prison. When I first went to jail you couldn't talk out the door. You would get done for "disturbing the peace of the prison." Less than a year later we were having singsongs out the door, giving the Gaelic lessons and the political lectures. We just broke down the whole prison discipline. They would threaten us with the "boards" [isolation]. The boards were in better condition than our cells, dry and clean with clean sheets and a hot meal. We go down there for a bit of holiday, a little peace and quiet. (INLA)

It is simplistic to view this process as cultural revivalism. On one level, the acquisition of Gaelic suggests the need to bridge the isolations and separations of the prison experience. Speaking Gaelic inserted the stigmatized and isolated prisoner into a historical lineage that endowed him with a crucial cultural identity, an identity that rectified his loss of self in the total institution. But to make this claim would be to identify as motive or rationale what was in effect one of the results of the acquisition of Gaelic. Gaelic speaking was born from the prison experience, and though it had a transcendental power, this power was first and foremost directed at the prison itself. The prison was the initial discursive object formed by the speaking of Gaelic.

Sound was a crucial medium that granted the prisoners a communicative mobility and sociation capacity denied to their bodies. The prison guards' initial rule of silence in the early days of the H-Blocks, their "peace of the prison," was a continuation of the interruption of human communication characteristic of prison architecture. The observed subject, constrained in the antiseptic laboratory of the prison cell, was not meant to disrupt the disciplinary experiment by speaking, by establishing a linkage with other cells. To do so would be tantamount to contaminating the conditions of a controlled experiment. Speech under such conditions takes on a special value intensity. But in contrast to the relative security of the defiled cell under the No Wash regime and the rationalization of auditory signs, covert speech in English was susceptible to interventions by the guards. The establishment of any communicative circuit among the inmates had first to confront the problems of its interception.

Much in the same manner that the prison had stratified and rarified a valued medium for empowerment, vision, the prisoners were impelled to develop methods for stratifying their informational media. Prison slang, pipe-tapping codes, and bangling were several responses to the necessity of communicative stratification. However, Gaelic was a much more comprehensive and mobile secret language within the surveilled environment. Unlike prison slang, it was completely divorced from any etymological inherence in English and therefore less susceptible to decodification. In comparison to pipe tapping, Gaelic had a vastly wider vocabulary and range of expression and could be deployed in prison spaces other than that of the cell. Bangled messages written in Gaelic were doubly covert. The linguistic trickery played upon those guards who sought to learn Gaelic testifies to the stratification effect of Gaelic acquisition.

Any mechanism that prevents the transgression of secret knowledge will be concerned with contamination. Thus, the practical efficiency of Gaelic as a secret language also participated in the dynamics of defilement in the prison. In a situation where language compensated for the immobilized and contaminated body, any purification of the linguistic domain was bound up with the impurities of the corporeal domain. The biological separatism of the scatological body was the ground upon which a variety of techniques and discourses of resistance were founded. *In the H-Blocks, the cultural separatism of the linguistic domain has first to be understood within the cultural separatism of the fecal body.*

Gaelic speaking should be apprehended as a language of purification. Its symbolic negation of political colonization endowed Gaelic speaking with a utopian vocation. The Dirty Protest, which neutralized the domination effects of the prison regime, still did not extricate the prisoner from a sense of defilement which had been the longstanding goal of this action. Quite the contrary: the protest intensified collective pollution. All the strategies of resistance participated in an anomalous condition. The prisoners exploited this defilement, investing it with inverting meanings, but they never transcended impurity. Yet Gaelic, inextricably tied to the mobility and transcendence of the disembodied voice, the solidarity of collective vocality, as well as deep historical resonances, overcame the semiotics of captivity. The acquisition of Gaelic, with all its multiple uses and manifold social meanings, functioned as a mechanism of decontamination. The fecal cell and body were renamed, or rather, in the context of cultural separatism, named for the first time through Gaelic. This act of naming divorced the prisoners from the sign systems of captivity. Gaelic speaking created a rupture with the semantics of imprisonment which were linked to "the cold English," the juridical language of penal enforcement, and before that, colonization. The Adamic act of "first" naming in Gaelic initiated a new historicity, a new beginning. The prison was no longer interminable, but a portal for historical exiting—an act enabled by the accumulated symbolic systems that ranged from new languages to ascetic disciplines of the body. With the acquisition of Gaelic, the Blanketmen truly began to leave the prison. Gaelic speaking finalized the conversion of the prison into something the prison administration, and particularly the guards, could no longer understand.

By shifting the prison into a new semiological order in which the cell door suddenly and "magically" became *doiris* (5.39), the prisoners journeyed to a mythic-historical locale that had been made accessible to them by the grammar and etymologies of Gaelic. Every object, every component of the defiled body and the prison, once transposed into Gaelic, was no longer linked solely to the determinations of captivity, but it also secretly participated in a historicity with anchorages that transcended both the time and place of imprisonment. By speaking Gaelic and transforming the prison into a pure communicative space, the Blanketmen may have been participating in a revivalist myth, but they were also enacting a "Cabalistic" model of language. The semiosis of material violence by sound, the power of language to overcome the fragmentations and constraints of the body and the prison cell, all contributed to the transcendent power of language. As in Cabalistic tradition, Gaelic speaking, its grammar, its lexicon, its phonetics, its "beat," once enunciated in the prison, enabled migration to alterity.

The prison leadership identified intensive Gaelic enculturation as the required cognitive preparation for the collective commitment to hunger striking. Gaelic was seen as the necessary precipitant of the political solidarity that would enable chosen prisoners to act materially on their own bodies as the central structure of their captivity. Gaelic enculturation was tied to hunger striking by a common utopian and eschatological impetus. Gaelic acquisition and hunger striking were complementary media for purifying the materiality of incarceration and the body. This is why the hunger strike had to be endowed with a Gaelic name—*Cealachan*. The prisoners renamed and historicized the body with this term.

The prison cell, already imprinted with a scatological writing, relinquished part of its wall space to the graphics of Gaelic acquisition. The prisoners scratched their accumulated learning alongside the fecal matter on the walls. This transformation of the cell into a pedagogical space was as strong an act of personalized political appropriation as its defilement with excreta. Alongside the scatological history of domination, the prison cell now bore the secret history of language acquisition. The reading of old Gaelic graffiti on the cell wall by each new inhabitant and the addition of new inscriptions became an act of sociation and a means for reproducing secret knowledge and an indigenous literary culture. The prisoners who were physically absent from each other, who may have never seen each other, were, present to each other on the cell wall. The textual presence of the invisible prisoner on the cell wall and his disembodied acoustic presence "on the air" finalized the shift of the prison into a spectacle of alternative representation.

Through the Gaelic and scatological writing, the cell became a historical membrane that secreted a record of prison experience and knowledge. The cell ceased to separate, to desocialize inmates. Through the sedimentation of its many strata—interrogation white, H-Block feces, Gaelic graffitti—it had become an archaeological artifact, a place for the storage and the liberation of memory. An entire genealogy of resistance was etched with pain and endurance into the material of imprisonment. Both the mind and the bodies of the prisoners passed into this cell membrane through the media of their writing and the fecal transcription of their political condition.

6 *Eschatology*

> The way the Hunger Strike worked was that the Brits sat and recorded every move the hunger striker made, everything he said, everything he done. . . . The doctors were doing it, the screws were doing it, the priests were doing it, and we were doing it. Everybody was into sussing it out.
>
> —PIRA Blanketman

The Republican tradition of hunger striking in this century can be traced to the 1917 Mountjoy Jail Strikes and the protest of Cork mayor and IRA man Terrence McSwiney who died after seventy-four days on hunger strike in 1920. In the current IRA campaign there have been several hunger strikes: In 1972, at Crumlin Road jail, Billy McKee and Pronsias McArt held a successful thirty-seven day hunger strike for political status, thus establishing the precedent for the Blanketmen's protest. In 1974, the Price sisters went on hunger strike for repatriation, which was terminated by forced-feeding. In 1973, Michael Gaughan died on hunger strike over the issue of repatriation of Irish prisoners in English jails, and again in 1976, Frank Stagg died for the same issue. On October 27, 1980, seven Blanketmen[1] initiated the first H-Blocks hunger strike for the "five demands": (1) the right to wear civilian clothes; (2) the right not to engage in prison work; (3) the right to free association with other prisoners; (4) 50 percent remission of their sentence (i.e., the erasure of lost remission time caused by their participation in the Blanket/No Wash protests); and (5) normal visiting schedules, parcels, recreational, and educational facilities (Coogan 1980:14–19).

On December 18, the men were pulled off the Hunger Strike without any fatalities. At the time it appeared as if the British were conceding to the demands. This agreement was never finalized by the British government, and the Blanketman were left in the same position as before the strike. Today, activists in the Republican movement like to point to this chain of protests and to the reference made to hunger striking (*Troscad* or *Cealachan*) in the ancient Brehon legal codes (*Senchus Mor*) as an ongoing jural tradition of corporeal protest against injustice in Ireland. Yet this historicization does not provide an exhaustive explanation of the 1980 and 1981 Hunger Strikes in the H-Blocks. It does, in effect, mask a profound rupture in the ideology and leadership of the Republican movement at that time, which the Hunger Strikes exemplified.

The 1981 Hunger Strike which led to the deaths of ten men can better be understood in terms of its chronological and performative position in the somatic forms that emerged from the H-Blocks. The fundamental issue of the H-Block situation is not what prior Republican ideologies contributed to the modes of protest in the prison, but what the Blanketmen's resistance contributed to the transformation of the Republican movement. This is not to deny that there were any external ideological and performative influences on the decision to protest prison conditions with hunger striking. But too much emphasis on an "event history" in this matter would efface the more pervasive underlying structural influences and indigenous performative codes which determined both the enactment and the ideological validity of the 1981 Hunger Strike.

Hunger striking is a dramatic and eloquent form of political expression, but its physical immediacy can obscure its performative contexts, particularly when one hunger strike is compared to or legitimized by another. Within the Republican movement, the 1920, 1972, 1973, and 1976 Hunger Strikes may have been retrospectively appropriated as expressing a single ideological message, but that does not necessarily imply that they had comparable ideological intentions, common structural origins, and shared performative codes.

Various commentators have described the 1981 Hunger Strike as an act of "expiation," a "ceremony of innocence," an act of some sort of religious transcendence (Collins 1986; O'Malley 1983). All such Christological models are highly problematic because they tend to assume an equivalence between the PIRA Hunger Strike and the type of protest associated with Ghandi, Martin Luther King, or traditions of Christian martyrdom. The Blanketmen, while insisting on a secular interpretation of the Hunger Strike, are well aware of the political benefits of the protest's sacralization. For them it is 'sacralized' to the extent that the protest can be positioned within an ideology that conflates the direction of Irish history with the ideological evolution of the IRA. At the same time that they point to the outpouring of popular grief and rage at the deaths of the hunger strikers, the ex-Blanketmen sharply demarcate their own interpretations and experience of the 1981 Hunger Strike from its reception by their supporters outside the prison. They are well aware that a multiplicity of meanings has been attached to the protest, many of which, though politically supportive, are not reconcilable with the prisoners' own experiences.

There is no single reductive historical truth to the 1981 Hunger Strike. A multiplicity of truths has been attached to this event. The multivalent potential of the Hunger Strike can be examined with the most clarity by paying attention to the manifold formation of the body in the H-Blocks and other modes of somatic violence contemporaneous with the political experience of the Blanketmen. A salient dimension of the 1981 Hunger Strike is its capacity to achieve symbolic generality and collective meaning through the engagement of polysemy.

A cultural analysis of the 1981 Hunger Strike must distinguish the following: its intentionality as a mode of political representation, as perceived by the Blanketmen; the ways it was eventually appropriated by the Republican movement outside the prison, by the media, and by the general population of Ireland; and the underlying forms of cognition and action that exceeded explicit ideological intention. The present analysis will not attempt an exhaustive historical reconstruction of the 1981 Hunger Strike both inside and outside the prison. The Hunger Strike mobilized significant segments of the Irish population that had previously been uninvolved in Republican politics. It also had a complex history of political negotiation, a good deal of which remains undisclosed in IRA[2] and British government archives and memories. All these factors demand extensive historical analysis. Consequently, this chapter focuses on the political intentionality of the 1981 Hunger Strike in the prison, and the encompassing structures of symbolic logic and ritual action which formed and exceeded this intentionality.

The Blanketmen viewed the 1981 Hunger Strike as a military campaign and organized it as such. For them, it was a modality of insurrectionary violence in which they deployed their bodies as weapons.[3] They fully expected a coupling of this act of self-directed violence with mass insurrectionary violence outside the prison. These two forms of violence were seen as semantically and ethically continuous. Thus, despite its surface similarity to the nonviolent and pacifist protests associated with Ghandi and Martin Luther King, the Hunger Strike in the H-Blocks was not a pacifist or religious action. For the Blanketmen, the 1981 Hunger Strike involved none of the moral superiority or obligations of a turn away from violence. It was to be a prelude to violence. This was a result of both self-conscious ideological decisions and the performative, but equally ideological, conditioning by the violence inherent in the H-Block situation.

Yet it was precisely the "pacifist" and/or "religious" iconography surrounding the 1981 Hunger Strike that gained it wide popular support and sympathy throughout Ireland and the international community. (Support in urban and rural Republican strongholds would not have been "pacifist.") Within the Hunger Strike, several antagonistic utopian methodologies and sets of expectations (the violent and the nonviolent, the secular and sacred) momentarily merged and then splintered off from each other. The subsequent inability of the IRA to maintain the same levels of widespread popular support that had appeared during the Hunger Strike can be traced to the conviction among its leadership and membership, both inside and outside the prison, that the sacrificial death of ten men legitimized a subsequent sustained campaign of political violence (modified somewhat by an electoral strategy). If this present analysis of the 1981 Hunger Strike is to remain with the cognitive and symbolic systems of paramilitary culture, then this event, despite any religious or nonviolent reception, should be viewed as a political technology of the body connected to paramilitary practice both inside and outside the prison. As such, the 1981 Hunger Strike must be analyzed within the general framework of the cultural construction of violence in Northern Ireland.

H6

With familiar H-Block logic, the Hunger Strike, in terms of its initial planning, originated in still another futile disciplinary tactic by the prison administration to "break" the Blanket Protest.

6.1   The philosophy of the need to politicize the Republican move-
       ment originated in the "group of 32." In 1978 they took thirty-
       two of us, all the OCs and adjutants, off of our various wings
       throughout the blocks and isolated us in a block of our own.[4]
       But what they done there aided us. We had everybody
       together—Brendan Hughes, Bobby Sands, John Dreen, Bik
       McFarlane, Thomas McElwee, and Richard O'Rourke and
       others—and what went on there was an intensive politicization
       process, a revamping of the whole thing. What they thought
       they were doing when they took all the OCs out and held us
       on our own—they thought they had the hard core, that they
       had taken the leadership away from the Blanket Protest and it
       would then fall apart. It didn't, and what happened was that it
       brought us together and gave us a full year on our own to sit
       and plan the whole strategy for the hunger strikes, to inten-
       sify our Gaelic, and to develop the whole approach to the po-
       liticization of the communities on the outside.
            While we were being held in H6 they upped the pressure against
       the guys in the other Blocks. There was guys going to fuckin'
       pieces. When they pulled us out into that Block on our own they
       gave us the noise treatment from the machines they had there. The
       pressure was all very psychological, but as they pulled us out the
       physical brutality increased in the other blocks.

The Hunger Strike was entirely planned from the inside. It was the inside pushing for it.[5] We saw the Hunger Strike as being far more than a jail issue. We saw that the Irish struggle had come to a stage where Sinn Fein needed a high political profile. We needed to form a base and politicize the movement. Put it into community politics, put it into politicizing and then channeling the support, building a whole alternative system of politics. Show people how you deal with bureaucracy. We realized that the most potent weapon people had in war was organization, competent forward-moving organization. That's what we had all been about in the jails, and that message had to go out from the jails into the community. One of the main planks of that program was the culture. The culture in the jails had defeated the Brits; it could do the same thing on the outside. Bobby Sands was the main advocate of that. We realized that with the Blanket a new phase of the campaign had begun—that the center of the Republican movement was in the jails. The Brits had attempted to isolate the prisoners as the weakest link in the Republican movement. They had tried to portray the IRA as a criminal conspiracy to the world, and the prisoners were supposed to be the symbol of that. They knew that the Irish people always very closely identified with their prisoners—that if they broke the morale of the prisoners they could break the morale of the people on the outside. We realized that it was a watershed period—that the Brits had chosen a battleground and that we from inside the prison might have to die to defeat them on it.

Ninety-nine percent of the people on the Blanket came into the jail when they were nineteen. You had very few over that age. We were the second generation of IRA people who had joined in '74 and '75. There was no old IRA, Catholic Nationalists on the blocks; we had become socialists, and individuals may have been Marxists. Our whole philosophy that developed that year was based on nationalism, socialism, separatism, secularism, and nonsectarianism.

After that year they broke us apart when they saw that their tactic to break the protest hadn't worked. They then split us up into all the wings so we were able to disseminate.[6] We were able to send men from that group of thirty-two into every wing. We separated among the wings and began intensive Irish lessons. The Gaelic was going to be the basis for politicizing the wings and preparing them for the Hunger Strike. (PIRA)

6.2   They took the OCs and IOs [Intelligence Officers] out of H3, 4, and 5 and put them into H6, another jail completely. It served no purpose. The blanket orderlies had wired the boys about the shift a week before it was supposed to take place. They knew about the shifts because of the brown bags that you were supposed to pack your gear in when they moved you from wing to wing. They were all in the new cells with the name tags of the guys to be moved. We knew who was going; it was obvious what they were trying to do. The whole structure had been set up for new OCs and IOs a week before the group left. (INLA)

6.3   The more active men had been moved off the wing into one particular wing away from the rest. They were hoping to break things up. But other commanders just took their place. But they moved the commanders back into the wings when they saw that segregation was having no effects on us. Bobby Sands, Bik McFarlane, and a few others came onto our wing and things began to pick up. I thought of Bobby Sands as a man who went out of his way to help others. Before he came onto the wing the morale of the wing was very low. We had taken a fair bit of hassle from the warders. Sands and McFarlane immediately organized Gaelic lessons, singsongs, story tellings, and lectures through the doors. Bobby Sands was the man who gave the Irish lessons, sung songs, told stories. He was like an old-time *seanachie* [story teller]. When he told a story from the old Gaelic times it was very vivid. You could picture it in your mind's eye.

     Other times there would be political lectures. Mainly about getting involved in community projects, identifying with people, and getting them to identify with the Republican movement. Mainly discussing what type of Ireland a socialist Ireland would be. They saw it as equal wages and opportunity for all. The Irish language would be the first language and English the second. Feminist issues were discussed. They had debates on contraception and abortion. There were a certain number of people elected to speak for it and against it. There were no conclusions about the debates; they were supposed to make us think about the issues.

     Sands envisioned that the Republican movement as a whole should be very much involved in all types of community work so that people could see that the IRA wasn't just interested in bombing and shooting. Yet he said to some extent there was a need for the violence, because there was no way they could overthrow the capitalist system without the use of force. There was no way they could hold what they won without the use of force. That America and the European community would never allow a left-wing socialist Ireland on their doorsteps. Eventually Sands said that we would need at the beginning a one-party state until such time as the situation settled down and you could hold elections. But they couldn't see people holding capitalistic views because exploitation wasn't right. Sands and the others believed that the people could be educated to believe in the state and be dedicated to one another rather than to themselves. It was all very well to say but difficult to put into practice. The man himself, I respected him. He was always writing and reading. He had done a lot for the men around him. He meant what he said; there were no other personal motives. (INLA)

6.4 I'm looking at the whole management of the H-Block situation as something that may have played into the hands of the British. When you consider the withdrawal of the leadership and their reintegration, it makes you wonder further. In that situation to deliberately take out a planning group, allowing them to develop expertise and time to develop a strategy, to get their act together, and then to reintegrate them. My God, what sort of sense does that make? The most blind idiot could have predicted that would have only aggravated an already unstable situation. It may well have been a job of bloody brilliance! I'm just considering the factors behind a governmental desire to escalate the conflict to create further communal polarization. What concerns me, at the point that I quit the prison I was pointing out that this situation would result in massive polarization. I'm not that smart; there must have been other people who saw this coming. The whole prison situation during the time I was there was handled in such a way as to create profound disturbances and animosities that weren't there previously. The withdrawal and reintegration of the prison leadership confirms this. Was there a master plan for this or were the prison and the government just stumbling around? (Ex–prison welfare officer, H-Blocks)

6.5 The Hunger Strike had always been a card. It was always on people's minds. Nobody wanted it, but it was always there. (INLA)

Among the Blanketmen, each stage of ideological rupture and development occurred within the context of increasingly intensified experiences of withdrawal and physical enclosure. The initial refusal to wear the prison uniform had resulted in the placement of the Blanketmen under twenty-four hour lockup and their segregation from the rest of the prison population. The staining of the cells with excreta and the stench of unwashed bodies in the Dirty Protest further intensified the isolation of the protesting prisoners. Gaelic acquisition transformed biological separatism into cultural separatism. The isolation of the commanding officers and the intelligence officers of the Blanket Blocks, unplanned by the inmates as it was, evokes the dynamics of the Gaeltacht (or "Jailtacht") huts of the Cages, the other (in this case voluntary) segregation of a Republican leadership elite within a prison. As in the Gaeltacht huts of the Cages, life in H6 centered around intensified exercises in language acquisition, political education, and the development of new modes of political representation (see chapter 5, n.1).

The hunger strike to the death was expected to complete the aborted biological breakdown that had been anticipated with the Dirty Protest (see narrative 5.5). Thus the Blanketmen intended to subvert the juridical time of the penalogical regime and the temporal liminality of the Blanket Protest with linear biological time. Further, the protest was expected to disseminate and expand its own temporal biological urgency and linear impetus into a widespread social movement. There was to be a translation of temporal schedules from the singular biological finitude of the dying hunger striker to the magnitudes of mass protest and even insurrection beyond the prison. Immersed in the political efficacy of the signifying body, the Blanketmen transcribed biological time into epochal time.

Death in the Hunger Strike was conceived as both the literal termination of biological functions and "the countdown," the long drawn-out sociobiological death that the endurance of starvation dramatically stretched into an iconic act of historical mediation. "Going to the edge" is a common phrase used by ex-Blanketmen in reference to the Hunger Strike. Reaching the "edge" was reaching the cusp of history; it was the creation of a new sociotemporal continuum arising out of the biological time of the dying prisoner. The Blanketmen, of course, did not desire the actual deaths of their comrades, but they did desire for themselves as a group the prolonged ascesis that witnessing and empathic participation would generate. The hunger striker by "going to the edge" would take his comrades and possibly Irish society to that edge. By manipulating biological imagery, the Hunger Strike would inject historical time as a radical and critical force into the static spatialized power configurations of the prison and of Northern Ireland society as a whole (see chapter 2).

The withdrawal of the Blanketmen's leadership into H6 and the transformation of their segregation into a renewed politicization/planning process formalized the aura of "monastic" retreat that permeated the political culture of the Blanketmen. The culture of "monastic retreat" is explicit once the factors of specialized techniques of the body, of a secret and sacralized language, and of an eschatological philosophy of history are considered. The renewed politicization of the Republican movement both inside and outside the prison was conceived as a secular conversion experience. While conversion inside the prison would be finalized by the intensified dissemination of Gaelic and its associative historicity, conversion of populations outside the prison would be effected by an eloquent incorporating sacrificial ritual. This sacrifice both presupposed and demonstrated the same technologies of the body that had been forged through years of resistance, institutional violence, and survival in a scatological environment. The conversion of social consciousness was, as in other matters, founded on the conversion of the body and the self through ascetic disciplines.

Asad's discussion of the relation between the ascetic technologies of the body developed by medieval monastics and the emergence of ideologies of conversion in the same period offers a historical parallel to the structural role of asceticism in the H-Blocks (Asad 1983:284–327). Asad traces the translation of penitential techniques of the monastics into religious renewal among secular populations. He also charts the origins of juridical torture in these same ascetic disciplines of the body. Whether one is concerned with conversion experience or inquisition violence, the privileged relation of technologies of the body to the production of "truth" during this period offers informative parallels to the ideology of conversion (politicization) associated with the 1981 Hunger Strike and to the ethical continuity of hunger striking with terrorist violence outside the prison. The Hunger Strike, state interrogation, and terrorist violence are practices united by the assumption that the inscription of violence on the human body (protracted or sudden violence) constitutes the production and display of truth. For Foucault (1979), this jural conjuncture formed by violence, body, and discourse is the ironic archeological site of the Western philosophical formula of truth as adequation or correspondence. (The exemplary site of competence for the performance of truth is subversively identified as the torture chamber.)

In the H-Blocks, the incorporation of ascetic disciplines of the body into the production of historical truth follows the same pattern described by Asad: withdrawal from the secular culture; construction of an emblematic social life based on the experience of enclosure; the development of enculturating ascetic disciplines of the body; the emergence of ideologies of conversion that sought to disseminate the truth disclosed by the ascetics of the body to the world beyond the cloistered institution.

The Blanketmen saw their passage through the disciplinary machinery of the prison as a journey to the inner truth of the British state. The prison system for them encapsulated a wider colonial power which had imprinted discourses of domination upon their bodies. There was a semantic and historical equivalence between the colonization of Ireland and the colonization of the Blanketmen's bodies. In their view, they had lived through a reenactment of the relation of domination that characterized Britain's historical relation to Ireland. And they had reversed that historical trajectory. Instead of losing a language and a culture, they had gained a language and a culture. Yet the Blanketmen knew that this drama which had been memorialized in their bodies remained locked up with those encoded bodies within the prison. The history of their passage through discipline and punishment had to be externalized and dramatized beyond prison space. This could only be accomplished through the exiting of emblematic bodies from that place and the resultant release of historical codes.

The prison discipline of corporeal debasement had led to the redemptive immersion into the Gaelic language and Irish cultural history; domination had been resisted by new forms of sociation, communalism, and separatism. All these components were identified by the Blanketmen (by Bobby Sands in particular) as central to nation building beyond the prison. Irish society, in turn, was depicted as a larger, more diffused and camouflaged "prison" of which the H-Blocks were but one paradigmatic component.[7] Their resistance had provided the elementary forms for sociocultural emancipation beyond the prison. In the eschatology of the planned hunger strike, Irish history was to shift its locus. It had passed through the force field of the H-Blocks and was to be reassembled there, through the medium of the Hunger Strike, into a new teleology. The prison had to be the topos for historical mediation and cultural intervention, because for the Blanketmen it was there that the embryo of the new Irish society had been formed.

By 1981 the Dirty Protest ceased to be an incendiary precipitant of political symbolization and meaning. The beatings and other disciplinary regimes inflicted by the guards devolved into a dead language that could no longer affect the Blanketmen. The guards seemed also to have exhausted the significative intensity of their own violence. After a period of intensification in February 1980, beatings deescalated. This only furthered the urgency of hunger striking. The suspensions of the prisoners' existence became even more oppressive once they were distanced from the more direct and interpersonal forms of penal intervention and coercion.[8]

Both the Blanket and No Wash protests had been constructed by the prisoners out of failed attempts at initiation by the prison regime. The Blanketmen had survived in the prison as anomalous entities, as unresolved initiates of an experience that demanded ritual synthesis, if not resolution. The Hunger Strike was planned as their own initiation ritual. It was to be simultaneously an inauguration of a new juridical order, a display of ideological separatism and integrity, a final resolution of their "criminality," and a dramatization of the disciplines of the body that had formed them in the prison.

The Hunger Strike, whether taken as initiation rite, a final resolution of jural-political-biological liminality, or as an eschatological rite of collective conversion, always returns to the same underlying issue of time. As the Blanketmen slowly exhausted the immediate and daily political significance of the Dirty Protest and inserted themselves deeper and deeper into an ideal Gaelicized cultural and historical order, the issue of time, its suspension and reactivation, became for them the lever upon which the mechanism of political action depended. The role that the body was to play in the reactivation of time would be crucial in the planning and experience of the hunger strike.

6.6   On the Blanket what you had was an existence; that's all it was. And you was conscious of the fact that it was an existence because one day was exactly the same as the next. People will tell you that the time of protest went in very quickly. We put it down to the fact that every day was the same. There were no markers to give you a sense of time passing. If you ask me a date or a time about anything to do with the protest I couldn't tell you anything. I had no sense of time at all. You didn't want it. Release didn't come into your mind during the protests; you were too wrapped up. It went on to one year, then two, then three. You were wondering seriously whether you were going to get out of there alive. (PIRA)

6.7   I could isolate exact days by the weather but not by the calendar. I do remember a meeting or a discussion taking place because of the weather that day. The only thing we used as stages and times was the stages of the protest. There was nothing else that meant fuck all. Days were measured on meals. Weeks were measured on fuck all. (PIRA)

6.8   What was essential in the long drawn-out process of the protest was the isolation. If the Brits could isolate the struggle in local terms and portray our movement internationally as a criminal conspiracy, they could get us into a position in which people in our communities would begin to reject us. "Youse are going nowheres. No one doubts your capacity to keep this

going, but where are you going?" Over the years of the protest we had made a great deal of propaganda mileage. To be
beat on that issue was going to have grave complications politically. The Brits are never going to stop me and some other
guys getting weapons and taking a crack at a soldier. But
you're pissing against the wind; you're never going to go nowhere. The Hunger Strike was the answer to all that. (PIRA)

6.9 The power had firmly shifted in our favor. The higher the
beatings, the stronger we were—that was their weakness.
The only thing that frightened us was that nobody knew how
long we could hold out. It wasn't that someone could come in
and knock your bollocks in today or next week but, "Could I
last another five years." We knew when the hunger strike
started we would be in our last year or two. (PIRA)

6.10 Some of the worst screws were genuinely sorry over the
whole thing. They didn't expect it to go as far as it did. They
were doing beatings from day to day. It got to the stage that
the beatings weren't going to work, that guys who had been
on the Blanket for three to five years weren't going to go off
of it just because of beatings. So the screws stopped the beatings and just let people vegetate. There was all these talks
going on, but they all broke down. So guys knew there was
fuck all else to do but hunger strike. The screws had become
apathetic. They wanted an end to the whole thing, just as
surely as we did. Apathy set in the whole prison. By this time
everybody had given up hope, and guys were saying we're
going to have to go on like this for ten years, for fifteen
years. Particularly the lifers. The Hunger Strike came about
as the only option. The Hunger Strike was the ace card.
(INLA)

The relative withdrawal of the figure of the screw as a political object
for the Blanketmen expanded their horizon of political action while at the
same time it accentuated their sense of suspension. Prior to the dimin-
ishment of routinized violence, the fundamental political polarities of
prison life were located in the subject positions of oppressive screw and
resisting Blanketman. In the planning period prior to the Hunger Strike,
the we/they opposition, that is, the screw/Blanketman polarity, that
structured political culture in the prison was subsumed by another
we/they polarity that demarcated the "inside" from the "outside," the
prison culture from the rest of Ireland and the British state.

The Hunger Strike was directed at a much wider audience than that of the prison regime. Within the performative framework of the Hunger Strike, the prison regime would mainly serve as an affective symbol for public identification outside the prison. The prison regime had become for the Blanketmen a symptom of deeper structural problems. They had grown beyond the politics of prison protest, but unfortunately the contradiction between their actual living conditions and the cognitive/ideological development persisted. For the Blanketmen, new oppositions, for which the prison topos was a useful lever, assumed political importance. The we/they, inside/outside opposition that animated the conceptualization of the Hunger Strike was first expressed in the ideological disjuncture between the Blanketmen and the IRA Army Council on the outside.

Technically most of the Blanketmen were subordinate to the IRA Army Council outside the prison. Yet the thesis of the "Breaker's Yard," advanced by Bobby Sands and accepted by the H6 planning group, established the prison struggle and the prison cadres as the axis of the current IRA campaign phase. The Hunger Strike, under the guise of an energizing injection into the military/political campaign on the street, implicitly relegated the military campaign to a supportive posture in relation to the prison struggle. The Breaker's Yard thesis contradicted the existing command structures of the PIRA unless the Army Council on the outside was in full concordance with the prison leadership inside. This potential internal conflict involved much more than territorial privilege and hierarchy. Given the specific conditions from which the Republican prison struggle emerged, it was inevitable that a good deal of tactical conflict was predicated on the symbolic media employed by the Blanketmen, the type of weapons they had become accustomed to wielding in their unique struggle. The conflict between the IRA "outside" and the IRA "inside" boiled down to the contradictions between instrumental technical actions such as rationalized military performance and symbolic expressive techniques that, due to their perceived dependence on emotional identification, could easily fall apart or move with equal rapidity beyond the explicit and immediate plans of the strategists. This type of differentiation between managed utilitarian violence with its rationalized controls and unmanageable symbolic warfare dependent on alterities of the body condensed a profound ideological rupture between the IRA's prison culture and the "outside" IRA's military thinking. The Blanketmen had come to experience, or at least they theorized, the political manipulation of their bodies as a managed project, though this logic understandably eluded the Army Council. The latter comprehended serial hunger striking as an unknown and unpredictable shift in their relationship to support populations.

The Stiff

6.11 We knew two things, the Hunger Strike was the last option
we had and that we would always get strong opposition from
the movement outside. Simply because hunger strikes unleash
forces you can't control, not to the same extent as violence.
When you have a situation in prison and everybody confined
so closely who became involved in the issue, nobody on the
outside can tell where a hunger strike was going to end.
When in '79 we were withdrawn up into H6, the Hunger
Strike was seen as inevitable at that point, but the communications we were having with the outside did not recognize
that. It had built to the point inside that people were looking
to years and years ahead; the Blanket wasn't ending. We were
in a situation where we believed we were in a stalemate—that
the Brits were prepared to let us lie to kingdom come on the
Blanket. Yet we knew we were on the verge of kicking the
Brits strategy from here to kingdom come. No matter what
they would do, we would win the moral victory.

But the outside was saying it can't be resolved. Nobody
outside understood the alternative to the Hunger Strike. We
were saying, "If we don't hunger strike, what are we going to
do?" The outside was scared to make the logical extension of
the struggle we were in. They felt fairly in control of the military campaign, but not of the Hunger Strike.

We were prepared to get the Hunger Strike to go into
1985. We eventually had at least fifty guys out of a Blanket
population of four hundred. Fifty guys who had cast-iron legal
guarantees that their families couldn't take them off the
strike. The outside was saying, "You have to understand the
effect this parade of death will have on the morale of the people on the outside." We weren't in touch with that, but we
were saying, "We can go on indefinitely, we can keep sending
coffins out of here every week if you give us a guarantee on
the outside that you can sustain the level of the political campaign." (PIRA)

6.12 It has been accepted that the tactic of the Blanket was at a
stalemate. There was dissatisfaction in many of the wings
with the liason guy from the outside, because he was coming
in, from a genuine sense of boosting morale, saying, "Everything's going fine!" But we couldn't see it from the inside.

> From the moment we entered the H-Blocks we had used our
> bodies as a protest weapon. It came from the understanding
> that the Brits were using our bodies to break us. It wasn't
> just a prison movement. We began to identify with the op-
> pressed all over the world. That's how full the circle had be-
> come. There was more entailed in it than the five demands. It
> wasn't just to get us out of the conditions we were living in.
> (PIRA)

The ideological and tactical debates between the IRA "inside" and the
IRA "outside" contain an underlying theme that is crucial to the analysis
of the cultural construction of violence by all Northern Ireland paramilitary organizations and not only the IRA. The Blanketmen were engaged
in a debate with the IRA Army Council that attempted to establish the
political-tactical equivalence of the self-directed symbolic violence of self-
willed starvation with the other-directed violence of the military operation. With the failure of the 1980 protest the prison leadership and the
majority of the Blanket population held no illusions that the British government would concede to their demands without any deaths. For the
Blanketmen, the ideological and tactical equivalence between hunger
striking and military violence was based on the corpse as a fundamental
unit of political communication. This is the assumption that informs the
grotesque mechanical imagery in narrative 6.11 of an assembly line of
coffins emerging on schedule, from the prison. For the Blanketmen, this
very rationalization of self-inflicted death, now rendered analogous to the
rationalized military operation, was sufficient to secure the tactical legitimacy and effectiveness of the Hunger Strike.

From the inception of the Northern Ireland conflict, whether we are
concerned with sectarian murders, indiscriminate civilian bombings, or
the picking off of individual members of the army and police, the corpse
or the "stiff" has been the elemental communicative unit of political
performance. "Stiffing" is a cognate term for paramilitary violence in
Belfast, and the production of "stiffs" is crucial to the legitimation of any
paramilitary organization. Take for instance the INLA, for which legitimation was a central issue because of its lack of funds and weapons and
its secondary position to the larger, more established, and well armed
PIRA. An Intelligence Officer of that organization informed me that there
was an consensus among INLA active service units that they would have
to "produce twenty-six stiffs a year, a minimal operational level of a stiff
every two weeks," in order to achieve local legitimacy and an effective
political presence. The production of stiffs is a rationalized enterprise
involving economic and political calculations. It was estimated by the
INLA that "for every stiff there would have to be five operations

planned," which in itself demands supporting operations, such as bank raids and holdups. If establishing a quota for stiffs is crucial for initiating and sustaining political legitimation, then we can understand the Blanketmen's investment in prolonged and rationalized corpse production—the "parade of death"—as the basis for the Hunger Strike's political and instrumental viability.

In the discourse on stiff production there is an explicit relationship between sequence and significance in which the stiff is comprehended as the bearer of qualitative time (see also chap. 3). The stiff, serialized by repeated violence, is a currency that measures historical alterity. The causal linkage of stiff to stiff advances an emergent alien temporal continuum through which political power is claimed, and the singular appearance of each stiff is an instantiation of an alterity that displaces and fractures the present. The stiff as a repeatable code is the passageway that paramilitaries construct in order to intervene in historical time and to demonstrate their ability to regulate the latter in a material form. Scheduling stiffs is scheduling historical transformation and alternative time signatures. Violence applied to the body in a visible manner is the literal movement of time across the somatic surface. In turn, a sequence of stiffs is the movement of alien time signatures across the social surface. The problematic of the stiff of paramilitary culture is the dual problematic of the materialization of historical time and of the ethnography of "historical" surfaces, those "spaces of representation" (see Harvey 1989) on which historical maps are made manifest.

Koselleck (1985:246) has coined the phrase "the temporalization of history" to account for the process by which historical time is consciously submitted to human action for instrumentation. The temporalization of history is the construction of history as a cultural object:

> Time is no longer simply the medium in which all histories take place, it gains a historical quality. Consequently history no longer occurs in time but through time. Time becomes a dynamic and historical force in its own right. (Koselleck 1985:246)

The Blanketmen sought a "temporalization" of history by displacing residual jural-political temporalities and their existential suspensions with the directional biological time of the hunger strike. The body altered by defilement and later starvation was the instrument by which the Republican prisoners were able to posit history as a cultural object susceptible to alteration. The hunger strike scenario corresponded to what Kosseleck terms the "acceleration" of history (1985:231–66), a process central to the performative interventions of any social movement.

The materialization of historical time in the body, in the process of stiff production, opens onto the related problematic of the historiographic surface—the spaces, stages, templates of representation where historical alterity is made to appear as an effective force. Foucault (1978a) treated the issue of the historiographic surface through the thesis of the "spatialization of history," which in modernity was grounded on the spatialization of power. Historical temporality for Foucault was the normative effect and discourse of regional enclosures of power: the body, the clinic, the asylum, the prison, the state. It is in these spaces that time is constructed as a cultural object and as an instrument of domination. Kosseleck's "temporalization" (instrumentation) of history would only be possible for Foucault in terms of its prior synchronic spatialization in specified sites of enclosure and competence. The instrumentation of historical time is coeval with the manipulation of material relations, artifacts, expanses, and surfaces that embody history as the prerequisite to its mobilization. That is why Foucault (1978a) understood his analyses as the subversion of the Hegelian concept of history. For Hegel, history is the negation of space by time. The Hegelian concept is inverted by Foucault to produce the problematic of the historical surface, the subordination of time to regional ontologies and spatial synchronies.

In Northern Ireland the ethnography of political violence is the ethnography of the historical surface, the somatics and erotics of historical alterity. There, political power first constructs itself by constructing surfaces and sites for the staging, display, and narration of power. These points of instantiation include the interrogation cell, the "interface," and the bodies of the tortured interogatee, the sectarian stiff, and hunger striker. The performance of these sites and bodies aims at "making history appear." Whoever seeks power must first control the apparatuses for the production and mimesis of history as material spectacle.

"Stiffing" is the mobilization of spectacle by which the paramilitary apparatus and the state apparatus display their possession of political exchange values. In Northern Ireland the "space of death" (Taussig 1984 and 1987) is the mobilized spectacle from which particular artifacts of historical alterity flow and circulate as bearers of political norms. Such artifacts, like the stiff, can be understood as political commodities. Thus the ethnography of the historical surface is also the ethnography of the historical fetish—those chosen text(ture)s where the formal movement of history is imagined, where history effects are stored and produced.

To speak of a political violence that circulates artifacts and spectacles of power is to call into question any rigid separation of ideological and repressive apparatuses. The spectacle of death in the paramilitary strike, in the counterinsurgency incision, or in the prison protests attests to the fusion of the repressive and the ideological. Contrary to the Althusserian thesis, the performative dynamics of violence in Northern Ireland and the analyses of Foucault (1979) and Taussig (1987) suggest that the expansion of spheres of domination frequently takes place through a ritualized resynthesis of ideological and repressive apparatuses. The stiff in Northern Ireland is the exemplary symbol of this conjuncture.

The production of stiffs is as much a statement about the possession of power as it is a demand for power. In this process of displaying, substantiating, and eliciting power, the iconic, the performative, and the material components of power become fused. The forms and substance of power are conflated, if indeed they were ever separable.

This fusion of the forms and substance of power, the synthesis of the performance, artifacts and command of power, is a profound rejection of abstract juridical power. The propensity to distinguish between the enactment of power and an idealized juridical reserve of power that has an independent relation to instantiation is contravened by the autonomous animation of power from out of the body. In its very being and nonbeing, the stiff is the perfect topos and conduit for self-constructing empowerment. The stiff is simultaneously the bearer of political value, a communicant, an inscribed surface, and an inscribing agency. It is both presence/absence, inert and active, a thing and a persona, a silence and a vocality. The stiff authors political power as pure effect. Covert forms of random violence particularly amplify the stiff as an archic presentation of effective power, power as pure presence without a tangible Archimedean point outside of the stiff's political aura. Yet this immediacy of effect also functions as a mimetic system that concretizes fictive sites and narratives of legitimation.

The performative and political immediacy of the stiff, the visible/invisible, the presence/absence oppositions that are united in the condition of the stiff, complement a political agency that must remain both clandestine and hegemonic, secret and public, visible and invisible, random and inevitable. The iconicity of the stiff echoes the political iconography of the paramilitary apparatus. Consider the masked absence of the clandestine killer and the heightened presence of the stiff, the effaced body of the Blanketmen and the miasma emanating from it, or the invisibility of the Blanketmen in their confinement and the visually symbolic emergence of the corpse of the dead hunger striker from behind prison walls in the mass funeral.

The legitimizing potential of the politically encoded corpse was deployed by the planners of the Hunger Strike. Corpses had become the customary spectacle of political power on the "outside." Thus, the media through which the PIRA (inside) was to establish its legitimacy and hegemony on the "outside" would be the externalization and production of corpses. Each dead and dying hunger striker was intended as a building block in an architecture of empowerment that would secure the legitimacy of the prison-based Republican movement. The Hunger Strike was planned as the Blanketmen's entrance into the generalized economy of violence within which all paramilitary groups in Northern Ireland sought to secure their legitimacy. The logic of corpse symbolism in the political theater of the Hunger Strike was a continuation of the symbolic logic of paramilitary violence outside of the prison, although in this case the template of the politically encoded corpse was to be enhanced by the truth claims of the ascetic formation of the body. There was very little cynical manipulation in their strategy. They did believe in the efficacy of their bodies defiled, dying, and dead inasmuch as they had believed in the political efficacy of their weapons and the stiff when they functioned on the "outside" in active service units.

The prisoner who starved to death achieved an act of purification that separated him irrevocably from the stigma of criminalization, and as subtext removed him from the defiling topos of the prison. This conviction on the part of the Blanketmen was the strongest motivating force behind the necessity of the Hunger Strike. It just about predetermined the death of the hunger striker, though it was also believed that those who experienced a hunger strike, who had "gone to the edge" and returned, would have achieved a radical act of separation culminating in both political and personal transformation.

The prison regime, which had intended first to criminalize and then to "normalize" and "rehabilitate" the "conforming" political prisoner, would be exposed as a machine for degradation and abuse. The performance of the hunger strike would stage the abuse and violence of the Other in the eviscerated flesh of the dying protester. The penal imperative to incorporate the panoptic presence of the Other as a form of compliance and subjugation would itself be subjected to deflating mimesis and a final ironic reversal. In turn, the corpse of the hunger striker would be one more jettisoned *sacrifecal* fragment of state violence. The act of hunger striking purified and decriminalized the striker, but the queue of corpses emerging from behind prison walls would shake the moral legitimacy of the British state. Time after time the Republican inmates, under interrogation and in prison, had been charged by state propaganda with "self-inflicted" violence. This charge would be subverted from within by a performance that diagrammed in a graphic *reenactment* the procedures of the state that drove men to abjection. The hunger strike was an epic act of emancipation. Yet no other action more eloquently demonstrated the condition and image of the human body infested with the state apparatus.

In this context the public sacralization of the dead hunger striker was inevitable, whether or not Christological codes were in play in the communities that physically and politically received the body of the protester. The dead hunger striker was a mimetic part of the state, it was the state itself in a concentrated form that had been ejected from the prison.

Starvation of the flesh in the hunger strike was the inverting and bitter interiorization of the power of the state. Hunger striking to the death used the body of the prisoner to recodify and to transfer state power from one topos to another. The corpse of the hunger striker was also the artifact of the contaminated Other. The act of self-directed violence interiorized the Other, neutralized its potency, enclosed its defiling power, and stored it in the corpse of the hunger striker for use by his support community. The subsequent sacralization of the dead hunger striker completed the process of purification and commemorated the subverting transfer of power from the state to the insurgent community with elaborate funeral processions and mortuary displays. Today in almost every Republican house the tokens, fragments, and storage artifacts of this recodified, inverted, and disseminated state power are present in the form of iconographic photographs, paintings, and posters of the dead hunger strikers. I was presented with one such poster which displayed the faces, names, and birth and death dates of the ten hunger strikers, that had been designed and printed in Libya.

If Christological motifs in the hunger strike ritual seem to pervade the performance, we have also to place into this schema the dead hunger striker as a new empowering origin site. From his dead and purified body, new cycles of violence were expected to flow. Military eschatology and biological eschatology were intertwined. This new violence would be founded on a renewed legitimacy; it would not be the same paramilitary violence that had preceded the hunger strike. This newly legitimized violence would be symbolically (and practically, once the Blanketmen were released) an extension of the same political technologies and ascetic disciplines of the body that would be so eloquently demonstrated in the forthcoming Hunger Strike.

The Hunger Strike was a rite of differentiation that directly addressed the cultural construction of violence. It repositioned what were in effect the same instrumental performances of paramilitary violence within a new biosymbolic framework, and in doing so effected a revaluation of subsequent Republican violence. The paramilitary violence that was to be based on the legitimacy of the dead hunger strikers was a material repetition of the paramilitary violence that had preceded the Hunger Strike. But this violence was now decriminalized through a purifying filter created by the self-sacrifice of the hunger striker.

The Lark

The period preceding the initiation of the 1981 Hunger Strike was characterized by intensive debates on the Blanket wings concerning the timing, structure, and implications of this new mode of resistance. These debates were attempts to construct and plan a ritual performance powerful enough to extract the Blanketmen from the current H-Block situation. The planning discussions were particularly volatile because of the failure of the 1980 Hunger Strike to attain the five demands. That failure ensured that the 1981 Hunger Strike would have fatal consequences for at least the first group of strikers. The Hunger Strike was also conceived as a renewal and regeneration of the Republican movement. The Hunger Strike bore the weight of a collective history that would be precariously distilled into the determination of a few men. The fundamental contradiction confronting the Blanketmen was that the performance that would emerge from the social solidarity of the prison collective and which could subsequently determine the collective experience of the entire Republican movement had to be organized in such a manner that the structures of collectivity were to be removed from the center of political action, the solitary dying hunger striker.

The most frustrating violence of the prison regime had been the sound of individual prisoners being beaten while the prison collective was forced to listen behind locked doors. When one prisoner was beaten, they all felt the blows. Likewise, hunger striking entailed sending individual prisoners one by one to their deaths as the prison collective waited for the political effect of each death.

The actual hunger strikers were to be chosen as emissaries and surrogates of the prison collective, but the status of the hunger striker as an encapsulating symbol of the experiences and ideology of the prison collective grated against the fact that in the Hunger Strike each participant died alone. These debates over the necessary separation of the hunger striker from the prison collective were organized around comparative performances of violence. As a death ritual, the Hunger Strike was subjected to comparisons with that other death ritual, the paramilitary operation. As a military strategy, the Hunger Strike introduced a new and disturbing individualization of death and proposed a new political division of labor.

6.13 The final discussions in the wing where everybody was giving their two d's worth. The "Dark" got up and said, "Before we begin here for anybody putting their name down for hunger strike we can rule out people who have missing livers and things like that. Anybody who's considering to go on it has to be in fairly sound physical condition." This had all been given out, and everybody was aware of it on the wing. There was a big reluctance for people to get up to the door and say, "We have to hunger strike," that we have no option. For years de-

cisions had been taken at the door; it was a collective responsibility. Nobody wanted to get up at the door and it would be
his fucking speech or his arguments that would push us over
the edge. As the "Dark" said, "We're blowing the whistle to
take the boys up the fucking trenches. When that whistle is
blown and starts the ball rolling, you were the guy who was
taking men to the edge of death."

People matured in those discussions. Some didn't. You also
got egotists. I mind one who had lost his liver when he was
shot. He knew he wasn't going on hunger strike. He got up to
the door and he says: "Anybody who doesn't put their name
down is a coward!" I flipped. I tore up to the door, "See,
you'll not be going on hunger strike, don't be going up to the
door with your sanctimonious attitudes! Don't be getting up
there and browbeating people into hunger strikes!"

In those discussions you could identify who was genuine
and who wasn't. But that shows how critical you can become
within that sort of condition. Here's a guy who's been lying
naked for five years, and I say he's looking for an easy way
out or that he's not genuine. It shows you how the severity of
things increases your perceptions of things. "This is nothing!
Laying around in a blanket under snow and getting beaten on
a regular basis!" that was normal; to hunger strike was going
beyond that. (PIRA)

6.14 Death became more sensitive in the Blocks than on operations, because you had to live with people day in and day out.
It was a family. When you're out on the street operating in a
squad you're tight knit. Death was something that you faced,
but it's not a foregone conclusion. You have a chance. In the
Blocks the guys who were saying "hunger strike," weren't
saying, "hunger strike and you might die." They were saying,
"Die! You, die for me!"

The big difference between that and an "op" is I turn
around and say to my mate, "This is an 'op,' this is your part
in it." He goes on the line and gets blown away. I do have a
responsibility, but at the same time there is not that finality
about it. I've planned the "op" to give him every chance to
live. I'm not just sending him out to die. "Go around and
stand in front of the police barracks and give a 'det' [detonate
a bomb], and he gets blown away." In an "op" I'm not saying
that. But in a hunger strike we knew you were dying. (PIRA)

6.15 A lot of the debates were concentrated on that aftermath of the Hunger Strike, its consequences. We were very analytical. We could pick different scenarios, analyzing where we would be going. We would draw out five different scenarios and one by one discuss those scenarios, the options we would be left with in a given situation. The thing we were talking about was if in the event of a death of a hunger striker you had massive widespread violence on the outside, and the IRA went out to try to channel that, to try to control that. What if the IRA was overrun? What if they became a secondary force and popular street violence took over from that? What if the Hunger Strike failed? If guys withdrew and didn't go to their death, we envisioned massive demoralization on the outside. In that situation we envisioned that the campaign would grind to a halt. That we would have to start the politicization process over again. If the Hunger Strike failed in its goals and didn't grant us immunity from the prison uniform, we would either continue on the Blanket till every one of us had done our sentences or wear the uniform and go for the maximum facilities for training people in prison for the war. (PIRA)

6.16 There were talks at that time between the Brits and Bishop Daly about the Blanket Protest. We had been told by the OCs not to place any hopes on those talks, even though we all had lots of hopes that something would happen to resolve the issue and break the deadlock. The Dirty Protest had been going on for two and a half years and the Blanket longer than that. When those talks collapsed there must have been a plan prearranged, because Brendan Hughes, after he had been informed about the collapse of the talks on the visit, went up to the door and put out that there should be a hunger strike.[9] Bobby Sands, his right-hand man at the time, immediately swung into action. Each man in the wing who could was delegated to write letters announcing the strike and its reasons. He then asked us that if we were prepared to die, to put our names on the list for the strike. If we weren't prepared to die, don't. My cell mate and I began to pace up and down. I started to think about dying, and I didn't know what good it would do if I came to that point. I would try to tell myself that I would be able to die, and then I wasn't sure. I kept putting off the decision. After a few days I couldn't come to any decision and I passed off thinking about it. About a week and a half later a note came down through the cells. There were wee holes scooped out around the pipes, and the notes were passed through them. The note was the list for the Hunger Strike. The cell below us, both of them put their names down. The note came to us and my cell mate put his name down. We had been together a long time. And then it came to me, and I knew at that moment that I could die if they were willing to. I was sort of convinced afterward it was taking the easy out of the prison situation. At the time I felt I had no right to leave people in the other cells to say they could do it and I couldn't do it.

Brendan Hughes and Bobby Sands were discussing the first hunger strikers. They had the list of people who wanted to go. They were deciding on the merits of where they came from, what they were in for, and what the guys knew of them, what they thought of them as people. People who had been on the Blanket, off of it, and then back on again were not accepted, only people who were on the Blanket from the start and stuck through it. How you carried yourself on the Blanket was important in their choice.

They drew up a short list of several names. Then there was a bit of hassle between the INLA and the Provos (IRA). The original seven on the list were all Provisionals and the INLA demanded that they get two men. The Provos on the list were all from their higher ranks. (INLA)

The Blanketmen knew quite well that the individual hunger striker was a representative of their collective condition, that he would sacrifice his individuality at the same time that he committed the most individual of acts. It was only by sustaining a representational ethic within his very being that the striker would be able to maintain his commitment to "the edge." Bobby Sands was perhaps the person most sensitive to the emblematic status of the hunger striker as a concentrate of historicized collectivity. Because of this awareness, Sands knew that the Hunger Strike had to be constructed as a ritual resynthesis not only for the world outside the prison but for the Blanketmen. Ritualization of the Hunger Strike was extended by Sands to the entire preparatory period. Sands emerged as the paradigmatic figure of the Hunger Strike, not only because he would be the first to go on strike, but because he was fully aware of the fact that the protest demanded a social and ideological reorganization of the Blanketmen themselves. Sands incarnated this organization in his very comportment and presentation of self to the other Blanketmen. Sands was the prison poet, myth maker, architect of the cultural separatist ideology within the H-Blocks, and one of the central authors of the politicization program. He generated the orienting myths and anchoring symbols of the prison situation which imparted an epic narrative to the Blanketmen's situation. It was Sands who constantly reiterated the eschatological and fatal consequences of hunger striking. In contrast to other prisoners who conceptualized the Hunger Strike as a purely instrumental political tactic, Sands saw it explicitly as a renewing death ritual. He was basically disinterested in the immediate objective gains of the protest.[10] Sands was well aware that a purely functional approach to the Hunger Strike would not be sufficient to maintain the ideological certitude of the individual striker once he was isolated from his comrades in the hospital ward of the prison and subject to the interventions of medical staff, priests, and family. Sands' fatalistic comportment in the face of death was meant to establish the paradigm of the "good death" of the Hunger Strike. Sands established death on the Hunger Strike as a poetic/epic figure, a ritual reenactment, a completion of a historical epoch in the Republican movement, and as the unification of the dying hunger striker with the past cultural and political traditions of a separatist and insurrectionary Ireland. For Sands, the Hunger Strike incarnated deeper passages than the attainment of political status. The Hunger Strike as performance was the final seal of irrevocable historical completion. Posthumous bureaucratic recognition of this was unimportant for Sands.

Sands deliberately, but without any cynicism, cultivated the imagery of the good Republican death by cultivating the imagery of his own death before he even began his hunger strike. This anticipatory dissemination of his death both manipulated the Blanketmen's emotions and signified the entering of a ritual condition. In a moment of foreclosure, Sands placed himself on the other side. In doing so, he socialized the prisoners to the inevitable eschatology imbedded in hunger striking. Sands saw his death as a pedagogical event, and by visibly displaying his crossing over the life/death boundary, he was able to pull the other prisoners over that boundary with him.

6.17 The first thing you noticed about Bobby Sands, in his lectures and political talks it was all done with incredible intensity. He got really worked up putting his point of view across. He couldn't abide apathy. He had a lot of sympathy for people who were slow; he always took the time to talk to them if he made a point you didn't see. Bobby would have spent a few hours and even days trying to convince you. But he wasn't a browbeater; he always wanted you to speak your piece. He was very very intense and very tied up in his own beliefs and view of life.

He talked about the *borachie,* the lark that he loved listening to outside the cell window. He had a story from his grand-
father. There was a lark captured by a cruel evil man. The
man put the lark into a cage. He wanted to trap the song of
the lark. That, Bobby said, was the freedom of the lark. The
man wanted the lark's song for himself, but the lark refused
to sing. But the man still kept the lark in the cage. He started
to break the lark, but the lark still wouldn't sing. He was
cruel to it. It never sang, and it eventually died in the cage.
There was a lark that used to fly above his cell and he used to
say to me, "You see, no matter what they do, my spirit is like
that lark, free and singing even if they kill me." He said he
had the spirit of freedom; like his "little friend" the lark, he
had a spirit that couldn't be broken. The symbol that came out
of the H-Blocks, the symbol of the freedom fighter, was the
lark singing on the barbed wire. That was the symbol everybody associated with the hunger strikers. (PIRA)

6.18   We were talking of upward of twenty people dead on the Hunger Strike. Bobby Sands himself got up to the door and said,
"Right, if anybody imagines that the British are giving in here
they better catch themselves on. What we're talking about
here is a battleground chosed by the Brits, and the Brits
aren't going to give in. You're talking about people who are
ruthless to the extent that they planted bombs in bars and
killed innocent people so as to put the blame on the IRA.
You're talking about people who will have no compunction in
allowing ten, twenty, thirty men to parade to their death on
Hunger Strike!" We had that mentality and a very sound
group majority that accepted that analysis. You had other people who were still hoping something would come out of it.
"That's brilliant. Bobby will just go on hunger strike, and he'll
go to the edge and get political status and everything will be
hunky dory." With that attitude and those types of people, as
the Hunger Strike progressed and people died you had a disil-
lusionment setting in, real depths of depression.

Bobby said out the door, "I'm going to die, make no two
ways about it. I know I am dying and I want to make it clear
what I am dying for. It's not about a suit of clothes or a food
parcel. I'm dying to make sure that the struggle continues,
that the struggle lives!" I mind Bobby saying, "My death will
only be in vain if you as Republicans fail to understand what
you're about and where you're going and fail to teach it to

others. It had fuck all to do with the uniform. For anybody to believe I died for five demands is madness! I am dying for those people who I'm proud to know as the risen people!" (PIRA)

6.19 All the ones who died on the Hunger Strike were very, very good people, and that's the way it had to be. Bobby Sands knew he was dying. On his last visit with his mother before the strike his Ma asked, "What do you think, will it work?" Bobby said, "Just go out and make funeral arrangements, I'm dead." She said, "Don't be talking like that!" He says, "I have to talk like that. I'm not coming out of here. That's me start the countdown from now." And that's the attitude he had.[11] (PIRA)

Bobby Sands translated the longstanding Republican tradition of endurance (Coogan 1980:14–30) into the evocative saga of the caged lark. In his story, the determination of the lark embedded political practice within the sphere of nature, the latter standing as a metonym of the body in the H-Blocks. Here the "good" Republican death was inserted into the transcendant domain of nature which imbued death by hunger strike with an autonomous trajectory. The body denatured by prison conditions would be renatured in hunger striking. Hunger striking was implicitly the return to the prepolitical body through a highly politicized action. Nature (in the form of the body) functions as the transcendent donor that reempowers those disenfranchised within the political domain. In starvation the hungar striker did not put divestiture before him but behind him.

Sands' story endowed the Hunger Strike, the Republican movement, and the insurrectionary history of Ireland with an organic teleology. This naturalization of subjective will was foregrounded by the topological polarity of the cage, symbol of both the H-Blocks and a colonized Ireland, and the lark—the poetic agency of biological self-determination. The lark's refusal to sing in the cage evokes the deployment of Gaelic in prison as a secret language and is a metaphor of cultural separatism made possible by biological separatism.

Sands established the lark as a totemic symbol of the Blanketmen and the Hunger Strike. The autonomy of biological process in the Dirty Protest and the Hunger Strike was advanced by Sands as *the structure* that could rupture the material and ideological constraints of captivity both within and outside the prison. The Hunger Strike was constructed by Sands as a performative display of the genealogy of the body in the H-Blocks. This genealogical depiction would be constituted by the serialization of hunger-striking bodies, the transfer of the sacrificial code from the body of each hunger striker to the next. It was to be a relay of death that symbolized, through the substitution of one body by another, the generational/historical continuity of Irish political resistance.

The necessity of this naturalization code can be found in the contrast between the performative structures of the Hunger Strike and the performative structures that dominated the Blanket and Dirty Protest. The sociation of Gaelic speakers created the necessary anchorages for maintaining political/cognitive solidarity among prisoners separated by cellular confinement and twenty-four-hour lockup. This sociation would be marginalized or absent altogether in the later stages of starvation. It was known, based on the 1980 Hunger Strike, that the fasting prisoner would be separated from the cell block and relocated in the prison hospital after twenty-odd days. The striker would not be allowed to die in his cell among his comrades. In the prison hospital he would be cut off from the collective except for visits from Sinn Fein representatives, smuggled "coms" (communiqués), and perhaps the company of one or two other advanced strikers who could have been in weak condition and even in coma by the time the new striker arrived.[12]

The hunger striker had to perform his singular act cut off from the unifying discourses of the Blanket culture "always on the air." Those who left the Blocks were described as going "off the air," a local idiom for death. The anticipation of separation gnawed at the empathetic solidarity of the Blanketmen. The departure of the hunger striker from the Blocks as well as his embarkation on a process of starvation was like an autonomous part of a collective body disengaging from the whole in order to construct its own specialized field of political action.

As Sands began his hunger strike on March 1, 1981, he performed the ultimate act of structural separation from the defiling past of the H-Blocks, and in doing so, presented the gathering audience of the Hunger Strike—prisoners, prison staff, the media, government officials, Republican sympathizers, and the people of Ireland—with an explicit sign of his utopian and eschatological intentions. In one gesture he demonstrated that the surface and extremities of the body had once belonged to the oppressor; they, the outside, had been neutralized by fecal disorder (the revenge of the inside), but the goal of the Hunger Strike was to reclaim the external body from all institutional objectifications through a radical process of interiorization—self-consumption.

6.20   Bobby went and got a haircut and a shave on the first day of
        his hunger strike. I thought at the time, "This is it. The
        body's wasted here. The body's going out."
            It was a marker that a phase had gone obsolete and a new
        phase had begun. We knew we were caught in the Blanket

situation and that was a definite ongoing thing. If we continued the dirt protest in parallel with the Hunger Strike, then when the Hunger Strike ended we would still be in the Blanket Protest, no matter what way the Hunger Strike ended. We had decided that we weren't going forward in that situation. The Hunger Strike was the ultimate weapon, and if that failed we would have just isolated ourselves and we would be into the slow grind of the Breaker's Yard. The men would just be gradually worn down having to face fifteen to twenty years on the Blanket.

We decided as the Hunger Strike commenced on March 1 that the Dirty Protest would end. We still had no clothes. We were still on the Blanket. If we had come off the Dirty Protest five days before the Hunger Strike, it would have been a massive political stunt for the Brits. But the day we went off the protest the media was splashed with, "Bobby Sands, OC and PRO (Public Relations Officer) of the H-Blocks, commences hunger strike." But it always stuck in my head, Bobby's haircut, and he said, "What do ye reckon kid, how do I look?" (PIRA)

6.21 The first day of Bobby Sands' hunger strike we went off the No Wash Protest. It was just my own view that the Provos were allowing for the fact that even if the Hunger Strike didn't work, guys would be sitting in better conditions as far as sitting in a clean cell and getting washed. It really fucked the screws up on that first day. For four years they had to deal with the smell and the stink of the Dirty Protest and the abuse from the guys day in and day out. Then one morning suddenly there we all were asking nicely for the breakfast, for a wash, a haircut, and the cell to be cleaned. What the screws were really thinking was their extra money for working in these conditions just got knocked in the head with the end of the No Wash Protest. (INLA)

Bobby Sands (PIRA) went on hunger strike on March 1, 1981. On March 2, the Blanket blocks went off the Dirty Protest. On March 8, Francis Hughes (PIRA) joined Sands on the Hunger Strike, to be followed by Raymond McCreesh (PIRA) and Patsy O'Hara (INLA) on March 22. On April 9, 1981, Bobby Sands was elected to Parliament as M. P. for Fermanagh/South Tyrone. On May 5, 1981, at 1:15 A.M., Bobby Sands, M. P., died while in coma. The night he died there was rioting in Belfast and throughout Northern Ireland, but the expected cathartic upsurge of popular and violent revolt did not emerge. Up to a hundred thousand people marched peacefully at his funeral two days later. The Blanketmen, as they mourned Sands, watched and waited for what the next few deaths would bring. Nine more men would follow Sands to their deaths before the strike was called off on October 3, 1981, after 217 days and ten dead.[13]

6.22   The slagging and practical joking stopped during the Hunger Strike. I minded Bobby saying the joking shouldn't decrease. But it was all dead artificial. There was no fucking singsongs. We tried but it wouldn't work. Bobby had asked us not to get into the silence. We were all in mourning for the duration. The thing was one massive period of death and mourning and saturation with death. (PIRA)

Biological Time, Prison Time, and Historical Time

The ending of the No Wash Protest furthered the imagery of ritual purification associated with the Hunger Strike. The prison collective no longer needed to wear the stigmata of its institutional condition on their bodies or on their cell walls. In the form of the dying hunger striker, the Blanketmen now possessed an encapsulating public bearer of their institutional defilement. That collective condition was transferred to a singular exemplary agent who, through the act of sacrificial expulsion, conveyed the collective defilement out of the prison and transferred this miasma to the British government and to Irish society as a whole.

The termination of the Dirty Protest was also an attempt to collectivize the personal passage encoded in the hunger striker's death. In following Sands' pedagogical example by accepting haircuts, showers, and cleaning of their cells, the prisoners crossed over the life/death boundary along with Bobby Sands. In this step, the new history had begun to flow outward from the sacrificial process, an event that was marked by the reactivation of time in the Blanket blocks.

6.23   When the strike started we had left a phase behind us. We had broken that sense of "the never ending." You were very conscious then that every day that went past was bringing the day of reckoning closer. There was that much happening and a new sense of urgency that set in all around. It meant that you were *scriobhing* [writing] all day. You had the skins [cigarette papers] put out and your mailing list, and everybody was banging away. The thing about the writing—it gave everybody a sense of doing something. (PIRA)

6.24   There was information available [on] how long an individual could last on the Hunger Strike and what physical stages would occur. We bangled the information in. During the Hunger Strike you were very very conscious of time. You knew that each day that went in was another day lost, another day somebody was closer to death. I mind going through that with Bobby's hunger strike particularly. We knew that roughly in their mid-twenties they [the strikers] was going to get shifted from the cell to the hospital. We thought that they would isolate them from the beginning of the strike. But they didn't; they kept them in the wing for twenty-one days, and that became the marker of death for everybody else. (PIRA)

6.25   Everything was urgent issues, happening all there and then. When a guy was on hunger strike in the wing, the noise level went down. Everybody was conscious all the time that there was someone next to you dying. When the food came around you had to be conscious about not shouting, "What do you think of the meat today?" Your complaints were relegated to something meaningless. You couldn't go to the door and shout, "There's something with this grub." (INLA)

6.26   We felt guilty about food; everytime you sat eating a meal, you felt guilty as fuck. You couldn't taste anything, just get the meal over and taken away. Once a striker died you couldn't eat at all; you just fucked the food in the corner. There was no basis for feeling guilt, yet at the same time there was a sense of it.

Until the Hunger Strike we found the thing by what one does, everybody does. If one's getting beat, we were all getting beat. If somebody smashed a cup in the cell accidentally, that meant that the screws would knock his bollocks in, as an excuse if he asked for a new cup. If somebody broke a cup the OC would say, "Right, everybody smash the cups!" Everybody smashed the cups. He wasn't on his own; he wasn't isolated. There was that security in numbers, that unification. Everybody acted together. But with the Hunger Strike you were dead aware about that separation between yourself and the guy laying in the cell dying.

The other thing that was thrown out was the mass hunger strike. Everybody going up to the edge, sixty to seventy days, then pulling back, four hundred guys traveling the road together. In that scenario you would of went your sixty days;

there would be no telling what the fuck you would of done when you got to the edge. You might have said, "Fuck it" and go all the way. Four hundred guys would have at least gone to that stage. There was that sense of the rush to get out of this fuckin' thing that we've been trapped in for five years. That rush toward it. It would have been like a jailbreak with the fuckin' Brit in the tower firing the machine gun, but you're all going in a rush, and you didn't care because what you were leaving behind isn't too nice anyway. (PIRA)

6.27   The night Bobby died I felt it was going to happen that night. But Jesus, I never believed it would happen. You had that feeling of disbelief even though you knew in your heart he was dying. I knew from the very start that it was just a matter of time. If you read his diary, he knows he's dying. He just accepts it. So did we, but at the same time when somebody you know so well is just dead you thought, "Bobby's not coming down on the wing no more." And he was the motivating force, a driving force. (PIRA)

6.28   The night Bobby Sands died was just . . . you never heard a sound for hours. Nobody spoke and nobody would go near the door. The way we knew he was dead, a screw came down and there was a grill at the end of the wing, and with his baton he started banging the grill slowly, Dong!—dong!—dong!—like a church bell. It was just a hollow sound. From that point on whenever someone died the screws would ring the grill and another one would walk up the wing slowly pulling a trolley behind him, saying, "Bring out your dead. How many dead do youse have for us today?" It was like the plague. (PIRA)

The highly revealing proposal of the mass hunger strike, that undifferentiated rush of the collective body to the "edge" and beyond, indicates the extent to which the Hunger Strike as a medium of political action was considered analogous to the prison escape. That sense of the "never ending" while on the No Wash Protest and the stalemate of negotiations with the British had convinced many men with long sentences that the only way they would ever leave the prison would be in their coffins. They pondered how long they could endure the No Wash Protest and the violence, and they knew well that despite their temporary biological mastery over the prison, the administration would devise new techniques of coercion. Going to the edge (the collective rush toward death) indicated the extent to which hunger striking was perceived as a newly acquired discipline of the body, a new experience of biological seccession from prison and from their own captive bodies that could sustain the prisoners through the long years of subsequent imprisonment if it did not culminate in death.

The Hunger Strike completed the textualization of the prisoner's body. As Bobby Sands and subsequent hunger strikers lay dying, the rest of the Blanketmen engaged in the intensified production of political texts that were smuggled out of the prison. These texts constituted a literature of conversion, letters to international organizations, political groups, unions, governments, and prominent individuals which publicized the Hunger Strike and asked support for the protest. Certain prisoners writing with pen refills on cigarette papers were able to produce 200 letters a day. It was a remarkable literary production which seemed to flow directly from the dying body of the hunger striker. The tortuous process of composing four thousand–word letters on cigarette rolling papers was an uncanny evocation of the equally tortuous production of monastic caligraphy in medieval Ireland. What connects the two forms of literary production was the dialectic between institutions of confinement, ascetic disciplines of the body, and the externalization of a culture through part objects of the body, emblems of an invisible totality.

Again, as in many other facets of their political culture, the conversion texts that emerged from the Hunger Strike were mediated by the body. The genesis of the letter of conversion, its conditions of production, repeated the genealogy of the recodified body. The letter of conversion originated in the body of the hunger striker as his proxy and double. It was produced through specialized manual techniques of miniaturization, and then "bangled" or "fagined" by other bodies out of the prison, just as the raw materials for literary production had been bangled by the body into the prison. The literary culture of the Blanketmen was based on a corporeal workshop of storage, graphics, and dissemination.

The Hunger Strike continued the H-Block tradition of extracting techniques, discourses, and systems of knowledge from the prisoner's body. The literary production of the Blanketmen was one component of this industry of the body. For all the adversary groups implicated in the Hunger Strike—the Blanketmen, the prison regime, the British government, and the media—the body in the process of starvation became a renewed source of ideology production. The starving body of the hunger striker had injected a new equation into the rigid political frameworks of the Northern Ireland situation. All parties invested in the general political culture were eager to integrate this equation into their existing systems of knowledge and representation:

6.29   The way the Hunger Strike worked was that the Brits sat and
recorded every move the hunger striker made, everything he
said, everything he done. It was a whole psychological wire-
up. They were trying to find out as much as they could from
every angle, just a whole in-depth study. The doctors were
doing it, the screws were doing it, the governors of the
prison were doing it, the priests were doing it, and we were
doing it. Everybody was into sussing it out.[14] (PIRA)

The Hunger Strike reactivated the political dynamic of hierarchical
observation and radical textualization of the body that had characterized
much of the H-Blocks' history. At the moment of the striking Blanketman's disappearance, he was to attain his highest condition of visibility.
But despite this parasitic swarming over his body, the hunger striker
became an isolate, dominated by the solitary ordeal of his dying body,
witnessing the submersion of his politically constructed self by the
decimations of biological process. The hunger striker slowly learned
that, beyond this one final political reorganization of his body, no further
codifications were possible this side of death, that this final act exhausted
the body as self-reflexive political discourse. In reaching the edge, death,
pain, blindness, and coma moved the body beyond all cultural/political
constructs. As he entered into the time of his death, the hunger striker
realized the politics of silence as the termination of his long passage
through the joined labyrinths of the prison and his body:

6.30   By the time Joe McDonnell died, [July 18, 1981] people were
going on strike even though they didn't expect anything. My
cell mate went on, and after seventy-one days I knew his
death was coming and I had to prepare myself for I was next.
I would go on anytime after seventy-one days. Before he died
I was in a preparation period for going on. I just got my mind
ready for death. To get myself into the frame of mind, I was
saying to myself, you can't turn back no matter what happens,
no matter what pain comes, no matter what hurt, no matter
what pressure.
   I had a good idea what was coming. My cell mate and I
didn't talk much about the process. It was a thing that you
kept to yourself. I prepared myself to die. I hardened myself
so when my cell mate died I didn't get emotional, I just felt
null. I said to myself, "He died and I'm going to die now, and
that's just the way it is. I wasn't happy about the prospect,
but it was something I had to do. I justified my going on Hun-

ger Strike and not breaking by thinking that in the last analysis
that if I didn't go on, someone else would go in my place. He
would suffer and die where I should be. There was no way in
my conscience I could allow someone else to go through that.

The first two weeks were fairly tough. There was a craving
for food and an overwhelming desire to eat one last pea or
one last chip.[15] But I kept fighting it all the time. The other
men hadn't broken and I wasn't going to break. After three
weeks the food craving eased up. During that time I was
praying each day, but not reading the Bible because I was trying to preserve my eyes. I knew that the eyesight of the hunger strikers was the first thing to go.

I was moved out into a single cell and left on my own. For
four weeks I was in that cell, and I didn't see anybody but
screws for that time. After that I was moved into the hospital
ward.

I had a visit with my mother. My mate had been buried,
and there had been a big controversy at his funeral. Shots had
been fired, and there had been an agreement that the military
salute wouldn't be given on chapel grounds. I had sent out to
the mother and said I wanted to see her and the priest to discuss funeral arrangements while I could. I didn't want a big
controversy when I was buried. I just wanted to be buried
quietly. My mother asked me where I would like to be buried.
I first said just throw me in a hole, I'm not worried about
where my body goes. Then I said I would like to be buried
alongside my cell mate. I thought afterward it was very hard
on her to come out with such an answer. She probably had
very little hope, but whatever hopes she might have held
were killed by what I said. What had happened at my cell
mate's funeral was so much on my mind that without thinking
I made things harder for her. She took it all very calmly and
didn't try to talk me out of it.

As time went on I was trying to keep as relaxed as possible, trying to lead a normal life, walking around the yard for
an hour a day, talking with the other men who were also on
strike. To go down and watch TV, which was the first time I
seen it for years. I didn't find much on it. I spent most of the
days praying and began to think a lot about people who were
dying on the outside and the inside, feeling sorry for them all.
Going toward death I began to identify with people who had
died in the Troubles and their families. Thinking all the time
I'm making a blunder here, that I'm going to have a long time

afterward to think about it. I began to see that in reality the
Hunger Strike was falling apart. A few men had been taken
off it by their parents, including the two men I had been with
in hospital. That left me in the hospital all alone. The Hunger
Strike was fast breaking down. It was the only means it could
have broken down—that somebody had to intervene between
the two parties because they weren't prepared to move an
inch.

On the forty-second day my eyesight started to go. I was
watching TV and the picture began to flicker. I was wondering
if it was the TV or me and looked around and the whole room
did the same. Just after that I was sick. That the beginning of
a weeklong cycle when my eyesight began to slowly fade.
This causes a seasickness effect. I was in bed all the time
holding a wee bowl, vomiting up water and green bile which
was very unpleasant. My eyesight started to go on Sunday,
and by Friday I was constantly heaving and heaving. I thought
that my whole insides would just drop out. I thought that if
this keeps going on much longer I'd not live long, because it
was a very weakening effect. The next morning, Saturday, I
woke up and I was blind, and because of that the sickness
stopped. Around this time my bowels and coordination started
to go downhill. I didn't realize though because I was blind.[16]

I knew I was going downhill fast. I just thought to myself
when I woke up in the morning, "This is how it feels like dying." And I was by no means pleased with the prospect.
Thinking at that time that the whole Hunger Strike was falling
apart anyway. I was as good as dead. But still I felt conscious
bound to keep going. I couldn't give up because I have given
my word to die if I had to. I didn't see a way out. So I kept
on going.

The priest came in and began to talk to me, saying various
things—that my mother had been in contact with an eye specialist, who said if I continued to that weekend I'd be blind for
the rest of my life. I thought to myself I'm going to die, I
don't have to worry about my eyesight. Then he told me that
when my cell mate was dying he had told this priest that he
shouldn't let me die the way he was dying. I was thinking on
the fact that he still had time to think of me when he was dying himself. It got me emotional inside, though I didn't show
anything on the outside. I kept a hard exterior. The priest
went out and my mother came in. I hadn't expected her that
day. She came in to me and said that she couldn't have my

death on her conscience. That there was no way she was going to allow me to die. That she would move to end my hunger strike as soon as I went into a coma. Then she asked me
to come off of it myself. My first reaction was not to come off
of it. That I had to keep going. And then I thought that there
was no point to leaving her to take the decision and leave me
off the hook, so that I could say, "I didn't go off," but that it
was the mother who took me off.

I decided then that the best thing was for me to go off myself. It was my fifty-fifth day into my hunger strike. Sands had
lasted sixty-six days; some men lasted fifty-odd days, others
sixty-odd days. I don't think I would have made sixty days. I
was going downhill fast. I was close. The blindness was doing
me harm and the bowel movements were a torture. I still had
a bit of weight to lose. I could still "pinch an inch." I went off
with mixed emotions. I remember the tears were streaming
out of me. Thinking of the men who died. Thinking of the men
who are still on the Blanket. That they still had to go through
all the same stuff. That a hunger strike had failed yet again. I
didn't know what to feel. I had an injection. A doctor had been
on standby just in case. The eyesight began to come back
slightly. It would be a couple of days before I could eat anything. The Hunger Strike ended exactly a week after I left it.
(INLA)

In the early 1970s, the basis of the IRA military strategy had been the
de-ghettoization of the war and the collectivization of the experience of
disruptive violence in all sectors of Northern Ireland society and the
British mainland. The Hunger Strike, staged from behind prison walls,
followed a similar strategy. It was an attempt to reawaken an overwhelming sense of historical violation in the Catholic communities, which would
push this population over the edge into an apocalyptic display of street
riots, intensified terrorist activity, and open armed revolt to be led by the
cadres of the PIRA and INLA. A crucial component of the planning of the
Hunger Strike had been a series of analyses in H6 that rehearsed all the
variations and tactical implications of this popular revolt. Yet with the
death of Sands, Hughes, McCreesh, and O'Hara, the prospects of violent
resolution receded dramatically:

6.31   When Bobby died it was just so hard to take in. A man went
out of the wing and he had been there for years with you, and
then suddenly he was dead. We lived with death. We had seen
death in the streets. When Bobby died, everybody was ex-

pecting a massive unleashing of armed force, riots, and all the rest. But it didn't happen. The Army Council on the outside told us later they weren't fuckin' militarily equipped to handle that. The Brits were so well prepared they could move in and wipe out the IRA militarily. The Army Council had to bide its time. There was that sense of anticlimax. The army had two options: to deliver what military resources they had to move it out and go for it; to try to give the people the momentum, to give a direction through the people themselves. (PIRA)

6.32 The Brits done a classic job during the Hunger Strike. The Provos, after Bobby Sands died, expected an intensification of operations and mass demonstrations. The Brits had all the Republican areas cut off from each other and from City Centre [in Belfast]. There was no way in and no way out. You couldn't hijack cars and take them from one area to another for a job. There was nobody going [driving] through the Republican areas. And the only people whose car they would of took would have been their own people, which would have alienated the community. That proved that you're never going to have a mass military confrontation here, just a Brit stiffed here and there.

 In jail the reason why they were expecting a doomsday situation with the Hunger Strike was because you were living it twenty-four hours a day. The news was screened. All you heard was that some Brit was whacked or there was this demonstration for the Blanketmen. All you were hearing was stuff related to the protest, nothing else. You were thinking about the Hunger Strike twenty-four hours a day and thinking everybody else was thinking the same way you were thinking. (INLA)

Throughout the Hunger Strike the prison collective projected an uninterrupted continuity between the self-directed violence of the starving prisoner and the other-directed violence of the military campaign. Even when the momentum of the Hunger Strike began to falter, and the expected upsurge of mass violent reaction failed to appear, the prison collective remained faithful to the ideology of the stiff as an efficacious agent of political causality. They still hoped that the dramatic display of the dead hunger striker would transsubstantiate into collective and cathartic uprising against the British state. The logic of political violence and that of the Hunger Strike were united in their attempt to produce catharsis through alterity.

In analyzing the failure of the protest to secure popular revolt, the prisoners pondered the failure of the biological eschatology of the hunger striker to translate itself into a generalized societal eschatology. In their attempts to link the two disparate dimensions of biological and historical time, to impose one upon the other, they revealed an inability to comprehend that the somatic history that organized political consciousnes in prison could not sublate the manifold and diffuse temporalities of social life and institutions beyond the incarceration. Their tactical dependency on a centralizing temporality is quite clear in the prisoners' critique of the Hunger Strike, which focused on the mutual management of time and death. These discussions reveal that though the Hunger Strike articulated a logic of rationalized and serialized corpse production, it presupposed the sympathetic magic of mimesis:

6.33 We were slow to appreciate that once four guys had died, that the initial impact started to slow. There were a hundred thousand people at Sands' funeral and fifty thousand people at Joe McDonnell's. It began to come to me then that we needed extra pressure here. It came to the OC too. He got up at the door, "Right men, any ideas here? There are four guys dead, what do you think?" It ran through my head that it was starting to peak, starting to slack off. We had expected a culmination each time somebody died. That there would actually be more and more people demonstrating on the outside. It seemed like everything else in this country, people become immune to death. Death is no stranger here. (PIRA)

6.34 The tactical mistake we made was the way the first four went on. They didn't go on one after another every week. What we didn't account for was that by the time the fourth died, the next guy still had fifty days to go before he dropped off. We should have had them coming on hunger strike week after week after week all the time. We should never have allowed four to die and give them [the state, the public] that fucking breather. That allowed the international organizations to come in and diffuse the issue. And then when Martin Hurson died unexpectedly at forty-five days, that created that gap in the timing. (PIRA)

Sacrifice Doubled

6.35 After the strike there was no sense of defeat, but it was an expensive victory, a phyrric victory. We knew we had won, but it was all too close and too personal. There was a great sense of reluctance to talk about it in the first few weeks after it ended. It was all "shift your attention elsewhere." "What are we going to do about segregation?" Diverting your attention. We were out of it. If our own clothes had come in to the prison six months earlier as they came after the strike, we would have lifted the roof off the fuckin' Blocks. But when they did, "So what." We were getting our parcels but it didn't matter. We got our remission back and just looked at them [the prison staff]. (PIRA)

6.36   What we had been hoping for was that the movement outside would pull out all stops and gain the momentum for a big military push. But basically on the outside what it was, the movement wasn't ready. The Army Council told us, "Granted that your analysis is dead sound, but you aren't in touch with political reality on the outside. The movement is only beginning to emerge and get to grips with its own problems. It's only beginning to sort itself out. Everybody is as much to blame as the next, that the level of community politicization wasn't reached at an earlier stage. Without the Hunger Strike we wouldn't have reached it. If we had reached it before, we mightn't have needed the Hunger Strike." The Hunger Strike came, and it injected in us inside a dose of reality. We were able after the Hunger Strike to say, "We're going out of this prison, and what we're going out into is a long hard struggle." (PIRA)

6.37   The continuation of the military struggle is built on a very very small but very solid base; that's never going to go away. You can take a dig at the Brits, and you can go to this base and they'll feed and water you, give you clothes, and send you on your way. You're into a tight base of people who understand the need to get rid of the Brits. It is a base that will never turn the "Boys" away from the door, be it 1996. But outside of that you have this massive middle ground who don't know where they're going, who don't understand the implications. For us, the Hunger Strike concentrated the whole Irish struggle into a small black-and-white understandable issue. There are these guys lying on protest who suffered all this. Why? They're starting to die. Why? What are they dying for? The Brits have been telling people for years that we were political maniacs, that we had no political understanding and that we were not going anywhere. People were beginning to say,

> "They can't be criminals; criminals don't die on hunger strike. Criminals don't lie five years on a protest." (PIRA)

For René Girard (1977), the sacrificial rite is a culturally generative performance and a reaction to collective states of desymbolization and undifferentiation. These retrograde cultural conditions are exemplified in the mimetic reproduction of violent reciprocity. Girard (1977:39–67) anchors his analysis of ritual violence in the opposition between the nondifference of reciprocating violent performances and the singular differentiation of the expelled sacrificial surrogate. In Girard, unending mimetic exchange is polarized to a terminal, rarified, and singularized act of violence that encloses itself as ritual. The exchange values mobilized by mimetic reciprocity are in effect devaluing because they do not promote hierarchy and hegemony.[17] With the advent of the sacrificial rite, these exchanges will be absorbed, overwhelmed, and rendered dépassé by one final exchange: the condensation of the many into the one; the concentration of collective contamination in a single bearer. The movement between the two poles of violence and exchange can be considered as simultaneously a dialectical, ritualized, and historical progression to new levels and dynamics of social structuration.

For Girard the desymbolization of social life by violent reciprocity

> coincides with the disappearance between the impure violence and purifying violence. When this difference has been effaced, purification is no longer possible and impure, contagious reciprocal violence spreads throughout the community . . . . the distinctions between the pure and the impure cannot be obliterated without obliterating all other differences as well. The sacrificial crisis can be defined, therefore, as a crisis of distinctions—that is, a crisis affecting the cultural order. (1977:49)

Girard's work offers the outlines of a theory of hegemony based on sacrificial intervention and symbolization. For Girard, the central political problematic of violent reciprocity is the thin membrane of division, reversibility, and doubling that both divides and conflates "legitimate" and "illegitimate" violence. Mimetically structured violence implies the deflation of political legitimacy, and mimetically structured conflicts are often about the relative legitimacy and illegitimacy of the violence being deployed to advance the conflict in the first place. The search for a legitimized violence in social orders afflicted by proliferating violent reciprocity can precipitate the forging of new social forms that address violence as an autonomous, culturally generative, and meaning-endowing practice. The search for legitimacy through the search for nonmimetic practice resolves into a new cultural construction of violence.

For Girard, the passage out of mimetic violence is the repetition of violence via a circumscribed form that terminates uncontrolled desymbolization. Because mimetic violence has dominated collective representation, the new modality resymbolizes by reorganizing social representation. The efficacy of sacrificial violence, then, is dependent on the prior prominence of generalized violence in mediating social relations.

In Northern Ireland the social consciousness of violent mimesis is registered in the characterization of "tit-for-tat" sectarian violence as a basic element of paramilitary practice. Republican paramilitaries react strongly against the imputation that they are engaged in reciprocating sectarian violence. The claim of nonsectarian violence is seen by this group as crucial to their legitimation as a revolutionary political movement deserving international recognition. The PIRA is quick to disassociate any of its operations from sectarian intent and circularity.

Related to the stigma of sectarian reciprocation was the imputed equation of the Republican inmate with the prison's criminal population. Here another form of mimesis and undifferentiation was involved. The Republican rejection of the uniform and the prison number—in themselves devices for mimetic socialization—was a strategy of hierarchical differentiation in relation to the criminal population of the prison. For Republican inmates, criminalization was tantamount to depoliticization. Similarly, sectarian violence is considered to be depoliticized violence and thus criminal violence. Criminalization in prison directly inferred a sectarian and apolitical cast to violence committed outside the prison.

The 1981 Hunger Strike united the two Republican issues of the illegitimacy of their violence and their criminalization within the prison system. The imputed devaluation of their "revolutionary" violence as sectarian and their jural equivalence to the ODCs were experienced by the Blanketmen as desymbolizing conditions. These situations emptied Republican violence and discourse of all its ideological and historically specific intentionality and singularity. The Hunger Strike can be seen as the ultimate resymbolization of the Republican movement. It erased the imputed stigma of criminality and founded their violence on a new origin myth. Resymbolization, revaluation, and singularization are evident in the ethics of "politicization," cultural separatism, and most importantly, in the individuated agency of the hunger striker.

Girard (1978) links the mythic code of sacrificial expulsion, exile, or differentiation to cosmogonic rites, salvation myths, and origin narratives. These narrative codes point to the formation of polity around excluded negativity or absence. All of these narrative codes have an operational presence in the performances and discourses that organized the 1981 Hunger Strike. What remains crucial for Girard is the double negation: the structural separation from a prior condition of negating undifferentiation and the expulsion of an emissary surrogate that effects a break and thereby founds a new significative order. The concept of a rupture from violence through an act of violence predominates in Girard's analysis:

> All such customs may appear to us unreasonable and absurd. In fact they adhere to a coherent logic. All of them concern themselves with formulating and practicing a form of violence incapable of serving as a connecting link between the violent act that preceded and the one that must follow. The aim is to achieve a radically new type of violence that will put an end once and for all to violence itself. . . . Primitive people try to break the symmetry of reprisal by addressing themselves directly to the question of form. (1977:27)

Legitimation here is tied to the capacity to effect a structural, ethical, and semiological break with all preceding and contemporary forms of violence in the performance sphere out of which the sacrificial rite will emerge. The central conundrum of sacrificial violence is predetermined by the necessity of posing a structural discontinuity with mimetic violence through a new form of violence. Violence still remains the founding language of social representation, and Girard, under the powerful imagery of sacrificial victimage, discloses one of the basic strategies for the construction of political mastery. The sacrificial act can only sublate other forms of violence and transgression by the ritual repetition of violence. It can only expel and delegitimize violence by legitimizing violence in a culturally encysted form which culminates in a double interiorization of violence: its containment and its reinscription as a cultural institution.

> The ritualistic elements disintegrate into actual events and it becomes impossible to distinguish history from ritual. This confusion is itself revealing. A rite retains its vitality only as long as it serves to channel political and social conflicts of unquestionable reality in a specific direction. On the other hand, it remains a rite only as long as it manages to restrict the conflictual modes of expression to rigorously determined forms. (1977:109–10)
> The ritualistic imagination strives to repeat the original generative process. . . . All sacrificial rites reproduce certain forms of violence and appropriate certain associations that seem more suitable to the sacrificial crisis itself than to its cure. (1977:114)

The sacrificial rite repeats violence and unavoidably confirms the performance of violence as hegemonic and legitimate. Within a dominant pattern of mimetic violent reciprocity, the sacrificial rite is vulnerable to new levels of mimetic appropriation precisely because it establishes a ritualized form of violence and surrogate victimage as hegemonic. The sacrificial rite, because of its dialectical and genealogical relation to mimetic violence, shifts the structures of mimetic objectification onto new levels of cultural and performative complexity. What Girard does not account for is that *with the advent of sacrificial ritual, what becomes emulated and subjected to mimesis is the sacrificial form itself as a semio-technique of political legitimation and as narrative code for the construction of historical reality.*

A Scene of Exchange from the Gospels

Both the pervasiveness of the sacrificial narrative code and its engagement with the problem of mimesis and exchange are evident in the following allegory given to me by an ex-Blanketman who, like the other protesters, was only allowed the Bible as reading material in the cell:

6.38   I would read the Gospels, take scenes out of the Gospels like the crucifixion and compare it to today. Who's being crucified? The boys on the right and left of Jesus weren't thieves. They were as much thieves as I was. They were political activists, activists against the Roman authorities. On one side you have a present-day Republican getting crucified and on the other a Loyalist paramilitary; you have the Brits into the thing of the Romans. You had different religious divisions, the Samaritans and the Jews who hated each other just as much as the Catholics and Protestants of Northern Ireland.

    The first person who would be welcomed into Heaven today would be a paramilitary, just as Jesus said to Dismus the thief: "You will be in Heaven with me today." It wouldn't be somebody out of the institutionalized church, it wouldn't be somebody out of the government, it would be a "terrorist." (INLA)

The triangulation presented in this mythic figure freezes the diachronic experience of violent exchange into a synchronic tableau. The understructure of paramilitary violence is initially presented as a spatial arrangement: the left side, the right side, the figure in the middle, and the polarized position of the Roman-Brits to the left-right-middle continuum. This areal division of figures and agencies into left, right, center, and Other infers the metaphor of singular embodiment that pervades the entire scenario. The symbolic division of left and right follows Hertz's (1960) formulation in linking the qualitative space of the individual body to the qualitative space of the social and cosmological body. Thus this spatial segmentation encodes, mystifies, and transposes the territorial-ethnic divisions of political violence in Northern Ireland, where belligerent interactions between the microspaces of confessional communities are understood as referring to the nationalist macrospaces of a United Ireland or a British Ulster.

Three different subject positions occupy the center of the theater of violence depicted here. (The "Brits" provoke the scene but remain marginal to the spectacle). There is the dyadic and polarized relation of Republican and Loyalist paramilitaries, and there is the central figure of Jesus who mediates the others. But it could also be pointed out that the triangulation is also that of the same body in three different subject positions. This dimension of the same, underlying body is signified by the position of the victim shared by all the figures. This mimetic imagery uses the shared position of the victim as a vehicle for indexing political value equivalence and exchange.

The imagery of crucifixion—the stigmatic marking of the body— effects the body's shift from one regime of valuation to another: from criminalization to politicization and/or sacralization. When the narrator asserts that only terrorists will pass into heaven, he is also stating that only those political subjects who have marked the eschatological direction of history on the bodies of others and have had this same graphic applied to their own bodies will achieve epochal transport. Here historical passage is portrayed as topological transfer in a manner analogous to Hertz's formula for sacrifice: "to make a material object or a living being pass from this world to the next, to free or create the soul [or the political subject], it must be destroyed" (1960:46).

The Lacanians (see Lemaire 1977) propose that a symbolic economy arises when a binary relation is mediated by a third term. In Northern Ireland the dyadic transactions of opposing paramilitary groupings (and their respective antagonistic exchanges with the state) are enacted through the vehicle of the emissary victim. Situated between the two paramilitaries, the figure of Jesus functions as the mediative agent that makes the exchanges between political protagonists possible. This emissary victim is arbitrary insofar as its major function is to supply a point of articulation between others. The victim is the template through which antagonists become present for each other. The choice of Jesus as the third term is attributable to a host of culturally overdetermined reasons, but the Christological symbol is appropriate here because Jesus, as victim, is the mechanism of epochal transport, that is, historical transformation for the other two figures.

This tableau is a diagram of the genetic mechanisms of victim processing. The two crucified paramilitaries with their binary coding— Republican/ Loyalist—represent the ideological partitioning of the object of violence. There are this side's victims and that side's victims. This differential valuation of victims (or the same victim) by one side or the other institutes the victim as a heterogeneous ideological composite and thus engenders the metaphorical body of the victim. Yet despite the ideological division of victims and their bodies, victimage is the generic institution shared by all sides of the conflict as their common material denominator and as the operator of all political exchange.

Jesus, situated between the two polarities of victimage (Protestant and Catholic), is the generic victim out of which the ideological energy of the other two is formed. In this sense Jesus, the incarnate, represents the invarient, unified institution of the partible body that underlies the ideological codings of particular bodies by paramilitary violence. The same body in three different stages of political codification is presented here as three different subject positions united by a uniform condition of violence. The materialist exchange of victims is the shared mimetic performance that engenders ideological differentiation, a differentiation dependent on the partitioning of the generic body. Here mimesis or equivalence is the mechanism by which the relations of antagonism are transformed into the conditions of antagonism, by which the exchangist organization of violence becomes the precondition for its own reproduction.

The dynamic of mimesis and commensuration in victim exchange both constructs and presupposes an essentialism that is crucial to the ideology of effective and socially transformative violence. This essentialism has a materialist and an institutional character. Victims are essentially the same because they participate in the shared invariant of the stiff, which prepares the political partitioning of the body and the circulation of bodies as ideological units. The essentialist discourse of the victim is isomorphic to the materialist discourse of historical alterity and transformation. To fetishize victimage and other material mutations as the motor of social transformation is to reduce the historical to an essentialist metaphysic and to rationalize matter as historical spectacle.

Interiorizing Subjects and Objects

I have explored the theme of surrogate victimage in a variety of situations and with a variety of political agents to a sufficient extent in this study to establish the typicality of this political logic. Each of the violent enactments described throughout this study claims a legitimacy that is materially dependent on the codified victim expunged through violence. In Northern Ireland the culturally constructed rhetoric of victimage is merely the other side of the cultural construction of mastery and domination. The structuration of each enactment of sacrificial violence into a binary iconography of mastery and victimage is the central source for the equivocal legitimation and delegitimation of all such acts of violence. The reciprocal production and exchange of sacrificial objects become the fundamental sign of the circularity of violent mimesis. It is also the central indication of the reduction of historical action to recursive ritualized closure.

The Blanketmen deployed a form of violence which effected a structural separation from all contemporary modalities of political practice. The hunger strike as self-inflicted violence short-circuited the ritual partition of victimizer and victim that characterized and stereotyped political hegemony in Northern Ireland by interiorizing this exchange. *By fusing the subject and object of violent enactment into a single body, the hunger striker effected the resymbolization of the Republican movement* (see also Lukács 1971:164–72).

But as Girard states, the subject of the sacrificial act is violence, and the sacrificial intervention is condemned to repeat violence, to legitimize it in specific forms as a central medium of social representation. The Hunger Strike and its victims both temporarily abolished the opposition of victimage and mastery and reinscribed them into new configurations.

The Hunger Strike was seen by the PIRA as authorizing subsequent violence that would flow from the self-inflicted sacrificial act as its excess, as the surplus value of a new historical legitimacy. Thus the 1981 Hunger Strike moved the cultural construction of Republican violence from subject/object (victimizer/victim) oppositions to subject/object fusion and then to a new partitioning of subject/object relations. The latter was perceived as sundered from mimetic contamination and desymbolization by its grounding in the inner-directed sacrificial act which functioned as a purification filter for subsequent Republican violence. Thus the exchanges between victim and victimizer which had been internalized were externalized and returned to the political culture as a replenished schema of empowerment.

The funerals of many of the hunger strikers were scenes of dramatic political confrontation that demonstrated the new centrality of the political language and symbolic systems the Blanketmen had forged for the entire society from behind prison walls. In one instance the corpse of a dead hunger striker was mysteriously disfigured prior to its departure from prison and before the funeral.[18] The mass funerals given to the dead hunger strikers were the final sealing of their decriminalization and of their political purification. In turn, the harassment of the funerals by the security forces and the desecration of one corpse were attempts to restigmatize the hunger striker, to prevent his return to his community as the bearer of empowerment. But even this obstruction demonstrated that the corporeal power of the Blanketmen had disseminated its fetishizing aura to all parties of the Northern Ireland conflict.

The ritualized circuit traveled by the hunger striker from agency of political violence to incarceration-criminalization, to biological defilement, to purifying sacrificial death and political sacralization, was a stylized movement from lower to higher orders and topologies. This topological progression established the hunger striker's corpse as a political force-field and as a meaning-endowing, culturally generative agency. This circuit constituted the movement from desymbolization to symbolic fecundity, measured out in a variety of biological and juridical transformations. This circuit was totally dependent for its transformational dynamics upon the construction of the body by violence, both in the prior enactment of violence by that body and in the enactment of violence onto that body by both the state and the protesting prisoner. In the end, the Hunger Strike returned Northern Ireland political culture to the customary insight that the manipulation of the human body as an erasable transparency is the utilitarian motor of historical alterity. In that sense, the Hunger Strike was condemned to perpetuate political violence.

The Reversal of Sacrifice

6.39 After the Hunger Strike, as we were split up and moved into wings that had a regular prison routine and mixed in with Loyalist prisoners, the segregation issue came up. What was important about it was both Republicans and Loyalists wanted their own separate wings for military and political training, like they had in the old Cages system. There was more discipline in a wing when everybody was under the one command. There was no real moral issue behind it like the Hunger Strike; they just wanted separate wings to train their own men. It had nothing to do about not wanting to mix with Protestant paramilitaries.

When the Hunger Strike failed, the Republican OCs all met together and decided to push for one issue at a time. Segregation of the Republicans from Loyalist prisoners and ODCs was first on their list. They also wanted segregation to facilitate escape. Now that we had our own clothes and could move around the jail more freely escapes were a nearer possibility than when we were on the Blanket and under twenty-four hour lockup.

When the Republican prisoners were moved out of the Blanket Blocks, they more or less threatened the Loyalist prisoners. The OCs of the Republicans began to meet with the Orangies' [Loyalist] OCs, telling them they wanted the populations in the wing split up by organization. Because of the Hunger Strike they were thought of as "hardmen" by the Loyalist OCs. The Orangies were afraid of being overrun and being told what to do by the Republican prisoners because the Republican prisoners outnumbered them in the prison. The Orangies also wanted segregation for sectarian reasons.

The Republicans had it organized in such a way so that they sat in the background throughout the segregation issue, that the Orangies were the ones who were visibly pushing for segregation. So it wouldn't look obvious to the outside world who was doing what.

The Republican OCs believed it was inevitable, before segregation could be accomplished, that a Loyalist prisoner would have to kill a Republican prisoner, and a Republican would have to kill a Loyalist to force the issue. An arrangement was made between the Republican and Loyalist OCs that the Loyalists would kill a Catholic who the Republicans considered to be an informer, a "tout." He would be pushed into the yard when the Orangies were exercising, and there they could do [kill] him. They would arrange it among themselves that the informer was thrown to the dogs. And the Loyalist OCs were to arrange the same thing for one of their informers so that the Republicans could stiff him. (Republican prisoner, H-Blocks, organizational affiliation withheld)

6.40   After the Hunger Strike, certain guys were sacrificed for the sake of segregation. Not only touts, but hoods, rapists, sex offenders. They [Republican OCs] wanted it to look like a Catholic/Protestant thing and not particularly a paramilitary issue. The actual paramilitaries [Republicans and Loyalists] were all right with each other. The RA [PIRA] would tell the UDA, "You can do him, this sex offender, in the showers tomorrow morning. He's a Catholic and you would be doing us a favor, and it helps the segregation thing." The strategy was that the Republicans would say, "Right, all Catholics use the showers or the exercise yard on such and such a day during such and such a time." Your man would go, but alone, and the Orangies would have a squad waiting for him. The Republicans would stay away from the place, and the whole incident would look like a sectarian murder. (Republican prisoner, H-Blocks, organizational affiliation withheld)

The fictionalization of sectarian violence by Republican and Loyalist paramilitaries in the aftermath of the Hunger Strike completes the genealogy of sacrificial process in the H-Blocks. The self-directed violence of the Hunger Strike, its autoinscription of political codes on the body of the dying prisoner, reversed itself in the mirror of the other-directed violence enacted against ODCs, sex offenders, and informers during the segregation campaign.

The chronological and structural movement from the Hunger Strike to the fabricated violence of the segregation issue reveals a disturbing symmetry to ritual process in the H-Blocks. This symmetry underscores their mutual determination by the logic of surrogate victimage. Coupled together, the shared emplotment of the two protests totalizes the ritualistic foundations of paramilitary political rationality.

Sacrificial strategy in the Hunger Strike and the segregation issue was based on the collective movement from pollution to purification and from undifferentiation to differentiation. Further, it must be taken into consideration that the tactical transition from the Hunger Strike to the segregation strategy, a movement from inner-directed violence to other-directed violence, was in itself based on the cultural construction of the body in the H Block protests.

The performance and termination of the Hunger Strike signified the Blanketmen's return to the generalized economies of violence of paramilitary culture. This return was expressed in their designation as "hardmen" (narrative 6.39), based on the endurance, commitment, and toughness they had displayed for five years on the Blanket and during the Hunger Strike. The "hardman" in Northern Irish lore was the individual who was willing to risk his body through violence for the sake of establishing his standing within his local community. The hardmen were known for their predilection for direct physical violence enacted within certain rules and juridical norms. The hardman's standing derived from both his mastery over a reputable opponent and his capacity to wager his body for the sake of status (see chap. 3).

The designation of the Blanketmen as hardmen by the Loyalist paramilitaries is striking when we consider that during the period of protests the Blanketmen had been for the most part the recipients and objects of violence and not its enactors. (With the exception of their distanced collaboration in the assassination of prison guards outside the prison.) The reconstruction of their bodies during the protracted hardship and violence of the Blanket Protest and the culmination of this conditioning in the willingness to hunger strike to the death were perceived by the prison population as immediately translatable to the practice of violence against others by the same hardened and enduring body. The Blanketmen, insofar as they were masters of their own bodies, were masters over the bodies of others. And this reversible mastery was codified in the term "hardmen."

The segregation issue engaged several practical, ideological, and symbolic concerns shared by both Republican and Loyalist paramilitaries. For the Republican prisoners, residential segregation complemented the socialization of cultural and biological separatism. Residential segregation for this group constituted a spatial representation of a society they sought to create outside the prison. It had utopian nuances. For the Loyalist paramilitaries, however, residential segregation replicated the spatial imagery of the existing social order they saw themselves as defending (see chap. 2). Both groups were united in their desire for residential segregation to the extent to which it addressed their political concerns over criminalization. The central trope of a delegitimizing and depoliticizing stain of criminality for all paramilitaries was their coresidence with the ODCs.

The expulsion of the ODC, the sex offender, and the suspected informer would remove several layers of pollution and stigmatization from the prison. Further, this violence could attain a wider political efficacy by recasting the expulsion of polluting entities from prison as the public propaganda of the "innocent" victim of sectarian murder. The sacrificial construction of the segregation issue not only replicated the ideological concerns of the Hunger Strike—decriminalization—but also the Hunger Strike's performative logic: the expulsion of surrogate victim as the personification and removal of defilement (criminal stigma). The political transformation of the fictionalized sectarian victim was a mirror image of the transformations of the hunger striker. The emissary victim of the segregation campaign began as the lowest category in the prison social order, the most stigmatized entity, and through the mediation of sacrificial exchange was transformed into a sanitized "political victim," a verification and advertisement of the disorderly residential administration of the prison. Here the state was artificially pitted against the cultural institutions of the ethnic community. In this fashion the fictive victim of segregation violence and the dead hunger striker were both "sandwichboard men," mimetic entities that circulated complex and multilayered political equations (see Buck-Morss 1989, and chapter 1).[19]

Given that the Blanketmen as an identifiable collective in the prison initiated this exchange of bodies in the period after their return to the general prison population, the segregation violence can be viewed as the diplomatic opening of formal contact and reciprocity with Loyalist paramilitaries from whom they had been largely isolated during the years of protest. In this context the rationalized exchange or victims ironically reenacted on the level of a fiction, the political transactions of Republican and Loyalist paramilitaries outside the prison (see chapter 3).

For the Republican inmates, this manipulation of sectarian "tit-for-tat" murder—a cultural institution with deep symbolic and political roots in both Protestant and Catholic communities—as if it were a war-game simulation was one more indication of their sublation of residual forms of stigmatized violence and of their entry into a new historical logic of purified and rationalized force. Here too, as in the Hunger Strike, the mimesis of what was other and contaminating reflected a newly acquired political mastery and an empowering encompassment of the negative through ritual form.

The fabricated segregation violence carved an exit from the political imaginary of the Hunger Strike through a ritual inversion. The political logic and symbolism of the Hunger Strike reappeared in the planning of segregation violence in its new secularized and rationalized form *as an institution*. The violence of the segregation campaign ended the Blanket-men's exile from the fields of sacrifice that extended beyond the prison walls and to which, through the medium of their bodies, they had always sought to return.

Appendix 1: Glossary

Armalite. U.S.-made semiautomatic rifle locally known as Armaduke.

ASU. Active Service Unit; four to five man community-based military unit of the PIRA or INLA.

Auchnacloys. Rhyming slang for "the Boys," that is, the PIRA or INLA.

Bang, banged. To shoot someone; to be shot.

Bangle, bangling. The anus; the act of hiding or smuggling using the anus or other orifices of the body.

Bear. Prison guard.

Bear, Polar. Prison Officer, named after the white shirt worn by this rank.

Big Bear. Governor of the prison.

Black bastards. Insult directed at the RUC, who wear black uniforms.

Black Taxi. Community-based taxi services run by Republican and Loyalist paramilitary organizations in their own communities and staffed by ex-prisoners.

Boards. Punishment cells, solitary confinement.

Boys, the. Local UDA, PIRA or INLA paramilitary unit or entire organization.

Break, to. To coerce someone into informing during interrogation; to depoliticize; to destroy the will to resist.

Breaker's Yard. Name coined by Bobby Sands for the H-Blocks.

Cages. Compounds located at Long Kesh containing Nissen huts for sentenced prisoners with political status.

Call house. A safe house where members of Active Service Units receive orders and general news of relevance to their activities and the organization.

Camels' humps. Rhyming slang for arms dumps.

Castlereagh. A major interrogation center located in Belfast.

Choochoos. A technique devised for passing messages and other items from cell to cell by using thread or string.

Circle, the. Administrative section of the H Block that corresponds to the crossbar of the H.

Com. Communiqué; message smuggled by prisoners.

Crack. Entertainment; excitement; the truth; hidden meaning of an event.

Crum, the. Crumlin Road Jail, used mainly for housing prisoners awaiting trial.

Cunt. Insult directed at males; the victim of violence; the effect of violence, as in "to knock his cunt in."

Det, to give a. To detonate an explosion.

Dig, diggings. To beat up; beatings; to attack with firearms.

Dirty weapon. A weapon with a history of prior use within the same organization.

Do. To beat up; to kill; to arrest; to raid.

Doctor Martens. Ankle-length work shoes supposedly favored by Loyalist paramilitaries.

Doing(s). Act(s) of violence; weapons (plural only).

Done. To receive violence; to be killed; to be arrested; to be raided.

Dummy-run. Practice of a planned military operation.

Dump, floating. Arms dump that is moved around from hiding place to hiding place.

Dump, open. Arms dump containing a small stash of weapons in current use.

Dump, pipe. Weapons placed in a buried drain pipe.

Dump, sealed. Arms dump used for long-term weapon storage.

Effort. Originally referred to males active in the IRA, but currently used to refer to any individual, as in "that effort," "this effort"; equivalent to "your man."

Emptying the mag. Rapid fire of an automatic weapon until all bullets in the magazine are expended.

Fagin, fagin bush. Penis; foreskin; scrotum.

Fagining. Smuggling items or message underneath the foreskin.

Failed job. A paramilitary operation that has been canceled.

Fill him in, filled in. To shoot someone; to kill; to be killed.

Fixer, the. The M15 rifle used by the PIRA.

Fuck-all. Nothing.

Gear. Weapons.

Giving the message. Killing; originally referred to sexual act by a male.

Go on a float. To ride around in a car searching for a suitable target for attack.

Grass. Informer; from a pop-song verse that refers to the "whispering grass."

Guddy, guddied. To beat; to be beaten; named after the brand name of a cleated shoe.

Hair-bear. Paramilitary who performs local law-and-order functions.

Hammered. To be beaten up; to suffer a hard attack.

Hammerhead shark. Prisoner who used his foreskin for smuggling.

Header. An insane person.

Hood. Local criminal.

Hooding. Committing apolitical criminal acts.

INLA. Irish National Liberation Army; see appendix 2.

Interview. Interrogation session.

IO. Intelligence Officer.

IRSP. Irish Republican Socialist party; see appendix 2.

Jailtacht. Gaelic-speaking sections of the Cages and H Block prisons. A pun on the term *Gaeltacht,* the Gaelic-speaking reserves mainly located in the west of Ireland.

Joyrider. Adolescent boy who steals cars for racing.

Long Kesh. Penological-military complex that houses the Cages, the H-Blocks, a military camp, and residences for prison staff.

Malood. To be blown up.

Monkey Suit. Prison uniform.

OC. Officer Commanding.

ODC. Ordinary Decent Criminal; nonpolitical prisoner.

Off the air. Prison slang for silence; departure from cell block; death.

On the air. To speak; an event taking place; to be alive.

One-shot wonder. A single-shot snipe that leaves the target wondering where it came from.

Op. Military operation.

Opening up. To open fire.

Orangies. Term for Protestants; derives from the Orange Order, a Loyalist secret society named after Prince William of Orange.

Peelers. Police.

PIRA. Provisional Irish Republican Army, Provisional IRA, IRA, the Ra; see appendix 2.

Punishments. Internal organizational or community disciplinary violence performed by paramilitaries.

Reagh, the. See Castlereagh.

Redlight. A civilian or paramilitary subjected to numerous police stops and interrogations; a paramilitary who is an ex-prisoner; a "retired" paramilitary.

RUC. Royal Ulster Constabulary; see appendix 2.

Runback. The planned escape route of a paramilitary operation.

Safe house. A place for receiving orders, weapons, disguises, stolen vehicles; a place for hiding.

Saracen. Armored car used by counterinsurgency forces.

Sceal(ing). Gaelic for news; anglified Gaelic for gossiping.

Scone, to. To shoot in the head.

Scooped. To be arrested.

Scorcher. Prisoner who shouts news.

Scriobhing. Prison slang and anglified Gaelic for writing.

Shoot-to-kill. Counterinsurgency arrest operation whose real purpose is assassination of targeted paramilitaries.

Short. A pistol.

Slag, Slagging. To insult; to make fun of.

Stick, giving. Abuse; insult; criticism.

Stiff, stiffing. A corpse; killing.

Supergrass. Informer in witness protection program who gives information and anonymously testifies against numerous members of his organization.

Taig. A Catholic.

Tanking. A beating.

Topping. Assassination.

Touch up. To beat up.

Tout. Informer.

UDA. Ulster Defense Association; see appendix 2.

UDR. Ulster Defense Regiment; see appendix 2.

UVF. Ulster Volunteer Force; see appendix 2.

Wash house. A safe house used to get rid of weapons and disguises and for the transfer of stolen vehicles after an operation; also used for debriefing.

Whack. To attack; to shoot.

Yo-yo. Weapon.

Appendix 2: Organizations Cited

INLA/IRSP: Irish National Liberation Army/Irish Republican Socialist party; the Irps; the Wyatt Irps. This group, formed by members of the Official IRA who wanted a return to a "physical force" strategy, broke from the Officials in 1974, leading to extremely violent feuding with the Officials over the issue of who controlled arms dumps. INLA is much smaller than the PIRA, and now that the latter has adopted a more left-wing and less Catholic Nationalist orientation, it is difficult to discern major ideological differences between the organizations. Militarily INLA is known for spectacular assassinations and a more politically reckless deployment of violence. They have engaged in more violence against Loyalist paramilitaries than the PIRA. Because of the lack of Irish-American financial support (which is monopolized by the PIRA), they are also known for running community protection services, bank robberies, and other problematic "political" fundraising activities. INLA has been subject to numerous internal feuds and unstable leadership. It is seen by many Republicans in Belfast as having degenerated into gangsterism. In 1986, internal feuding broke out led by a recently released H Block inmate, "The Doctor," and a faction that sought to "repoliticize" the organization and steer it in the direction of a more concerted offensive military campaign. The IRSP, the political wing of INLA, initially attracted younger Marxist activists who subsequently left the organization because of internal disputes over whether the political or military wing of the INLA/IRSP complex held ultimate control. The military wing won out.

Official IRA: The Officials; the Stickies; the Workers' party. A lineal descendant of the IRA of the 1920s–50s, the Official IRA of the 1960s developed an increasingly Marxist orientation involving a stage theory of Irish national development which precluded unilateral insurgency by the Catholic minority of Northern Ireland and advocated working-class alliances with Ulster Protestants. It declared a unilateral ceasefire in 1972, and prior to this conducted defensive operations against the British army and subsequently feuded with the INLA and the PIRA. Despite their abandonment of the "physical force" strategy, it is well known in Belfast that the Officials have numerous weapons dumps. The organization also maintains economic interests in drinking clubs and monopolizes the subcontracting of building sites in certain areas of Belfast, as do other paramilitary groups.

Orange Order: A Protestant political-religious organization with a hierarchy of secret initiation rites resembling Masonic ceremony. The Orange Order has between 80,000 to 100,000 members and is a main organizing and ideological force behind the summer season of commemorative parades and ceremonies which celebrate the military victories of William of Orange (King William III). The organization was formed in 1795, and its processions were temporarily banned in the 1860s. It has strong links with Official Unionist party, and many of its members hold joint membership in the RUC, the UDR, the UDA, and the UVF. The Orange Order has branches in the Republic of Ireland, England, Scotland, Australia, Togoland, and Ghana.

PIRA: Provisional Irish Republican Army; IRA; Provos; Provies; and the RA. Formed in 1970 by a breakaway "physical force" faction in reaction to the abandonment of a renewed military campaign at the Sinn Fein Conference of that year, the PIRA is currently the largest and most active Republican paramilitary organization. From 1970 to 1973, the PIRA developed from a community defense group to an insurgency force. From 1971 to 1973 it engaged in an "economic campaign" based on the bombing of commercial districts, utilities, and government buildings. Between 1972 and 1976 the PIRA increasingly abandoned its community-defense posture and was severely hampered by more efficient counterinsurgency activity. During this period it advocated a Federal Ireland solution. With a decreased capacity for effective military action in Northern Ireland, the PIRA initiated a bombing campaign in England in 1974. Also, in response to Loyalist sectarian violence, in 1975, the PIRA for the first time initiated an official, systematic campaign of sectarian retaliation. The PIRA reached a ceasefire agreement with the British government in 1975. Sinn Fein, the political wing of the PIRA, was recognized as a political party in the same year. During this period, the PIRA established community-based economic enterprises in West Belfast such as pubs and the black taxi service. The truce with the British broke down in 1975. In 1975 the PIRA engaged in violent feuding with the Official IRA. During this period, community support decreased drastically. New counterinsurgency programs and the criminalization policy initiated in 1976 by the British contributed to a major attrition of organizational membership. In 1977, ex-prisoners from the Cages reorganized the PIRA into the cell model in order to create a greater level of security and to put the organization back into a military offensive. The cell model enabled the organization to limit its membership base and its logistical interface with local communities. In 1980 the federal solution for Northern Ireland was rejected by the left-wing leadership that emerged from the prison cadres. During this period and in the aftermath of the 1981 Hunger Strike, the politicization program was undertaken. This new program highlighted the role of Sinn Fein as a community service organization and political party. Sinn Fein contested elections in Northern Ireland from 1981 onward.

RUC: Royal Ulster Constabulary. Established in 1922 as a Loyalist paramilitary police force, the RUC basically remained a Protestant organization (10 percent Catholic membership), despite its status as an official arm of governmental law enforcement. In the late 1960s its role as an anti-Catholic counterinsurgency force was radically attenuated with the deployment of the British army. With the advent of the Criminalization, Ulsterization, and Normalization program, the RUC was retrained as a front-line counterinsurgency force in order to generate popular perceptions of the Northern Ireland situation as basically one of local, limited criminal violence. In its surveillance, crowd-control technologies, and specialized urban counterinsurgency training (including covert assassinations), the RUC should be appreciated as an extremely politicized law enforcement unit. It is probably the most sophisticated urban counterinsurgency force in the world today.

UDA: Ulster Defense Association. Originally began as an alliance of various Loyalist community defense groups in 1969, the UDA, despite an open paramilitary ethos and imagery, has never been banned like the PIRA and INLA. It is the largest (12,000 members) paramilitary organization in Northern Ireland. It was instrumental in the territorial shifting of Catholic populations from mixed areas in the early 1970s and is considered responsible for the vast majority of sectarian murders of Catholics. It played a central role in the 1974 strike against the power-sharing policies of the Sunningdale Agreement. Despite its role in the 1974 strike, it has not been able to expand into an electoral power base. Currently the UDA advocates a federated, independent Ulster, based on the federal model of the United States. It claims no sectarian bias against Catholics, but declares Republican paramilitaries and political activists as legitimate targets. The UDA has been active in the prison segregation campaign and has sought alliances with sectarian-racist groups in Belgium, Israel, and South Africa.

UDR: Ulster Defense Regiment. This locally recruited reserve unit of the British army, akin to the American National Guard, supposedly replaced the infamous B Specials, a Protestant militia that functioned as a police reserve and was known for extreme anti-Catholic bigotry and indiscriminate anti-Catholic violence. The UDR was formed in 1970 and, despite its official nonsectarian recruitment policy, is mainly composed of Protestant volunteers. Many of its members have been exposed as holding dual membership in Loyalist paramilitary organizations and have been involved in sectarian murders. It is especially feared by Catholics in rural Northern Ireland where its duties consist of maintaining road checkpoints and patrolling isolated areas. Its on-duty and off-duty members are frequently targeted by the PIRA.

Ulster Special Constabulary, A, B, C Specials: Set up in 1920 by the British government, the "Specials" functioned as a paramilitary reserve to the police. The specials served on a full-time basis and lived in barracks; the B Specials served on a part-time basis in mounted patrols. The C Specials, mobilized in crisis situations, were exclusively recruited from the Orange Order and the first UVF. The A and C Specials were demobilized in 1925, but the B Specials were in operation until 1969.

UVF: Ulster Volunteer Force. Formed in 1966, this Loyalist organization attempted to revive the populist UVF formed in 1913. The organization, flirting with socialist ideology, is explicitly sectarian and is currently informally associated with the National Front. The UVF is known for sectarian torture and assassinations of Catholics. It has units in both Northern Ireland and Scotland (Glasgow). The UVF recruits among ex-soldiers of the British army and has close underground contacts with the Ulster Defense Regiment. It is smaller than the UDA and has not engaged in building large-scale community-based economic and political support. The UVF is frequently short of funds and has been known to sell arms to the UDA.

Appendix 3

Republican (PIRA and INLA) Paramilitary Cohort

Informant	Born	Joined Organization	Significant Arrests	Charge	Incarcerated
INLA	1957	1969	1974		
			1976	Possession of explosives	7 years
INLA	1958	1970	1976	Possession of weapons	5 years
PIRA	1955	1969	1974		
			1976	Attempted murder	6 years
PIRA	1953	1971	1976	Possession of weapons	5 years
PIRA	1955	1970	1975		
			1976	Hijacking of vehicles; possession of weapons	8 years
INLA	1956	1969	1977	Possession of weapons	7 years
PIRA	1960	1971	1973		
			1976		
			1977	Vehicle theft	5 years
INLA	1958	1971	1976	Attempted murder	3 years; released on appeal
PIRA	1959	1970	1976	Attempted murder	8 years

Informant	Born	Joined Organization	Significant Arrests	Charge	Incarcerated
PIRA	1957	1970	1974	Bombing	1 year on remand
			1975	Attempted murder	1½ years on remand
INLA	1957	1970	1974	Interned	1 year
			1977	Possession of explosives	10 months on remand
			1979	Possession of explosives	6 years
PIRA	1956	1971	1976	Hijacking of vehicles; possession of weapons	10 years
PIRA	1951	1971	1972	Interned	2 years
			1976	Bombing	10 years
INLA	1957	1969	1976	Attempted murder	7 years, including remand time
PIRA	1958	1969	1974		
			1976	Possession of weapons	5 years

Notes: All informants are male. Many informants originally joined the youth wing, the *Fianna,* of the OIRA and the PIRA where they received military training and political indoctrination, and then graduated into active service units. INLA members originally joined the Official IRA and left this organization in 1974 when the INLA emerged from an internal split within the Official IRA. All interned informants were "charged" with membership in banned organizations. Charges are only listed with arrests that resulted in indictment and incarceration. Time served includes 50 percent remission of original sentence due to good behavior.

Notes

1 / Artifacts and Instruments of Agency

1. Benjamin's original somatic model for this mythic mass communication was the prostitute as mass article. See Buck-Morss 1989:190.

2. Appadurai's (1986) notion of the cultural biography of the artifact—the diverse trajectories that mediate a commodity's origins and ends—was thoroughly anticipated by Nietzsche's genealogical method as a critique of domination and fetishism. For Nietzsche the historical and semantic genealogy of concepts and things was indispensable to theorizing political orders as self-regulating economies, as systems of value commensuration. Genealogical method traces the lines of descent by which the "whole history of an organ, a custom, a thing becomes a continuous chain of reinterpretations and rearrangements . . . a sequence of more or less profound, more or less independent processes of appropriation" (Nietzsche 1956:210).

3. For Hegel paradigmatic spaces are formed by the slave's performance of labor and the master's performance of consumption; see Kojéve 1969. For Lukács (1971) it is the factory floor where the worker's body is bifurcated into commodified-rationalized elements and subjective "idiosyncratic" elements. Foucault's (1979) spaces for the formation of the body are the plague-infested town, the prison, the asylum, and the clinic.

4. David Harvey (1989) distinguishes between material spatial practices, representations of space, and spaces of representation, crediting these categories to the social historian Henri Lefebvre. My inspiration for this tripartite model has been the Lacanian distinction between the Real, the Symbolic, and the Imaginary; see Lemaire 1977.

5. This viewpoint can be contrasted to the fieldwork strategies of Burton (1978) and Sluka (1989), who resided in urban Catholic communities. This strategy prevented both from conducting research in Protestant communities. I also feel, from interpretive readings of their ethnographies, that these field-workers were strategically insulated from paramilitary culture by their resident communities, local paramilitary organizations, and their own sense of tact and survival. Both Burton and Sluka, however, were not directly concerned with the cultural construction of violence but rather with the fluctuations of paramilitary political legitimacy on the level of community perceptions.

6. The so-called postmodern discourse of the "new ethnography" is decidedly *not* poststructuralist, Derridean, or Foucauldian. This discourse perpetuates the theodicy of writing that Derrida (1976) identifies as the central mytheme of Western metaphysics and phonocentrism. A good deal of the "new ethnography" discourse is concerned with the recuperation of presence as embodied by the fieldwork encounter (which is a naïve reading of this encounter). This discourse reads the textualization process as an analogue of the Marxist theory of alienation, where the producer (the informant) is alienated from his product (discourse) by the ethnography. Needless to say the realist representation of a dialogical encounter is a simulation as culturally specific and morally ethnocentric as any other narrative mode of forging presence (as is the Western concept of dialogue). Neither Foucault nor Derrida has shied away from translating, representing (objectifying and deobjectifying) systems of representation in other historical epochs of Western culture, epochs that constitute our internal and anterior others.

7. Therefore, to submit a dialogue as event to a literary representation does not necessarily mean the discourses represented or the text in which this depiction is found is dialogical in itself. In this book the dialogical process is indexed in the fact that neither the informant's discourse nor the theoretical discourse of Western academe (Foucault, Hegel, Nietzsche, etc.) are reducible to each other. Neither sphere of discourse functions as a metalanguage; rather, they transform each other through a fictive interface. My editing and juxtapositions of oral histories and theorists present one strategy of reading which has its normative preferences representing my cultural contexts. Many aspects of the oral histories have been left in silence in recognition that no particular strategy of reading can exhaust a discourse in whole or part. Dialogical discourse should disclose the mutation of signifiers and signifieds as the effect of historical experience. This is valid for the discourses that emerge within and from the fieldwork process. This book also reconstructs or fabricates dialogical encounters and ramifications between oral histories, so that Republican, Loyalist, and state discourses are juxtaposed in a manner that renders explicit what is in effect a tacit intertextual reference between antagonistic discourses in political practice.

8. Any naïve acceptance of linear temporality is highly problematic insofar as this time signature governs the ideological relation between acts of violence and the political narratives that function as the authorizing referent of the act in the political culture of Northern Ireland. (See chapters 2, 4, and 6 for discussions of the ideological functions of linear time in the political culture.) The work of both Derrida and Lyotard uses the critique of linear time to call into question the model of a prediscursive subject and any notion of correspondence between truth and origination.

9. See Clifford 1988 for the usual phonocentric misreading of this text. Ricoeur has in mind not only the dynamic by which the text renders the act or event polysemic and transformative, but also the in-place "spontaneous" readings of coactors who share the same social space. Such decentralizing readings always come up against the constraints of culture and historical particularity which restricts their interpretive gauge.

2 / Spatial Formations of Violence

1. I was told by one informant that the civil rights marches had been "beaten to the ground" by Protestant mobs and the police. This metaphor captures the sensibility of territoriality. Being beaten to the ground, among other things, is to be pushed back into the sectarian enclave that has been reserved for you.

2. The Campaign for Social Justice, the founding organization of the civil rights movement, was based in the politically moderate Catholic middle class. The Northern Ireland Civil Rights Association (NICRA), which superseded the Campaign for Social Justice, in 1967 combined the Catholic professional middle class, Catholic and Protestant university students, and trade unionists who were predominantly Protestant. Certain figures in the Republican movement (the Wolf Tone societies) and the IRA, who were instrumental in the original process of setting up the federation, were distanced from leadership positions by 1969.

3. In 1969, 74 percent of Belfast's population was Protestant. The Catholic minority was and still is located mainly in the Falls and Ardoyne districts, though there were numerous pockets of Catholic settlement in other parts of the city, such as the Short Strand (Poole and Boal 1973:14).

4. Between August and September 1969, about 3,750 families were forced out of their home districts by direct and indirect intimidation. Approximately 83 percent of these emigrants were Catholic (Poole 1971). The majority of Catholics were ejected from mixed districts with a Protestant majority. The majority of emigrating Protestants left in anticipation of large-scale Catholic settlement in their areas, which were usually isolated among Catholic enclaves (Darby and Morris 1974). By 1973 up to 15,000 people had been relocated (Darby and Morris 1974).

5. Darby calls this the "nostalgia myth" (1987:82) and finds it current mainly among persons who underwent forced displacement. Leaving aside questions concerning the myth, reality, and levels of intercommunal fraternization, whatever exchanges that did take place between Catholics and Protestant always ran up against dramatic limits. Interviews I conducted with Catholic women who had worked in the linen factories between the 1930s and the 1950s all referred to the abrupt social withdrawal of Protestant female workers from close contact with Catholic counterparts during the period immediately prior to the annual Loyalist marching season in the summer. The curtailment of interaction was a ritualized form of social death. Relations were resumed by Protestants just as arbitrarily after the marching season, with no references made to the suspension of social contact.

6. They were both involved in political and/or sectarian violence during that period.

7. On August 19, 1969, a nine-year-old boy, Patrick Rooney, was killed by random machine-gun fire by the B Specials (a Protestant-dominated police reserve), who were firing at Divis Flats, a high-rise housing project with a Catholic population. The gunfire was indiscriminate and was not precipitated by any violence from Divis Flats.

8. The figure of the empty house in the confessional enclave implies not only the emigration of neighbors or kin but the possibility of its resettlement by incoming groups. The empty house is a frontier zone and automatically a militarized space.

9. Prior to 1969, large-scale rioting between Catholics and Protestants in Belfast took place in 1835, 1857, 1864, 1872, 1898, 1920–22, and 1935. Interethnic rioting emerges with the stabilization of Catholic settlement in the city at the end of the eighteenth century. A report on the 1857 riots contains the first clear-cut reference to self-imposed segregation by Catholic and Protestant communities. Forced displacement of ethnic populations on a large scale is first mentioned in an 1864 inquiry (Darby 1987).

10. Before the 1969 riots, two-thirds of Belfast families lived on streets in which 90 percent of the population were ethnically homogeneous.

11. It was not unusual for paramilitary organizations to encourage the desertion of particular streets on the grounds that they were indefensible against attack from the other side. The militarization of streets as interface zones reflected the recasting of communal conflict into a war of position.

12. This refers to the emergence of local district-based Loyalist paramilitary groupings like the Shankill and Woodvale Defense Associations. These groups were centralized as the Ulster Defense Association in September 1971.

13. Disraeli Street cuts into the Crumlin Road which separates the Protestant Woodvale district from the Catholic sections of the Ardoyne. There had been rioting between the two communities on the previous night. An armored car of the B Specials had smashed through Catholic barricades, followed by a Protestant mob that fired several shops and homes. On August 15 the Catholic streets adjacent to the Protestant sector began evacuating. This incident with the bus seems to have been both revenge for the intrusions of the armored car and a covering operation for the Catholic evacuation. Though it is unclear, the narrator implies that the Catholic crowd commandeered the bus and used it to break the Protestant barricades.

14. This process was refracted in the renaming of social space, in the shift from ethnic codifications to military codifications. Communities became defensible or indefensible because of their geography; families that lived near interfaces or were resettled at these sectors were considered "frontier" families capable of resisting intimidation, and the desertion of streets by the populace was viewed by observers from the opposing community as a sure sign of impending paramilitary attack from that space. Informants from the Short Strand, a small Catholic enclave among larger Protestant districts, relate to their community as a social space and as a military liability to the IRA. They were all quite literate in the logistics of defense and evacuation over the Albert Street bridge, which was considered the only way out in the face of a Protestant attack. The Short Strand has the mentality of a military outpost superimposed on the sensibility of a tight-knit working-class community.

15. There were the Hanaways of the Falls Road, the Adamses of Pound Loney and Ballymurphy, the McCanns of the Markets area, and the McGuigans of the Ardoyne among others.

16. This paramilitary police volunteer reserve was founded in 1920, before the establishment of the Northern Ireland state. Known as the Ulster Special Constabulary, it was in effect the creation of the British state, which used the Specials as a community-based deterrent to the IRA in the early 1920s. In 1969 the Specials numbered ten thousand men. Each volunteer owned a uniform and a weapon that was kept at home. A significant number of these personal weapons were automatic. The Specials were clearly a government-sanctioned counterinsurgency force, and many of its volunteers held dual membership in the emerging nongovernmental paramilitary organizations and activists groups of the period such as the Ulster Protestant Volunteers and the Ulster Constitution Defense Committee.

17. In 1969 the existing nongovernmental paramilitary organizations—the Irish Republican Army and the Ulster Volunteer Force—could hardly be characterized as involved in populist politics or populist paramilitary mobilization. The UVF engaged in clandestine sectarian assassination and was not organized as a community defense apparatus, in contrast to the defense organizations that sprang up in Protestant working-class comunities from 1969 onward. In 1969 the leadership of the IRA had all but abandoned the "physical force" strategy and was committed to a Marxist stage theory of social transformation, predicated on a projected working-class alliance between Catholics and Protestants. The IRA was totally unprepared, ideologically and logistically, for the military threat to the Catholic community that emerged with the Protestant rioting of the summer of 1969.

18. An increase in both sectarian killings and armed resistance to the British army occurred in the aftermath of Operation Motorman in July 1972. British army troops, aided by the RUC and the UDR and equipped with armored vehicles, swept away the barricades in Derry and Belfast. Despite the removal of these physical boundaries, the cognitive mapping of urban space remained in effect and informed the structure of sectarian killing and aggression against the British troops by Republican and Loyalist forces.

3 / Hardmen, Gunmen, Butchers

1. The narrator is making an indirect reference to the Tartan Gangs, neighborhood organizations of Protestant youths who wore tartan scarfs as a commemoration of three soldiers of the Royal Highland Fusiliers killed in Belfast on March 10, 1971, supposedly by Republican paramilitaries. The Tartan Gangs were used as a recruitment base by the UDA (Ulster Defense Association) and the UVF (Ulster Volunteer Force), though the gangs and the paramilitaries frequently clashed over their different positions on rioting and the timing of sectarian violence.

2. The paired imagery of the mask and the gun is the cathartic moment in the funerals of Republican "volunteers" killed in action. The dead are supposed to receive a three-to-six-man military salute. The honor guard are masked and in uniform and are expected to fire their weapons as the official military salute. Usually this performance takes place at the grave site as part of the funeral service. But the British army and the police are on the look out for the honor

guard. The salute, the possession of firearms, and the display of paramilitary insignia such as the uniform and masks are all illegal. The honor guard is made up of active service volunteers whom the security forces would like to take in for general questioning. All these factors make the display of uniforms, masks, and guns by the honor guard the political highpoint of the Republican death ritual. The gunmen are usually secreted into the procession as it marches up the Falls Road to Milltown Cemetery. The crowd screens the paramilitaries from the surveillance of the police and army, though they can do little about the army helicopter overflights that harass the funeral, monitor the crowd with aerial photography, and drown out the funeral orations at the gravesite. The procession stops for a moment while the honor guard performs the salute, firing their weapons in the air over the coffin in the street or at the grave. As this occurs the security forces, warned by the shots, lookouts, or the helicopter, try to break through the crowd. This usually precipitates rioting at the edge of the procession. During this confusion the honor guard is snuck out of the procession by the cooperating crowd into a nearby safe house, where the uniforms, masks, and weapons are gotten rid of by another unit. This performance reclaims public space from the state. It is also a mimesis of the surprise-trickster tactics of urban guerrilla war.

3. See Appendix B.

4. On July 17, 1973, a British army patrol in Divis Flats was blown up by an IRA thirty-pound bomb placed near an elevator shaft. A resident of the housing complex was injured in the explosion and numerous apartments were destroyed. The placement of the bomb within the complex was protested by the local residents, who are staunchly Republican in their politics.

5. Another phrase for political shootings which objectifies the victim as an orifice is "to fill him in." In Belfast I have heard this phrase used in reference to inflicting a beating as well as in reference to shooting someone.

6. This ratio has to be understood within the context the geographers are applying—a spatial categorization of this violence and not a strictly political denotation. Thus not all doorstep murders are in response to other doorstep killings or other forms of homicide that could be defined clearly as sectarian. From the Loyalist point of view, everytime the PIRA or the INLA kills a Protestant policeman, Protestant member of the UDR, or even a Protestant member of the British army, this is classified as a sectarian murder committed by Republicans. Conversely, Loyalist paramilitaries will assert that the Catholic victim of a Loyalist assassination was secretly a member of the PIRA or the INLA and thus the killing was "political" and not sectarian. The PIRA counterposition is that once a person puts on the uniform of the state, he or she is a representative of that apparatus and that person's assassination is explicitly political. The PIRA would add that they have assassinated Catholic members of the security forces (who amount to around 11 percent of RUC recruitment). The Republican paramilitary position also asserts that they always "claim" their killed active service volunteers and that if they do not claim the victim, then he or she was not a member of the PIRA or INLA.

7. The other major form of sectarian assassination is the targeting of victims who work in integrated factories. The victim (usually Catholic) is killed on the way home from work. Accepting car lifts from strangers or accepting a ride from

an acquaintance of the other community with unknown passengers in the car and using unknown taxi-cab firms are situations to be avoided in the context of sectarian assassination campaigns. Construction sites, which are usually strictly segregated, are also favored targets for sectarian assassination.

8. Murphy was jailed in 1979, released from prison in 1983 and resumed his prior activities. At that time he was known to be involved in the torture and death of Joe Donegan, a Catholic with no political connections. Murphy was killed when automatic rifles sprayed his car as he drove down the Shankill Road, the heart of a militant Loyalist sector. The RUC claims that the UDA and UVF allowed a PIRA active service unit into the area to stake out Murphy and kill him. For similar arrangements between Republican and Loyalist paramilitaries, see chapters 5 and 6.

9. Reinforcing this mimetic replication between the agent and object of violence is the fact that victims of sectarian torture and assassination are found dumped in back streets with their heads hooded. Interrogation detainees are also hooded (see chap. 4). The mutual masking of paramilitaries and stiffs is part of the iconography of induced alterity.

10. I use the categories the Symbolic, the Real, and the Imaginary as a way of conceptualizing the relationship between cultural formation and the subjective experience of diachronic transformation. For the Lacanians, the symbolic order is formed by the convergence between linguistic and social symbolism (Lemaire 1977), that is, the fusion of structures of representation and institutional structures, as in Lévi-Strauss's linguistic model of kinship systems.

> The homologous character of linguistic symbolism and social symbolism derives from the fact that both are structures of oppositional elements capable of being combined, that both establish the possibility of recognition between subjects, and, finally, that both necessitate the passage from an immediate "dual" relationship to a mediate relationship through the intervention of a third term: the concept in language, and the Ancestor, the Sacred cause, the God or Law in Society. (Lemaire 1977:55–56)

It is the mediacy of the symbolic order that is at issue here. Its disjuncture with the Real is grounded in the dynamic that the symbolic order regulates representations of "reality," the process of cultural construction as it is termed today. Yet "[a] symbol . . . is only an operator within a structure . . . it is essentially an indirect expression. Its condition is that of not being what it represents" (p. 55).

The symbolic order is the relational positioning and articulation of identities, between subjects and between subjects and objects.

> The symbolic—i.e., overdetermined—character of social relations therefore implies that they lack an ultimate literality which would reduce them to necessary moments of an immanent law. There are not two planes, one of essences and the other of appearance, since there is no possibility of fixing an ultimate literal sense for which the symbolic would be a second and derived plane of signification. . . . The objective world is structured in relational sequences which do not necessarily have a finalistic sense. (Laclau and Mouffe 1985:98 and 111)

The symbolic order is the representational limit formed by institutionalized closure that allows codes to operate, relationality to take place, and commensurations to be stabilized. Representational closure here is also distantiation from the Real, which is

> the fullness of inert presence, positivity; nothing is lacking in the Real—that is, the lack is introduced only by the symbolization; it is a signifier which introduces a void, an absence in the Real. But at the same time the Real is in itself a hole, a gap, an opening in the middle of the symbolic order. The Real . . . as a product, a leftover of symbolization. (Žižek 1989:170)

The Real is uncodifiable excess; it precedes the symbolic order, which cuts itself out from the Real through rules of inclusion and exclusion. Thus the Real is subsequently structured by the symbolic as the excess and repressed effects of symbolization. The Real is both internal and external to the symbolic order. It is "pressupposed and posed" by the symbolic (Žižek 1989:169). The Real is both the precondition of symbolization and failed symbolization, that density which is encountered in the historical exhaustion of symbolic modes. It is a material-experiential surplus beyond any socially prescribed set of descriptions. The Real is also historicity, the condition of possibility for any particular history or narrative closure, and that which "resists symbolization absolutely. We must therefore propose that history . . . as an absent cause, . . . is inaccessible to us except in textual form, and that our approach to it and to the Real itself necessarily passes through its prior textualization, its narrativization in the political unconscious" (Jameson 1981:35). But the so-called absence or externality of the Real is in part a function of the symbolic order, which detaches elements of its interiority to construct both extrinsic, authorizing sites of legitimation and external sites of negative alterity which permit the self-definition of the symbolic. The latter can break out of binary grids and carve out autonomous semantic spheres. "Defilement is what is jettisoned from the 'symbolic system.' It is what escapes that social rationality, that logical order on which a social aggregate is based" (Kristeva 1982:65). Modes of radical objectification such as violence precipitate the abject, those fragments which elude, exceed, and resist the differential structuring and coupling of subject-object totalities within the symbolic order.

11. The decentering encounter between the symbolic order and the Real precipitates the mediation of the imaginary in Lacanian theory. Transferred into sociopolitical process, the imaginary moves beyond the failed closure of the symbolic, but does so by attempting to erase the now-exposed gap, disjuncture, or rupture between the symbolic and the Real. In my analysis this rupture is precipitated by the disorder of the material domain. The incursions of the Real expose the articulated character of the social, its symbolic structuration, its fragile metaphorical hold on itself. The erasure of discontinuity, the repression of differential or articulated relations, is the function of the instrumental imaginary. Semantic fixity is reached through the effacement of symbolic distance. Yet this dynamic also implies the overdetermination of material orders by symbolic violence or other discursive practices. The materialism of terrorist practice involves a totalizing overcoding, or symbolic overdetermination of material orders, a

denial of its relative autonomy or elision of social codes. This denial is the mirror relation that political ideology as the instrumental imaginary constructs through discourse and violence. In this book the instrumental imaginary is a practice of mimetic transcription through violence that denies its own symbolic foundation, that is, it denies the metaphorical transfer of value forms from one body to another through the effectivity of violence.

> The image given back to us by the imagination is characterized by its dissimulation of the system of reference, by its fusion of figure and ground. . . . The imaginary hides consciousness's own operations and attitudes from it: in its representation consciousness sees something other than itself, whereas there is nothing in this other except what consciousness has put there. In other words consciousness dissimulates itself from itself in this other. . . . Lacan defines the essence of the imaginary as a dual relationship, a reduplication in the mirror, an immediate opposition between consciousness and its other in which each term becomes its opposite and is lost in the play of the reflections. (Lemaire 1977:60)

In the political culture of Northern Ireland's paramilitaries and counterinsurgency state, history and power are the effects of the transformation of the material sphere into a mimetic template, a mirror apparatus of ideological intentionality. The emergence of new relationships between ideology and materiality is itself a novel historical structure, an event, a shift into an alien narrative relation. This shift presupposes the refiguration and reassemblage of disparate and diverse elements of the residual symbolic order. The instrumental imaginary of the paramilitaries and the state attempts, through violence, to simulate presences that are absent—the completed community of nationalist identification in its prospective or retrospective modalities, or civil order. Thus there is a nostalgic nuance to all this simulation of what does not actually exist.

12. In the following narrative, nature is militarized and the military domain is organicized. These heterogeneous metaphors refract the liminal condition of material spheres in historical transit.

3.22 During the feud between the Officials [IRA] and INLA [a splinter group] there was lots of gear floating about; there was always stacks of guns, mainly sawed-off shotguns. The Brits would let them shoot each other and then move in and get the gear and the guys who done it. So the Brits would hit [raid] the Flats. You called the INLA the IRPS [Irish Republican Socialist party] or "Wyatt" IRPS, and Divis Flats, where there was a lot of IRPS, was called Planet of the IRPS. So when the Brits hit Divis Flats they would have went to the front door, and the next thing we would toss the shotguns out the window. It happened a few times, no problem; the Brits never caught on. One day they hit one of the top flats where there was three sawn-off shotguns. They were thrown out the window, but one of them went off whenever it hit the bottom. The fucking Brits bounce down the stairs, and there behind the building in the grass is two shotguns with the butts stuck into the ground and the double barrels pointing up, standing upright in a row. The Brits put the word around after seeing that: "Things are that bad that they're growing shotguns in Divis Flats!" (INLA)

4 / Being Done

1. Autonomization can be considered from a variety of theoretical perspectives. Laclau and Mouffe (1985) locate it in the mutation of political interests (the signified) by modes of representation (the signifier). This results in a deauthorization of ideological referents by prescribed modes of representation. Castoriadis (1987) identifies autonomization with the "alienation of a society to its institutions" and links this to a "special logic of symbolism" which imposes independent consequences that negate any notion of the symbolic as a neutral surface covering or as an adequate instrument of preexisting content. The issues of autonomization engage the internal shift from performatives—the reenactment of a preexisting code or narrative to performances—modal action with no dependency on a residual code. This tension can also be conceptualized as the disjunctive emergence of presentation from out of representation (understood as the failure of mimesis). For discussions of autonomization in relation to performance see Ricouer 1973. In relation to social organization see Zeleny 1980 and Livingston 1984. Jameson 1981 periodizes autonomization within the incremental processes of reification. In this study the representational mediation of originary political interest, Castoriadis's symbolism with independent consequences and Jameson's dynamic of reification, can be encountered in the exchange relations embedded in interlocking systems of violent performance.

2. Subsequent to the eradication of the barricades and no-go areas in working-class Protestant and Catholic districts, the British government initiated a program of self-barricading. The state now assumes the posture of the sanctuary, with its fortified police and army outposts or "forts" scattered throughout urban Belfast. These usually take the form of concrete and steel blockhouses protected by blast-resistant walls, wire mesh, steel gates, and video camera surveillance mounted on the buildings and on street corners. This self-barricading by the state is complemented by the panoptic colonization of public space with advanced mobile and stationary surveillance technology. With this barricading, all working-class communities, but particularly the Catholic areas, are constructed as frontier zones, as peripheries of a fictive civil order that exists solely within the physical edifices of the state as its internal space. Thus the counterinsurgency apparatus is as efficient in forestalling the generation of civil space as was the confessional division of urban space in the recent past.

3. Only 50 percent of those initially interned had any affiliation with the IRA (McGuffin 1973:86). Within thirty-six hours after the operation, protests erupted and seventeen people were killed in Belfast and Derry. In Belfast, buses were burned, barricades were set up in Catholic sectors, and the army was subjected to widespread sniper fire. Recruitment for the IRA swelled. The Social Democratic Labor Party, an anti-Republican electoral group, set up a civil dis-

obedience campaign against internment, and the Catholic ghettos went on a rent and rates strike against the government.

4. Rubber and plastic bullets have replaced C.S. gas and high-powered waterhoses as riot control and general street clearance weapons. Though intended as riot control technology, rubber and plastic bullets are used indiscriminately by the security forces in many situations that cannot be classified as riots. These weapons are frequently fired at under a twenty-five yard range; they travel at 160 miles per hour and weigh about five ounces. Plastic bullets have a greater range than rubber bullets and a stronger impact. Both these bullets can seriously main or kill their human targets.

5. For the historical background of rough music and its connection to the inversion of gender codes in the British Isles, see Ingram 1982.

6. By citing Bazin 1974 I am making no claims for a strict homology between enslavement and counterinsurgency practices in Northern Ireland. Rather with Bazin I am dealing with the experience of capture as an interstitial moment at which point political subjects are transformed and created as they pass from one social status and institution to another. The use of violence as a mechanism of passage, detachment, and differentiation is a focus I share with Bazin.

7. The Special Air Services (SAS) is an elite counterinsurgency regiment analogous to the American Green Berets and the French 10th Parachute Regiment. In Northern Ireland the SAS officially specializes in rural counterinsurgency operations and is unofficially associated with a specialized assassination program in which killings of Republicans are made to appear as the work of Loyalist paramilitaries.

8. Republican activists assert that many stop-and-search and arrest operations are merely facades for political assassination. See Boyle, Hadden, and Hillyard 1980 for statistics that support this charge. There is also the specialized RUC unit, E4A located in Gough barracks, which was supposedly trained by the SAS in England. Republicans consider this unit a state-sponsored death squad. In June 1986, John Stalker, the deputy chief constable of the city of Manchester, was removed from an almost completed inquiry into the existence and practice of an RUC shoot-to-kill policy. Stalker's preliminary report delivered prior to his removal was highly critical of the RUC.

9. The cell system was largely devised by IRA officer Ivor Bell when he was incarcerated in the Maze prison during the mid-1970s. In 1976, a systematic program to replace the community-based brigade system was advanced by Martin McGuinness of the IRA. During this period the "Green Book," the definitive PIRA training manual, was also composed in the Maze prison (Long Kesh). The introduction of the cell system in the late 1970s entailed a drastic reorganization of the interface between the PIRA and base communities.

The Belfast Brigade of the PIRA divides the city into three battalions. The First battalion covers the Upper Falls, Ballymurphy, and Andersontown. The Seond Battalion covers the Lower Falls, Divis Flats, and Clonard. The Third Battalion is responsible for the Ardoyne, the Bone, and the Short Strand. The backbone of the battalion was the active service unit formed into neighborhood companies. The units and the companies were community-based structures with a recruitment drawn from the local area. Thus they were highly vulnerable to informers and the interrogation methods instituted by the RUC in the mid-1970s. The new cell system detached the active service unit (ASU) from the company. The ASU no longer had a neighborhood affiliation but would be called upon to function in various segments of an operation in any area of the city, in tandem with other ASUs. The new ASU structure was formed by a commander and three or four subordinates. The commander is the only link to other sections of the organization. Thus any informing from within the unit would ideally have a limited gauge. With this reorganization, the community-based company was relegated to the less glamorous role of policing neighborhoods, carrying out local-level intelligence work, and providing logistical support for any operations occurring in their area. The cell system finalized the shift of the IRA away from a community defense posture and decidedly lessened the organization's dependence on large-scale practical support from base communities. The cell system also decreased the political-discursive interface between the military wing and the base community. Thus the cell system has to be seen in relation to the emergence of Sinn Fein as a community-based activist organization with an agenda surpassing that of simple political support of the "physical force" campaign. The INLA adopted the cell system, and there is growing evidence that Loyalist paramilitaries are deploying this structure too, though most Republican paramilitaries have a low opinion of Loyalist operations on the level of logistics.

10. The narrator is referring to a 1984 firefight between the RUC and an INLA unit whose safe house was the object of a raid by the security forces. Two RUC men died in the operation, and the entire INLA unit was wiped out.

11. On November 11, 1982, Eugene Tolman, Sean Burns, and Gervais McKerr were killed by an E4A unit while allegedly running the police roadblock near Lurgan. No weapons were found in the car which was riddled with automatic-weapons fire. The three men were active service volunteers of the PIRA and known to the police at the time of the encounter.

12. See chapter 5 for a more detailed discussion of the physical force/political polarity in Republican ideology.

13. Since the state has downplayed the role of the army and foregrounded the role of the police, courts, and prison, the discussion here is centered on demonstrating the political structure underneath the civil and juridical facade of police practices. Locating police violence as political places paramilitary violence on the same footing as the violence of the state. This essentially "decriminalizes" the violence of the paramilitary. Thus the political in Northern Ireland is set off from the juridical and from the sectarian. The admissibility of the "political space" forged by paramilitary discourse and practice is an ongoing issue in the conflict for all parties. The admissibility and hegemonization of this space testify to its emergent character for all parties, despite the use of "tradition" in making legitimation claims for the political space of paramilitary practice.

14. A "P" check is a "personal identity" check or computerized verification. "P" checks are authorized by the Emergency Provisions Act of 1978 which requires subjects to provide data concerning their identities and residence to the security forces. The subject under a "P" check is obligated to give information on the purpose of his or her presence in public space, including point of origin and destination. The security forces can interrogate the subject as to his or her

knowledge of terrorist activity. Refusal to answer any of the inquiries renders the subject vulnerable to arrest at the discretion of the security forces.

15. The RUC are insulted as "black" because of the color of their uniform. The term does not have a racial connotation here.

16. Thus the parts of the captive's body are made to circulate in a system of equivalence; the name as a detachable part of the captive's memory is commensurate to the detachable parts of the captive's body. Both the name and the body parts threatened with detachment are understood as value-imbued units of a debt to the state the captive must pay. The centrality of substitution and simulation in these episodes marks the captive's entry into a new regime of valuation in which the relation between language and the body will be altered (see Nietzsche 1956).

17. See chapters 3, 5, and 6 for more extensive examples and analysis of political violence and medical rationality and iconography.

18. This refers to the disciplinary regime of the H-Blocks where a program to depoliticize and criminalize the paramilitary prisoners was implemented. Many of the disciplinary techniques of interrogation centers were transposed to the prison regime. See chapters 5 and 6.

19. Arrest and interrogation procedures and coercions frequently include the disruption of families and the domestic space as part of the repertoire of intimidation. The wives of interrogatees are subject to arrest, and children in this situation are remanded to public child care agencies. The RUC notifies employers about the detention of employees, and of course repeated arrests render the suspect and family visible to Loyalist paramilitary assassination squads if the suspect is Catholic. There have been frequent cases of the largely Protestant RUC and Special Branch sharing the dossiers of suspects with Loyalist paramilitaries.

20. Gerry Adams, M.P., leads the executive committee of Provisional Sinn Fein, the political wing or party of the PIRA. Adams also holds a position on the Army Council, the executive branch of the PIRA. Adams was wounded in a Loyalist assassination attempt in March of 1984. The narrator, as a member of the UDA, was detained as part of a general roundup of UDA activists. This interview took place in April 1984.

21. It is standard procedure for interogatees, paramilitaries and civilians, to ask for a medical examination of each day of the captivity and before leaving the interrogation center on the last day of detention (usually denied). Detainees also request medical examinations at the court hearing when they are charged, which occurs during or at the end of their detention period.

22. On January 2, 1969, a civil rights march sponsored by Peoples' Democracy, a student activist group, was attacked by a mob of Protestants at Burntollet Bridge outside the village of Claudy. It turned out that about 100 participants in the mob were off-duty members of the B Specials organized by Major Bunting.

5 / The Breaker's Yard

1. The accommodations for both the internees and sentenced prisoners at Long Kesh consisted of Nissan huts laid out in wire-rimmed compounds. Each hut held up to ninety prisoners in an open dormitory space. Because of the

generous use of barbed wire around the compounds, the prisoners dubbed their accommodations "the Cages." A popular song of the period referred to inmates as "The Men Behind the Wire"; having conversations across compounds was termed "wirelessing," a phrase that eventually came to be used for all conversations.

The compounds were organized into separate political-ethnic sectors. Internees and sentenced prisoners were separated from each other during internment (see chap. 4). Within the internee and sentenced prisoner sectors, compounds were segregated first by religious affiliation and secondly by membership in one of the Republican and Loyalist paramilitary organizations. A small section was reserved for nonpolitical sentenced prisoners who were termed Ordinary Decent Criminals or ODCs. This group, segregated from the political prisoners, served as prison orderlies.

The compound huts were self-governing communities. Political prisoners had little contact with prison staff. All prison administration–prisoner interaction was mediated by the paramilitary officer commanding each hut. Within the compound, military hierarchies and ranks prevailed. This social structure replicated and intensified the paramilitary social structure on the outside. The Republican compounds engaged in extensive political and military education-training programs. Most noteworthy were the Gaeltacht or Jailtacht huts, dormitories where only Gaelic was spoken. Prisoners would enter into a Gaeltacht hut for regular cycles of language immersion. Some prisoners resided permanently in the Gaeltacht huts.

The conversation recounted in narrative 5.1 took place in Cage 11. Gerry Adams, current leader of Sinn Fein and then OC of Cage 11, Bobby Sands, and other inhabitants were part of the leadership group that radicalized and revitalized the political philosophy of the IRA from the late 1970s onward.

2. In 1975 the OC of the Republican prisoners at Long Kesh, Larry Marley, met with officials of the Northern Ireland Office concerning the shift to cellular incarceration and the possibility of phasing out Special Category status. The Provisionals were offered a two-thirds reduction of their sentences in exchange for the acceptance of the new regime.

3. Northern Ireland Office figures set the reconviction rate for IRA men during the 1970s as 10–15 percent, in contrast to the 60 percent level of recidivism for nonpolitical prisoners (Bishop and Mallie 1987:274).

4. Long Kesh, formerly a World War II air force base, now functions as a penal-military complex formed by the Cages, military barracks, the residences of prison staff, and the H-Blocks facility. The spatial adjacency between the Cages and the H-Blocks and the fact that many of the paramilitaries incarcerated in the H-Blocks had also served time under the Cages regime combined to obscure the radical transformations implied by the new criminalization policy in the prisons.

5. The removal of political status and the criminalization regime were first implemented in Crumlin Road Jail in 1976, where Republican paramilitaries were held on remand awaiting trial and/or sentencing.

6. The prison uniform was also referred to as "gear." In paramilitary slang, "gear" refers to weapons. Thus the term links the uniform to instruments of violence and coercion.

7. One dynamic that may have inhibited the establishment of a separate H-Block brigade command autonomous from the brigade structure of the Cages was the customary loss of rank IRA men undergo when they enter prison. This practice automatically granted command seniority to the IRA in the Cages. However, when Brendan "Darkie" Hughes, former Officer Commanding of the Cages, was incarcerated in the H-Blocks in early 1978, he was placed in command of the H-Block IRA prisoners.

8. By refusing to wear the uniform, "noncooperation" as it was termed, the resisting prisoner automatically had his sentence doubled, because he would have lost his 50 percent remission of sentence awarded for cooperative behavior. The prisoner also lost four visits a month (one of which was statutory) by "noncooperating," and by not wearing the uniform to take the statutory visit. A prisoner was entitled to one letter per month even during the resistance. Compromising on the visits did not relieve a prisoner's social deprivations. Frequently the "family member" or girlfriend who visited the prisoner was in effect an IRA volunteer who used the visit to receive and convey communiqués between the prisoners and the outside IRA command.

9. PIRA procedure differed from INLA procedure in this matter. Narrative 5.33 describes the smuggling out of a written list of prison staff assassination targets by the PIRA.

10. This was the required statutory visit. To take this visit required putting on the uniform, so the narrator is referring to conditions in 1978.

11. The narrator is placing this experiment in the winter of 1978, but he is most likely confusing it with events that took place at the end of January 1981. See Collins 1986:116–17 and Beresford 1989:32–33.

12. This was referred to as "giving the furniture the message." See Beresford 1989:35.

13. There were 837 Republican prisoners incarcerated in the H-Blocks and the total prison population was about 1,300 prisoners altogether. More than half the Republican prison population was not on the protest.

14. The prison guards were paid extra to do the mirror searches since in the context of the protest it was considered hazardous duty. See narrative 5.25 for a discussion of the relationship between the financial incentives of the guards and their ideological interactions with prison conditions and the prisoners.

15. This manifold, economic formation of the subject is termed *Herrschaftsgebilde,* a "formation of domination" (Schürmann 1984:375–76). The *Herrschaftsgebilde* is constituted on the distinction between force and power. It is a historically determinate combinatory of forces.

> Formation means that power forms itself into a configuration and domination means that the constituents of such configuration are forces. A formation of domination is the ordering of power. In that ordering . . . the moral subject is only an instance. . . . From the viewpoint of power it is not one type that is nomothetical but the coming together, the gathering of forces in a determinate formation. . . . Power does not occur unless translated into forces . . . this originative translation functions as normative determination. (P. 379)

Thus in Nietzschean political anthropology there is no dichotomy between a repressive and ideological apparatus. They are different moments of a normative and nomothetic practice or ensemble of practices: "Norms are born from power through one force and for another force" (p. 379).

16. In a communiqué smuggled out of the H-Blocks and addressed to the IRA Army Council, Bik McFarlane, then Officer Commanding of the H-Blocks, characterized the hunger strikers as "human Armalites." (Beresford 1989:276). The Armalite is the automatic rifle frequently used by the PIRA and INLA.

17. Clement Freud is the grandson of Sigmund Freud and Liberal party spokesman on Northern Ireland during 1976–79. The historical irony of this meeting is worth further investigation and comment insofar as the Blanketmen's scatological systems transgress the Freudian theory of the scatological.

18. Many of the techniques of sensory coercion developed in Castlereagh were tried out in the H-Blocks, including sleep deprivation through manipulation of the lights at night. Particularly salient here was the division between physical versus psychological coercive techniques. When the prison leadership was isolated from the rest of the Blanketmen in 1978,they were subjected to continuous exposure to a white noise apparatus at night. During the same period, physical brutality against the rank-and-file Blanketmen was intensified. In Castlereagh, "case-hardened" detainees are subjected to psychological interventions, while the new detainee is more frequently coerced through direct physical violence.

19. Albert Miles, Governor of the Maze prison, was assassinated by the PIRA on December 20, 1978.

20. During 1976–80, nineteen Prison Officers were assassinated by the PIRA in a campaign that attempted to retaliate for specific cases of brutality in the H-Blocks prison. See narratives 5.29 and 5.33.

21. On August 27, 1979, eighteen British soldiers were killed by a PIRA radio bomb explosion near Warrenpoint, County Down. On the same day at Mullaghmore, County Sligo, in the republic of Ireland, Earl Mountbatten, his grandson, and grandson's friend (both teenagers) were blown up by an IRA radio bomb planted in the earl's yacht. Another passenger died later from injuries.

22. Despite this the Loyalist prisoners and the prison guards held each other in contempt. An INLA informant claims that the addresses of prison guards were frequently supplied to them by Loyalist prisoners who wanted certain guards set up for assassination. In an interview with a UDA member and ex-inmate of the H-Blocks, he recounted how, some months after his release, he assaulted an off-duty prison officer encountered drinking in his local pub. Republican prisoners claim that the guards thought the Loyalist prisoners were "soft" in relation to those Republican prisoners who had undergone the prison protests. In 1978 some Loyalist prisoners initiated a Blanket protest that lasted only several weeks.

23. The charge of self-inflicted violence was also brought against the tortured detainees of Castlereagh. The relation of this discourse of "self-infliction" to the ideology of state violence bears further inquiry and analysis. For now this ideologeme indicates that the Other to which state violence is directed is the construct of the state. Thus state violence becomes intrinsic to the Other, an

element of the Other's ontological condition, despite the origin of both this violence and the Other in the state. The transfer of this violence, emanating from the state to the topos of the Other, is part of the process by which the Other is essentialized, the dialectical counterpart to the essentialization of the state. This essentialization, enabled by practices of domination and their fictions, is axial to the formation of a material culture of the state.

24. The term "crack" used here is significant. It can infer entertainment, excitement, pleasure, diversion, gossip, and the truth or exact character of a situation.

25. To the melody of "Brown Girl in the Rain," a hit song during this period by the group Boney M.

26. These crystal sets picked up signals from the BBC antennae located near Long Kesh. One wire was placed outside the cell window as aerial and another was attached as a ground to the heating pipes that ran through the cells. The radios were placed in plastic pharmaceutical vials. The radios usually picked up BBC Radio 4 and a local station. By placing the set in their mouths, prisoners, depending on their cell location, were able to receive other stations.

27. Inmates who smuggled "coms" (communiqués) were termed "pilots." The interception of a smuggled communiqué was characterized as "crashing," and the guards who intercepted the smuggler were called "Germans." This terminology relates to the phrase "on the air" discussed extensively below.

28. Sound was the modality through which the prisoner registered and semi-oticized the bodies of the prison guards. In this process, prison administration was reduced to its effects and could no longer be located as an ideal juridical reserve or center. The audio texture of prison administration foregrounded the prison itself as a stage and the penal regime itself as a daily performance that had no existence outside the effective structure of the act. The prison structure was enacted; the guards did not act within a structure. This foundational re-cognition of the penal regime was axial to the prisoners realizing their own potential for reorganizing the prison via an alternative structure of enactment. To act was to generate structure; to act was to autonomize. It was not simply a re-presentation but a presentation capable of referring to nothing outside itself. This tension between representation and presentation formed the infrastructure of the act in the prison resistance.

6 / Eschatology

1. Six of the hunger strikers were members of the PIRA and were meant to represent the six counties of Northern Ireland. The seventh was an INLA man.

2. One aspect of this archive has been recently disclosed in Beresford's (1989) journalistic account of the 1981 Hunger Strike. He was provided with a shopping bag of "coms," communiqués that Bik McFarlane, Officer Commanding of the H-Blocks, and other prisoners had written to the IRA Army Council outside the prison. Beresford, unfortunately, was not provided with the replies of the council. Beresford's book was published in the United States after this chapter was written. The H-Block communiqués upon which his book is largely based confirm the theses advanced in this chapter.

3. In the 1980 Hunger Strike the PIRA Army Council held back on military operations so as not to draw attention away from the prison protest. In the planning of the 1981 Hunger Strike the prison command agreed with the Army Council that military operations should continue as normal during the protest. The two operations had to be seen as continuous and complementary. This was, in effect, the ending of the breach between the "physical force" and "political" approaches (see chap. 5). This articulation anticipated the joining of electoral politics with a military campaign, initiated by the election of Bobby Sands to Parliament while he was hunger striking. In a communiqué to the PIRA council on June 14, 1981, Bik McFarlane classified the hunger strike action under the ethic of "acceptable levels of violence" to which the PIRA military operation had long been assimilated (Beresford 1989:195). See also chapter 5, n.16.

4. This occurred in January 1979.

5. The anti–hunger strike propaganda promoted by the state, the Loyalists, the Church, and some family members of the strikers stated that the Army Council had ordered the prisoners on strike and thus could order them off the strike. In fact the opposite was the case. The Army Council was opposed to the strike and reluctantly agreed, after the advocacy of Gerry Adams and assertions by the prisoners, that individual Blanketmen would go on strike without council approval. The Army Council expressly vetoed a strike at Armagh women's prison. One ex-Blanketman informed me that he felt betrayed by the posture of the Army Council during the planning discussions of the protest.

6. The breaking up of the H6 collective took place in September of 1979.

7. The H-Block ideology of politicization thus effectively abandoned or sublated the residual model of the colonial relationship based on a nineteenth-century model of economic imperialism. Postcapitalist reality emerged with the advent of the disciplinary-surveillance systems of the total counterinsurgency apparatus. The dialectical interaction of communities of resistance with this disciplinary regime generated the "Gnostic" model of the dominated community as a prison topos. Corresponding to this ideological shift away from the economic imagery of the imperialist model was the new centrality of cultural structures as the cornerstone of emancipation. As in the relations of resistance in interrogation, a rupture within the neocolonial relation has to be preceded by a rupture in cultural consciousness (see chap. 4). Thus even though the H-Block veterans are more positive about socialism than the older Provisionals, this ideological shift has little in common with the Marxist stage theory of the Official IRA during the middle and late 1960s. That program called for the sublation of ethnicity in favor of a common class alliance between the Catholic and Protestant proletariat. The H-Block philosophy was implicitly asking the Protestants to share an archaeological Irish ethnicity. But an ethnicity in which religion was irrelevant insofar as it would be based on the cultural structures of language, music, literature, and geographical separatism from Britain and the rest of Europe. Not surprisingly, from the late 1970s onward the leadership of the UDA and local Loyalist scholars developed discourses on the Cruit, a pre-Christian ethnic group distinguishable from the Celts, who resided in Ulster long before the seventeenth-century Protestant plantation and are deemed the native ancestors of a doubly displaced "lowland Scot" population that was the backbone of the later plantation.

8. In the summer of 1981, in an attempt to break the hunger strike, the penal regime escalated repressive practices. Beatings were intensified during increased cell shifts, cell searches occurred about three times a day, food rations were cut, and visits were arbitrarily delayed by the guards.

9. The call for volunteers for a second hunger strike went out through the cells on January 5, 1981. On February 2, 1981, the second hunger strike was officially announced for March 1. In February the PIRA Army Council vetoed a hunger strike at Armagh women's prison because of the poor physical conditions of the proposed volunteers. A Blanket protest had been underway there since February 1980.

10. Supporting this depiction of Sands' expectations in the oral histories is the following communiqué written by Sands on March 9, 1981:

> As you should know I don't care much to entering any discussion on the topic of "negotiations" or for that matter "settlements.". . . I've told Bik [McFarlane, OC PIRA, H-Blocks] to let me or anyone else die before submitting to a play like that [a last-minute agreement in order to save the hunger striker in the last stage before death]. (Beresford 1989:65)

11. Supporting this view is a communiqué to the Army Council, unsigned but dated March 3, 1981: "He [Sands] seems to have totally accepted the fact that he will die, this has come across in his speech. He has mentioned it a few times in a quite matter of fact manner," (Beresford 1989:67).

12. At the beginning of his strike, Sands requested that furniture, books, and other-hospital-type amenities be moved into his cell on the block in order to delay his removal to the prison hospital, which was understood as a varient of the punitive isolation treatment used in Castlereagh and in the prison.

13. Francis Hughes (PIRA) died on May 12 after fifty-nine days on strike. Raymond McCreesh (PIRA) and Patsy O'Hara (INLA) died on May 21, within a few hours of each other. Joe McDonnell (PIRA) died on July 8, and Martin Hurson (PIRA) died on July 13. Kevin Lynch (INLA) died on August 1; Keiran Doherty (PIRA) died on August 2. Tom McElwee (PIRA) died on August 8, and on August 19 Mickey Devine (INLA) was the last hunger striker to die.

14. Bik McFarlane registered the resurgence of hierarchical observation and occular penetration in a communiqué written at the time of Bobby Sands' death: "Well mate, it's been a heartbreaking day for us all. We lost someone we all loved dearly and *we can't cry in case someone is looking. Who made these rules?"* [emphasis mine] (Beresford 1989:101). The prison also replicated Castlereagh surveillance techniques by frequently turning the lights on in the hospital ward at night, when the hunger strikers were sleeping.

15. The prison guards would leave trays of food over night at the bottom of the hunger striker's bed.

16. At this stage of physical degeneration, the loss of sight indicated the body was feeding off of brain protein.

17. Serres (1982) sees exchange as the democratization of the sacrificial ritual, its de-singularization. Appadurai (1986) identifies an element of sacrificial deferment in the act of commodity exchange. Girardian sacrifice in this framework would be a modality of singularization (Appadurai 1986), the removal of an

artifact from a system of commensuration within which it previously circulated, though from another vantage point singularization of a mimetically appropriated artifact is merely another form of valuation. In this case it is singularity itself as a value that becomes commodified, that is placed in a differential, that is, exchange relation, to systems of general equivalence.

18. The body of hunger striker Patsy O'Hara was disfigured prior to its departure from the prison to be buried. The face had been beaten, the nose was broken, and cigarette burns were visible on the body.

19. The agreed exchange of undesirable prisoners removed the paramilitaries from recriminations by communities of their coreligionists outside the prison. The punishment shooting of informers, sex offenders, and hoods [petty thieves] was alternately an act acclaimed by the community or subjected to vociferous criticism. The ordering of punishment killings in the prison through the insulation of exchange removed the respective paramilitary organizations from these controversies.

References

Adorno, Theodor. 1973 *Negative dialectics*. New York: Continuum Books.

Allison, David B. 1977. *The new Nietzsche: Contemporary styles of interpretation.* Cambridge: M.I.T. Press.

Appadurai, Arjun, ed. 1986. *The social life of things: Commodities in cultural perspective.* Cambridge: Cambridge University Press.

Ardener, Edward. 1978. Some outstanding problems in the analysis of events. In *The yearbook of symbolic anthropology*, pp. 103–21. Montreal: McGill-Queens University Press.

Ariès, Philippe. 1981. *The hour of our death.* New York: Penguin Books.

Asad, Talal. 1983. Notes on body, pain and truth in medieval Christian rituals. *Economy and Society* 12:285–327.

Bazin, Jean. 1974. War and servitude in Segou. *Economy and Society* 28:107–43.

Beattie, G. 1982. A drink with your own kind: On Belfast sectarian drinking clubs. *New Society* 61(1033):413–14.

Bell, Desmond. 1987. Acts of union: Youth subculture and ethnic diversity amongst Protestants in Northern Ireland. *British Journal of Sociology* 34(3):158–83.

Benhabib, S. 1986. *Critique, norm and utopia: A study of the foundations of critical theory.* New York: Columbia University Press.

Beresford, David. 1989. *Ten men dead: The story of the 1981 Hunger Strike.* New York: Atlantic Monthly Press.

Bew, Paul. 1985. *The British state and the Ulster crisis from Wilson to Thatcher.* London: Verso.

Bew, Paul, Peter Gibbon, and Henry Patterson. 1979. *The state in Northern Ireland: Political forces and social class.* New York: St. Martin's Press.

Bishop, Patrick, and Eammon Mallie. 1987. *The Provisional Ira.* London: William Heinemann Ltd.

Bloch, Maurice, and Jonathan Parry. 1982. *Death and the regeneration of life.* New York: Cambridge University Press.

Boal, F. W., and Neville Douglas. 1982. *Integration and division: Geographical perspectives on the Northern Ireland problem.* London: Academic Press.

Boal, F. W., and Russell Murray. 1977. A city in conflict. *Geographical Magazine* 44:364–71.

Bonanate, Luigi. 1979. Some unanticipated consequences of terrorism. *Journal of Peace Research* 16:197–211.

Boyle, K., R. Chesney, and T. Hadden. 1976. Who are the terrorists? *New Society* 36(709):29.

Boyle, K., T. Hadden, and P. Hillyard. 1979. *Law and state: The case of Northern Ireland.* London: Martin Robertson.

———. 1980. *Ten years in Northern Ireland: The legal control of political violence.* London: Cobden Trust.

Buckley, A. D. 1985–86. The chosen few: Biblical tests in the regalia of an Ulster secret society. *Folklife* 26:5–24.

Buckley, A. D., and M. C. Kenney. N.d. Fighting and fun: Stone throwers and spectators in Ulster riots. Typescript.

Buck-Morss, Susan. 1984. The flaneur, the sandwichman and the whore: The politics of loitering. *New German Critiique,* 99–153.

———. 1989. *The dialectics of seeing: Walter Benjamin and the arcades project.* Cambridge: M.I.T. Press.

Burton, Frank. 1978. *The politics of legitimacy: Struggles in a Belfast community.* London: Routledge and Kegan Paul.

———. 1979. Ideological social relations in Northern Ireland. *British Journal of Sociology* 30:61–80.

Cahn, Michael. 1984. Subversive mimesis: Theodore W. Adorno and the modern impasse of critique. In Mihai Spariosa, ed., *Mimesis in contemporary theory: An interdisciplinary approach.* Philadelphia: D. Benjamin Publishing.

Castoriadis, Cornelius. 1987. *The imaginary institution of society.* Cambridge: M.I.T. Press.

Clifford, James. 1988. *The Predicament of Culture: Twentieth-century Ethnography, literature, and art.* Cambridge, Mass.: Harvard University Press.

Collins, Tom. 1986. *The Irish hunger strike.* Dublin: White Island Books Company.

Comaroff, Jean. 1985. *Body of power, spirit of resistance: The culture and history of a South African people.* Chicago: University of Chicago Press.

Comaroff, John, and Jean Comaroff. 1987. The madman and the migrant. *American Ethnologist* 12(2):191–209.

Coogan, T. P.

———. 1971. *The IRA.* London: Fontana.

———. 1980. *On the blanket: The H-block story.* Dublin: Ward River Press.

Corbin, Alain. 1986. *The foul and the fragrent: Odor and the French social imagination.* New York: Berg Publishers.

Craigie, William Alexander, Sir. 1937. *A dictionary of the older Scottish tongue, from the twelfth century to the end of the seventeenth.* Chicago: University of Chicago Press.

Crapanzano, Vincent. 1984. Life histories. *American Anthropologist* 86(4):933–60.

Darby, John. 1987. *Intimidation and the control of conflict in Northern Ireland.* Syracuse: Syracuse University Press.

Darby, J., and G. Morris. 1974. *Intimidation in housing.* Belfast: Northern Ireland Community Relations Commission.

Dean, Carolyn. 1986. Law and sacrifice: Baitaille, Lacan and the critique of the subject. *Representations* 12 (Winter):43–62.

Certaeu, Michel. 1986. *Heterologies: Discourse on the other.* Minneapolis: University of Minnesota Press.

Deleuze, Gilles. 1977. Active and reactive. In Allison David, ed., *The new Nietzsche: Contemporary styles of interpretation.* Cambridge: MIT Press.

Derrida, Jacques. 1976. *Of grammatology.* Baltimore: Johns Hopkins University Press.

_____. 1986. But beyond . . . (open letter to Anne McClintock and Rob Nixon). *Critical Inquiry* 13(1):155–70.

Douglas, Mary. 1968. The social control of cognition: Some factors in joke perception. *Man* 2:361–76.

Easthope, Gary. 1976. Religious war in Northern Ireland. *Sociology* 10:427–50.

Fairweather, Ellen. 1981. A visit to Patrick on the blanket. *New Society* 56(964):219–23.

Feldman, Allen. 1985. *The northern fiddler: Music and musicians of Donegal and Tyrone, with photography and illustrations by Eammon O'Doherty.* New York: Oak Publications. First published in 1979 by Blackstaff Press, Belfast.

_____. N.d. Self acting instruments: Body, commodity form and automaton in the 18th and 19th centuries. Typescript.

Firestone, Joseph M. 1974. Continuities in the theory of violence. *Journal of Conflict Resolution* 18:117–42.

Foucault, Michel. 1978a. The eye of power. *Semiotext* 3:6–19.

_____. 1978b. *Language, counter memory and practice: Selected essays and interviews.* Ithaca: Cornell University Press.

_____. 1979. *Discipline and punish: The birth of the prison.* London: Perigrin Books.

_____. 1980. *The history of sexuality.* New York: Vintage Books.

Franco, Jean. 1985. Killing priests, nuns, women, children. In Marshall Blonsky, ed., *On signs,* 414–20. Baltimore: Johns Hopkins University Press.

Girard, René. 1977. *Violence and the sacred.* Baltimore: Johns Hopkins University Press.

_____. 1978. *To double business bound: Essays on literature, mimesis and anthropology.* Baltimore: Johns Hopkins University Press.

Glassie, Henry. 1982. *Passing the time in Ballymenone: Culture and history of an Ulster community.* Philadelphia: University of Pennsylvania Press.

Goffman, Erving. 1961. *Asylums: Essays on the social situations of mental patients and other inmates.* New York: Anchor Books.

Hadden, T., P. Hillyard, and K. Boyle. 1980. How fair are the Ulster trials? *New Society* 54(938):320–22.

_____. 1980. The communal roots of violence. *New Society* 54(938):268–70.

Hamill, Desmond. 1985. *Pig in the middle: The army in Northern Ireland, 1969–1985.* London: Methuen.

Harris, Rosemarie. 1972. Prejudice and tolerance in Ulster: A study of neighbours and "strangers." In *A border community.* Manchester: Manchester University Press.

Harvey, David. 1989. *The urban experience*. Baltimore: Johns Hopkins University Press.

Heald, Suzette. 1986. The ritual use of violence: Circumcision among the Gisu of Uganda. In D. Riche, ed., *The anthropology of violence*. Oxford: Basil Blackwell.

Hechter, Michael. 1975. *Internal colonialism: The Celtic fringe in British national development, 1536–1966*. Berkeley: University of California Press.

Hertz, Robert. 1960. *Death and the right hand*. Aberdeen: Cohen and West.

Hewitt, Christopher. 1981. Catholic grievances and violence in Northern Ireland. *British Journal of Sociology* 32(3):362–80.

———. 1983. Discrimination in Northern Ireland. *British Journal of Sociology* 38(1):88–93.

———. 1985. Catholic grievances and violence in Northern Ireland. *British Journal of Sociology* 36(1):102–5.

———. 1987. Explaining violence in Northern Ireland. *British Journal of Sociology* 38(1):88–93.

Hillyard, Paddy. 1983. Law and order. In John Darby, ed., *Northern Ireland: The background to the conflict*, 32–60. Belfast: Apple Tree Press.

Holland, Jack. 1981. *Too long a sacrifice: Life and death in Northern Ireland*. Middlesex: Penguin Books.

Hubert, Henri, and Marcel Mauss. 1964. *Sacrifice: Its nature and function*. Chicago: University of Chicago Press.

Ingram, Martin. 1982. Ridings, rough music and the reform of popular culture. *Past and Present* 105:79–113.

Jameson, Fredric. 1981. *The political unconscious: Narrative as a socially symbolic act*. Ithaca: Cornell University Press.

Johnston, R. J. 1986. *On human geography*. Oxford: Basil Blackwell.

Kafka, Franz. 1976. *The penal colony*. New York: Schocken Books.

Kitson, Frank. 1971. *Low intensity operations: Subversion, insurgency and peace keeping*. London: Faber and Faber.

Kojéve, Alexandre. 1969. *Introduction to the reading of Hegel: Lectures on the phenomenology of the spirit*. Ed. Allan Bloom. Ithaca: Cornell University Press.

Koselleck, Reinhart. 1985. *Futures past: On the semantics of historical time*. Cambridge: M.I.T. Press.

Kristeva, Julia. 1982. *Powers of horror: An essay on abjection*. New York: Columbia University Press.

Lacan, Jacques. 1977. *Ecrits: A selection*. New York: W. W. Norton.

Laclau, Ernesto, and Chantal Mouffe. 1985. *Hegemony and socialist strategy: Towards a radical democratic politics*. London: Verso.

Lemaire, Anika. 1977. *Jacques Lacan*. London: Routledge and Kegan Paul.

Leyton, Elliot. 1974. Opposition and integration in Ulster. *Man*, n.s. 9:185–98.

Lima, Luis Costa. 1985. Social representation and mimesis. *New Literary History* 16:447–66.

Lincoln, Bruce. 1985. Revolutionary exhumations in Spain, July 1936. *Comparative Studies in Society and History* 27:241–68.

_____. 1989. *Discourse and society: Comparative studies of myth, ritual and classification.* New York: Oxford University Press.

Livingston, Paisley. 1984. *Disorder and order: Proceedings of the Stanford International Symposium.* Saratoga, Calif.: Anma Libri.

Lukács, Georg. 1971. *History and class consciousness: Studies in Marxist dialectics.* Cambridge: M.I.T. Press.

Lyotard, Jean François. 1973. *Des dispositifs pulsionnels.* Paris: Union Générale d'Editions.

McFarlane, Graham. 1986. Violence in rural Northern Ireland. In David Riches, ed., *The Anthropology of Violence,* 184–203. Oxford: Basil Blackwell.

McGuffin, John. 1973. *Internment.* Tralee: Anvil Press.

Makarius, Laura. 1970. Ritual clowns and symbolical behavior. *Diogenes* 69:44–73.

Maranhão, Tullio. 1990. *The interpretation of dialogue.* Chicago: University of Chicago Press.

Mauss, Marcel. 1973. Techniques of the body. *Economy and Society* 2:70–89.

Murray, Russell. 1982. Political violence in Northern Ireland, 1969–1977. In F. W. Boal and J. N. H. Douglas, eds., *Integration and division: Geographical perspectives on the Northern problem,* 309–31. London: Academic Press.

Murray, R., and F. W. Boal. 1979. The social ecology of urban violence. In D. T. Herbert and D. M. Smith, eds., *Social problems and the city: Geographical perspectives,* 139–57. Oxford: Oxford University Press.

Nietzsche, Friedrich. 1956. *The birth of tragedy and the genealogy of morals.* Garden City, N.Y.: Doubleday.

_____. 1968. *The will to power* New York: Vintage Books.

O'Hearn, Denis. 1983 Catholic grievances, Catholic nationalism: Comments. *British Journal of Sociology* 34(3):438–45.

_____. 1985 Again on discrimination in Northern Ireland: A reply to the rejoinder. *British Journal of Sociology* 36(1):94–100.

_____. 1987. Catholic grievances, Catholic Nationalism: A comment. *British Journal of Sociology* 37(1):94–100.

O'Malley, Padraig. 1983. *The uncivil wars: Ireland today.* Boston: Houghton Mifflin.

_____. 1990. *Biting at the grave: The Irish hunger strikes and the politics of despair.* Boston: Beacon Press.

Partridge, Eric. 1961. *A dictionary of slang and unconventional English.* New York: Macmillan.

Passerini, Luisa. 1987. *Fascism in popular memory: The cultural experience of the Turin working class.* Cambridge: Cambridge University Press.

Poole, Michael. 1971. Riot displacement in 1969. *Fortnight* 34:17.

Poole, M. A., and F. W. Boal. 1973. Religious residential segregation in Belfast in mid-1969: A multi-level analysis. In B. D. Clark and M. B. Gleave, eds. *Social patterns in cities,* 1–40. Special Publication No. 5. London: Institute of British Geographers.

Popular Memory Group. 1982. Popular memory: Theory, politics, method. In Richard Johnson, ed., *Making histories.* Minneapolis: University of Minnesota Press.

Poulantzas, Nicos. 1980. *State, power, socialism.* London: Verso.

Price, Edward H., Jr. 1977. The strategy and tactics of revolutionary terrorism. *Comparative Studies in Society and History* 19:52–66.

The Provos have second thoughts. 1982. *Fortnight* 187:4–5.

Ricoeur, Paul. 1973. The model of the text: Meaningful action considered as text. *New Literary History* 5:91–120.

———. 1979. *The rule of metaphor: Multi-disciplinary studies of the creation of meaning in language.* Toronto: University of Toronto Press.

———. 1984. *Time and narrative.* Vol. 1. Chicago: University of Chicago Press.

———. 1986. *Lectures on ideology and utopia.* Ed. George H. Taylor. New York: Columbia University Press.

Rosaldo, Renato. 1986. Ilongot hunting as story and experience. In Victor Turner and Edward Bruner, eds., *The anthropology of experience.* Urbana: University of Illinois Press.

Sack, Robert David. 1980. *Conceptions of space in social thought: A geographic perspective.* Minneapolis: University of Minnesota Press.

Sands, Bobby. 1981. *The diary of Bobby Sands.* Dublin: Sinn Fein Publicity Department.

Santoli, Al. 1981. *Everything we had: An oral history of the Vietnam War By thirty-three American soldiers who fought it.* New York: Random House.

Scarry, Elaine. 1985. *The body in pain: The making and unmaking of the world.* New York: Oxford University Press.

Schürmann, Reiner. 1984. Legislation-transgression: Strategies and counter strategies in the transcendental justification of norms. *Man and World* 17:361–98.

Seremetakis, C. Nadia. 1991. *The last word: Women, death and divination in Inner Mani.* Chicago: University of Chicago Press.

Serres, Michel. 1982. *The parasite.* Baltimore: Johns Hopkins University Press.

Shallice, T. 1973. The Ulster depth interrogation techniques. *Cognition* 1:385–405.

Sluka Jeffrey. 1989. *Hearts and minds, water and fish: Support for the IRA and INLA in a Northern Irish ghetto.* Greenwich, Conn.: AI Press.

Smadar, Lavrie. 1990. *The Poetics of military occupation: Mzeina allegories of Bedouin identity under Israeli and Egyptian rule.* Berkeley: University of California Press.

Spivak, Gaytari Chakravorty. 1976. Translator's preface. In Jacques Derrida, *Of grammatology,* ix–lxxxvii. Baltimore: Johns Hopkins University Press.

Sunday Times Insight Team. 1972. *Ulster.* London: Penguin.

Taussig, Michael. 1984. Culture of terror—Space of death: Roger Casement's Putayamo report and the explanation of torture. *Comparative Studies in Society and History* 26:467–97.

———. 1987. *Shamanism, colonialism and the wild man: A study in terror and healing.* Chicago: University of Chicago Press.

Taylor, P. 1980. *Beating the terrorists? Interrogation in Omagh, Gough and Castlereagh.* Middlesex: Penguin.

Thompson, E. P. 1977. Folklore, anthropology and social history. *Indian Historical Review* 3:247–66.

Timerman, Jacobo. 1982. *Prisoner without a name, cell without a number*. New York: Vintage Books.

Touraine, Alain. 1988. *Return of the actor: Social theory in postindustrial society*. Minneapolis: University of Minnesota Press.

Tyrie, A., and J. McMichael. 1981. Conformers the key. *Fortnight* 179:4.

Veyne, Paul. 1984. *Writing history: An essay in epistomology*. Middletown, Conn.: Wesleyan University Press.

Virilio, Paul. 1989. *War and cinema: The logistics of perception*. London: Verso.

Warren, Mark. 1988. *Nietzsche and Political Thought*. Cambridge, Mass.: M.I.T. Press.

Watson, Lawrence, and Maria Watson-Franke. 1985. *Interpreting life histories: An anthropological inquiry*. New Brunswick, N.J.: Rutgers University Press.

White, Hayden. 1973. *Metahistory: The historical imagination in nineteenth century Europe*. Baltimore: Johns Hopkins University Press.

Wilden, Anthony, ed. 1968. *The language of the self: The functions of language in psychoanalysis*. Baltimore: Johns Hopkins University Press.

Wright, Steve. 1978. New police technologies: An exploration of the social implications and unforeseen impacts of some recent developments. *Journal of Peace Research* 15:305–22.

Wyshogrod, Edith. 1985. *Spirit in ashes: Hegel, Heidegger and man-made mass death*. New Haven: Yale University Press.

Zeleny, Milan, ed. 1980. *Autopoeisis, dissipative structures and spontaneous social orders*. Boulder, Colo.: Westview Press.

Žižek, Slavoj. 1989. *The sublime object of ideology*. London: Verso.

Index

Action, social. *See* Agency; Body; Exchange; Violence

Adorno, T., 64, 120, 144

Agency, political, 1–10; of the corpse, 69–70, 232–37; of the dead, 65–70; of historical force, 53–54; in hunger striking, 219–20, 232–37, 244–55; Nietzschean concept of, 3–4, 176–78; removal of, 136–38; sensory formation of, 56–59, 126–28, 136–38, 195–96, 205–6, 209–10; of the tortured, 142–46; in violence, 44, 53–54, 68–71, 78–79, 81–84, 94–97, 99–110, 114–15, 119–21, 123, 127–28, 138–46, 176–80, 232–37, 244–55, 261–65; of weaponry, 53–56, 101–3, 138–46, 176–80

Alterity: historical, 63–70, 72–74, 79–84, 232–37, 244–45, 250–51, 258–59, 261–63; personifications of, 53–54, 59–71, 73–74, 77–84, 88–89, 93–104, 106–10, 114–15, 119–23, 127–28, 136–38, 142–46, 176–80, 232–37, 244–45, 250–51, 258–59, 261–63, 268–69; sensory formation of, 56–65, 119–20, 123–38, 195–96, 205–6, 209–10; violent formation of, 35–37, 39, 44–45, 53–54, 59–74, 77–84, 88–89, 93–104, 106–10, 114–15, 119–46, 176–78, 232–37, 244–45, 250–51, 258–59, 261–63, 268–69

Antagonism: conditions of, 4–5, 18–20; and ideology, 1–4, 6–7; and material practice, 1–4, 6–7; relations of, 4–7, 18–22, 26–37, 41–45, 63–65, 68–70, 72–74, 76–81, 83–84, 96–97, 99–104, 137–38, 142–46, 176–80, 227–30,

234–37, 244–45, 258–65, 267–69, 288n.6

Appadurai, A., 9, 56, 283n.2, 301n.17

Asad, T., 226

Autonomization, 4–6, 292n.l; of the body, 59–65, 138–46, 176–81, 234–35. 244–45; of the senses, 56–59, 123–27, 136–37, 205–11, of space, 26–31, 35–36, 38–39, 41–45, 65–68, 71–78, 126–28; of the state, 40–41, 86–89, 93–94, 103–10, 114–15, 121–22, 126–28, 137–38, 143–45, 292n.2; of violence, 26–27, 31, 35–36, 39, 41–45, 53–54, 56, 99–103, 112–28, 137–46, 174–81, 185–86, 189–90, 195–96, 209–11, 226–27, 232–37, 244–45, 258–65

Bakhtin, M., 12

Bazin, J., 98, 293n.6

Belfast: barricading of, 30–37, 80–81, 287n.18; doorstep murders in, 72–76; ethnic homogeneity in, 21–23, 26–27, 56–59, 72–73, 76–77, 285n.3; fieldwork in, 10–16, 283n.5; industrial culture of, 5–6, 71; internment in, 86–87, 292n.3; PIRA brigades in, 293n.9; population dislocation in, 23–28, 30–31, 285nn. 4, 5, 286nn. 8, 9, 11, 13, 14; Protestant and Catholic residence in, 21–22, 26–30, 35–37, 56–59, 72–73, 285n.3; Republican families of, 38, 286n.15; rioting in, 23–28, 30–31, 285n.1, 286nn. 9, 13, 287n.17, 292n.3; sectarian violence in, 18–19, 21–37, 40–45, 54, 57–68, 71–78, 80–81; state occupation of, 67–68, 87–97, 287n.18, 292n.2

311